BRITISH UNION-CATALOGUE OF PERIODICALS

incorporating

World List of Scientific Periodicals

NEW PERIODICAL TITLES

Edited for the British Library

by

Mrs J. Gascoigne, A.L.A.

LONDON
BUTTERWORTHS
1974

THE BUTTERWORTH GROUP

ENGLAND: BUTTERWORTH & CO. (PUBLISHERS) LTD.
LONDON. 88 Kingsway, WC2B 6AB
AUSTRALIA: BUTTERWORTH & CO. (AUSTRALIA) LTD.
SYDNEY: 586 Pacific Highway, Chatswood, NSW 2067
MELBOURNE: 343 Little Collins Street, 3000
BRISBANE: 240 Queen Street, 4000
CANADA: BUTTERWORTH & CO. (CANADA) LTD.
TORONTO
NEW ZEALAND: BUTTERWORTH & CO. (NEW ZEALAND) LTD.
WELLINGTON: 26-28 Waring Taylor Street, 1
SOUTH AFRICA: BUTTERWORTH & CO. (SOUTH AFRICA) (PTY) LTD.
DURBAN: 152-154 Gale Street

DISTRIBUTORS FOR THE U.S.A. AND CANADA
Archon Books, The Shoe String Press, Inc.
995 Sherman Avenue, Hamden, Connecticut 06514

Quarterly issues numbered 1 to 4 within each calendar year. Annual cumulations dated by year of preceding issues. First year of publication: 1964

Typeset by Computaprint Ltd., London

Printed in Great Britain by Clarke, Doble & Brendon Ltd., Plymouth

ISBN 0 408 70697 X

ISSN 0007-1919

Published by Butterworths, 88 Kingsway, London W.C.2. Published quarterly
with Annual Comprehensive Volume. Basic Annual subscription, including
postage, £10·50; U.S.A. $31.50

Introduction

1. ABOUT THE PUBLICATION

The *British Union-Catalogue of Periodicals* (*BUCOP*) appeared originally in four volumes from 1955–1958, with a Supplement published in 1962, bringing the coverage of serial publications in British libraries down to 1960. The *World List of Scientific Periodicals* (*WLSP*) appeared in its fourth edition in three volumes issued 1963–1965, covering scientific, technical and medical serials in British libraries for the period 1900–1960. The current computer-produced publication, which unites *BUCOP* and *WLSP* and carries the secondary title 'New Periodical Titles' began to appear in 1964. It is published in quarterly issues, which are cumulated annually into two volumes: one including all the titles appearing in the quarterlies, and the other (in effect continuing *WLSP*) including the scientific, technical and medical titles only.

2. SCOPE

2.1 The current publication (referred to below as *BUCOP*) is concerned with recording new periodical titles for the period in and after 1960. This embraces periodicals and serials which began publication for the first time, or which changed their titles, or which began a new series. Serials which ceased publication in this period are also noted. Where it has not proved possible to establish the commencing date of a particular new title of which we have been notified, the publication date may be taken as that of the earliest issue in our records.

2.2 *BUCOP* includes all periodicals and most categories of serial publications, with certain reservations, as described below:

2.2.1 *Reports.* Administrative reports are in general excluded, but research and development reports are included, as well as the annual reports of research organizations and learned societies.

2.2.2 *Monographic series.* Publishers' series, and un-numbered series are excluded, but monographic series issued by a learned body or research organization are included under the series title. Since libraries normally record their holdings of such material by specific, individual entries, it should be pointed out that these entries are likely to be partial, at best, as far as the recorded holdings are concerned.

2.2.3 *Limited interest.* Material of ephemeral, or of narrowly local or sectional interest, is normally excluded.

2.2.4 *Newspapers.* These are included, unless they fall into the 'limited interest' category.

2.2.5 *Editions.* Works issued in successive editions are not normally regarded as serials, except where the changes from issue to issue, as in the case of certain statistical publications, suggest that they qualify for entry here.

2.2.6 *Conference proceedings.* These are not regarded as serials, except where they form part of an editorially independent serial publication with an individual title; e.g. the 'Advances in . . .' type of title.

2.2.7 *Reprints.* These are not regarded as new publications.

3. TEXT

3.1 The main text of *BUCOP* comprises the following sections: New Periodical Titles (NPT), which gives main entries for each title, with publication details, and indication by symbols of libraries holding the title (but a title can be included where no U.K. holdings are known); Index of Sponsoring Bodies (ISB), listing the bodies responsible for the titles in NPT, with the titles issued by them; and in the cumulations only, an Index of Library Symbols (ILS) providing a key to the holding libraries indicated by symbols in NPT.

3.2 The NPT entry comprises the following elements, as required, in the order shown:
Title with title abbreviation.
Sponsoring body (or bodies); publisher.
Imprint (place of publication; numbers and dates of first and last issues).
Remarks (frequency of publication, previous and subsequent titles, etc.)
Holding libraries.

3.3 The ISB section lists the sponsoring bodies, in the form in which they appear in the second element of the NPT entry, as headings, with the titles, in the form in which they appear in the first element of the NPT entry, below.

3.4 The ILS gives the name and address of the library concerned after the symbol by which it is indicated in NPT, together with information, where known, on the library's policy concerning loans and access and on its facilities for making photocopies/microfilms.
Details of the NPT entry, and of the ILS code for loans/access/photocopying/microfilming appear below.

4. TITLE

4.1 Serials are entered under their published titles. The 'corporate author' approach is never used: its place is supplied by the ISB which also shows 'distinctive' titles issued under the sponsorship of a body.

4.2 Separate entries are made in the case of a title change; but not in the case of a change in the name of the sponsoring body, except where the body name forms part of the title. However, a uniform title may be used in the case of a title change, if the circumstances appear to justify it; e.g. where the change is slight, not materially altering the position of the title in an alphabetical sequence, and where the numbering is continuous over the change. The use of a uniform title is indicated by a following asterisk; e.g.:

HISTORICAL STUDIES.* [originally HISTORICAL STUDIES, AUSTRALIA & NEW ZEALAND.]

4.3 A title which is inadequate without the name of the sponsoring body (which may appear in a separate position on the title-page) attached to it, is expanded according to the following pattern: Title word or phrase, Subordinate body (where required), Parent body; e.g.:

OCCASIONAL PUBLICATION, GRADUATE SCHOOL OF CONTEMPORARY EUROPEAN STUDIES, UNIVERSITY OF READING.

However, where the normal pattern for a concrete title in a particular language happens to take the opposite form (e.g. Hungarian, Japanese, Turkish, etc.), then that pattern is followed in expanding the title, thus:

(EOTVOS LORAND TUDOMANYEGYETEMI) KONYVTAR EVKONYVEI.

4.4 Where a serial has alternative titles in two or more languages, and these are also the languages of the text, preference is normally given to the English title where there is one. All the titles concerned are shown in the NPT entry thus:

INTERNATIONAL YEARBOOK OF CARTO-GRAPHY. = ANNUAIRE INTERNATIONALE DE CARTOGRAPHIE. = INTERNATIONALES JAHRBUCH FUR KARTOGRAPHIE.

References are made from the alternative titles. However, alternative titles are not shown, nor are references made, in the case of United Nations publications, and those of U.N. agencies.

4.5 Where a serial gives an alternative title in another language, but this is not one of the languages of the text, the vernacular form is preferred. The alternative title is shown in such cases as if it were a subtitle, but references are made as required.

4.6 A separate entry is made for each subdivision of a main title, and the secondary title is shown, where there is one, as follows:

JOURNAL OF POLYMER SCIENCE: PART A: GENERAL PAPERS.

4.7 A separate entry is made for each successive series of a main title, with the series indication attached to the main title in the same form as in 4.6. This indication may be reduced to NS (for 'new series', 'nuova seria', etc.), 2S for 'second series', etc. E.g.:

MEDICAL WORLD NEWSLETTER: NS.

4.8 A serial which is issued as part of a more general series is entered under the more specific title, if it is independently numbered, and is not lettered or numbered as part of the main title, with the series indicated in brackets after the title, thus:

FAR EASTERN AFFAIRS. (ST. ANTONY'S PAPERS.)

4.9 Additions to the title: official or authoritative serials whose contents pertain to a particular area, and this is not otherwise clear from the title, may have the name of that area added to the end and used as an additional filer word. The usual English form is normally used in such cases, e.g.:

BOLETIN ESTADISTICO (CHILE).

4.10 Omissions from the title: serial numbers and dates, together with the phrase containing them, are omitted from the title. Lengthy titles may be reduced to a significant phrase, if this is adequate for identification, and does not materially affect the placing of the title in an alphabetical sequence.

4.11 Absence of title: if a serial is issued without a title, but with the name of the sponsoring body, then the name of the body in brackets is used as the title, e.g.:

(LIST & INDEX SOCIETY).

4.12 If an alphabetical and/or numeric code is the only distinguishing feature of a serial (e.g. in the case of a research and development report series), the code is used as the title.

4.13 Subtitles are shown following the main title where the title consists of a single word, where the subtitle contains the name of the sponsoring body and might be assumed to be the main title, or where there is room to include it in the same line as the title. Otherwise, it is disregarded, or, if it contains useful information, it is given in the 'Remarks' section following S/T:.

4.14 References are made in cases where a published title deviates from the 'normal' pattern (cf. 4.3), e.g.:

JOURNAL, AMERICAN INSTITUTE OF AERO-NAUTICS & ASTRONAUTICS. SEE: AIAA JOURNAL.

4.15 The following devices are used in the right hand margin opposite the last line of the title as required: XXX, to indicate a change of title (normally against the superseded title), or to show that the title has ceased publication; 000, to indicate a reference (primarily for the use of BUCOP editorial staff).

5. SPONSORING BODY

5.1 Sponsoring bodies are entered as the second element of the NPT entry and as headings in the ISB under the names by which they are normally identified in their publications, or, where this varies, under their official names. The native form is normally used; but an English form is preferred in the case of international organizations, or where English is an official language of the country concerned.

5.2 In the case of changes of name of a body, the form used in association with a particular title is used. Where there has been a change of name in association with a title which is itself unchanged, the latest form of name is normally preferred. A uniform name, with references, may be used if justified by circumstances. Such cases are indicated by an asterisk (cf. 4.2).

5.3 Additions to the name: an identifying characteristic which may be abbreviated, may be added if required to distinguish between bodies of the same name in different places, or where amplification appears desirable. A place-name (normally preference is given to a larger over a smaller unit) or the name of a superior body may be used; e.g.:

CORPUS CHRISTI COLLEGE (UNIV. OF CAMBRIDGE).
CORPUS CHRISTI COLLEGE (UNIV. OF OXFORD).
NATIONAL RESEARCH COUNCIL (CANADA).
NATIONAL RESEARCH COUNCIL (US).
MANCHESTER COLLEGE (OXFORD).

5.4 Omissions from the name: certain elements in a body's official name, of an 'honorific' nature, or which are often dispensed with when the name is shown in publications, may be omitted from the form used in *BUCOP*. Where such elements appear to have become an integral part of the name, and affect the placing of the name in an alphabetical list, they are retained. e.g.:

UNIVERSITA DI GENOVA. *Not* UNIVERSITA DEGLI STUDI DI GENOVA.

GOSUDARSTVENNAJA BIBLIOTEKA SSSR. *Not* GOSUDARSTVENNAJA ORDENA LENINA BIBLIOTEKA SSSR IMENI V.I. LENINA.

But

UNIWERSYTET IM. ADAMA MICKIEWICZA W POZNANIU.

5.5 Subordinate bodies are entered directly under their own names, if these are adequate for identification (with an added identifying characteristic if necessary) and unless the name itself implies subordination. *But* bodies subordinate to a commercial firm are always entered under the name of the parent body, whether their names are distinctive or not.

5.6 A subordinate body whose name does not (necessarily) imply subordination, but whose identification requires the addition of the name of the parent body is entered as an extension of the parent body's name the whole name then filing as a unit. But if such a name has been made distinctive by the inclusion of a place or personal name, it is entered directly under that name; e.g.:

UNIVERSITY OF LONDON: INSTITUTE OF EDUCATION.

COURTAULD INSTITUTE OF ART.

But libraries with distinctive names are entered as an extension of the parent body's name, unless they are well known under their own names; e.g.:

UNIVERSITY OF LEEDS: BROTHERTON LIBRARY.

BODLEIAN LIBRARY.

5.7 A subordinate body whose name implies subordination is omitted from the name of the sponsoring body, and mentioned in the 'Remarks' section only; *except* where such a body is one of the departments,

etc., of a government, or where it indicates a branch of the parent body located in another area. An example of the latter case:

ROYAL ASIATIC SOCIETY (HONG KONG BRANCH).

5.8 Where there is a hierarchy of subordinate bodies, and the specific sponsoring body cannot be entered directly under its own name (cf. 5.6), intermediary bodies between the parent body and the subordinate body concerned may be omitted from the entry.

5.9 In the case of 'jurisdictional' entries, the name of the jurisdiction, in its English form, is inserted before the body's actual name. This name is enclosed in brackets if it represents the name of a place. But if the official name of the body begins with the jurisdictional name in any form, it is entered directly under that name. Entries with an added jurisdictional name are filed as a unit. The title of an officer may be used instead of the name of his department if this appears to be the better known form. The name of a subordinate body may be given immediately after the jurisdictional name if the name is adequate for identification. Examples:

UNITED NATIONS: HIGH COMMISSIONER FOR REFUGEES.

(UNITED STATES) BUREAU OF MINES.
(UNITED STATES) DEPARTMENT OF STATE.
UNITED STATES INFORMATION SERVICE.

5.10 Bodies created and controlled by a government are entered directly under their names where they are of one of the types described in rule 78A of the *Anglo-American Cataloguing Rules: British Text* (London, The Library Association, 1967). However, contrary to rule 84 of that publication, *BUCOP* also enters armed forces directly under their names if these seem adequate for identification. An added identifier is normally used in these cases. E.g.:

AERONAUTICAL RESEARCH COUNCIL (GB).
NATIONAL AERONAUTICS & SPACE ADMINISTRATION (US).
ROYAL AIR FORCE (GB).
WARREN SPRING LABORATORY.

5.11 A body may be entered under an acronym or group of initials (regarded as a word), particularly if it is an international organization, if it is well known by those initials. E.g.:

GATT.
NATO.
UNESCO.

5.12 The name of a commercial publisher, or a university press, may appear in the entry enclosed in square brackets, in place of or together with the name of a sponsoring body.

5.13 If the vernacular form of the name of a body, or part of it, cannot be determined at the time of a title's inclusion, the name or part concerned is shown in round brackets.

5.14 The following devices are used in the right-hand margin opposite the last line of the body's name as required (cf. 4.15): XXX, to indicate a change in the body's name (normally against the superseded name); 000, to indicate a reference.

6. IMPRINT

The 'imprint' element of the NPT entry comprises:

6.1 Place of publication. Normally a specific city, or cities, or the name of a country in brackets if the place is variable, or cannot be determined. A serial published simultaneously in several places may be shown by one place only followed by &C.

6.2 The issue numbering and date of the first (and last) issue for that particular *title*. The numbers and dates are shown together for each issue concerned. Months are indicated according to the following abbreviated forms: JA, F, MR, AP, MY, JE, JL, AG S, OC, N, D. A day is shown with a month thus: 15/JL (to avoid confusion with issue numbers). A year of publication differing from the year pertaining to the contents of a work (normally affecting annuals) is shown in brackets after the date pertaining to the text. Volumes and issues are shown thus: 1(1). Some examples:

1(1), OC 1960–
[title in progress]
1(1), OC 1960– 3(4), JA 1964.//
[ceased publication]
1(1), OC 1960– 3(4), JA 1964.
[ceased publication, continued by another title]
1(1), OC 1960– 3(4) JA 1964 . . .
[ceased publication, continued by another title with continuous numbering]
3(5), F 1965–
[first issue of a new title continues numbering from a previous title]
1, 1959/60 (1962)–
[contents of first issue concern 1959/60, actual publication date 1962]
NO. 1, 1960– *or* [NO.]1, 1960–
[issues consecutively numbered without volume numbering]
1960 (1)–
[issues numbered from 1 each year, without volume numbering]

7. REMARKS

This section of the NPT includes the following information:

7.1 An indication of the frequency of publication, shown by a suitable abbreviation. Note the use of forms such as 2M, 2A for bi-monthly and biennial respectively. and 2/M, 2/A for semi-monthly and semi-annual, etc

7.2 The language(s) of the text, if not indicated by the language of the title. These are shown by suitable abbreviations, e.g. ENGL., FR., GER., ITAL., JAP., RUSS. A form such as ENGL. = FR. shows that the same text is given in the languages named.

7.3 In the case of a title change, previous and subsequent titles, shown following the abbreviations PREV and SUBS. All the previous titles from the first issue of a particular sequence of numbering are shown where the numbering continues through several changes.

7.4 Other information of importance in relation to the title is given as required.

8. HOLDINGS

8.1 Holding libraries are represented by symbols, for which the key is given in the ILS. The symbol comprises two letters representing the place where the library is located, e.g. LO for London, and one letter indicating the type of library, as follows: N, National libraries, museums and art galleries, major government libraries; P, Public and county libraries; U, University libraries, including departmental and university college libraries; C, 'Collegiate' libraries, that is, educational institutions not of university status; S, special libraries in general, learned societies and professional associations; M, Medical libraries (including dentistry and veterinary science), and including university medical libraries; R, Research associations research stations, and the like, not covered by other categories; T, Trade and technological associations, major technical libraries; F, commercial firms, with their laboratories and research stations. The number in the library symbol distinguishes libraries of the same category in the same place.

8.2 Holding libraries in the NPT entry are shown in groups, as categorized by a, b and c below. A selection principle is exercised by the computer: if at least twelve libraries are represented in category a, categories b and c are not printed; if at least twelve libraries are represented in categories a and b together, category c is not printed.

(a) Libraries with complete runs from the first issue of the title shown to date. These are printed four to a line, the symbols alone being shown.

(b) Libraries with a continuous run from some issue after the first of that title. These are printed two to a line, with an open entry from the first issue held.

(c) Libraries with partial, or temporary holdings, with a specific indication of the holding. These are printed one to a line.

A library's holding may appear in both the b and c categories above if warranted. A single asterisk follows the symbol or precedes the holding to indicate issues missing in the run shown. A double asterisk follows the symbol to indicate that the title is held, but the precise holding is not known.

9. ARRANGEMENT OF ENTRIES

9.1 The order of filing of title (NPT) and sponsoring bodies (ISB) is alphabetical, word-by-word, with numerals preceding letters.

9.2 Articles are disregarded in the filing order throughout.

unless they form an integral part of a place-name (cf. LOS ANGELES). They are not normally shown at the beginning of a title, unless it seems useful to indicate them; cf. AL-ANDALUS, filed as ANDALUS

9.3 Prepositions and conjunctions are disregarded in the filing order, except where they begin a title.

9.4 Groups of initials are filed as if they were words whether they form a vocable or not.

9.5 Hyphenated words are filed as single words, unless each element also constitutes a word which can occur in isolation. Compound words which sometimes occur as separate words, or with a hyphen, or as single words, are normally filed as single words. Words with detached prefixes are filed as complete single words, E.g.:

INTER-AMERICAN files as INTERAMERICAN
FAR-EAST   files as FAR EAST
YEAR BOOK   files as YEARBOOK
YEAR-BOOK   files as YEARBOOK
PAN AMERICAN   files as PANAMERICAN

9.6 Diacritical marks are omitted in *BUCOP*, and neither the spelling nor the filing is modified to indicate their presence.

OSTERREICHISCHE is shown and filed as OSTERREICHISCHE and not as OESTER-REICHISCHE

9.7 The filing is modified as appropriate to interfile cognate forms in the same or different languages; e.g plurals are normally filed with and as the singular forms. Words like ARCHIV, ARCHIVE, ARCHIVES, ARCHIVIOS, etc., are interfiled., as are BOLETIM and BOLETIN, etc., JAPAN and JAPANESE are interfiled. Words with different, inflected endings are interfiled, e.g. DEUTSCHE, DEUTSCHER DEUTSCHES.

Normally this procedure affects words which differ only in their endings; in some cases, however, it is extended to words where the variation occurs near the beginning. E.g. AARBOK files with ARBOK; NIHON with NIPPON; SWENSKA with SVENSKA; etc.

10. TRANSLITERATION

Non-roman alphabets are transliterated, or other forms of script transcribed, according to systems generally established in the United Kingdom. However, the Hanyu Pinyin system is normally used in preference to the Wade-Giles for Chinese, especially for mainland China publications, which often carry a transcription in the Hanyu Pinyin form. The British standard *BS 2979*:1958 is used for Cyrillic according to the 'British' system, but with the modification that the letter y is used only for the vowel sound shown in the standard as ȳ; otherwise, j is used in place of y, for instance in the forms ja, ju and (Ukrainian) ji, and also for the short i.

11. ILS CODING

An indication is given in the ILS after the library's name and address of their policy concerning loans and access, and their facilities for making photocopies and microfilms, as follows:

L   The library lends most of its serials, either direct to other libraries, or through the National Central Library.
*L   The library makes certain conditions concerning the loan of its serials, or will lend only some of its holdings.
XL   The library lends only to authorized users, or does not lend.
F   The library will lend its serials to libraries in foreign countries.
*F   The library will lend to foreign countries in special circumstances.
XF   The library will not lend its serials abroad.
A   The library permits access to callers in general.
*A   Access for reference is permitted to individuals suitably introduced.
XA   Access is restricted to authorized users of the library.
P   The library has photocopying facilities.
*P   The library has limited photocopying facilities.
XP   The library has no photocopying facilities.
M   The library has microfilming facilities.
*M   The library has limited microfilming facilities
XM   The library has no microfilming facilities.

12. TITLE ABBREVIATIONS

12.1 The title abbreviations given in the NPT entry immediately after the full title (following the + + sign) accord with the revised British Standard, *BS 4148*:1969, and its associated *Word-Abbreviation List*. The revised British standard conforms in all particulars to the revised American standard in this field, *Z39.5*–1969.

12.2 The major differences from the previous standard, and from earlier British practice, are as follows:

(a) There is no distinction between word forms implied by the use of upper and lower case; in *BUCOP* the abbreviation, like the rest of the main text, is in upper case throughout.

(b) Full stops are used after all abbreviations, even where the last letter of the original word is retained.

(c) The final element only of a compound word is abbreviated, unless hyphenation occurs; in such a case each element affected may be abbreviated.

12.3 Abbreviations have been assigned to titles in all subject fields, but not to all titles; in some cases it appears unsuitable to assign an abbreviated form, but users of *BUCOP* are invited to query any such decision with the editor if they wish.

12.4 The added identifier required in some cases to distinguish or to clarify abbreviations, may be a place—and normally a larger unit, such as a country, is preferred over a city—or an abbreviation for the name of the sponsoring body. The body is always shown in an added identifier in an abbreviated form based on the full name where it appears in the title in the form of initials. In such a case it need not necessarily be regarded as part of the abbreviation, unless distinction is required. E.g.:

AIAA JOURNAL.
++AIAA J. (AM. INST. AERONAUT. & ASTRO-NAUT.)

12.5 Where it has been established, the Coden for a title appears after the abbreviation in square brackets. E.g.:

JOURNAL OF MACROMOLECULAR CHEMISTRY.
++J. MACROMOL. CHEM. [JMCC-A]

12.6 The ampersand (&) is used for 'and' and its equivalent in all languages in the title abbreviation, but has no filing significance.

13 INTERNATIONAL STANDARD SERIAL NUMBERS.

The International Standard Serial Number relating to a title appears as the final element of the NPT entry for that title. E.g.

PARNASSUS. POETRY IN REVIEW.
NEW YORK 1, 1972-
OX/U-1.

ISSN 0048-3028

New Periodical Titles

ABERDEEN HARBOUR BULLETIN.
+ +ABERDEEN HARBOUR BULL.
ABERDEEN HARBOUR BOARD.
 ABERDEEN 1, 1973-
 AD/U-1.

ABERDEEN LEOPARD.   000
 SEE: LEOPARD.

ABERDEEN STUDIES IN DEFENCE ECONOMICS.
+ +ABERDEEN STUD. DEF. ECON.
UNIVERSITY OF ABERDEEN: DEPARTMENT OF POLITICAL
ECONOMY.
 ABERDEEN 1, 1973-
 AD/U-1.

ABSTRACTS, BRISTOL CITY ART GALLERY.
+ +ABSTR. BRISTOL CITY ART GALLERY.
 BRISTOL NO.1, 1964-
 OX/U-1.   ED/N-1. NO.40, JA/MR 1974-

ABSTRACT JOURNAL IN EARTHQUAKE ENGINEERING.
+ +ABSTR. J. EARTHQUAKE ENG.
UNIVERSITY OF CALIFORNIA: EARTHQUAKE ENGINEER-
ING RESEARCH CENTER.
 BERKELEY, CALIF. 1, 1971(1972)-
 ANNU.
 GL/U-2.   LO/N14.

ABSTRACT REVIEW, NATIONAL PAINT & COATINGS
ASSOCIATION.   XXX
+ +ABSTR. REV. NATL. PAINT & COAT. ASSOC.
 WASHINGTON, D.C. NO.390/400, JA 1972-
PREV: ABSTRACT REVIEW, NATIONAL PAINT, VARNISH
& LACQUER ASSOCIATION FROM NO.23, 1934- 389,
1971.
 LO/N14.

ABSTRACT REVIEW, NATIONAL PAINT, VARNISH &
LACQUER ASSOCIATION.   XXX
 SUBS(1972): ABSTRACT REVIEW, NATIONAL PAINT
 & COATINGS ASSOCIATION.

ABSTRACTS OF WORLD MEDICINE.   XXX
+ +ABSTR. WORLD MED.
BRITISH MEDICAL ASSOCIATION.
 LONDON 1, 1947- 45, 1971.//
 BH/U-1.   LD/U-1.   LO/M19.   LO/N13.
 LO/U-2.   LV/U-1.   NW/U-1.   SH/U-1.   ISSN 0301-3898

ACCOUNTANTS REVIEW.   XXX
+ +ACCOUNT. REV.
SOCIETY OF COMPANY & COMMERCIAL ACCOUNTANTS.
 BRISTOL 25(3), S 1974-
Q. PREV:THE COMMERCIAL ACCOUNTANT FROM
1, 1947- 25(2), JE 1974. S/T: JOURNAL OF
THE SOCIETY OF COMPANY & COMMERCIAL
ACCOUNTANTS.
 ED/N-1.   HL/U-1.   ISSN 0305-2087

ACERT NEWSLETTER.
+ +ACERT NEWSL.
ADVISORY COMMITTEE FOR THE EDUCATION OF ROMANY
& OTHER TRAVELLERS.
 LONDON NO.1, 1974-
 HL/U-2.

ACIERS SPECIAUX.
+ +ACIERS SPEC.
CHAMBRE SYNDICALE DES PRODUCTEURS D'ACIERS FINS
ET SPECIAUX.
 PARIS NO.1, 1967-
 LO/N14.

ACTA ALIMENTARIA.   XXX
+ +ACTA ALIMENT.
MAGYAR TUDOMANYOS AKADEMIA.
 [AKADEMIAI KIADO]
 BUDAPEST 1(1), JA/MR 1972-
Q. PREV: ELELMISZERTUDOMANY FROM
1, 1967- 4(1-2), 1970.
 CA/U-1.   LO/N-6.   LO/R-6.

ACTA ASTRONAUTICA. JOURNAL OF THE INTER-   XXX
NATIONAL ACADEMY OF ASTRONAUTICS.
+ +ACTA ASTRONAUT.
 [PERGAMON P.]
 NEW YORK & LONDON 1, 1974-
PREV: ASTRONAUTICA ACTA FROM 1, 1955-
18, 1973.
 BR/U-1.   GL/U-1.   LD/U-1.   LO/U12.   SO/U-1.

ACTA CHEMICA SCANDINAVICA.   XXX
 SUBS (1974): CONTINUED IN SERIES A & SERIES B.

ACTA CHEMICA SCANDINAVICA: SERIES A.   XXX
+ +ACTA CHEM. SCAND., A.
 COPENHAGEN 28, 1974-
FROM 1, 1947- ISSUED AS A SINGLE TITLE
THEN FROM 1974 CONTINUED IN SERIES A &
SERIES B.
 GL/U-1.   HL/U-1.   LO/N14.   LO/R-6.   MA/U-1.

ACTA CHEMICA SCANDINAVICA: SERIES B.   XXX
+ +ACTA CHEM. SCAND., B.
 COPENHAGEN 28, 1974-
SEE NOTES FOR SERIES A.
 GL/U-1.   HL/U-1.   LO/N14.   LO/R-6.

ACTA EUROPAEA FERTILITATIS.
+ +ACTA EUR. FERTIL.
 [MORGAGNI EDIZIONI SCIENTIFICHE]
 ROME 1, 1969-
 Q.
 SO/U-1.   ISSN 0587-2421

ACTA MEDICA AUXOLOGICA.
+ +ACTA MED. AUXOL.
CENTRO AUXOLOGICO ITALIANO DI PIANCAVALLO.
 MILAN 1(1), 1969-
3/A. GER., ENGL., FR. OR ITAL., WITH ITAL.,
ENGL., FR. OR GER. SUMM.
 OX/U-8. 2(3), 1970-   LO/U-1. 1(3), 1969; 2(3), 1970-

ACTA NEOPHILOLOGICA.
+ +ACTA NEOPHILOL.
UNIVERZA V LJUBLJANA: FILOZOFSKA FAKULTETA.
 LJUBLJANA 1, 1968-
 OX/U-1.   ISSN 0567-784X

ACTA NEUROVEGETATIVA.   XXX
 SUBS (1968): JOURNAL OF NEURO-VISCERAL
 RELATIONS.

ACTA OCEANOGRAPHICA TAIWANICA.
+ +ACTA OCEANOGR. TAIWAN.
NATIONAL TAIWAN UNIVERSITY: INSTITUTE OF OCEAN-
OGRAPHY.
 TAIPEI NO.1, 1971-
ENGL. WITH CHIN. SUMM. TITLE ALSO IN CHINESE.
AT HEAD OF TITLE, 1971- SCIENCE REPORTS OF THE
NATIONAL TAIWAN UNIVERSITY.
 LO/N-2.

ACTA PALAEOBOTANICA.
+ +ACTA PALAEOBOT.
POLSKA AKADEMIA NAUK: INSTYTUT BOTANIKI.
 CRACOW 1(1), 1960-
 OX/U-8.   LO/U-2. 4(2), 1963- 5(1-2), 1964.   ISSN 0001-6594

ACTA PHYTOMEDICA.
+ +ACTA PHYTOMED.
 BERLIN NO.1, 1973-
 BN/U-2.   CA/U-7.   LO/N-2.   SO/U-1.   XS/U-1.

ACTA PHYTOTHERAPEUTICA.   XXX
+ +ACTA PHYTOTHER.
 AMSTERDAM 1, JA 1954- 19(9), 1972.//
ENGL., FR. & GER. S/T: SCIENTIFIC JOURNAL OF
BOTANICAL MEDICINE.
 LO/N-4.   LO/N13.   ISSN 0001-6802

ACTA PRAEHISTORICA ET ARCHAEOLOGICA.   XXX
++ACTA PRAEHIST. & ARCHAEOL.
BERLINER GESELLSCHAFT FUR ANTHROPOLOGIE, ETH-
NOLOGIE UND URGESCHICHTE.
BERLIN 1, 1970-
ENGL., FR. & GER. PREV: PART OF BERLINER
BEITRAGE ZUR VOR- UND FRUHGESCHICHTE FROM 1,
1957- 13, 1969. SPONS. BODIES ALSO: IBERO-
AMERIKANISHE INSTITUT PREUSSISCHER KULTUR-
BESITZ (BERLIN); & STAATLICHE MUSEEN PREUSSIS-
CHER KULTURBESITZ (BERLIN).
CA/U-1. LO/S10.

ACTA UNIVERSITATIS PALACKIANAE OLOMUCENSIS:
GEOGRAPHICA-GEOLOGICA.   XXX
++ACTA UNIV. PALACKI. OLOMUC., GEOGR.-GEOL.
PALACKEHO UNIVERSITA: PRIRODOVEDECKA FACULTA.
PRAGUE 1, 1960-
ENGL., GER. OR RUSS. SUMM. PREV: SBORNIK
PRIRODNE VEDY: OBORY GEOLOGIE, GEOGRAFIE,
BIOLOGIE FROM 1, 1956- 3, 1959.
BH/U-1. BL/U-1. GL/U-1. LO/N-4.

ACTA VERTEBRATICA.   XXX
++ACTA VERTEBR.
NORDISKA MUSEET & SKANSEN.
SKANSEN 1, 1957- 3, 1964.//
VARIOUS LANGUAGES.
DR/U-1. LO/N-2. ISSN 0065-1680

ACTA WASAENSIA: GEOGRAPHY.
++ACTA WASAENSIA, GEOGR.
UNIVERSITAS ECONOMICA WASAENSIS.
VAASA NO.1, 1971-
AD/U-1.

ACTIVITIES AT TURRIALBA.
++ACT. TURRIALBA.
INTER-AMERICAN INSTITUTE OF AGRICULTURAL
SCIENCES: CENTRO TROPICAL DE ENSENANZA
E INVESTIGACION.
TURRIALBA, COSTA RICA 1(1), 1972-
LO/R-6.

ACTUAL.
UNIVERSIDAD DE LOS ANDES.
MERIDA 1, JA/AP 1968-
3/A.
OX/U-1. 11(8/9), 1971- ISSN 0001-7639

ACTUALIDAD ANTROPOLOGICA.
++ACTUAL. ANTROLOP.
MUSEO ETNOGRAFICO MUNICIPAL DAMASO ARCE.
OLAVARRIA, ARGENT. 1, JL/D 1967-
2/A. ISSUED AS A SUPPLEMENT TO: ETNIA.
LO/S10. 2, 1968- ISSN 0567-8560

ACTUALIDADES BIOLOGICAS.
++ACTUAL. BIOL.
MEDELLIN 1, 1972-
LO/N-2.

ADAB. JOURNAL OF THE FACULTY OF ARTS, UNIV-
ERSITY OF KHARTOUM.
[KHARTOUM UNIV. P.]
KHARTOUM 1, 1972-
ANNU.
LO/U14.

ADVANCES IN AGRONOMY & CROP SCIENCE.   000
SEE: FORTSCHRITTE IM ACKER- UND PFLANZENBAU.

ADVANCES IN NEUROLOGY.
++ADV. NEUROL.
[RAVEN P.]
NEW YORK 1, 1973-
ANNU.
CA/U-1. SO/U-1. SO/U-1. 2, 1973.

ADVANCES IN NUCLEAR QUADRUPOLE RESONANCE.
++ADV. NUCL. QUADRUPOLE RESON.
[HEYDON]
LONDON 1, 1974-
CA/U-1. GL/U-1. SF/U-1.

ADVANCES IN SLEEP RESEARCH.
++ADV. SLEEP RES.
[SPECTRUM]
FLUSHING, N.Y. 1, 1974-
LO/U-2.

AFGHANISTAN JOURNAL.
++AFGHAN. J.
[AKADEMISCHE DRUCK- U. VERLAGSANSTALT]
GRAZ 1(1), 1974-
LO/N12. LO/U14.

AFRICAN ADMINISTRATIVE ABSTRACTS.
++AFR. ADM. ABSTR.
CENTRE AFRICAIN DE FORMATION ET DE RECHERCHE
ADMINISTRATIVES POUR LE DEVELOPPEMENT:
LIBRARY & DOCUMENTATION SERVICES.
TANGIER 1, 1974-
Q.
LD/U-1.

AFRICAN GEOGRAPHICAL STUDIES.
++AFR. GEOGR. STUD.
NAIROBI 1, 1971-
OX/U-9.

AFRICAN RESEARCH & DOCUMENTATION.   XXX
++AFR. RES. & DOC.
AFRICAN STUDIES ASSOCIATION OF THE UNITED
KINGDOM.
BIRMINGHAM 1, 1973-
3M. PREV: PART OF LIBRARY MATERIALS ON AFRICA
FROM 1, 1962- 10(3), 1972; & BULLETIN OF THE
AFRICAN STUDIES ASSOCIATION OF THE UNITED
KINGDOM FROM NO.1, JA 1964- NO.22, 1972.
SPONS. BODY ALSO: STANDING CONFERENCE ON LIB-
RARY MATERIALS ON AFRICA.
AD/U-1. BL/U-1. ED/N-1. LO/N-2. LO/R-6. LO/U-8.
MA/U-1. OX/U-8. OX/U17. ISSN 0305-862X

AFRICA-TERVUREN.   XXX
AMIS DU MUSEE ROYAL DE L'AFRIQUE CENTRALE.
TERVUREN 7, 1961-
DUTCH & FR. PREV: CONGO-TERVUREN FROM 1,
1955- 6, 1960.
LO/N-2. LO/S10. 17, 1971- ISSN 0001-9879

AFRICAN THEATRE.
[AFRICAN PUBL. HOUSE]
NAIROBI NO.1, 1972-
OX/U-1.

AGRARTECHNIK INTERNATIONAL.   XXX
++AGRARTECH. INT.
[VOGEL-VERLAG]
WURZBURG 53, 1974-
PREV: LANDMASCHINEN-MARKT FROM 30(10), [1944]-
52, 1973.
LO/N14.

AGRICOLE.   XXX
PARIS NO.1, 1974-
PREV: FIGARO AGRICOLE.
LO/N13.

AGRICULTURA TROPICAL.   XXX
++AGRIC. TROP.
ASOCIACION COLOMBIANA DE INGENIEROS
AGRONOMOS.
BOGOTA 1(1), F 1945- 26(12), 1970.//
LO/R-6. 26(1), 1970-

AGRICULTURAL ADMINISTRATION.
++AGRIC. ADM.
[APPLIED SCIENCE PUBL. LTD]
LONDON 1(1), JA 1974-
Q.
CA/U-1. ED/N-1. EX/U-1. LO/N13. LO/R-6. OX/U-1.

AGRICULTURAL ECONOMICS & FARM MANAGEMENT
OCCASIONAL PAPER.
++AGRIC. ECON. & FARM MANAGE. OCCAS. PAP.
UNIVERSITY OF QUEENSLAND: DEPARTMENT OF
AGRICULTURE.
ST. LUCIA, QUEENSL. 1, AG 1970-
BL/U-1.

AGRICULTURAL RECORD, DEPARTMENT OF AGRICULT-
URE (SOUTH AUSTRALIA).   XXX
++AGRIC. REC. DEP. AGRIC. (SOUTH AUST.).
ADELAIDE 1(1), JA 1974-
PREV: EXPERIMENTAL RECORD, DEPARTMENT OF
AGRICULTURE (SOUTH AUSTRALIA) FROM NO.1, 1963-
7, 1973.
AB/U-2. LO/R-6.

AGRICULTURAL RESEARCH, GUYANA.
++AGRIC. RES. GUYANA.
(GUYANA) MINISTRY OF AGRICULTURE & NATURAL
RESOURCES: CENTRAL AGRICULTURAL STATION.
MON REPOS 1, 1969-
3RD- ANNUAL REPORT OF THE RESEARCH DIVISION
OF THE MINISTRY OF AGRICULTURE & NATURAL RES-
OURCES. REPORTS FOR 1967-68 ISSUED AS PART
OF: REPORT, MINISTRY OF AGRICULTURE & NATURAL
RESOURCES (GUYANA).
CA/U-1. 4, 1970-

AGRICULTURE HONG KONG.   XXX
++*AGRIC. HONG KONG.*
(HONG KONG) DEPARTMENT OF AGRICULTURE &
FISHERIES.
HONG KONG 1, 1972-
PREV: AGRICULTURAL SCIENCE, HONG KONG FROM
1(1), 1968- 1(5/6), 1971.
LO/N13.   LO/R-6.

AGRO-ECOSYSTEMS.
AMSTERDAM 1, 1974-
Q.
LO/N13.   LO/R-5.

**AGROMETEOROLOGICAL MEMORANDUM, METEOROLOGICAL
SERVICE (EIRE).**
++*AGROMETEOROL. MEMO. METEOROL. SERV. (EIRE).*
DUBLIN NO.1, 1969-
XS/N-1 NO.1, 1969.

AICHI IKA DAIGAKU IGAKKAI ZASSHI.
[NAGOYA] 1, 1973-
ENGL. TITLE: JOURNAL OF THE AICHI MEDICAL
UNIVERSITY ASSOCIATION.
LO/N13.

AIR ENTHUSIAST INTERNATIONAL.   XXX
++*AIR ENTHUSIAST INT.*
[PILOT P. LTD.]
LONDON 6, 1974...
PREV: AIR ENTHUSIAST FROM 1, 1971- 5, 1973.
SUBS: AIR INTERNATIONAL.
LO/N14.

AIR INTERNATIONAL.   XXX
++*AIR INT.*
[PILOT P. LTD.]
LONDON 7, 1974-
PREV: AIR ENTHUSIAST INTERNATIONAL
FROM 6, 1974.
LO/N14.

**AIR STRUCTURES BIBLIOGRAPHY/ LIGHTWEIGHT
ENCLOSURES UNIT.**
++*AIR STRUCT. BIBLIOGR./ LIGHTWEIGHT ENCLOSURES
UNIT.*
LIGHTWEIGHT ENCLOSURES UNIT.
LONDON [NO.1], AP 1973-
ED/N-1.

AKROS. POETRY MAGAZINE.
PRESTON, LANCS. 1, 1965-
3/A.
CA/U-1.   GL/U-1. ‡W. 5(13)- 6(18)A   ISSN 0002-3728

**AKTUAL'NYE PROBLEMY PROFESSIONAL'NOJ PATOL-
OGII.**
++*AKTUAL. PROBL. PROF. PATOL.*
DONETSKIJ MEDITSINSKIJ INSTITUT.
KIEV 1, 1970-
LO/N13.

ALBERTINA INFORMATIONEN.
++*ALBERTINA INF.*
[GRAPHISCHE SAMMLUNG ALBERTINA]
VIENNA 1(1), 1968-
5/A.
OX/U-2.

ALCOHOL & HEALTH NOTES.
NATIONAL INSTITUTE ON ALCOHOL ABUSE & ALCOHOL-
ISM (US).
ROCKVILLE, MD. 1, 1972-
SPONS. BODY ALSO: NATIONAL INSTITUTE OF MENTAL
HEALTH (US).
BL/U-1.   ISSN 0090-2969

ALCOHOL HEALTH & RESEARCH WORLD.
++*ALCOHOL HEALTH & RES. WORLD.*
NATIONAL INSTITUTE ON ALCOHOL ABUSE & ALCOHOL-
ISM (US).
ROCKVILLE, MD. 1(1), 1973-
Q.
LO/N-1.   ISSN 0090-838X

ALIVE. CMS YOUTH MAGAZINE.
CHURCH MISSIONARY SOCIETY: YOUTH DEPARTMENT.
LONDON 1, S/OC 1973-
6/A.
CA/U-1.   ED/N-1.

**ALL SPORTS INTERNATIONAL. THE SPORT &
LEISURE NEWSPAPER.**
++*ALL SPORTS INT.*
[ASSET PROMOTIONS LTD.]
LONDON NO.1, 1971-
CA/U-1. NO.18, 1974-   ED/N-1. NO.19, 1974-

ALLIANCE JOURNAL.   XXX
++*ALLIANCE J.*
COCOA CHOCOLATE & CONFECTIONERY ALLIANCE.
LONDON 1(1), 1949- 24(8), 1972.//
MON.
LO/R-6.

**ALLIANZ BERICHTE FUR BETRIEBSTECHNIK UND
SCHADENVERHUTUNG.**   XXX
++*ALLIANZ BER. BETRIEBSTECH. & SCHADENVERHUTUNG.*
ALLIANZ VERSICHERUNGS.
MUNICH 3, 1967-
PREV: ERFAHRUNGSBERICHTE, ALLIANZ VERSICHER-
UNGS FROM 1-2, 1965.
LO/N14. ‡W. 8, 1968; & 10, 1969A   ISSN 0569-0692

ALLIED IRISH BANKS REVIEW.
++*ALLIED IR. BANKS REV.*
DUBLIN NO.1, JL 1973-
Q.
ED/N-1.   OX/U-1.

ALLPANCHIS PHUTURINQA.
INSTITUTO DE PASTORAL ANDINA.
CUZCO 1, 1969-
S/T: REVISTA ANUAL.
LO/N-1.

AL'MANAKH NAUCHNOJ FANTASTIKI.
++*ALM. NAUCHN. FANTASTIKI.*
[IZDATEL'STVO £ZNANIE£]
MOSCOW 1, 1964- 10, 1971.
SUBS: SBORNIK NAUCHNOJ FANTASTIKI.

ALUMINIUM (COPENHAGEN).
[ALUMINIUMRADETS FORLAG]
COPENHAGEN MR 1972-
Q.
LO/N14. 2, 1973-

**AMAZONIANA. LIMNOLOGIA ET OECOLOGIA REGION-
ALIS SYSTEMAE FLUMINIS AMAZONAS.**
INSTITUTO NACIONAL DE PESQUISAS DA AMAZONIA
(BRAZIL).
[KOMMISSIONS-VERLAG WALTER G. MUHLAU]
KIEL 1, 1965-
ENGL., FR., GER., PORT. OR SPAN. VOL.1(1)
SPONS. BODY ALSO: HYDROBIOLOGISCHE ANSTALT,
MAX-PLANCK-GESELLSCHAFT ZUR FORDERUNG DER
WISSENSCHAFTEN, WHICH FROM 1(2)- CHANGED TO
ABTEILUNG TROPENOLOLOGIE, MAX-PLANCK-INSTITUT
FUR LIMNOLOGIE. ISSUES A SUPPLEMENT: BIBLIO-
GRAFIA AMAZONICA.
LO/N-2.   LO/N-4.   LO/N13.   LO/U-4.   ISSN 0065-6755

AMAZONISCHE BIBLIOGRAPHIE.   000
SEE: BIBLIOGRAFIA AMAZONICA.

**AMENAGEMENT DU TERRITOIRE ET DEVELOPPEMENT
REGIONAL.**
++*AMENAGEMENT TERRIT. & DEV. REG.*
UNIVERSITE DE GRENOBLE: CENTRE D'ETUDE ET DE
RECHERCHE SUR L'ADMINISTRATION ECONOMIQUE ET
L'AMENAGEMENT DU TERRITOIRE.
GRENOBLE 1, 1965/1966(1968)-
ANNU. CENTRE SUBORD. TO: INSTITUT D'ETUDES
POLITIQUES.
LO/U-3.   OX/U-1.

AMERICAN CARTOGRAPHER.
++*AM. CARTOGR.*
AMERICAN CONGRESS ON SURVEYING & MAPPING.
WASHINGTON D.C. 1, AP 1974-
2/A.
CA/U-1.   ED/N-1.   LO/U-1.   ISSN 0094-1689

AMERICAN ETHNOLOGIST.
++*AMER. ETHNOL.*
AMERICAN ANTHROPOLOGICAL ASSOCIATION.
WASHINGTON, D.C. 1, 1974-
LO/U-2.   LO/U14.

AMERICAN HIGHWAY & TRANSPORTATION MONTHLY.   XXX
++*AM. HIGHW. & TRANSP. MON.*
AMERICAN ASSOCIATION OF STATE HIGHWAY & TRANS-
PORTATION OFFICIALS.
WASHINGTON, D.C. 53, 1974-
PREV: AMERICAN HIGHWAYS FROM 1, AG 1922- 52,
1973.
LO/N14.

AMERICAN HIGHWAYS.   XXX
SUBS (1974): AMERICAN HIGHWAY & TRANSPORTATION
MONTHLY.

AMERICAN JOURNAL OF ARABIC STUDIES.
+ +AM. J. ARABIC STUD.
LEIDEN 1, 1972-
OX/U-1.

AMERICAN JOURNAL OF CHINESE MEDICINE.
+ +AM. J. CHIN. MED.
GARDEN CITY, N.Y. 1(1), 1973-
2/A.
LO/U14.   OX/U-8.

AMERICAN JOURNAL OF POLITICAL SCIENCE.   XXX
+ +AM. J. POLIT. SCI.
[WAYNE STATE UNIV. P.]
DETROIT 17, 1973-
PREV: MIDWEST JOURNAL OF POLITICAL SCIENCE
FROM 1, 1957- 16, 1972.
GL/U-2.   HL/U-1.   OX/U-1.   SA/U-1.

AMERICAN REVIEW OF EAST-WEST TRADE.
+ +AM. REV. EAST-WEST TRADE.
[SYMPOSIUM P.]
WHITE PLAINS, N.Y. 1(1), 1968-
MON.
LA/U-1. 2(1), 1969-   LO/N17. 3(1), 1970-   ISSN 0003-0783

AMERICAN STUDIES. AN INTERNATIONAL NEWS-
LETTER.   XXX
+ +AM. STUD. (WASH., D.C.).
CONFERENCE BOARD OF THE ASSOCIATED RESEARCH
COUNCILS: COMMITTEE ON INTERNATIONAL EXCHANGE
OF PERSONS.
WASHINGTON, D.C. 8, 1970-
3/A. PREV: AMERICAN STUDIES NEWS FROM 1,
1962.
BL/U-1.   DN/U-1.   NO/U-1.   SO/U-1.   ISSN 0003-1321

AMERICAN STUDIES (STUTTGART).   000
SEE: AMERIKASTUDIEN.

AMERICAN STUDIES NEWS.   XXX
SUBS (1970): AMERICAN STUDIES. AN INTERNAT-
IONAL NEWSLETTER.

AMERIKANSKIJ ETNOGRAFICHESKIJ SBORNIK.
+ +AM. ETNOGR. SB.
AKADEMIJA NAUK SSSR: INSTITUT ETNOGRAFII.
MOSCOW 1, 1960-
SUBSERIES OF: TRUDY, AKADEMIJA NAUK SSSR:
INSTITUT ETNOGRAFII: NOVAJA SERIJA. NO.1 OF
ABOVE + TOM 58 OF TRUDY.
LO/U15.

AMERIKANSKIJ EZHEGODNIK.
+ +AM. EZHEG.
AKADEMIJA NAUK SSSR: INSTITUT VSEOBSHCHEJ
ISTORII.
MOSCOW 1971-
TITLE ALSO IN ENGL.: ANNUAL STUDIES OF
AMERICA.
CA/U-1.   CC/U-1.

AMERIKASTUDIEN. AMERICAN STUDIES.   XXX
DEUTSCHE GESELLSCHAFT FUR AMERIKASTUDIEN.
STUTTGART 19, 1974-
PREV: JAHRBUCH FUR AMERIKASTUDIEN FROM 1,
1956- 18, 1973.
OX/U-1.

AMERIKASTUDIEN: BEIHEFT.   XXX
DEUTSCHE GESELLSCHAFT FUR AMERIKASTUDIEN.
STUTTGART 38, 1974-
PREV: JAHRBUCH FUR AMERIKASTUDIEN: BEIHEFT
FROM 1, 1957- 37, 1972. ALSO ENTITLED: AMER-
ICAN STUDIES.
OX/U-1.

AMPERA REVIEW.
+ +AMPERA REV.
[PUTERA PUBL. INST.]
DJAKARTA NO.1, 17/AG 1964-
S/T: TRANSMITTER OF THE MESSAGE OF THE
PEOPLE'S SUFFERINGS & ASPIRATIONS.
*HL/U-1.**   ISSN 0569-9568*

AMSTERDAM IN DE MARKT.
+ +AMST. MARK.
KAMER VAN KOOPHANDEL EN FABRIEKEN VOOR
AMSTERDAM.
AMSTERDAM 1968(1)-
LO/N-1. 1969(2)-   ISSN 0003-2069

ANAIS, SOCIEDADE ENTOMOLOGICA DO BRASIL.
+ +AN. SOC. ENTOMOL. BRAS.
ITABUNA, BRAZ. 1, 1972-
LO/N-2.   LO/N13.

ANALECTA VETERINARIA.   XXX
+ +ANALECTA VET.
UNIVERSIDAD NACIONAL DE LA PLATA: FACULTAD DE
CIENCIAS VETERINARIAS.
LA PLATA 1, JA/AP 1969-
PREV: REVISTA, FACULTAD DE CIENCIAS VETERINAR-
IAS, UNIVERSIDAD NACIONAL DE LA PLATA: TERCERA
EPOCA FROM 1, JA/AP 1959- 10(24), 1968.
LO/N13.

ANALES, ARCHIVO NACIONAL (HONDURAS).
+ +AN. ARCH. NAC. (HONDURAS).
TEGULIGALPA 1, S 1967-
OX/U-1. 10, 1971-   ISSN 0441-1331

ANALES, COMISION DE INVESTIGACION CIENTIFICA
(BUENOS AIRES, PROVINCE).
+ +AN. COM. INVEST. CIENT. (B. AIRES PROV.).
LA PLATA 1, 1960-
ENGL. SUMM.
LO/N13.   ISSN 0524-9880

ANALES DE LA FACULTAD DE MEDICINA, UNIV-
ERSIDAD DE SALAMANCA.
+ +AN. FAC. MED. UNIV. SALAMANCA.
SALAMANCA 1, 1964/65-
GL/U-1.   ISSN 0581-3794

ANALIZ ASSOTSIATIVNOJ DEJATEL'NOSTI GOLOVNOGO
MOZGA.
+ +ANAL. ASSOTS. DEJAT. GOLOVN. MOZGA.
MOSKOVSKIJ GOSUDARSTVENNYJ UNIVERSITET.
MOSCOW 1, 1972-
LO/N13.

ANALYTICAL ADVANCES.
+ +ANAL. ADV.
[HEWLETT-PACKARD CO.]
AVONDALE, PA. 1968-
LO/N14.   ISSN 0570-0027

ANALYTICAL SCIENCES MONOGRAPH.
+ +ANAL. SCI. MONOGR.
SOCIETY FOR ANALYTICAL CHEMISTRY.
LONDON NO.1, 1973-
CA/U-1.   ISSN 0583-8894

ANBAR YEARBOOK.
+ +ANBAR YEARB.
[ANBAR PUBL. LTD.]
WEMBLEY 1, [1972]-
CA/U-1.   OX/U-1.

ANESTHESIOLOGY BIBLIOGRAPHY.
+ +ANESTHESIOL. BIBLIOGR.
AMERICAN SOCIETY OF ANESTHESIOLOGISTS.
PARK RIDGE, ILL. [1, 1968]-
BL/U-1. 5, 1972-   ISSN 0572-3795

ANGLICAN THEOLOGICAL REVIEW: SUPPLEMENTARY
SERIES.
+ +ANGLICAN THEOL. REV., SUPPL. SER.
[ANGLICAN THEOLOGICAL REVIEW, INC.]
NEW YORK 1, 1973-
HL/U-1.   OX/U-1.   ISSN 0097-4951

ANIMAL BEHAVIOUR ABSTRACTS.   XXX
+ +ANIM. BEHAV. ABSTR.
[INFORMATION RETRIEVAL LTD.]
LONDON 2(1), F 1974-
PREV: BEHAVIOURAL BIOLOGY ABSTRACTS: SECTION A
ANIMAL BEHAVIOUR FROM 1(1-4), MY- N 1973.
ED/N-1.   HL/U-1.   LO/N13.   LO/U-2.   LO/U-4.   RE/U-1.

ANNALS OF BIOMEDICAL ENGINEERING.
+ +ANN. BIOMED. ENG.
BIOMEDICAL ENGINEERING SOCIETY.
[ACADEMIC P.]
NEW YORK & LONDON 1, S 1972-
LO/N13.

ANNALES CISALPINES D'HISTOIRE SOCIALE.
+ +ANN. CISALP. HIST. SOC.
UNIVERSITA DEGLI STUDI DI PAVIA.
PAVIA S.1. NO.1, 1970-
OX/U-1.

ANNALES DE L'ECOLE DES LETTRES DE L'UNIV-
ERSITE DU BENIN.
+ +ANN. EC. LETT. UNIV. BENIN.
LOME 1, 1972-
LO/S10.

ANNALI DELLA FACOLTA DI ECONOMIA E COMMERCIO
IN VERONA.
++ANN. FAC. ECON. & COMMER. VERONA.
UNIVERSITA DI PADOVA: FACOLTA DI ECONOMIA E
COMMERCIO IN VERONA.
VERONA S.1. 1, 1964/65(1965)-
LO/N-1.   ISSN 0552-7686

ANNALS OF HUMAN BIOLOGY.
++ANN. HUM. BIOL.
SOCIETY FOR THE STUDY OF HUMAN BIOLOGY.
[TAYLOR & FRANCIS]
LONDON 1, 1974-
S/T: FOR THE STUDY OF HUMAN ECOLOGY, DEMO-
GRAPHY & GROWTH & THE GENETICS & PHYSIOLOGY OF
HUMAN POPULATIONS.
ED/N-1.   LD/U-1.   LO/U12.   MA/U-1.   SF/U-1.   SH/U-1.

ANNALES, INSTITUT DE PHILOSOPHIE, UNIVERSITE
LIBRE DE BRUXELLES.
++ANN. INST. PHILOS. UNIV. LIBRE BRUX.
BRUSSELS 1969-
OX/U-1.

ANNALI DE MEZZOGIORNO.
++ANN. MEZZOGIORNO.
UNIVERSITA DI CATANIA: CENTRO DI STUDI E RIC-
ERCHE SUL MEZZOGIORNO E LA SICILIA.
CATANIA 1, 1961-
CENTRO SUBORD. TO: INSTITUTO DI STORIA ECON-
OMICA.
LO/U-3.   OX/U-1.   ISSN 0066-2259

ANNALS OF NUCLEAR SCIENCE & ENGINEERING.   XXX
++ANN. NUCL. SCI. & ENG.
[PERGAMON P.]
OXFORD 1(1), 1974-
PREV: JOURNAL OF NUCLEAR ENERGY.
ED/N-1.   LD/U-1.   LO/N14.   LO/U12.   OX/U-8.   RE/U-1.
XS/R10.   ISSN 0302-2927

ANNALS OF OPHTHALMOLOGY (CHICAGO).
++ANN. OPHTHALMOL. (CHIC.).
[ANNALS OF OPHTHALMOLOGY PUBL. CORP.]
CHICAGO 1, JE/JL 1969-
MON.
OX/U-8.   ISSN 0003-4886

ANNALS OF OTOLOGY, RHINOLOGY & LARYNGOLOGY:
SUPPLEMENT.
++ANN. OTOL. RHINOL. & LARYNGOL., SUPPL.
[ANNALS PUBL. CO.]
ST. LOUIS, MO. NO.1, 1971-
LO/U-1.

ANNALS OF THE ROYAL COLLEGE OF PHYSICIANS &
SURGEONS OF CANADA.
++ANN. R. COLL. PHYSICIANS & SURG. CAN.
OTTAWA 1, JA 1968-
Q.
OX/U-8.   LO/M13. 1(4), 1968-   ISSN 0035-8800

ANNALES DE L'UNIVERSITE D'ABIDJAN: SERIES I:
HISTOIRE.
++ANN. UNIV. ABIDJAN, I.
ABIDJAN 1, 1972-
AD/U-1.   LO/U14.   OX/U-1.

ANNEE AFRICAINE.
++ANNEE AFR.
FONDATION NATIONALE DES SCIENCES POLITIQUES
(FRANCE): CENTRE D'ETUDES DES RELATIONS INTER-
NATIONALES.
[EDITIONS A. PEDONE]
PARIS 1963-
SPONS. BODIES ALSO: CENTRE D'ETUDES D'AFRIQUE
NOIRE, UNIVERSITE DE BORDEAUX; & CENTRE DES
HAUTES ETUDES ADMINISTRATIVES SUR L'AFRIQUE ET
L'ASIE MODERNES.
LO/N-1.   LO/S14.   LO/U-3.   LO/U14.   RE/U-1.

ANNEE ECONOMIQUE.
++ANNEE ECON. (PARIS).
FONDATION NATIONALE DES SCIENCES POLITIQUES
(FRANCE): SERVICE D'ETUDES DE L'ACTIVITE ECON-
OMIQUE.
PARIS 1966-
DB/U-2.   LO/U-3.   ISSN 0066-233X

ANNOTATED BIBLIOGRAPHY OF RESEARCH IN
EDUCATION.
++ANNOT. BIBLIOGR. RES. EDUC.
HUMAN SCIENCES RESEARCH COUNCIL (SOUTH
AFRICA).
PRETORIA 1, 1970-
BL/U-1.

ANNUAIRE DU MUSEE NATIONAL DU CANADA.
++ANNU. MUS. NATL. CAN.
OTTAWA NO.1, 1965/1966-
LO/N-1.   ISSN 0576-2812

ANNUAL ART SALES INDEX.
++ANNU. ART SALES INDEX.
[ART SALES INDEX LTD.]
WEYBRIDGE, SURREY 1971/72-
ED/N-1.

ANNUAL BIBLIOGRAPHY OF EUROPEAN ETHNOMUSIC-   000
OLOGY.
   SEE: MUSIKETHNOLOGISCHE JAHRESBIBLIOGRAPHIE
EUROPAS.

ANNUAL BIBLIOGRAPHY OF THE HISTORY OF THE PRINT-
ED BOOK & LIBRARIES.
++ANNU. BIBLIOGR. HIST. PRINTED BOOK & LIBR.
THE HAGUE 1, 1970-
BL/U-1.   EX/U-1.   LO/N-2.   OX/U-1.

ANNUAL BULLETIN OF THE FRIENDS OF THE LIBRARY,   XXX
TRINITY COLLEGE, DUBLIN.
   SUBS (1970): LONG ROOM.

ANNUAL EDITIONS: READINGS IN ECONOMICS.
++ANNU. ED., READINGS ECON.
[DUSHKIN PUBL. GROUP]
GUILDFORD, CONN. 1, 1972-
AD/U-1.

ANNUAL, HEBREW UNION COLLEGE BIBLICAL & ARCH-
AEOLOGICAL SCHOOL.
++ANNU. HEB. UNION COLL. BIBLICAL & ARCHAEOL.
SCH.
JERUSALEM 1, 1970-
AD/U-1.

ANNUAL OF JEWISH STUDIES.
++ANNU. JEW. STUD.
GRATZ COLLEGE (PHILADELPHIA).
PHILADELPHIA 1, 1972-
OX/U-1.

ANNUAL, MUSEUM OF ART (BALTIMORE).
++ANNU. MUS. ART (BALTIMORE).
BALTIMORE 1, 1966-
OX/U-2.   ISSN 0067-3080

ANNUAL OF POWER & CONFLICT.
++ANNU. POWER & CONFLICT.
INSTITUTE FOR THE STUDY OF CONFLICT.
LONDON 1971(1972)-
SPONS. BODY ALSO: NATIONAL STRATEGY INFORMAT-
ION CENTER (US).
AD/U-1.   CA/U-1.   EX/U-1.   SO/U-1.   OX/U-1. 1972/73-

ANNUAL OF PSYCHOANALYSIS.
++ANNU. PSYCHOANAL.
CHICAGO INSTITUTE FOR PSYCHOANALYSIS.
[QUADRANGLE]
NEW YORK 1, 1973-
LO/U-1.   ISSN 0092-5055

THE ANNUAL REGISTER OF INDIAN POLITICAL
PARTIES.
++ANNU. REGIST. INDIAN POLIT. PARTIES.
[ORIENTALIA (INDIA)]
NEW DELHI 1, 1972/73-
LO/N12.

ANNUAL REPORT, ADVISORY BOARD FOR RESEARCH
COUNCILS.
++ANNU. REP. ADVIS. BOARD RES. COUNC.
[HMSO]
LONDON IST, 1974-
LO/R-5.

ANNUAL REPORT, ESSEX RIVER AUTHORITY.
++ANNU. REP. ESSEX RIVER AUTH.
CHELMSFORD 1, 1965/66-
LO/R-5.   ED/N-1. 6, 1971-

ANNUAL REPORTS IN INORGANIC & GENERAL SYNTHESES.
++ANNU. REP. INORG. & GEN. SYNTH.
[ACADEMIC P.]
NEW YORK & LONDON 1972(1973)-
LO/N14.   LO/S-3.

ANNUAL REPORT, NATIONAL GALLERY OF ART (US).   xxx
++*ANNU. REP. NATL. GALLERY ART (US).*
WASHINGTON, D.C. 1969/70.
REPORT YEAR ENDS 30 JE 1970. PREV: REPORT &
STUDIES IN THE HISTORY OF ART, NATIONAL GALL-
ERY OF ART (US) FROM 1967- 1969. SUBS:
STUDIES IN THE HISTORY OF ART, NATIONAL GALL-
ERY OF ART (US).
RE/U-1.

ANNUAL REPORT, POLITICAL & ECONOMIC PLANNING.
++*ANNU. REP. POLIT. & ECON. PLANN.*
LONDON 1960/61[1961]-
BH/U-1. HL/U-1. ISSN 0085-4964

ANNUAL REPORT, SOCIETY FOR LIBYAN STUDIES.
++*ANNU. REP. SOC. LIBYAN STUD.*
LONDON 1, 1969/70-
REPORT YEAR ENDS MR 31.
LO/S10. LO/U14.

**ANNUAL REVIEW OF BEHAVIOR THERAPY: THEORY &
PRACTICE.**
++*ANNU. REV. BEHAV. THER., THEORY & PRACT.*
[BRUNNER/MAZEL]
NEW YORK 1973-
CA/U-1. OX/U-8. ISSN 0091-6595

**ANNUAL REVIEW, EUROPEAN COMMISSION OF HUMAN
RIGHTS.**
++*ANNU. REV. EUR. COMM. HUM. RIGHTS.*
STRASBOURG 1972(1973)-
ENGL. & FR.
LO/U-2. OX/U15.

**ANNUAL REVIEW, RUBBER RESEARCH INSTITUTE
OF SRI LANKA.**   xxx
++*ANNU. REV. RUBBER RES. INST. SRI LANKA.*
AGALAWATTA 1972(1973)-
PREV: ANNUAL REVIEW, RUBBER RESEARCH
INSTITUTE OF CEYLON FROM 1960(1961)-
1971(1972).
LO/N14.

ANNUAL STUDIES OF AMERICA.   000
SEE: AMERIKANSKIJ EZHEGODNIK.

ANNUAL SURVEY OF INDIAN LAW.
++*ANNU. SURV. INDIAN LAW.*
INDIAN LAW INSTITUTE.
NEW DELHI 1, 1965(1966)-
OX/U15.

ANTARTIDA.
(ARGENTINA) DIRECCION NACIONAL DEL ANTARTICO.
BUENOS AIRES NO.1, D 1971-
LO/N-2. XS/N-1.

**ANTHOS. VIERTELJAHRES-ZEITSCHRIFT FUR
GARTEN- UND LANDSCHAFTSGESTALTUNG.**
INTERNATIONAL FEDERATION OF LANDSCAPE
ARCHITECTS.
ZURICH 1, MR 1962-
GER. FR. & ENGL. SPONS. BODIES ALSO:
BUND SCHWEIZERISCHER GARTEN- UND LAND-
SCHAFTSARCHITEKTEN; & VEREINIGUNG
SCHWEIZERISCHER GARTENBAUAMTER
BL/U-1. 13, 1974- XS/U-1. 8, 1969- ISSN 0003-5424.

ANTI DEAR FOOD CAMPAIGNER.
ANTI DEAR FOOD CAMPAIGN.
EPSOM, SURREY NO.1, JL 1973-
MON.
ED/N-1.

ANTIKITETE TE KOSOVE E METOHIS.   000
SEE: STARINE KOSOVA I METOHIJE.

ANTIPODE MONOGRAPHS IN SOCIAL GEOGRAPHY.
++*ANTIPODE MONOGR. SOC. GEOGR.*
WORCESTER, MASS. NO.1, 1972-
SH/U-1.

ANTIQUARIAN BOOK MONTHLY REVIEW.
++*ANTIQ. BOOK MON. REV.*
OLNEY, BUCKS. NO.1, F 1974-
CA/U-1. ED/N-1. LO/U-3. NO/U-1. SH/U-1.

ANTIQUITES DE KOSOVO ET METOHIJA.   000
SEE: STARINE KOSOVA I METOHIJE.

**ANUARIO, INSTITUTO DE CIENCIAS PENALES Y CRIM-
INOLOGICAS, UNIVERSIDAD CENTRAL DE VENEZUELA.**
++*ANU. INST. CIENC. PENALES & CRIMINOL. UNIV.
CENT. VENEZ.*
CARACAS 1, 1967-
INSTITUTO SUBORD. TO: FACULTAD DE DERECHO.
OX/U15. ISSN 0507-570X

APPLIED SCIENCES & DEVELOPMENT.
++*APP. SCI. & DEV.*
INSTITUTE FOR SCIENTIFIC CO-OPERATION
(TUBINGEN).
TUBINGEN 1, 1973-
2/A. S/T: COLLECTION OF RECENT GERMAN CON-
TRIBUTIONS CONCERNING DEVELOPMENT THROUGH
APPLIED SCIENCES.
OX/U-8.

APPROPRIATE TECHNOLOGY.   xxx
++*APPROPRIATE TECHNOL.*
[INTERMEDIATE TECHNOL. PUBL.]
LONDON 1(1), 1974-
PREV: ITDG BULLETIN FROM 1, 1966- 10, 1973.
CA/U-4. ED/N-1. LO/N14. LO/R-6. OX/U-8.

AQUARIUM HOBBYIST.
[FORGE ASSOCIATION PUBL. INC.]
PHILLIPSBURG, N.J. 1, S 1971-
MON.
LO/N13. ISSN 0044-8532

AQUATIC MAMMALS.
++*AQUAT. MAMM.*
HARDERWIJK, NETH. 1, 1972-
LO/N-2.

ARABLE FARMING.
[FARMING P.]
IPSWICH 1, 1974-
ED/N-1. LO/N13.

ARCHAEOLOGY MONOGRAPH, ROYAL ONTARIO MUSEUM.
++*ARCHAEOL. MONOGR. R. ONT. MUS.*
TORONTO [NO.]1, 1974-
LO/U-1. ISSN 0316-1285

ARCHAEOLOGISTS' YEAR BOOK.
++*ARCHAEOL. YEAR BOOK.*
[DOLPHIN P.]
CHRISTCHURCH, HANTS. 1973-
S/T: AN INTERNATIONAL DIRECTORY OF ARCHAEOLOGY
& ANTHROPOLOGY.
GL/U-1.

ARCHIEF VOOR ANTROPOLOGIE.   000
SEE: ARCHIVES D'ANTHROPOLOGIE.

**ARCHIFACTS. BULLETIN OF THE ARCHIVES COMMITTEE
OF THE NEW ZEALAND LIBRARY ASSOCIATION.**
DUNEDIN NO.1, 1974-
LO/U-1 LO/U-8. ISSN 0303-7940

ARCHITECTURAL COMPETITIONS NEWS.
++*ARCHIT. COMPET. NEWS.*
ROYAL INSTITUTE OF BRITISH ARCHITECTS.
LONDON 1, 1974-
BL/U-1.

ARCHITECTURAL JOURNAL (PEKING).   000
SEE: CHIEN-CHU HSUEH-PAO.

ARCHITECTURAL PERIODICALS INDEX.   xxx
++*ARCHIT. PERIOD. INDEX.*
ROYAL INSTITUTE OF BRITISH ARCHITECTS.
LONDON 1(1), AG/D 1972-
Q. PREV: PART OF RIBA LIBRARY BULLETIN FROM
1(1), 1946- 26, 1972; & RIBA ANNUAL REVIEW OF
PERIODICAL ARTICLES FROM 1, 1965/66(1967)- 7,
1972.
ED/N-1. GL/U-2. LO/N14. LO/U-2. OX/U-1.

ARCHITECTURAL PSYCHOLOGY NEWSLETTER.
++*ARCHIT. PSYCHOL. NEWSL.*
KINGSTON POLYTECHNIC: SCHOOL OF ARCHITECTURE.
KINGSTON-UPON-THAMES 1, JL 1969-
PRODUCED BY THE SCHOOL'S PSYCHOLOGY RESEARCH
UNIT.
LO/U-1. SH/U-1. ISSN 0305-8603

**ARCHIVES D'ANTHROPOLOGIE. ARCHIEF VOOR ANT-
ROPOLOGIE.**   xxx
++*ARCH. ANTHROPOL.*
MUSEE ROYAL DE L'AFRIQUE CENTRALE.
TERVUREN NO.16, 1972-
PREV: ARCHIVES D'ETHNOGRAPHIE FROM 1, 1960.
LO/N-1.

ARCHIVES DE L'INSTITUT BOTANIQUE DE L'UNIV-
ERSITE DE LIEGE.   XXX
+ +ARCH. INST. BOT. UNIV. LIEGE.
 LIEGE 1, 1897- 34, 1972.//
 CA/U-2.   LO/N-1.   LO/N-2.   NO/U-1.

ARCHIVES INTERNATIONALES DE FINANCES PUB-
LIQUES.   XXX
+ +ARCH. INT. FINANC. PUBL.
 PADUA &C. 1, 1954- 4, 1964.//
 OX/U-1.   ISSN 0518-3405

ARCHIVES INTERNATIONALES D'HISTOIRE DES IDEES:
SERIES MINOR.
+ +ARCH. INT. HIST. IDEES, SER. MINOR.
 [NIJHOFF]
 THE HAGUE 1, 1972-
 OX/U-1.

ARCHIVO DE LENGUAS PRECOLOMBINAS.
+ +ARCH. LENGUAS PRECOLOMB.
 CENTRO DE ESTUDIOS LINGUISTICOS (BUENOS AIRES).
 BUENOS AIRES 1, 1966-
 LO/U-1.   ISSN 0570-7072

ARCHIVES OF MICROBIOLOGY.   XXX
+ +ARCH. MICROBIOL.
 [SPRINGER]
 BERLIN &C. 95, 1974-
 PREV: ARCHIV FUR MIKROBIOLOGIE FROM 1, 1930-
 94, 1973.
 LD/U-1.   LO/N13.   SO/U-1.

ARCHIV FUR MIKROBIOLOGIE.   XXX
 SUBS (1974): ARCHIVES OF MICROBIOLOGY.

ARCHIVUM OTTOMANICUM.
+ +ARCH. OTTOMANICUM.
 THE HAGUE 1, 1969-
 CA/U-1.   MA/U-1.   OX/U-1.

ARCHIV FUR PHYTOPATHOLOGIE UND PFLANZENSCHUTZ.XX
+ +ARCH. PHYTOPATHOL. & PFLANZENSCHUTZ.
 [AKADEMIE VERLAG]
 BERLIN 9, 1973-
 PREV: ARCHIV FUR PFLANZENSCHUTZ FROM 1, 1965-
 8, 1972.
 LO/N13.   LO/R-6.

ARCHIVES DE SCIENCES SOCIALES DES RELIGIONS.   XXX
+ +ARCH. SCI. SOC. RELIG.
 CENTRE NATIONAL DE LA RECHERCHE SCIENTIFIQUE
 (FRANCE).
 PARIS NO.35, 1973-
 PREV: ARCHIVES DE SOCIOLOGIE DES RELIGIONS
 FROM NO.1, JA/JE 1956- 34, 1972.
 HL/U-1.   OX/U-1.   ISSN 0335-5985

ARCHIVOS DE LA SOCIEDAD ESPANOLA DE OFTALMOL-
OGIA.   XXX
+ +ARCH. SOC. ESP. OFTALMOL.
 MADRID 31, 1971-
 PREV: ARCHIVOS DE LA SOCIEDAD OFTALMOLOGICA
 HISPANO-AMERICANA FROM 1, 1942- 30(11), 1970.
 LD/U-1.   LO/U-1.

ARCHIVOS DE LA SOCIEDAD OFTALMOLOGICA HISPANO-
AMERICANA.   XXX
 SUBS (1971): ARCHIVOS DE LA SOCIEDAD ESPAN-
 OLA DE OFTALMOLOGIA.

ARCHIVES DE SOCIOLOGIE DES RELIGIONS.   XXX
 SUBS (1973): ARCHIVES DE SCIENCES SOCIALES
 DES RELIGIONS.

ARCHIVIO DEL TEATRO ITALIANO.
+ +ARCH. TEATRO ITAL.
 [EDIZIONI IL POLIFILO]
 MILAN 1, 1968-
 CA/U-1.   ISSN 0066-6661

ARCHIVNI ZPRAVY, USTREDNI ARCHIV, CESKOSLOV-
ENSKA AKADEMIE VED.
+ +ARCH. ZPR. USTRED. ARCH. CESK. AKAD. VED.
 PRAGUE NO.1, 1970-
 GER. & RUSS. SUMM.
 OX/U-1.

ARCTIC BULLETIN.
+ +ARCT. BULL.
 WASHINGTON, D.C. 1(1), 1973-
 AD/U-1.   CA/U12.   LO/N-2.   LO/N13.   LO/S13.

AREAS.
 ASSOCIATION FOR RADICAL EAST ASIAN STUDIES.
 LONDON NO.1, 1971-
 LO/U14.*

ARGUMENTA PALAEOBOTANICA.
+ +ARGUMENTA PALAEOBOT.
 [CRAMER; REMY]
 LEHRE & MUNSTER 1, 1966-
 ENGL. OR GER.
 LO/N-2.   LO/N13.   ISSN 0587-5404.

ARGUMENTO.
 RIO DE JANEIRO NO.1, 1973-
 OX/U-1.

ARHITEKTURA UN PILSETBUVNIECIBA LATVIJAS PSR,
RAKSTU KRAJUMS.
+ +ARHIT. PILSETBUVNIECIBA LATV. PSR RAKSTU
 KRAJUMS.
 RIGAS POLITEHNISKAIS INSTITUTS: ARHITEKTURAS
 KATEDRA.
 RIGA 1, 1969-
 LATV. & RUSS. TITLE ALSO IN RUSS.: ARKHIT-
 EKTURA I GRADOSTROITEL'STVO V LATVIJSKOJ SSR.
 OX/U-1.

ARIS. ART RESEARCH IN SCANDINAVIA.
 LUNDS UNIVERSITET: INSTITUTE OF ART HISTORY.
 LUND 1, 1969-
 2/A.
 BT/C-1.   ISSN 0044-5711

ARKHITEKTURA I GRADOSTROITEL'STVO V LATVIJSKOJ
SSR (RIGA).   000
 SEE: ARHITEKTURA UN PILSETBUVNIECIBA LATVIJAS
 PSR, RAKSTU KRAJUMS.

ARKWRIGHT'S FIRST MAGAZINE.
+ +ARKWRIGHT'S FIRST MAG.
 [ARKWRIGHT]
 LONDON NO.1, 1973-
 CA/U-1.   ED/N-1.

ARMAGH POETRY PRESS.
+ +ARMAGH POETRY P.
 [J. MACKEY]
 ARMAGH 1, 1974-
 BL/U-1.

ARNOLD NEWSLETTER.
+ +ARNOLD NEWSL.
 EASTERN MICHIGAN UNIVERSITY: DEPARTMENT OF
 ENGLISH.
 YSPILANTI, MICH. 1, 1973-
 3/A.
 OX/U-1.

ARRAN BANNER.
 WHITING BAY NO.1, MR 1974-
 ED/N-1.

ARSBOK, MALMO MUSEUM.
+ +ARSB. MALMO MUS.
 MALMO 1, 1970-
 LO/N-2.

ART & ARCHAEOLOGY TECHNICAL ABSTRACTS.   XXX
+ +ART & ARCHAEOL. TECH. ABSTR.
 INTERNATIONAL INSTITUTE FOR CONSERVATION
 OF HISTORIC & ARTISTIC WORKS.
 LONDON & NEW YORK 6, 1966-
 2/A. PREV: IIC ABSTRACTS FROM 2, 1958-
 5, 1965. PUBL. FOR THE INSTITUTE BY
 NEW YORK UNIVERSITY INSTITUTE OF FINE ARTS.
 GL/U-1.   DB/U-2. 7, 1968-   LO/N12. 8(2), 1970-

ART BIBLIOGRAPHIES: CURRENT TITLES.
+ +ART BIBLIOGR., CURR. TITLES.
 AMERICAN BIBLIOGRAPHICAL CENTER.
 [CLIO P.]
 SANTA BARBARA &C. 1(1), S 1972-
 10/A.
 CA/U-1.   EX/U-1.   OX/U-1.   SA/U-1.   AD/U-1. 2, 1973-

ART INVESTMENT GUIDE.
 [ART SALES INDEX LTD.]
 WEYBRIDGE [NO.]1, SUMMER 1973-
 Q.
 CA/U-1.

ARTS D'AFRIQUE (VILLIERS-LE-BEL).   000
 SEE: ARTS D'AFRIQUE NOIRE.

ARTS D'AFRIQUE NOIRE.   XXX
+ +ARTS AFR. NOIRE.
 VILLIERS-LE-BEL 1, 1971-
 VOL.1 ENTITLED: ARTS D'AFRIQUE.
 CA/U-3.   LO/S10.

ASHER'S GUIDE TO BOTANICAL PERIODICALS.
++*ASHER'S GUIDE BOT. PERIOD.*
[A. ASHER & CO.]
AMSTERDAM 1973-
3W.
CA/U-2. LO/N-2. LO/N13.

**ASIAN CULTURE. BULLETIN OF THE ASIAN CULT-
URAL CENTRE IN TOKYO.**
++*ASIAN CULT.*
[MAINCHI NEWSPAPERS]
TOKYO NO.1, 1972-
Q.
HL/U-1.

ASIAN CULTURE QUARTERLY. YA-CHOU WEN HUA.
++*ASIAN CULT. Q.*
ASIAN CULTURAL CENTRE (TAIPEI).
TAIPEI 1, 1973-
OX/U-1.

ASIEN, AFRIKA, LATEINAMERIKA.
++*ASIEN AFR. LATEINAM.*
ZENTRAAL RAT FUR ASIEN-, AFRIKA- UND LATEIN-
AMERIKAWISSENSCHAFTEN IN DER DDR.
[AKADEMIE VERLAG]
BERLIN 1, 1973-
Q.
LO/U14. OX/U-1.

**ASKLEPIJ. BOLGARO-SOVETSKIJ EZHEGODNIK ISTORII
I TEROII MEDITSINY.**
[MEDITSINA I FIZKUL'TURA]
SOFIA 1, 1970-
ENGL. SUMM.
LO/M24. 1972-

ASPIRANTU ZINATNISKIE RAKSTI.
++*ASPIR. ZINAT. RAKSTI.*
LATVIJSKIJ GOSUDARSTVENNYJ UNIVERSITET.
RIGA 1, 1963-
TITLE ALSO IN RUSSIAN: UCHENYE ZAPISKI ASPIR-
ANTOV.
LO/U-3. OX/U-1. 3, 1965-

ASSEGA1.
[POETRY ONE]
BILLERICAY, ESSEX NO.1, 1974-
ED/N-1.

ASTRONAUTICA ACTA.   XXX
   SUBS (1974): ACTA ASTRONAUTICA.

ATMOSPHERIC TECHNOLOGY.   XXX
++*ATMOS. TECHNOL.*
NATIONAL CENTER FOR ATMOSPHERIC RESEARCH (US).
BOULDER, COLO. NO.1, MR 1973-
PREV: FACILITIES FOR ATMOSPHERIC RESEARCH FROM
NO.1, 1966- 22, 1972.
XS/N-1. ISSN 0091-2026

ATOMIC DATA & NUCLEAR DATA TABLES.   XXX
++*AT. DATA & NUCL. DATA TABLES.*
[ACADEMIC P.]
NEW YORK & LONDON 12(1), AG 1973-
PREV: NUCLEAR DATA TABLES FROM 9(4/5), 1971-
11, 1973; INCORP. ATOMIC DATA FROM 1(1), S
1969- 5, 1973.
LO/N14. OX/U-8. XS/R10.

AUDIOVISUAL LIBRARIAN.   XXX
LIBRARY ASSOCIATION: AUDIOVISUAL GROUP.
LONDON 1(1), 1973-
Q. PREV: BULLETIN, AUDIOVISUAL GROUP, LIBRARY
ASSOCIATION FROM NO.7, N 1972. SPONS. BODY
ALSO: AUDIO-VISUAL GROUP OF ASLIB.
BL/U-1. CA/U-1. ED/N-1. OX/U-1. SH/P-1. SH/U-1.
LO/U-2 1974- ISSN 0302-3451

**AUSGRABUNGEN IN BERLIN. FORSCHUNGEN UND FUNDE
ZUR UR- UND FRUHGESCHICHTE.**   XXX
++*AUSGRABUNGEN BERL.*
[HESSLING]
BERLIN 1, 1970-
PREV: PART OF BERLINER BEITRAGE ZUR VOR- UND
FRUHGESCHICHTE FROM 1, 1957- 13, 1969.
CA/U-1. LO/S10.

AUSTRALASIAN OIL & GAS JOURNAL.   XXX
   SUBS (1968): AUSTRALASIAN OIL & GAS REVIEW.

AUSTRALASIAN OIL & GAS REVIEW.   XXX
++*AUSTRALAS. OIL & GAS REV.*
[TRACER PETROLEUM & MINING PUBL. PTY. LTD.]
SYDNEY 14(5), 1968- 19(1), 1972 ...
PREV: AUSTRALASIAN OIL & GAS JOURNAL FROM 1,
1954- 14(4), 1968. SUBS: OIL & GAS.
LO/N13. ISSN 0004-8429

AUSTRALIAN BUSINESS LAW REVIEW.
++*AUST. BUS. LAW REV.*
SYDNEY 1, 1973-
OX/U15. SO/U-1.

AUSTRALIAN FOREIGN AFFAIRS.   XXX
++*AUST. FOR. AFF.*   XXX
(AUSTRALIA) DEPARTMENT OF EXTERNAL AFFAIRS.
CANBERRA 44, JA 1973-
MON. PREV: CURRENT NOTES ON INTERNATIONAL
AFFAIRS FROM 1, JA 1936- 43, 1972.
HL/U-1.

AUSTRALIAN GOVERNMENT DIGEST.
[GOVERNMENT PRINTER]
CANBERRA 1, 1972(1973)-
CA/U-1.

AUSTRALIAN JOURNAL OF OPHTHALMOLOGY.   XXX
++*AUST. J. OPHTHALMOL.*
AUSTRALIAN COLLEGE OF OPHTHALMOLOGISTS.
GLEBE, SYD. 1, F 1973-
PREV: TRANSACTIONS, AUSTRALIAN COLLEGE OF
OPHTHALMOLOGISTS FROM 1, 1969(1970)- 3, 1971
(1972).
LO/M17.

AUSTRALIAN JOURNAL OF PLANT PHYSIOLOGY.
++*AUST. J. PLANT PHYSIOL.*
CSIRO (AUSTRALIA).
VICTORIA, N.S.W. 1(1), MR 1974-
AB/U-2. BH/P-1. BL/U-1. CA/U-1. CA/U-2. CA/U-7.
LO/N-2. LO/N-6. LO/N13. OX/U-8. RE/U-1. SA/U-1.
SO/U-1. SW/U-1.

AUSTRALIAN MARXIST REVIEW.
++*AUST. MARXIST REV.*
SOCIALIST PARTY OF AUSTRALIA.
MEREWETHER, N.S.W. 1(1), F 1972-
2/M.
LO/U-8. ISSN 0004-9654

AUSTRALIAN PAINT JOURNAL.   XXX
++*AUST. PAINT J.*
[BELL PUBL.]
SYDNEY 5, 1960- 19(1), 1974.//
PREV: PAINT JOURNAL OF AUSTRALIA & NEW ZEALAND
FROM 1, 1956- 4, 1959.
LO/N13. ISSN 0004-9948

AUSTRALIAN WELDING RESEARCH.
++*AUST. WELD. RES.*
AUSTRALIAN WELDING RESEARCH ASSOCIATION.
SYDNEY 1, JE 1969-
2M.
LO/N14. 1(2), 1969- ‡W.2(1)Å ISSN 0045-0960

AUSTRALIND.
UNIVERSITY OF WESTERN AUSTRALIA: REID LIBRARY.
NEDLANDS, PERTH 1971-
LO/U-1. OX/U-9.

AUTOMATIC CONTROL THEORY & APPLICATIONS.
++*AUTOM. CONTROL THEORY & APPL.*
[ACTA P.]
CALGARY 1, JA 1972-
LO/N14.

AUTOMEDICA.
[GORDON & BREACH]
NEW YORK & LONDON 1, 1970-
CA/U-1. ED/N-1. GL/U-2. 1974- ISSN 0045-1045

AUTOMOTIVE EMISSION CONTROL.
++*AUTOMOT. EMISS. CONTROL.*
[R.H. CHANDLER LTD.]
BRAINTREE, ESSEX 1, 1973-
LO/N14. CA/U-1. 2, 1974- ED/N-1. 2, 1974-

AUTOSAFE.
(NEW SOUTH WALES) DEPARTMENT OF MOTOR TRANSPORT
[MAXWELL PRINTING PTY. LTD.]
ROSEBERY, N.S.W. 1972-
MON.
LO/N14. CURRENT BOX ONLY.

AVIAN PATHOLOGY.
++*AVIAN PATHOL.*
BELGRADE 1(1), OC 1972-
Q.
LO/M18.

AVTOMATIZATSIJA PROEKTIROVANIJA V ELEKTRONIKE.
++*AVTOM. PROEKT. ELEKTRON.*
(UKRAINE) MINISTERSTVO VYSSHOJI I SEREDN'OJI
SPETSIAL'NOJI OS'VITY.
KIEV 1, 1970-
S/T: RESPUBLIKANSKIJ MEZHVEDOMSTVENNYJ
NAUCHNO-TEKHNICZESKIJ SBORNIK.
LO/N13.

BACTERIOLOGIA, VIRUSOLOGIA, PARAZITOLOGIA,   XXX
EPIDEMIOLOGIA.
++*BACTERIOL. VIRUSOL. PARAZITOL. EPIDEMIOL.*
UNIUNEA SOCIETATILER DE STIINTE MEDICALE.
BUCHAREST 19, 1974-
PREV: MICROBIOLOGIA, PARAZITOLOGIA, EPIDEMIO-
LOGIA FROM 1, JA/AG 1956- 18, 1973.
LO/N13.

BAIT.
CHICHESTER & DISTRICT ANGLING SOCIETY.
CHICHESTER NO.1, MR 1973-
ED/N-1.   OX/U-8.

BAKERY WORKER.   XXX
++*BAKERY WORK.*
BAKERS' UNION.
LONDON 22, 1969-
PREV: JOURNEYMAN BAKER FROM NS.1, 1928- 21,
1968.
BH/U-1.

BANK OF LONDON & SOUTH AMERICA REVIEW.   XXX
++*BANK LOND. & SOUTH AM. REV.*
LONDON NO.85, JA 1974-
PREV: BOLSA REVIEW FROM NO.1, JA 1967- 84, D
1973.
SH/P-1.

BANKERS' DIGEST.   XXX
SUBS (1973): SPECIAL OFFICE BRIEF.

BARCLAYS BANK REVIEW.   XXX
SUBS (1971): BARCLAYS REVIEW.

BARCLAYS INTERNATIONAL REVIEW.   XXX
++*BARCLAYS INT. REV.*
BARCLAYS BANK, LTD.
LONDON OC 1971- S 1974.//
PREV: BARCLAYS OVERSEAS REVIEW FROM
MY 1968- S 1971.
DB/U-2.   LD/U-1.   LO/N35.   LO/R-6.   NW/U-1.   RE/U-1.

BARCLAYS OVERSEAS REVIEW.   XXX
++*BARCLAYS OVERSEAS REV.*
BARCLAYS BANK, LTD.
LONDON 1968- S 1971...
PREV: OVERSEAS REVIEW FROM MR 1946- 1967.
SUBS: BARCLAYS INTERNATIONAL REVIEW.
MA/U-1.   NW/U-1.   RE/U-1.   DB/U-2. S 1969-
XS/T-4.   ‡ONE YEAR ONLY‡

BARCLAYS REVIEW.   XXX
++*BARCLAYS REV.*
BARCLAYS BANK, LTD.
LONDON 46(3), 1971-
PREV: BARCLAYS BANK REVIEW FROM 22, 1947-
46(2), 1971.
GL/U-1.   HL/U-1.   LO/U-1.   LO/U-3.   RE/U-1.

BARLEY GENETICS NEWSLETTER.
++*BARLEY GENET. NEWSL.*
COLORADO STATE UNIVERSITY: DEPARTMENT OF
AGRONOMY.
FORT COLLINS 1, 1971-
ANNU.
AB/U-2.

BASIC ASSET.
SOIL & WATER MANAGEMENT ASSOCIATION.
KENILWORTH SUMMER 1973-
LO/N14.

BDSA INDUSTRY TREND SERIES.
++*BDSA IND. TREND SER.*
(UNITED STATES) BUSINESS & DEFENSE SERVICES
ADMINISTRATION.
WASHINGTON, D.C. 1, OC 1968-
OX/U-9.

BEARINGS DIGEST.
++*BEAR. DIG.*
WORTHING NO.1, 1973-
LO/N14.

**BEITRAGE ZUR AUFFUHRUNGSPRAXIS. SCHRIFTENREIHE
DES INSTITUTS FUR AUFFUHRUNGSPRAXIS DER HOCH-
SCHULE FUR MUSIK UND DARSTELLENDE KUNST IN GRAZ.**
++*BEITR. AUFFUHRUNGSPRAXIS.*
AKADEMIE FUR MUSIK UND DARSTELLENDE KUNST
(GRAZ): INSTITUT FUR AUFFUHRUNGSPRAXIS.
GRAZ 1, 1972-
MONOGR.
LO/N-1.

**BEITRAGE ZUR GESCHICHTE DER DEUTSCHEN SOZIAL-
ISTISCHEN LITERATUR IM 20. JAHRHUNDERT.**
++*BEITR. GESCH. DTSCH. SOZ. LIT. 20. JAHRHUNDERT*
DEUTSCHE AKADEMIE DER KUNSTE: ABTEILUNG GES-
CHICHTE DER SOZIALISTISCHEN LITERATUR.
[AUFBAU-VERLAG]
BERLIN & WEIMAR 1, 1971-
ABTEILUNG SUBORD. TO: SEKTION DICHTKUNST UND
SPRACHPFLEGE.
LO/N-1.

**BEITRAGE ZUR SEMITISCHEN PHILOLOGIE UND LING-
UISTIK.**
++*BEITR. SEMANTISCH. PHILOL. & LINGUIST.*
[GEORGE OLMS VERLAGSBUCHHANDLUNG]
HILDESHEIM 1, 1968-
MONOGR.
LO/N-1.

BEITRAGE ZUR SOZIAL- UND WIRTSCHAFTSGESCHICHTE.
++*BEITR. SOZ.- & WIRTSCHAFTSGESCH.*
KIEL 1, 1970-
OX/U-1.

BEITRAGE ZUR TROPISCHEN LANDWIRTSCHAFT UND   XXX
VETERINARMEDIZIN.
++*BEITR. TROP. LANDWIRTSCH. & VETERINARMED.*
KARL MARX-UNIVERSITAT (LEIPZIG).
LEIPZIG 11, 1973-
GER. OR ENGL. WITH ENGL., FR., RUSS., GER. OR
SPAN. SUMM. PREV: BEITRAGE ZUR TROPISCHEN
UND SUBTROPISCHEN LANDWIRTSCHAFT UND TROPEN-
VETERINARMEDIZIN FROM 1, 1963- 10, 1972.
CA/U11.   GL/U-1.

BELARUSKAJA LINHVISTYKA.
++*BELARUS. LINHVISTYKA.*
AKADEMIJA NAVUK BELARUSKAJ SSR: INSTYTUT MOVAZ-
NAUSTVA.
MINSK 1, 1972-
TITLE ALSO IN ENGL.: BYELORUSSIAN LINGUISTICS.
CA/U-1.   SA/U-1. 4, 1973.

**BERICHTE, INSTITUT FUR STEUERUNGSTECHNIK DER
WERKZEUGMASCHINEN UND FERTIGUNGSEINRICHTUNGEN,
UNIVERSITAT STUTTGART.**
++*BER. INST. STEUERUNGSTECH. WERKZEUGMASCH. &
FERTIGUNGSEINRICHTUNGEN UNIV. STUTTG.*
[SPRINGER]
BERLIN &C. ISW 1, 1972-
LO/N14.

BERLINER BEITRAGE ZUR VOR- UND FRUHGESCHICHTE.XX
SUBS (1970): PART OF ACTA PRAEHISTORICA ET
ARCHAEOLOGICA; & AUSGRABUNGEN IN BERLIN.

BETTER BREEDING.
MILK MARKETING BOARD.
THAMES DITTON, SURREY 1966-
Q.
CA/U-1. 1973-   ED/N-1. SUMMER 1973-
OX/U-8. AUTUMN 1973-

BFI TELEVISION MONOGRAPHS.   000
SEE: TELEVISION MONOGRAPHS, BRITISH FILM
INSTITUTE.

**BIBLIOGRAFIA AMAZONICA. PUBLICACOES LIMNOL-
OGICAS ECOLOGICAS E DE CIENCIAS AFINS SOBRE A
REGIAO AMAZONICA.**
++*BIBLIOGR. AMAZONICA.*
INSTITUTO NACIONAL DE PESQUISAS DA AMAZONIA
(BRAZIL).
KIEL [NO.1], 1965-
ISSUED AS A SUPPLEMENT TO: AMAZONIANA. ALSO
ENTITLED: AMAZONISCHE BIBLIOGRAPHIE.
LO/N13.

BIBLIOGRAFIA BOLIVIANA.
++*BIBLIOGR. BOLIV.*
[LOS AMIGOS DEL LIBRO]
 COCHABAMBA, BOLIV. 1962(1963)-
 OX/U-1.   LO/U-3. 1966-   SO/U-1. 1966- 1972.

BIBLIOGRAFIA URUGUAYA.
++*BIBLIOGR. URUG.*
BIBLIOTECA DEL PODER LEGISLATIVO (URUGUAY).
 MONTEVIDEO JA/AP 1962-
 3/A.
 LO/U-3.   SO/U-1. 1962; 1962/68.   ISSN 0523-1957

**BIBLIOGRAPHY, AERONAUTICAL RESEARCH LABORAT-
ORIES (AUSTRALIA).**
++*BIBLIOGR. AERONAUT. RES. LAB. (AUST.).*
 MELBOURNE ARL/MET.1, 1973-
 LO/N14. NON-CONFIDENTIAL ISSUES ONLY.

BIBLIOGRAPHY, BEE RESEARCH ASSOCIATION.
++*BIBLIOGR. BEE RES. ASSOC.*
 GERRARDS CROSS, BUCKS. NO.1, 1963-
 OX/U-8. NO.12, 1971-   ISSN 0408-7755

BIBLIOGRAPHIEN ZUR DEUTSCHEN BAROCKLITERATUR.
++*BIBLIOGR. DTSCH. BAROCKLIT.*
[FRANCKE VERLAG]
 BERN 1, 1972-
 CA/U-1.

BIBLIOGRAPHIE PHILOSOPHIE.
++*BIBLIOGR. PHILOS. (BERL.).*
INSTITUT FUR GESELLSCHAFTSWISSENSCHAFTEN: ZENT-
RALSTELLE FUR DIE PHILOSOPHISCHE INFORMATION
UND DOKUMENTATION.
 BERLIN 1(1), 1967-
 LO/U-1.   OX/U-1.

BIBLIOGRAPHIE PHILOSOPHIE: BEIHEFT.
++*BIBLIOGR. PHILOS., BEIH.*
INSTITUT FUR GESELLSCHAFTSWISSENSCHAFTEN: ZENT-
RALSTELLE FUR DIE PHILOSOPHISCHE INFORMATION
UND DOKUMENTATION.
 BERLIN 1, 1967-
 OX/U-1.

BIBLIOGRAPHY OF VERTEBRATE PALEONTOLOGY.   XXX
++*BIBLIOGR. VERTEBR. PALEONTOL.*
SOCIETY OF VERTEBRATE PALEONTOLOGY.
[GEOSYSTEMS]
 LONDON 1(1), 1973-
 Q. PREV: BIBLIOGRAPHY OF VERTEBRATE PALEONT-
 OLOGY & RELATED SUBJECTS FROM [1], 1945/46-
 26, 1970/71(1972).

BIBLIOTECA DI STORIA SOCIALE.
++*BIBL. STOR. SOC.*
 ROME 1, 1973-
 CA/U-1.

BIBLIOTECA DI STUDI MERIDIONALI.
++*BIBL. STUDI MERIDIONALI.*
 NAPLES 1, 1969-
 OX/U-1.

**BIBLIOTEKA MUZEALNICTWA I OCHRONY ZABYTKOW:
ZABYTKI ARCHITEKTURY I BUDOWNICTWA W POLSCE.**   000
  **SEE: ZABYTKI ARCHITEKTURY I BUDOWNICTWA W
  POLSCE.**

**BIG FLAME. MERSEYSIDE REVOLUTIONARY SOCIALIST
NEWSPAPER.**
 LIVERPOOL NO.1, 1973-
 20/A.
 CA/U-1. NO.19, 1974-   ED/N-1. NO.15, 1974-

**BILTEN OBAVEZNOG PRIMERKA JUGOSLOVENSKE
KNJIGE.**
++*BILT. OBAVEZNOG PRIMERKA JUGOSL. KNJIGE.*
NARODNA BIBLIOTEKA SR SRBIJE.
 BELGRADE 1, 1971-
 BD/U-1.

BIOGRAFICKE STUDIE.
++*BIOGR. STUD. (MARTIN).*
MATICA SLOVENSKA V MARTINE: BIOGRAFICKY USTAV.
 MARTIN 1, 1970-
 GER. & RUSS. SUMM.
 GL/U-1.

**BIOLOGICHESKIE AKTIVNYE VESHCHESTVA MIKRO-
ORGANIZMOV.**
++*BIOL. AKT. VESHCHESTVA MIKROORG.*
AKADEMIJA NAUK MOLDAVSKOJ SSR: OTDEL MIKROBIOL-
OGII.
 KISHINEV 1, 1970-
 LO/N13.

**BIOMATERIALS, MEDICAL DEVICES, & ARTIFICIAL
ORGANS.**
++*BIOMATER. MED. DEVICES & ARTIF. ORGANS.*
[DEKKER]
 NEW YORK 1, 1973-
 LO/N14.   MA/U-1.

BIOMEDICAL MASS SPECTROMETRY.
++*BIOMED. MASS SPECTROM.*
[HEYDEN]
 LONDON 1(1), F 1974-
 6/A.
 CA/U-1.   ED/N-1.   LO/N14.   LO/R-6.   OX/U-8.

BIOPHYSICAL CHEMISTRY.
++*BIOPHYS. CHEM.*
[NORTH HOLLAND]
 AMSTERDAM 1972-
 MA/U-1.   SH/U-1. 1973-

**BLACK IMAGES. A CRITICAL QUARTERLY ON BLACK
CULTURE.**
 TORONTO 1, JA 1972-
 Q.
 LO/U-2.   MA/U-1.

BLACK LIBERATOR.
[BLACK LIBERATOR ALLIANCE INC.]
 CHICAGO 1969-
 MON.
 CA/U-1. 1971-   ISSN 0006-4181

BLACK PERSPECTIVE IN MUSIC.
++*BLACK PERSPECT. MUSIC.*
FOUNDATION FOR RESEARCH IN THE AFRO-AMERICAN
CREATIVE ARTS, INC.
 NEW YORK 1(1), 1973-
 2/A.
 EX/U-1.

BNF BULLETIN.   XXX
++*BNF BULL.*
BRITISH NUTRITION FOUNDATION LTD.
 LONDON NO.7, 1972-
 PREV: BNF INFORMATION BULLETIN FROM NO.1,
 1968- 6, 1971.
 CA/U11.   LO/N-6.   BL/U-1. NO.8, 1973-

BOARD MANUFACTURE & PROCESSING.   XXX
++*BOARD MANUF. & PROCESS.*
[PRESSMEDIA LTD.]
 DORCHESTER 15(5), S 1973-
 PREV: BOARD MANUFACTURE & PRACTICE FROM 13,
 1970- 15(3/4), 1972.
 ED/N-1.   LO/R-6.   LO/N14. CURRENT BOX ONLY.

BOAT ENGINEERING (TOKYO).   000
  SEE: BOTO ENJINIARINGU.

**BOLETIN, ARCHIVO GENERAL DE LA NACION
(GUATEMALA).**
++*BOL. ARCH. GEN. NAC. (GUATEM.).*
 GUATEMALA, C.A. 1, 1967-
 VOLS. FOR MR 1967- CALLED SEGUNDA EPOCA IN
 CONTINUATION OF THE BOLETIN ISSUED BY THE
 ARCHIVES UNDER ITS EARLIER NAME: ARCHIVO GEN-
 ERAL DEL GOBIERNO FROM 1, 1935-.
 OX/U-1.

BOLETIM DO COMERCIO EXTERIOR.
++*BOL. COMER. EXTER.*
(BRAZIL) SECRETARIA DA RECEITA FEDERAL: CENTRO
DE INFORMACOES ECONOMICO.
 RIO DE JANEIRO 1, 1970-
 CC/U-1. ‡W. 1(2-4)‡A

**BOLETIM, DEPARTAMENTO DE MATEMATICA, FACUL-
DADE DE FILOSOFIA, CIENCIAS E LETRAS DE PRES-
IDENTE PRUDENTE.**
++*BOL. DEP. MAT. FAC. FILOS. CIENC. & LET. PRES.
PRUDENTE.*
 PRESIDENTE PRUDENTE, BRAZ. NO.1, 1970-
 LO/N14.

**BOLETIN DEL INSTITUTO DE DERECHO COMPARADO,
UNIVERSIDAD NACIONAL AUTONOMA DE MEXICO.**   XXX
  **SUBS (1968): BOLETIN MEXICANO DE DERECHO
  COMPARADO: NUEVA SERIE.**

**BOLETIN MENSUAL, DIRECCION GENERAL DE ESTAD-
ISTICA (VENEZUELA).**
++*BOL. MENS. DIR. GEN. ESTAD. (VENEZ).*
 CARACAS JE 1973-
 LO/U-3.

**BOLETIN MEXICANO DE DERECHO COMPARADO: NUEVA
SERIE.**   xxx
++*BOL. MEX. DERECHO COMP., NS.*
UNIVERSIDAD NACIONAL AUTONOMA DE MEXICO: INST-
ITUTO DE INVESTIGACIONES JURIDICAS.
MEXICO, D.F. 1(1), 1968-
PREV: BOLETIN DEL INSTITUTO DE DERECHO COMP-
ARADO, UNIVERSIDAD NACIONAL AUTONOMA DE MEXICO
FROM 1, 1948- 20, 1967. PRODUCED BY THE INST-
ITUTO'S SECCION DE DERECHO COMPARADO.
OX/U15. ISSN 0041-8633

**BOLETIN DEL MUSEO NACIONAL DE ANTROPOLOGIA Y
ARQUEOLOGIA (PERU).**
++*BOL. MUS. NAC. ANTROPOL. & ARQUEOL. (PERU).*
LIMA 1, 1964-
LO/S10. 3, 1965- ISSN 0459-4061

BOLETIM DA SOCIEDADE BRASILEIRA DE GEOLOGIA.   xxx
++*BOL. SOC. BRAS. GEOL.*
SAO PAULO 1, 1952- 19, 1970.//
LO/N-2 LO/N-4. XY/N-1. ISSN 0583-7804*

BOLETIM TECNICO, INSTITUTO FLORESTAL (BRAZIL).
++*BOL. TEC. INST. FLORESTAL (BRAZ.).*
SAO PAULO 1, 1972-
OX/U-3.

**BOLETIN TECNICO, SECCION DE DIVULGACION CIENT-
IFICA, CENTRO NACIONAL DE INVESTIGACIONES DE
CAFE (COLOMBIA).**
++*BOL. TEC. SECC. DIVULG. CIENT. CENT. NAC.
INVEST. CAFE (COLOMB.).*
CHINCHINA, COLOMB. NO.1, 1972-
LO/N13.

BONNER ZOOLOGISCHE MONOGRAPHIEN.
++*BONN. ZOOL. MONOGR.*
ZOOLOGISCHES FORSCHUNGSINSTITUT UND MUSEUM
ALEXANDER KOENIG.
BONN NO.1, 1971-
LO/N-2.

BOOK FORUM.
[HUDSON RIVER P.]
NEW YORK 1, 1974-
AD/U-1.

BOOK WINDOW.
SCOTTISH CHILDREN'S BOOK ASSOCIATION.
GLASGOW 1, D 1973-
ED/N-1. ISSN 0306-2341

BORDER TORY.
ROXBURGH, SELKIRK & PEEBLES CONSERVATIVE &
UNIONIST ASSOCIATION.
GALASHIELS NO.1, 1973-
ED/N-1. OX/U-1.

**BOTANICHESKIE ISSLEDOVANIJA ZA POLJARNYM
KRUGOM.**
++*BOT. ISSLED. POLJARN. KRUGOM.*
POLJARNO-AL'PIJSKIJ BOTANICHESKIJ SAD.
APATITY 1, 1969-
SPONS. BODY ALSO: VSESOJUZNOE BOTANICHESKO
OBSHCHESTVO (KOL'SKOE OTDELENIE).
LO/N13.

**BOTANY LEAFLET, BRITISH MUSEUM (NATURAL
HISTORY).**
++*BOT. LEAFL. BR. MUS. (NAT. HIST.).*
LONDON NO.1, 1974-
LO/N-2. ISSN 0305-4187

BOTO ENJINIARINGU. BOAT ENGINEERING.
SHUTEI KYOKAI SHUPPANBU.
TOKYO NO.1, 1971-
LO/N13.

BOUNDARIES.
SCOTTISH COUNCIL FOR CIVIL LIBERTIES.
GLASGOW NO.1, OC/N 1973-
ED/N-1. OX/U-1. MR/AP 1974-

BOUNDARY 2. A JOURNAL OF POSTMODERN LITERATURE.
STATE UNIVERSITY OF NEW YORK AT BINGHAMTON:
DEPARTMENT OF ENGLISH.
BINGHAMTON 1, 1972-
3/A.
OX/U-1.

BRAIN & LANGUAGE.
++*BRAIN & LANG.*
[ACADEMIC P.]
NEW YORK & LONDON 1, 1974-
Q.
AD/U-1. LO/U-2. OX/U-8. SH/U-1.

BRENESIA.
MUSEO NACIONAL (COSTA RICA).
SAN JOSE, COSTA RICA NO.1, 1972-
LO/N-2.

BREWING & DISTILLING INTERNATIONAL.   xxx
++*BREW. & DISTILL. INT.*
[WILLIAM REED]
LONDON 4, 1974-
PREV: INTERNATIONAL BREWING & DISTILLING FROM
1, 1971- 3, 1973.
ED/N-1. LO/N14.

BRISTOL ORNITHOLOGY.
++*BRISTOL ORNITHOL.*
BRISTOL 1, 1968-
BR/P-1. LO/R-5. CA/U-1. 1(2), 1969-

BRITISH AMNESTY.   xxx
++*BR. AMNESTY.*
AMNESTY INTERNATIONAL: BRITISH SECTION.
LONDON JA 1973
PREV: BRITISH AMNESTY NEWS FROM NO.1, MY 1970-
8, D 1972.
LO/U-3. ED/N-1. NO.9, 1973-

BRITISH ARCHAEOLOGICAL REPORTS.
++*BR. ARCHAEOL. REP.*
OXFORD 1, 1974-
MONOGR.
BL/U-1. GL/U-1. LO/U25. NO/U-1. SO/U-1.

BRITISH CLAYWORKER.   xxx
SUBS (1973): CLAYWORKER.

BRITISH CLOTHING MANUFACTURER.
++*BR. CLOTH. MANUF.*
[TEXTILE TRADE PUBL. LTD.]
LONDON 1, 1965-
MON.
LD/P-1. 1967- XS/R10. 8(5), 1972- ISSN 0007-0467

BRITISH JOURNAL OF CLINICAL PHARMACOLOGY.
++*BR. J. CLIN. PHARMACOL.*
[MACMILLAN]
LONDON 1(1), F 1974-
BH/U-3. BL/U-1. CA/U-1. ED/N-1. LO/N13. OX/U-8.

BRITISH JOURNAL OF LAW & SOCIETY.
++*BR. J. LAW & SOC.*
LONDON 1(1), 1974-
Q.
AD/U-1. BL/U-1. BN/U-1. CA/U-1. CA/U-3. ED/N-1.
GL/U-2. LD/U-1. LO/U-2. LO/U-3. ISSN 0306-3704

BRITISH JOURNAL OF OCCUPATIONAL THERAPY.   xxx
++*BR. J. OCCUP. THER.*
ASSOCIATION OF OCCUPATIONAL THERAPISTS.
LONDON 37(5), MY 1974-
PREV: OCCUPATIONAL THERAPY (LONDON) FROM
1, 1936- 37(4), AP 1974.
ED/N-1.

BRITISH JOURNAL OF ORTHODONTICS.   xxx
BRITISH SOCIETY FOR THE STUDY OF ORTHODONTICS.
[LONGMAN]
LONDON 1, 1973-
Q. INCORP: ORTHODONTIST FROM 1, 1969- 4,
1972; & TRANSACTIONS OF THE BRITISH SOCIETY
FOR THE STUDY OF ORTHODONTICS FROM 1, 1908-
57, 1970/71. SPONS. BODY ALSO: BRITISH ASSOC-
IATION OF ORTHODONTISTS.
BL/U-1. ED/N-1. GL/U-1. LD/U-1. OX/U-8. SH/U-1.

BRITISH JOURNAL OF PHYSICAL EDUCATION.   xxx
++*BR. J. PHYS. EDUC.*
PHYSICAL EDUCATION ASSOCIATION OF GREAT
BRITAIN & NORTHERN IRELAND.
LONDON 1(1), JA 1970-
2M. PREV PART OF: PHYSICAL EDUCATION FROM
48(143), 1956- 61, N 1969; LEAFLET, PHYSICAL
EDUCATION ASSOCIATION OF GREAT BRITAIN &
NORTHERN IRELAND FROM 57, 1956- 70(10), D
1969; & RESEARCH IN PHYSICAL EDUCATION
FROM 1(1), OC 1966- 1(4), 1969.
BN/U-1. 1(2), 1970- CA/U-9. 3, 1972-

**BRITISH JOURNAL OF PSYCHIATRY: SPECIAL
PUBLICATIONS.**
++*BR. J. PSYCHIATR., SPEC. PUBL.*
ROYAL MEDICO-PSYCHOLOGICAL ASSOCIATION.
ASHFORD NO.1, 1967-
OX/U-8. ISSN 0068-2225

BRITISH JOURNAL OF SEXUAL MEDICINE.
++BR. J. SEX. MED.
[MEDICAL NEWS-TRIBUNE LTD.]
  LONDON 1(1), S/OC 1973-
  PRELIMINARY ISSUE DATED MR 1973.
  CA/U-1.   ED/N-1.   ISSN 0301-5572

BRITISH PLASTICS YEAR BOOK.   XXX
  SUBS (1973): EUROPLASTICS YEAR BOOK.

BRITISH POLITICAL SOCIOLOGY YEARBOOK.
++BR. POLIT. SOCIOL. YEARB.
[CROOM HELM]
  LONDON 1, 1974-
  HL/U-1.   LD/U-1.   NO/U-1.   SO/U-1.

BRIXTON'S OWN BOSS.   XXX
  LONDON NO.1, MR 1971- 25, MY 1973.//
  MON.
  LO/U-3.   ‡W.NO.2, AP 1971A

BROWNING INSTITUTE STUDIES.
++BROWNING INST. STUD.
  PRINCETON, N.J. 1, 1973-
  AD/U-1.   ED/N-1.

BRUNEL BULLETIN.
++BRUNEL BULL.
  BRUNEL UNIVERSITY.
  LONDON NO.1, 1966-
  OX/U-1.   ED/N-1. NO.8, 1971-   LD/U-1. NO.6, 1970-
  BL/U-1. CURRENT YEAR ONLY.

BUDUSHCHEE NAUKI. MEZHDUNARODNYJ EZHEGODNIK.
[IZDATEL'STVO ZNANIE]
  MOSCOW 1, 1966-
  BH/U-1. 2, 1968-   BD/U-1. 5, 1972.   LO/U15. 5, 1972.

BUILDING APPOINTMENTS.
++BUILD. APPOINTMENTS.
[BUILDING (PUBL.) LTD.]
  LONDON NO.1, 5/OC 1973-
  WKLY. S/T: FOR THE ARCHITECTURAL & BUILDING
  PROFESSIONS.
  ED/N-1. NO.6, 1973-

BUILDING PROGRESS.
++BUILD. PROG.
  INSTITUTE FOR INDUSTRIAL RESEARCH & STANDARDS
  (EIRE).
  DUBLIN 1, 1974-
  BL/U-1.   CA/U-1.   ED/N-1.

BULGARIAN HISTORICAL REVIEW.
++BULG. HIST. REV.
  BULGARSKA AKADEMIJA NA NAUKITE: UNITED CENTRE
  FOR RESEARCH & TRAINING IN HISTORY.
  SOFIA 1, 1973-
  TITLE ALSO IN FRENCH: REVUE BULGARE D'HISTOIRE
  LO/N-1.   OX/U-1.

BULLETIN OF THE AMERICAN HISTORICAL COLLECT-
ION.
++BULL. AM. HIST. COLLECT.
  AMERICAN ASSOCIATION OF THE PHILIPPINES.
  MANILA 1(1), 1972-
  OX/U-1.

BULLETIN, ARCHEOLOGICKY USTAV, CESKOSLOVENSKA
AKADEMIE VED.
++BULL. ARCHEOL. USTAV CESK. AKAD. VED.
  PRAGUE 2, 1964-
  PRODUCED BY THE ZACHRANNE ODDELENI OF THE
  ARCHEOLOGICKY USTAV. NO DATA AVAILABLE CON-
  CERNING VOL.1.
  OX/U-1. 3, 1966-

BULLETIN DE L'ASSOCIATION FRANCAISE POUR LES
RECHERCHES ET ETUDES CAMEROUNAISES.
++BULL. ASSOC. FR. RECH. & ETUD. CAMEROUNAISES.
  BORDEAUX 1, 1965-
  LO/S10. 4, 1969-   ISSN 0571-5806

BULLETIN, ASSOCIATION FOR RELIGIOUS EDUCATION.
++BULL. ASSOC. RELIG. EDUC.
  SUTTON COLDFIELD, WARWICKS. [NO.]1, 1969-
3/A
  ED/N-1.   HL/U-2. ‡NO.A5, 1970-   MA/U-1. ‡NO.A6, 1971-

BULLETIN, ASSOCIATION FOR RELIGIOUS EDUCATION:
EXTENDED SUPPLEMENT.
++BULL. ASSOC. RELIG. EDUC., EXTENDED SUPPL.
  SUTTON COLDFIELD, WARWICKS. NO.1, 1972-
  ED/N-1.

BULLETIN OF BALTIC STUDIES.   XXX
++BULL. BALTIC STUD.
  ASSOCIATION FOR THE ADVANCEMENT OF BALTIC
  STUDIES.
  [BROOKLYN, N.Y.] 1, 1970- 2, 1971 ...
  Q. SUBS: JOURNAL OF BALTIC STUDIES.
  CA/U-1.   ISSN 0007-4772

BULLETIN, BRITISH CAVE RESEARCH ASSOCIATION.   XXX
++BULL. BR. CAVE RES. ASSOC.
  BRIDGEWATER NO.1, 1973-
  Q. PREV: NEWSLETTER, CAVE RESEARCH GROUP OF
  GREAT BRITAIN FROM NO.1, 1947- 134, 1973.
  LO/N-2.   LO/N-4.   OX/U-8.

BULLETIN, BRITISH PTERIDOLOGICAL SOCIETY.   XXX
++BULL. BR. PTERIDOL. SOC.
  LOUGHTON, ESSEX 1(1), 1973-
  ANNU. PREV: NEWSLETTER, BRITISH PTERIDOLOG-
  ICAL SOCIETY FROM NO.1, 1963- 10, 1972.
  GL/U-1.   HL/U-1.   LD/U-1.   LO/N13.   MA/U-1.   OX/U-8.

BULLETIN, BUILDING CENTRE GROUP.
++BULL. BUILD. CENT. GROUP.
  LONDON &C. NO.1, JA 1973-
  OX/U-1.

BULLETIN OF CANADIAN WELFARE LAW.
++BULL. CAN. WELFARE LAW.
  UNIVERSITY OF BRITISH COLUMBIA: FACULTY OF LAW.
  VANCOUVER 1, F 1972-
  Q.
  OX/U15.

BULLETIN, CENTRE ELECTRONIQUE HORLOGER.   XXX
++BULL. CENT. ELECTRON. HORLOGER.
  NEUCHATEL, SWITZ. NO.1, 1963- 24, 1971.//
  LO/N13. NO.3, 1964-   ISSN 0069-1887

BULLETIN DE LA COLONIE FRANCAISE EN GRANDE-
BRETAGNE.
++BULL. COLON. FR. G.B.
  LONDON S/OC 1972-
  CA/U-1.   ED/N-1.

BULLETIN, CONSULTATIVE COMMITTEE ON THE CURR-
ICULUM, SCOTTISH EDUCATION DEPARTMENT.
++BULL. CONSULT. COMM. CURRICULUM SCOTT. EDUC.
  DEP.
  (GREAT BRITAIN) SCOTTISH EDUCATION DEPARTMENT:
  CONSULTATIVE COMMITTEE ON THE CURRICULUM.
  EDINBURGH NO.1, 1973-
  MONOGR. SPONS. BODY ALSO: CENTRAL COMMITTEE
  ON SOCIAL SUBJECTS.
  CA/U-1.   LO/N-1.

BULLETIN DE CORRESPONDANCE HELLENIQUE: SUPPLE-
MENT.
++BULL. CORRESP. HELL., SUPPL.
[EDITIONS E. DE BOCCARD]
  PARIS &C. 1, 1973-
  BL/U-1.   OX/U-1.

BULLETIN OF ETHIOPIAN MANUSCRIPTS.
++BULL. ETHIOP. MANUSCR.
  ETHIOPIAN MANUSCRIPT MICROFILM LIBRARY.
  ADDIS ABABA 1(1), 1974-
  LO/U14.

BULLETIN/ETUDES ETHNIQUES DU CANADA.   000
  SEE: CANADIAN ETHNIC STUDIES.

BULLETIN, GEOLOGICAL & MINERALOGICAL SURVEY
(AFGHANISTAN).
++BULL. GEOL. & MINERAL. SURV. (AFGHANISTAN).
  KABUL NO.1, 1964-
  GER.
  LO/N-2.   ISSN 0568-0824

BULLETIN, GLASGOW ARCHAEOLOGICAL SOCIETY.
++BULL. GLASGOW ARCHAEOL. SOC.
  GLASGOW 1, 1972-
  ED/N-1.

BULLETIN OF THE INSTITUTE OF JAMAICA: SCIENCE
SERIES.   XXX
++BULL. INST. JAM., SCI. SER.
  KINGSTON, JAM. NO.1, 1940- 21, 1972.//
  CA/U-1.   LO/N-2.   LO/S19.   OX/U-8.   XY/N-1.

BULLETIN, INTERNATIONAL COUNCIL ON ARCHIVES.
++BULL. INT. COUNC. ARCH.
  PARIS NO.1, 1973-
  2/A.
  LO/N12.

BULLETIN, INTERNATIONAL WATERFOWL RESEARCH BUREAU.   XXX
++ *BULL. INT. WATERFOWL RES. BUR.*
SLIMBRIDGE NO.33, JL 1972-
PREV: BULLETIN, INTERNATIONAL WILDFOWL RES-
EARCH BUREAU FROM NO.27/28, JL/D 1969- 32, D
1971.
LO/N-2.

BULLETIN OF MATHEMATICAL BIOLOGY.   XXX
++ *BULL. MATH. BIOL.*
NEW YORK & OXFORD 35(1/2), F/AP 1973-
PREV: BULLETIN OF MATHEMATICAL BIOPHYSICS FROM
1, MR 1939- 34, 1973.
ED/N-1.   SO/U-1.

BULLETIN OF MATHEMATICAL BIOPHYSICS.   XXX
SUBS (1973): BULLETIN OF MATHEMATICAL BIOLOGY.

BULLETIN MENSUEL D'INFORMATION, AMBASSADE DE FRANCE A LONDRES.   XXX
SUBS (1974): NEWS FROM FRANCE.

BULLETIN OF THE MONUMENTAL BRASS SOCIETY.
++ *BULL. MONUMENTAL BRASS SOC.*
[LONDON] NO.1, D 1972-
NW/U-1.   ISSN 0306-1612

BULLETIN OF THE NAGASAKI AGRICULTURAL & FORESTRY EXPERIMENT STATION: SECTION OF AGRICULTURE.   000
SEE: NAGASAKI-KEN SOGO NORIN SHIKENJO
KENKYU HOKOKU: NOGYO BUMON.

BULLETIN, NATIONAL SPELEOLOGICAL SOCIETY.   XXX
SUBS (1974): NSS BULLETIN.

BULLETIN OF THE NORTH STAFFORDSHIRE LABOUR STUDIES GROUP.
++ *BULL. NORTH STAFFS. LABOUR STUD. GROUP.*
STOKE-ON-TRENT 1, 1973-
CA/U-1.   ED/N-1.   LO/U-3.   OX/U-1.

BULLETIN OF QUANTITATIVE & COMPUTER METHODS IN SOUTH ASIAN STUDIES.
++ *BULL. QUANT. & COMPUT. METHODS SOUTH ASIAN STUD.*
LONDON NO.1, 1973-
2/A.
CA/U-1.   ED/N-1.   LO/N12.   LO/U-8.   LO/U14.

BULLETIN OF SCANDINAVIAN PHILOLOGY.
++ *BULL. SCAND. PHILOL.*
[MUNKSGAARD]
COPENHAGEN [NO.1], 1970-
SUPPL. TO ACTA PHILOLOGICA SCANDINAVICA.
DB/U-2.   LD/U-1.   LO/U-1.   OX/U-1.

BULLETIN OF THE SOCIETY FOR CO-OPERATIVE STUDIES.
++ *BULL. SOC. CO-OP. STUD.*
LOUGHBOROUGH NO.1, JE 1967-
GL/U-2.

BULLETIN OF THE SOCIETY FOR LATIN AMERICAN STUDIES.   XXX
++ *BULL. SOC. LAT. AM. STUD.*
LONDON NO.8, 1967-
PREV: INFORMATION BULLETIN, SOCIETY FOR LATIN
AMERICAN STUDIES FROM NO.1, 1964- 7, 1967.
GL/U-1.

BULLETIN OF SUGAR BEET RESEARCH: SUPPLEMENT.   000
SEE: TENSAI KENKYU HOKOKU: HOKAN.

BULLETIN TRIMESTRIEL, BANQUE DE FRANCE.
++ *BULL. TRIMEST. BANQUE FR.*
PARIS NO.1, N 1971-
4/A.
LO/U-3.

BULLETIN, UNIVERSITY OF STIRLING.
++ *BULL. UNIV. STIRLING.*
STIRLING 1, 1968/69-
LO/U-1.   *GL/U-1. 1(4), 1968-*

BURNS. JOURNAL OF THE INTERNATIONAL SOCIETY FOR BURN INJURIES.
[J. WRIGHT & SONS]
BRISTOL 1(1), S 1974-
ED/N-1.   ISSN 0305-4179

BUSINESS & ECONOMY OF CENTRAL & EAST AFRICA.   XXX
++ *BUS. & ECON. CENT. & EAST AFR.*
[KINGSTONS (NORTH) LTD.]
NDOLA 1(1), JA 1967-
PREV: FINANCIAL MAIL OF ZAMBIA.
LO/N17.   ISSN 0525-2636

BUSINESS EDUCATION REVIEW.
++ *BUS. EDUC. REV.*
ROBERT GORDON'S INSTITUTE OF TECHNOLOGY: SCHOOL
OF BUSINESS MANAGEMENT STUDIES.
ABERDEEN 1(1), 1974-
3/A.
CA/U-1.   ED/N-1.   SH/U-1.

BUSINESS SCOTLAND.   XXX
++ *BUS. SCOTL.*
EDINBURGH 18(4), AP 1974-
PREV: SCOTLAND FROM 1, 1947- 18(2/3), F/MR
1974.
ED/N-1.   HL/U-1.

BYELORUSSIAN LINGUISTICS.   000
SEE: BELARUSKAJA LINHVISTYKA.

CAC DOCUMENT.
++ *CAC DOC.*
UNIVERSITY OF ILLINOIS AT URBANA-CHAMPAIGNE:
CENTER FOR ADVANCED COMPUTATION.
URBANA NO.1, 1970-
ISSUED ALSO AS THE CENTER'S ECONOMIC RESEARCH
GROUP WORKING PAPER & SOME ALSO AS THE UNIV-
ERSITY'S DEPARTMENT OF COMPUTER SCIENCES
REPORT.
LO/N14.

CAHIERS D'ANTHROPOLOGIE ET D'ECOLOGIE HUMAINE.
++ *CAH. ANTHROPOL. & ECOL. HUM.*
SOCIETE FRANCAISE D'ANTHROPOLOGIE ET
D'ECOLOGIE HUMAINE.
[HERMANN EDITEURS]
PARIS NO.1, 1973-
LO/N13.

CAHIERS D'HISTOIRE.
++ *CAH. HIST. (OTTAWA).*
UNIVERSITY OF OTTAWA.
OTTAWA NO.1, 1968-
ALSO ENTITLED: HISTORICAL STUDIES.
LO/N-1.

CAHIERS, INSTITUT DE LINGUISTIQUE, UNIVERSITE CATHOLIQUE DE LOUVAIN.
++ *CAH. INST. LINGUIST. UNIV. CATHOL. LOUV.*
LOUVAIN 1(1), 1972-
2M.
OX/U-1. 1(5), 1972-

CAHIERS JEAN GIRAUDOUX.
++ *CAH. JEAN GIRAUDOUX.*
SOCIETE DES AMIS DE JEAN GIRAUDOUX.
[GRASSET]
PARIS 1, 1972-
GL/U-1.

CAHIERS DE LA TERRE CUITE.   XXX
++ *CAH. TERRE CUITE.*
CENTRE TECHNIQUE DES TUILES ET BRIQUES.
PARIS NO.1, 1974-
PREV: TERRE CUITE FROM [NO.]1, 1959- 59, 1973.
LO/N14.

CALIFORNIA WESTERN INTERNATIONAL LAW JOURNAL.
++ *CALIF. WEST. INT. LAW J.*
UNITED STATES INTERNATIONAL UNIVERSITY:
CALIFORNIA WESTERN SCHOOL OF LAW.
SAN DIEGO 1, 1970-
AD/U-1.   BL/U-1. 3, 1972-

CAMBRIA. A WELSH GEOGRAPHICAL REVIEW.
LAMPETER 1, 1974-
ED/N-1.   SH/U-1.   SW/U-1.

CAMBRIDGE ANTHROPOLOGY.
++ *CAMB. ANTHROPOL.*
CAMBRIDGE 1, 1973-
CA/U-3.   ED/N-1.   ISSN 0305-7674

CAMBRIDGE INDUSTRIAL ARCHAEOLOGY.
++ *CAMB. IND. ARCHAEOL.*
CAMBRIDGE SOCIETY FOR INDUSTRIAL ARCHAEOLOGY.
CAMBRIDGE [NO.1], 1973-
ANNU.
ED/N-1.   LO/N-4.

CAMBRIDGE MONOGRAPHS IN PHYSICAL CHEMISTRY.
++CAMB. MONOGR. PHYS. CHEM.
[CAMBRIDGE UNIV. P.]
 CAMBRIDGE 1, 1972-
 CA/U-1.

CAMBRIDGE TRACTS IN MATHEMATICS.   XXX
++CAMB. TRACTS MATH.
[CAMBRIDGE UNIV. P.]
 CAMBRIDGE NO.64, 1973-
 MONOGR. PREV: CAMBRIDGE TRACTS IN MATHEMATICS
 & MATHEMATICAL PHYSICS FROM NO.1, 1905- 63,
 1972.
 GL/U-1.

CAMBRIDGE TRACTS IN MATHEMATICS & MATHEMATICAL
PHYSICS.   XXX
 SUBS: CAMBRIDGE TRACTS IN MATHEMATICS.

CAMEROON LAW REVIEW.   000
 SEE: REVUE CAMEROUNAISE DE DROIT.

CANADIAN BAR NATIONAL.
++CAN. BAR NATL.
CANADIAN BAR ASSOCIATION.
 OTTAWA 1, 1974-
 MON.
 RE/U-1.

CANADIAN ETHNIC STUDIES. BULLETIN/ETUDES
ETHNIQUES DU CANADA.
++CAN. ETHN. STUD.
UNIVERSITY OF CALGARY: RESEARCH CENTRE FOR
CANADIAN ETHNIC STUDIES.
 CALGARY 1, 1969-
 2/A. ENGL. OR FR.
 LO/S10.   ISSN 0008-3496

CANADIAN HISTORIC SITES. OCCASIONAL PAPERS
IN ARCHAEOLOGY & HISTORY.
++CAN. HIST. SITES.
(CANADA) NATIONAL HISTORIC SITES SERVICE.
 OTTAWA NO.1, 1970-
 BL/U-1.   GL/U-1.   LO/U-2.   MA/U-1.

CANADIAN INHALATION THERAPY.   XXX
++CAN. INHALAT. THER.
CANADIAN SOCIETY OF INHALATION THERAPY TECHNIC-
IANS.
 EDMONTON 1, AP 1965- 7(1), 1971 ...
 Q. SUBS: RESPIRATORY TECHNOLOGY.
 ISSN 0008-3852

CANADIAN JOURNAL OF NEUROLOGICAL SCIENCES.
JOURNAL CANADIEN DES SCIENCES NEUROLOGIQUES.
++CAN. J. NEUROL. SCI.
[PUBLIC P. LTD.]
 WINNIPEG, MAN. 1, 1974-
 LD/U-1.

CANADIAN JOURNAL OF OTOLARYNGOLOGY. JOURNAL
CANADIEN D'OTOLARYNGOLOGIE.
++CAN. J. OTOLARYNGOL.
CANADIAN OTOLARYNGOLOGICAL SOCIETY.
 DON MILLS 1, JA 1972-
 Q.
 BL/U-1. 3, 1974-   ISSN 0045-5083

CANADIAN JOURNAL OF OTOLARYNGOLOGY: SUPPLE-
MENTS.
++CAN. J. OTOLARYNGOL., SUPPL.
CANADIAN OTOLARYNGOLOGICAL SOCIETY.
 DON MILLS 1, 1974-
 BL/U-1.

CANADIAN LIBRARY PROGRESS. PROGRES DE LA
BIBLIOTHEQUE CANADIENNE.
++CAN. LIBR. PROG.
 VANCOUVER 1, 1973-
 OX/U-1.

CANTIUM. A MAGAZINE OF KENT LOCAL HISTORY.
[THOMAS BECKET BOOKS]
 DOVER 1(1), JA 1969-
 Q.
 CB/U-1.   ED/N-1. 2, 1970-   LO/U-1. 2, 1970-

CARBOHYDRATE CHEMISTRY & METABOLISM ABSTRACTS.XX
++CARBOHYDR. CHEM. & METAB. ABSTR.
[INFORMATION RETRIEVAL LTD.]
 LONDON 2(1), JA 1974-
 MON. PREV: CARBOHYDRATE METABOLISM ABSTRACTS
 FROM 1(1-12), JA-D 1973.
 LO/N13.   ED/N-1. 2(2), 1974-   ISSN 0301-8679

CARDIOLOGY DIGEST.
++CARDIOL. DIG.
[CARDIOLOGY DIGEST INC.]
 NORTHFIELD, ILL. 1, 1966-
 S/T: A MONTHLY SUMMARY OF THE WORLD MEDICAL
 LITERATURE FOR THE CARDIOLOGIST.
 BL/U-1. 8, 1973-   LO/N13. 4(11), 1969-   ISSN 0008-6347

CARDIOVASCULAR PROJECTS.
++CARDIOVASC. PROJ.
WORLD HEALTH ORGANIZATION: IBADAN CARDIAC
REGISTRY.
 IBADAN 1, 1971-
 LD/U-1.

CARGO SYSTEMS.   XXX
++CARGO SYST.
INTERNATIONAL CARGO HANDLING COORDINATION
ASSOCIATION.
[C.S. PUBL. LTD.]
 LONDON 1(1), N 1973-
 MON. PREV: ICHCA MONTHLY JOURNAL FROM JA
 1967- S/OC 1973.
 ED/N-1.   OX/U-1.   ISSN 0306-0985

CARIBBEAN GEOGRAPHER. A REGIONAL NEWSLETTER.
++CARIBB. GEOGR.
UNIVERSITY OF THE WEST INDIES: GEOGRAPHY
DEPARTMENT.
 KINGSTON, JAM. 1, 1971-
 ANNU.
 BL/U-1.

CARLETON GERMANIC PAPERS.
++CARLETON GER. PAP.
CARLETON UNIVERSITY.
 OTTAWA 1, 1973-
 BL/U-1.   LO/U12.   SH/U-1.   SW/U-1.

CARNETS DE L'ENFANCE.   XXX
UNITED NATIONS CHILDREN'S FUND: EUROPEAN OFFICE
 NEUILLY-SUR-SEINE NO.1, 1963- 5, 1966 ...
 SUBS: PART OF CARNETS DE L'ENFANCE. ASSIGN-
 MENT CHILDREN.
 ISSN 0576-7989

CARNETS DE L'ENFANCE. ASSIGNMENT CHILDREN.   XXX
UNITED NATIONS CHILDREN'S FUND: EUROPEAN OFFICE
 NEUILLY-SUR-SEINE NO.6, JE 1967-
 ENGL. OR FR. WITH SPAN., GER. & ENGL. OR FR.
 ABSTR. PREV: THE SEPARATE LANGUAGE EDITIONS
 CARNETS DE L'ENFANCE; & ASSIGNMENT CHILDREN;
 OF WHICH THE NUMBERING IS CONTINUED.
 ED/N-1.   LO/U-3.   EX/U-1. 17, 1972-   LV/U-1. 11, 1970-
 OX/U16. 17, 1972-   ISSN 0590-5931

CARNYX.
COUNCIL FOR BRITISH ARCHAEOLOGY: SCOTTISH
REGIONAL GROUP.
 EDINBURGH NO.1, N 1970-
 ED/N-1.

CASE STUDIES IN ATOMIC COLLISION PHYSICS.   XXX
++CASE STUD. AT. COLLIS. PHYS.
[NORTH-HOLLAND]
 AMSTERDAM 1, 1969- 2, 1972 ...
 SUBS: CASE STUDIES IN ATOMIC PHYSICS.
 OX/U-8.

CASE STUDIES IN ATOMIC PHYSICS.   XXX
++CASE STUD. AT. PHYS.
[NORTH-HOLLAND]
 AMSTERDAM &C. 3(1), JL 1972-
 2M. PREV: CASE STUDIES IN ATOMIC COLLISION
 PHYSICS FROM 1, 1969- 2, 1972.
 CA/U-2.   GL/U-2.   OX/U-8.   RE/U-1.   ISSN 0300-4503

CASE STUDIES IN THE MANAGEMENT OF ECONOMIC
DEVELOPMENT.
++CASE STUD. MANAGE. ECON. DEV.
UNIVERSITY COLLEGE, DAR ES SALAAM: INSTITUTE OF
PUBLIC ADMINISTRATION.
[OXFORD UNIV. P.]
 NAIROBI & LONDON 1, 1968-
 GL/U-1.

CASHEW NEWS TELLER.
(INDIA) DEPARTMENT OF AGRICULTURE: DIRECTORATE
OF CASHEWNUT DEVELOPMENT.
 CALCUTTA 1(1), 1967-
 Q.
 LO/R-6. 4(1), 1970-   ISSN 0045-5911

**CATENA. AN INTERDISCIPLINARY JOURNAL OF GEO-
MORPHOLOGY-HYDROLOGY-PEDOLOGY.**
[LENZ-VERLAG]
GIESSEN 1, D 1973-
LO/U-4.   SH/U-1.

CAVE SCIENCE (1971).   XXX
++*CAVE SCI. C1971).*
BRITISH SPELEOLOGICAL ASSOCIATION.
SETTLE NO.48, D 1971- 52, N 1973.
PREV: JOURNAL, BRITISH SPELEOLOGICAL
ASSOCIATION FROM NO.41, 1967- 47, D 1971.
SUBS. PART OF: TRANSACTIONS, BRITISH CAVE
RESEARCH ASSOCIATION.
LO/N13.

CEDA SAMACHAR. A NEWSLETTER.
TRIBHUVAN UNIVERSITY: CENTRE FOR ECONOMIC
DEVELOPMENT & ADMINISTRATION.
KATHMANDU 1(1), AP 1974-
Q.
LO/N12.

C.E.G.B. RESEARCH.
++*C.E.G.B. RES.*
CENTRAL ELECTRICITY GENERATING BOARD (GB).
LONDON NO.1, D 1974-
CA/U-1.   CA/U-2.   ED/N-1.   SH/P-1.   XS/R10.   XS/T-4.

CELL.
[MASSACHUSETTS INST. TECHNOL. P.]
CAMBRIDGE, MASS. 1, JA 1974-
GL/U-1.   LD/U-1.   LO/U-2.   MA/U-1.

CEMENT, LIME & GRAVEL.   XXX
SUBS (1974): PART OF QUARRY MANAGEMENT &
PRODUCTS.

CENTRAL ASIAN MONOGRAPHS.
++*CENT. ASIAN MONOGR.*
CENTRAL ASIAN RESEARCH CENTRE.
LONDON 1, 1973-
CA/U-1.

CENTRAL COMPUTER AGENCY GUIDE.
++*CENT. COMPUT. AGENCY GUIDE.*
(GREAT BRITAIN) CIVIL SERVICE DEPARTMENT:
CENTRAL COMPUTER AGENCY.
LONDON NO.1, 1973-
LO/N-1.

CERAMIC INDUSTRIES JOURNAL.   XXX
++*CERAM. IND. J.*
[TURRET P.]
LONDON 83(987), AG/S 1974-
PREV: CLAYWORKER FROM 82(976), 1973- 83(986),
1974. INCORP: CERAMICS (LONDON).
ED/N-1.   LO/N14.   ISSN 0305-7623

CERAMICS (LONDON).   XXX
SUBS (1974) INCORP. IN: CERAMIC INDUSTRIES
JOURNAL.

CERCETARI MARINE.
++*CERCET. MAR.*
CONSTANTIANA NO.1, 1971-
LO/N-2.

CEREBROVASCULAR BIBLIOGRAPHY.
NATIONAL INSTITUTE OF NEUROLOGICAL DISEASES
& BLINDNESS (US).
BETHESDA, MD. 1, 1961-
SPONS. BODY ALSO: NATIONAL HEART INSTITUTE(US)
PREPARED WITH THE COOPERATION OF THE NATIONAL
LIBRARY OF MEDICINE (US).
LO/M-1 6, 1966-   SO/U-1. 8, 1968-   ISSN 0090-1407

CERES (COLUMBUS, OHIO).
(OHIO) DEPARTMENT OF AGRICULTURE.
COLUMBUS, OHIO 1(1), MR 1973-
LO/N-1.

**CESKOSLOVENSKE NEJKRASNEJSI KNIHY. THE MOST
BEAUTIFUL BOOKS OF CZECHOSLOVAKIA.**
++*CESK. NEJKRASNEJSI KNIHY.*
CESKOSLOVENSKE USTREDI KNIZNI KULTURY.
PRAGUE 1965-
SPONS. BODIES ALSO: SLOVENSKE USTREDIE KNIZNEJ
KULTURY; & PAMATNIK NARODNIHO PISEMNICTVI.
ED/N-1.   SA/U-1.

CESKOSLVENSKO-SOVETSKE VZTAHY.
++*CESK.-SOV. VZTAHY.*
KARLOVA UNIVERSITA V PRAZE.
PRAGUE 1, 1972-
OX/U-1.

CEYLON FORESTER.   XXX
SUBS (1972): SRI LANKA FORESTER.

CEYLON TRADE JOURNAL.   XXX
COLOMBO 1, 1935- 35(8-12), 1970.//
*LO/R-6.   LO/U-3.**

**CHAKIDAH. IRANDOC SCIENCE & SOCIAL SCIENCE
ABSTRACT BULLETIN.**
(IRAN) MINISTRY OF SCIENCE & HIGHER EDUCATION:
IRANIAN DOCUMENTATION CENTRE.
TEHERAN 1(1), 1970-
PERSIAN. CENTRE SUBORD. TO: INSTITUTE FOR
RESEARCH & PLANNING IN SCIENCE & EDUCATION.
LO/U14.

CHARLATAN. INTERDISCIPLINARY JOURNAL.   XXX
ST. CLOUD, MINN. NO.1, 1964- 4/5, 1968.//
2/A. MAINLY ENGL. OCCASIONALLY FR., GER. OR
SPAN. NO.1 ENTITLED WHAT CAN THIS CHARLATAN
BE TRYING TO SAY.
OX/U-1.

CHARLES LAMB BULLETIN: NS.   XXX
++*CHARLES LAMB BULL., NS.*
CHARLES LAMB SOCIETY.
LONDON NO.1, JA 1973-
PREV: C.L.S. BULLETIN FROM NO.51, 1941- 216,
OC 1972.
SH/U-1.

**CHARTERED SURVEYOR: BUILDING & QUANTITY
SURVEYING QUARTERLY.**
++*CHART. SURV., BUILD. & QUANT. SURV. Q.*
ROYAL INSTITUTION OF CHARTERED SURVEYORS.
LONDON 1(1), 1973-
S/T: SUPPLEMENT TO THE JOURNAL OF THE ROYAL
INSTITUTION OF CHARTERED SURVEYORS.
BL/U-1.   CA/U-1.   LO/N-4.   ED/N-1. 1(3), 1974-

**CHARTERED SURVEYOR: LAND HYDROGRAPHIC & MIN-
ING QUARTERLY.**
++*CHART. SURV., LAND HYDROGR. & MIN. Q.*
ROYAL INSTITUTION OF CHARTERED SURVEYORS.
LONDON 1, OC 1973-
ED/N-1.   CA/U-1. 1(3), 1974-   ISSN 0306-3186

CHARTERED SURVEYOR: URBAN QUARTERLY.
++*CHART. SURV., URBAN Q.*
ROYAL INSTITUTION OF CHARTERED SURVEYORS.
LONDON 1(1), 1973-
S/T: SUPPLEMENT TO THE JOURNAL OF THE ROYAL
INSTITUTION OF CHARTERED SURVEYORS.
BL/U-1.   LO/N-4.   ED/N-1. 1(2), 1973-

C.H.E.C. NEWS.
COMMONWEALTH HUMAN ECOLOGY COUNCIL.
LONDON NO.1, JA 1974-
LO/U-8.

CHEMICAL AGE (LONDON, 1972).   XXX
++*CHEM. AGE (LOND., 1972).*
[BENN BROTHERS]
LONDON 108(2846), 1974-
PREV: CHEMICAL AGE INTERNATIONAL FROM
105(2774), 1972- 108(2844/45), 1974.
ED/N-1.   LO/N14.   XS/R10.   SF/U-1.   ISSN 0302-2900

CHEMICAL PROCESSING (LONDON).   XXX
SUBS (1974): PROCESSING.

CHEMICAL SENSES & FLAVOR.
++*CHEM. SENSES & FLAVOR.*
[REIDEL PUBL. CO.]
DORDRECHT 1(1), JA 1974-
4/A. S/T: A JOURNAL DEVOTED TO THE CHEMICAL
SENSES & TO THE SENSORY EVALUATION OF THE
GUSTATORY, OLFACTORY, TACTILE & VISUAL PROP-
ERTIES OF MATERIALS.
LO/N13.   RE/U-1.

CHESHIRE FAMILY HISTORIAN.
++*CHESHIRE FAM. HIST.*
FAMILY HISTORY SOCIETY OF CHESHIRE.
CHESTER NO.1, JA 1974-
Q.
ED/N-1.   ISSN 0305-9057

CHIEN-CHU HSUEH-PAO. ARCHITECTURAL JOURNAL.
CHUNG-KUO CHIEN-CHU HSUEH-HUI.
PEKING NO.1, 1973-
CHIN. WITH SOME ENGL. ABSTR.
LO/U14.

CHILDREN'S LITERATURE.
MODERN LANGUAGE ASSOCIATION OF AMERICA: SEMINAR
ON CHILDREN'S LITERATURE.
STORRS, CONN. 1, 1972-
SPONS. BODY ALSO: CHILDREN'S LITERATURE
ASSOCIATION.
OX/U-1.

CHILDREN'S LITERATURE ABSTRACTS.
++*CHILD. LIT. ABSTR.*
INTERNATIONAL FEDERATION OF LIBRARY ASSOCIAT-
IONS: SUB-SECTION ON LIBRARY WORK WITH CHILDREN
BIRMINGHAM NO.1, MY 1973-
Q.
CA/U-1.   GL/U-2.   HL/U-2.   OX/U-1.
ISSN 0306-2015

CHILE MONITOR.
++*CHILE MONIT.*
CHILE SOLIDARITY CAMPAIGN.
LONDON NO.1, N 1973-
OX/U-1.   CA/U-1. NO.3, 1974-   ED/N-1. NO.3, 1974-

CHINA AKTUELL.
INSTITUT FUR ASIENKUNDE (HAMBURG).
HAMBURG 1, 1972-
MON.
OX/U-1.

CHINA MONTHLY.   000
SEE: TSU-KUO.

CHINESE LITERATURE.
++*CHIN. LIT.*
[FOREIGN LANGUAGES P.]
PEKING 1, 1973-
MON. FR. TITLE: LITTERATURE CHINOISE.
BH/P-1.   SW/U-1. 1974-   ISSN 0009-4617

CHRISTIAN PEACE CONFERENCE.   XXX
++*CHRIST. PEACE CONF.*
CHRISTIAN PEACE CONFERENCE: INTERNATIONAL
SECRETARIAT.
PRAGUE NO.1, N 1962- 35, AG 1971.//
ENGL. & GER.
LO/U-3. ‡W. NO.26 & 27A   ISSN 0009-5567

CIRCULATION RESEARCH: SUPPLEMENT.
++*CIRC. RES., SUPPL.*
AMERICAN HEART ASSOCIATION.
NEW YORK 1964(1)-
GL/U-1. 1967(1)-   LO/N-4. 1971(1)-   SO/U-1. 1969(1)-

CIS ABSTRACTS.
++*CIS ABSTR.*
INTERNATIONAL OCCUPATIONAL SAFETY & HEALTH
INFORMATION CENTRE.
GENEVA 1, 1974-
LO/N13.

CIVIL ENGINEERING HYDRAULICS ABSTRACTS.   XXX
++*CIVIL ENG. HYDRAUL. ABSTR.*
BRITISH HYDROMECHANICS RESEARCH ASSOCIATION:
FLUID ENGINEERING.
CRANFIELD 7(1), JA 1974-
PREV: CHANNEL FROM 1, 1968- 6, 1973.
ED/N-1.   LO/N14.   XS/R10.
ISSN 0305-9456

**CIVIL ENGINEERING RESEARCH REPORTS, MONASH
UNIVERSITY.**
++*CIV. ENG. RES. REP. MONASH UNIV.*
MELBOURNE NO.1, 1970-
LO/N14.

CIVIL RIGHTS.
NORTHERN IRELAND CIVIL RIGHTS ASSOCIATION.
BELFAST 1(1), 1972-
2W.
CA/U-1. 2, 1973-   ED/N-1. 2, 1973-

CLASS AGAINST CLASS.   XXX
MARXIST-LENINIST ORGANISATION OF BRITAIN.   XXX
LONDON NO.1, 1973-
Q. PREV: RED FRONT FROM 1(1), OC 1967- NS.
NO.1, JA/F 1973.
HL/U-1.   OX/U-1.   OX/U17.

CLASSIC PAPERS IN PHYSICS.
++*CLASSIC PAP. PHYS.*
[TAYLOR & FRANCIS]
LONDON 1, 1972-
LO/N-1.

CLAYWORKER.   XXX
[TURRET P.]
LONDON 82(976), 1973- 83(986), 1974...
PREV: BRITISH CLAYWORKER FROM 1, 1892-
82(975), 1973. SUBS: CERAMIC INDUSTRIES
JOURNAL.
ED/N-1.   LO/N14.   OX/U-8.

CLIMATIC RESEARCH UNIT OCCASIONAL BULLETIN.   XXX
++*CLIM. RES. UNIT OCCAS. BULL.*
UNIVERSITY OF EAST ANGLIA: CLIMATIC RESEARCH
UNIT.
NORWICH 1972 (1)- 1974 (1). //
LO/U12.   XS/N-1. NO.1, 1972.

CLINICAL CYTOLOGY.   000
SEE: MONOGRAPHS IN CLINICAL CYTOLOGY.

**CLINICAL & EXPERIMENTAL PHARMACOLOGY & PHYSIOL-
OGY.**
++*CLIN. & EXP. PHARMACOL. & PHYSIOL.*
[BLACKWELL]
OXFORD 1, 1974-
CA/U-1.   ED/N-1.   GL/U-2.   LO/N13.   LO/U-2.   OX/U-8.

C.L.S. BULLETIN.   XXX
SUBS (1973): CHARLES LAMB BULLETIN:NS.

COAL & ENERGY QUARTERLY.
++*COAL & ENERGY Q.*
NATIONAL COAL BOARD (GB).
LONDON NO.1, 1974-
Q.
LO/U-3.

COARSE GRAIN SITUATION.   XXX
SUBS (1972): COARSE GRAINS & OILSEEDS
SITUATION.

COARSE GRAINS & OILSEEDS SITUATION.   XXX
++*COARSE GRAINS & OILSEEDS SITUAT.*
(AUSTRALIA) BUREAU OF AGRICULTURAL ECONOMICS.
CANBERRA NO.17, 1972...
PREV: COARSE GRAIN SITUATION FROM JE 1954-
NO.16, 1971. SUBS: COURSE GRAINS: SITUATION
& OUTLOOK.
GL/U-1.   HL/U-1.

COARSE GRAINS: SITUATION & OUTLOOK.   XXX
++*COARSE GRAINS, SITUAT. & OUTLOOK.*
(AUSTRALIA) BUREAU OF AGRICULTURAL ECONOMICS.
CANBERRA 1974-
PREV: COARSE GRAINS & OILSEEDS SITUATION
FROM NO.17, 1972.
GL/U-1.   HL/U-1.

COCO Y PALMA.
FONDO PARA EL DESARROLLO DEL COCO, DE LA
COPRA Y DE LA PALMA AFRICANA.
CARACAS, VENEZ. 1, 1973-
LO/R-6.

**COFFEE INTERNATIONAL. BUSINESS JOURNAL OF THE
INTERNATIONAL COFFEE INDUSTRY.**
++*COFFEE INT.*
[INTERNATIONAL TRADE PUBL.]
LONDON 1(1), AP 1974-
CA/U-1.   ED/N-1.   OX/U-1.

**COGWORDS. BULLETIN OF THE KEGWORTH VILLAGE
ASSOCIATION.**
KEGWORTH 1, 1972-
NO/U-1.

**COLLECTION DE TRAVAUX ET DE DOCUMENTS POUR
SERVIR A L'HISTOIRE DU MANTOIS ET DU VEXIN.**
++*COLLECT. TRAV. & DOC. SERVIR HIST. MANTOIS &
VEXIN.*
MEULAN NO.1, 1971-
MONOGR.
LO/N-1.

**COLLECTION DES VOYAGEURS OCCIDENTAUX EN
EGYPTE.**
++*COLLECT. VOYAGEURS OCCIDENT. EGYPTE.*
INSTITUT FRANCAIS D'ARCHAEOLOGIE ORIENTALE.
PARIS 1, 1970-
CA/U-1.   OX/U-1.

COLLECTIVE PHENOMENA.
++*COLLECT. PHENOM.*
[GORDON & BREACH]
NEW YORK & LONDON 1(1), AG 1972-
Q.
CA/U-1.   CA/U-2.   LO/N14.   LO/U-2.   OX/U-8.   SW/U-1.

COLLEGIAN.
DANIEL STEWART'S & MELVILLE COLLEGE (EDINBURGH)
EDINBURGH 1(1), JE 1974-
ED/N-1.   ISSN 0305-1064

COLOUR REVIEW.
++*COLOUR REV.*
[WINSOR & NEWTON LTD.]
HARROW MR 1966-
3/A. S/T: THE ART TEACHERS' JOURNAL.
CA/U-1.   LD/U-2.   OX/U-1.   ISSN 0018-1818

COLUMBIA HUMAN RIGHTS LAW REVIEW.   XXX
COLUMBIA UNIVERSITY: SCHOOL OF LAW.
NEW YORK 4, 1972-
PREV: COLUMBIA SURVEY OF HUMAN RIGHTS LAW
FROM 1, 1967/68- 3, 1971. SPONS. BODY ALSO:
COLUMBIA UNIVERSITY INSTITUTE OF HUMAN RIGHTS.
OX/U15.   BL/U-1. 5, 1973   SO/U-1. 5, 1973-

**COMITATUS. STUDIES IN OLD & MIDDLE ENGLISH
LITERATURE.**
UNIVERSITY OF CALIFORNIA AT LOS ANGELES:
ENGLISH MEDIEVAL CLUB.
LOS ANGELES 1(1), D 1970-
LO/U-1.

COMLA NEWSLETTER.
++*COMLA NEWSL.*
COMMONWEALTH LIBRARY ASSOCIATION.
KINGSTON, JAMAICA NO.1, 1973-
LO/N12. NO.3, 1974-

COMMERCIAL ACCOUNTANT.   XXX
SUBS (1974): ACCOUNTANTS REVIEW.

COMMERCIAL RABBIT.
++*COMMER. RABBIT.*
COMMERCIAL RABBIT ASSOCIATION.
[CONE PUBL.]
LONDON 1(1), 1973-
CA/U-1.   ED/N-1.   LO/R-6.   OX/U-8.

COMMONWEALTH ECONOMIC PAPERS.
++*COMMONW. ECON. PAP.*
COMMONWEALTH SECRETARIAT.
LONDON NO.1, 1972-
MONOGR.
CA/U-1.   LO/N-1.

COMMONWEALTH JUDICIAL JOURNAL.
++*COMMONW. JUDICIAL J.*
COMMONWEALTH MAGISTRATES' ASSOCIATION.
LONDON 1, 1973-
LO/U14.

**COMMUNICATION RESEARCH. AN INTERNATIONAL
QUARTERLY.**
++*COMMUN. RES.*
[SAGE PUBL.]
BEVERLY HILLS, CALIF. &C. 1, 1974-
CB/U-1.   LD/U-1.   SH/U-1.

COMMUNICATIONS IN ALGEBRA.
++*COMMUN. ALGEBRA.*
[DEKKER]
NEW YORK 1, 1974-
2/M.
OX/U-8.   SH/U-1.   SW/U-1.   ISSN 0092-7872

COMMUNICATIONS SERVICE BULLETIN.
++*COMMUN. SERV. BULL.*
(CANADA) STATISTICS CANADA.   XXX
OTTAWA 1, JE 1971-
MON. FR. & ENGL. FR. TITLE: COMMUNICATIONS,
BULLETIN DE SERVICE. PREV. FORM OF BODY NAME:
BUREAU OF STATISTICS.
CA/U-1.

COMMUNICATIONS IN STATISTICS.
++*COMMUN. STAT.*
[DEKKER]
NEW YORK 1, 1973-
6/A.
GL/U-1.   LO/U-2.   SH/U-1.   ISSN 0090-3272

COMMUNIST REVIEW.
++*COMMUNIST REV. (BELFAST).*
BRITISH & IRISH COMMUNIST ORGANISATION.
BELFAST NO.1, MR 1974-
CA/U-1. NO.2, 1974-   ED/N-1. NO.2, 1974-

COMMUNITY CARE. SOCIAL WORK IN ACTION.
[IPC BUILDING & CONTRACT JOURNALS LTD.]
LONDON NO.1, AP 1974-
CA/U-1.   ED/N-1.   OX/U-1.

COMMUNITY DENTISTRY & ORAL EPIDEMIOLOGY.
++*COMMUNITY DENT. & ORAL EPIDEMIOL.*
[MUNKSGAARD]
COPENHAGEN 1, 1973-
GL/U-1.   LD/U-1.   LO/N13.   MA/U-1.

**COMMUNITY NOW. MONTHLY NEWSLETTER OF THE
EDINBURGH COMMUNITY RELATIONS COUNCIL.**
EDINBURGH NO.1, F 1974-
ED/N-1.

COMPASS (KUTZTOWN, PA.).
KUTZTOWN STATE COLLEGE.
KUTZTOWN, PA. NO.[1], 1971-
LO/U-2. NO.5/6, 1974.

COMPUTERIZED SERIALS SYSTEMS SERIES.
++*COMPUT. SERIALS SYST. SER.*
[LARC ASSOCIATION]
TEMPE, ARIZ. 1, 1973-
LO/N14.

COMPUTERS & AUTOMATION.   XXX
SUBS (1974): COMPUTERS & PEOPLE.

COMPUTERS & ELECTRICAL ENGINEERING.
++*COMPUT. & ELECTR. ENG.*
[PERGAMON]
OXFORD 1(1), JE 1973-
S/T: AN INTERNATIONAL JOURNAL.
CA/U-1.   ED/N-1.   LO/U-2.

**COMPUTERS & OPERATIONS RESEARCH. AN INTERNAT-
IONAL JOURNAL.**
++*COMPUT. & OPER. RES.*
[PERGAMON P.]
NEW YORK & OXFORD 1(1), MR 1974-
Q.
CA/U-1.   ED/N-1.   LO/N14.   OX/U-1.   ISSN 0305-0548

COMPUTERS & PEOPLE.   XXX
++*COMPUT. & PEOPLE.*
[BERKELEY ENTERPRISES]
NEWTONVILLE, MASS. 23, JA 1974-
MON. PREV: COMPUTERS & AUTOMATION FROM 2(1),
1953- 22, 1973.
LO/N14.

CONCH REVIEW OF BOOKS.
++*CONCH REV. BOOKS.*
STATE UNIVERSITY COLLEGE (NEW PALITZ, N.Y.):
DEPARTMENT OF AFRICAN STUDIES.
[CONCH MAGAZINE LTD.]
NEW YORK I(1), MR 1973-
Q. S/T: A LITERARY SUPPLEMENT ON AFRICA.
SUPPL. TO THE CONCH.
LO/U14.

CONDUCTOR.   XXX
SUBS (1972): PART OF SOUNDING BRASS ø THE
CONDUCTOR.

CONGO.   XXX
CENTRE DE RECHERCHE ET D'INFORMATION SOCIO-
POLITIQUES (BELGIUM).
BRUSSELS 1959- 1967.//
ANNU.
LO/U-3.

CONGO-TERVUREN.   XXX
SUBS (1961): AFRICA-TERVUREN.

CONNECTIONS.   XXX
MADISON, WIS. 1, MR 1967- 3(9), MY 1969.//
2/M. VOL.2(11) ENTITLED TARTUFFLES.
LO/U-2. 3(7-8), 1969.

CONTEMPORARY CHINA PAPERS.
++*CONTEMP. CHINA PAP.*
AUSTRALIAN NATIONAL UNIVERSITY: CONTEMPORARY
CHINA CENTRE.
CANBERRA NO.1, 1971-
CENTRE SUBORD TO: RESEARCH SCHOOL OF PACIFIC
STUDIES.
CA/U-1.   OX/U-1. NO.4, 1972-

CONTEMPORARY TOPICS IN IMMUNOCHEMISTRY.   XXX
++*CONTEMP. TOP. IMMUNOCHEM.*
[PLENUM P.]
NEW YORK & LONDON 1, 1972 ...
SUBS: CONTEMPORARY TOPICS IN MOLECULAR IMMUN-
OLOGY.
LO/N13.

CONTEMPORARY TOPICS IN MOLECULAR IMMUNOLOGY.　XXX
++CONTEMP. TOP. MOL. IMMUNOL.
[PLENUM P.]
　NEW YORK & LONDON　2, 1973-
　PREV: CONTEMPORARY TOPICS IN IMMUNOCHEMISTRY
　FROM 1, 1972.
　LO/N13.　OX/U-1.

CONTREBIS. BULLETIN OF THE LANCASTER ARCH-
AEOLOGICAL SOCIETY.
　LANCASTER　1(1), MY 1973-
　2/A.
　ED/N-1.　OX/U-1.

CONTRIBUTIONS FROM THE BIOLOGICAL LABORATOR-
IES, PRINCETON UNIVERSITY.　XXX
++CONTRIB. BIOL. LAB. PRINCETON UNIV.
　PRINCETON　2, 1912- 20, 1959/67.//
　PREV: PRINCETON MORPHOLOGICAL STUDIES FROM 1,
　1883- 1892.
　LO/N-2.　OX/U-8.　CA/U-1. 2, 1912- 17, 1949.
　MA/U-1. 2, 1912- 17, 1949.

CONTRIBUTIONS, DEPARTMENT OF GEOLOGY & MINERAL-
OGY, NIIGATA UNIVERSITY.　000
　SEE: NIIGATA DAIGAKU RIGAKUBU CHISHITSU KOBUT-
SUGAKU KYOSHITSU KENKYU HOKOKU.

CONTRIBUTIONS IN HUMAN BIOLOGY, MUSEUM OF
ANTHROPOLOGY, UNIVERSITY OF MICHIGAN.
++CONTRIB. HUM. BIOL. MUS. ANTHROPOL. UNIV.
　MICH.
　ANN ARBOR　NO.1, 1973-
　GL/U-1.

CONTRIBUTIONS TO MICROBIOLOGY & IMMUNOLOGY.　XXX
++CONTRIB. MICROBIOL. & IMMUNOL.
[KARGER]
　BASLE &C.　1, 1973-
　PREV: BIBLIOTHECA MICROBIOLOGICA FROM NO.1,
　1960- 10, 1972.
　LO/N13.

CONTRIBUTIONS TO PHYSICO-CHEMICAL PETROLOGY
(MOSCOW).　000
　SEE: OCHERKI FIZIKO-KHIMICHESKOJ PETROLOGII.

CONTRIBUTIONS TO PRIMATOLOGY.　XXX
++CONTRIB. PRIMATOL.
[S. KARGER]
　BASLE　1, 1974-
　PREV: BIBLIOTHECA PRIMATOLOGICA FROM 1, 1962-
　14, 1971.
　LO/N-2.　LO/N-4.

CONTRIBUTIONS TO SEDIMENTOLOGY.
++CONTRIB. SEDIMENTOL.
[SCHWEITZERBART'SCHE VERLAGSBUCHHANDLUNG]
　STUTTGART　NO.1, 1973-
　GL/U-1.　LO/N-2.　LO/U-2.　SO/U-1.

CONTRIBUTIONS TO THE SOCIOLOGY OF LANGUAGE.
++CONTRIB. SOCIOL. LANG.
[MOUTON]
　THE HAGUE & PARIS　NO.1, 1971-
　LO/N-1.

CONTROL MAGAZINE.
++CONTROL MAG.
CENTRE FOR BEHAVIOURAL ART.
　LONDON　NO.1, 1973-
　ED/N-1. NO.6, ‡1974A-

CORPORATE PLANNING.
++CORP. PLANN.
UNIVERSITY OF BIRMINGHAM: INSTITUTE OF LOCAL
GOVERNMENT STUDIES.
　BIRMINGHAM　1(1), F 1974-
　2/A. S/T: A REVIEW OF CORPORATE PLANNING &
　MANAGEMENT IN LOCAL GOVERNMENT.
　LO/U-3.　SH/U-1.　ISSN 0305-3695

CORPUS SCRIPTORUM ECCLESIASTICORUM LATINORUM:
BEIHEFT.
++CORPUS SCR. ECCLESIASTICORUM LAT., BEIH.
　VIENNA　1, 1973-
　OX/U-1.

CORREO GEOGRAFICO.
++CORR. GEOGR.
ASOCIACION COLUMBIANA DE GEOGRAFOS.
　TUNJA, COLOMB.　1, JA 1968-
　OX/U-1.　ISSN 0590-885X

CORSTORPHINE CHRONICLE.
++CORSTORPHINE CHRON.
[CAROLINE PUBL. CO.]
　EDINBURGH　NO.1, JL 1973-
　ED/N-1.

CORSTORPHINE NEWSLETTER.
++CORSTORPHINE NEWSL.
CORSTORPHINE LIBERAL ASSOCIATION.
　EDINBURGH　NO.1, [1971]-
　ED/N-1.

COSMETIC WORLD NEWS.　XXX
++COSMET. WORLD NEWS.
　LONDON　1, 1974-
　PREV: INTERNATIONAL PERFUMER FROM
　1, 1950- 22(1), 1974.
　LO/R-6.　ISSN 0305-0319

CPC OUTLINE SERIES.　XXX
++CPC OUTLINE SER.
CONSERVATIVE POLITICAL CENTRE.
　LONDON　NO.1, 1967- 7, 1969.//
　MONOGR.
　HL/U-1.

CRANFIELD RESEARCH PAPERS IN MARKETING &
LOGISTICS.
++CRANFIELD RES. PAP. MARK. & LOGIST.
　CRANFIELD　1, 1973/74-
　NO/U-1.

CRC JOURNAL.
++CRC J.
COMMUNITY RELATIONS COMMISSION (GB): INFORMAT-
ION DEPARTMENT.
　LONDON　NO.1, JE 1972-
　MON.
　CA/U-1.**　ED/N-1.

CRIME & DELINQUENCY LITERATURE.　XXX
++CRIME & DELINQ. LIT.
NATIONAL COUNCIL ON CRIME & DELINQUENCY (US).
　HACKENSACK, N.J.　2(1), F 1970-
　2/M. PREV: PART OF: INFORMATION REVIEWS ON
　CRIME & DELINQUENCY FROM 1, S 1968- 9, 1969; &
　SELECTED HIGHLIGHTS OF CRIME & DELINQUENCY
　LITERATURE FROM NO.1, OC 1968- 8, D 1969.
　SH/U-1.　NO/U-1. 6, 1974-　ISSN 0037-1327

CRITICA LETTERARIA.　XXX
++CRIT. LETT. (NAPLES).
　NAPLES　1, 1973-
　PREV: FILOLOGIA E LETTERATURA FROM 8, 1962-
　17, 1971.
　CA/U-1.　HL/U-1.　LD/U-1.　LO/U-2.　MA/U-1. 2, 1974-

CRITICAL CARE MEDICINE.
++CRIT. CARE MED.
[J.N. KOLEN INC.]
　NEW YORK　1, JA/F 1973-
　2/M.
　LO/N13.

CRITIQUE OF ANTHROPOLOGY.
++CRIT. ANTHROPOL.
LONDON ALTERNATIVE ANTHROPOLOGY GROUP.
　LONDON　NO.1, SPRING 1974-
　CA/U-1.　ED/N-1.　LO/U-2.　LO/U-3.　OX/U-1.

CRKVA U SVIJETU.
SPLITSKA NADBISKUPIJA.
　SPLIT　1, 1966-
　BD/U-1. 7, 1972-

CSIRO FOOD RESEARCH QUARTERLY.　XXX
++CSIRO FOOD RES. Q.
CSIRO (AUSTRALIA): DIVISION OF FOOD RESEARCH.XX
　NORTH RYDE, N.S.W.　31(1/2), 1971-
　PREV: FOOD PRESERVATION QUARTERLY FROM 1,
　1941- 30, 1970.
　LO/R-6.

CUADERNOS DE ESTUDIOZ MEDIEVALES.
++CUAD. ESTUD. MEDIEVALES.
UNIVERSIDAD DE GRANADA.
　GRANADA　1, 1973-
　LO/U17.

CUADERNOS DE HISTORIA DEL ARTE.
++CUAD. HIST. ARTE.
UNIVERSIDADE NACIONAL AUTONOMA DE MEXICO:
INSTITUTO DE INVESTIGACIONES ESTETICAS.
　MEXICO, D.F.　1, 1973-
　OX/U-1.

CUADERNOS NACIONALES (BUENOS AIRES).
+ + *CUAD. NAC. (BUENOS AIRES).*
UNIVERSIDAD NACIONAL Y POPULAR DE BUENOS AIRES:
FACULTAD DE DERECHO Y CIENCIAS SOCIALES.
BUENOS AIRES 1, 1974-
LO/U-3.

CUBAN JOURNAL OF AGRICULTURAL SCIENCE.   XXX
+ + *CUBAN J. AGRIC. SCI.*
INSTITUTO DE CIENCIA ANIMAL (CUBA).
HAVANA 7, 1973-
PREV: REVISTA CUBANA DE CIENCIA AGRICOLA
(ENGL. ED.) FROM 1, 1967- 6, 1972.
LD/U-1. LO/N13. LO/R-6.

CUBAN NEWS.
(CUBA) EMBASSY, LONDON: PRESS & INFORMATION
DEPARTMENT.
LONDON 1(1), MR/AP 1974-
2/M.
LO/U-3.

CULTURES.   XXX
UNESCO.
[EDITIONS DE LA BACONNIERE]
PARIS 1, 1973-
PREV: JOURNAL OF WORLD HISTORY FROM 1, 1953-
14, 1972.
AD/U-1. CA/U-1. OX/U-1. RE/U-1.

CUMULATED BIBLIOGRAPHY SERIES.
[PIERIAN P.]
ANN ARBOR, MICH. 1, 1970-
OX/U-1.

CUNEIFORM TEXTS FROM NIMRUD.
BRITISH SCHOOL OF ARCHAEOLOGY IN IRAQ.
LONDON 1, 1972-
CA/U-1. GL/U-1.

CURRENT BIBLIOGRAPHICAL INFORMATION.   XXX
+ + *CURR. BIBLIOGR. INF.*
DAG HAMMARSKJOLD LIBRARY.
NEW YORK 1, 1/JA 1971-
2/M. INCORP: CURRENT ISSUES FROM NO.1, D
1965- 11, 1970; & NEW PUBLICATIONS IN THE DAG
HAMMARSKJOLD LIBRARY FROM 1, 1949- 21, 1970.
ED/N-1. GL/U-2. LO/S14. SH/U-1.
ISSN 0041-7343

**CURRENT BIBLIOGRAPHY & ABSTRACTS OF HEBREW LAW
& ALLIED SUBJECTS.**
+ + *CURR. BIBLIOGR. & ABSTR. HEB. LAW & ALLIED
SUBJ.*
[WAHRMANN BOOKS]
JERUSALEM &C. NO.1, F 1966-
2/A. NO.1 ENTITLED CURRENT BIBLIOGRAPHY OF
HEBREW LAW & ALLIED SUBJECTS.
LO/U14.

**CURRENT BIBLIOGRAPHY OF HEBREW LAW & ALLIED
SUBJECTS.**   000
SEE: CURRENT BIBLIOGRAPHY & ABSTRACTS OF HEB-
REW LAW & ALLIED SUBJECTS.

**CURRENT CLINICAL CHEMISTRY. A CURRENT AWARE-
NESS SERVICE FOR CLINICAL CHEMISTS & MEDICAL
BIOCHEMISTRY.**
+ + *CURR. CLIN. CHEM.*
ASSOCIATION OF CLINICAL BIOCHEMISTS.
[PERGAMON]
OXFORD 1(1), JL 1974-
BL/U-1. ISSN 0305-0165

CURRENT FOOD ADDITIVES LEGISLATION.   XXX
+ + *CURR. FOOD ADDIT. LEGIS.*
FOOD & AGRICULTURAL ORGANIZATION (UN).
ROME NO.1, 1956- 150, 1972.//
LO/R-6. LO/N13. NO.11, 1957- MA/U-1. NO.96, 1966-
RE/U-1. NO.99, 1966- ISSN 0011-3506

CURRENT NOTES ON INTERNATIONAL AFFAIRS.   XXX
SUBS (1973): AUSTRALIAN FOREIGN AFFAIRS.

CURRENT PROGRAMS.
+ + *CURR. PROGRAMS.*
WORLD MEETINGS INFORMATION CENTER.
CHESNUT HILL, MASS. 1, JA 1973-
MON.
LO/N14. MA/U-1. OX/U-8. SH/U-1. SO/U-1.
CA/U-2. 1(10), OC 1973- ISSN 0091-0139

CYCLIC AMP.
UNIVERSITY OF SHEFFIELD: BIOMEDICAL INFORMATION
PROJECT.
SHEFFIELD 1(1), 1970-
MON.
OX/U-8. 4(1), 1973-

**CZECHOSLOVAK BIBLIOGRAPHY ON INDUSTRIAL HY-
GIENE & OCCUPATIONAL DISEASES.**   XXX
+ + *CZECH. BIBLIOGR. IND. HYG. & OCCUP. DIS.*
INSTITUTE OF HYGIENE & EPIDEMIOLOGY (PRAGUE).
PRAGUE 16, 1971(1972)-
PREV: SCIENTIFIC REPORTS ON INDUSTRIAL HYGIENE
& OCCUPATIONAL DISEASES IN CZECHOSLOVAKIA FROM
[2], 1957- 15, 1970. SPONS. BODY ALSO: RES-
EARCH INSTITUTE OF INDUSTRIAL HYGIENE & OCC-
UPATIONAL DISEASES (BRATISLAVA).
LO/N13.

DACOROMANIA.
FREIBURG &C. 1, 1973-
OX/U-1.

DALARNAS MUSEUMS SERIE AV SMASKRIFTER.
+ + *DALARNAS MUS. SER. SMASKR.*
[FALUN] NO.1, 1971-
LO/N-1.

DALHOUSIE LAW JOURNAL.
+ + *DALHOUSIE LAW J.*
DALHOUSIE UNIVERSITY: FACULTY OF LAW.
HALIFAX, N.S. 1, 1973-
LO/U-2. OX/U-1. OX/U15.

DANKO. ALMANAKH.
[MOLODAJA GVARDIJA]
MOSCOW 1, 1968-
CC/U-1.

DATA PROCESSING PRACTITIONER.
+ + *DATA PROCESS. PRACT.*
INSTITUTE OF DATA PROCESSING.
LONDON 2(11), 1970-
Q. NO.1, 1967- 10, 1970 PUBLISHED AS IN-
SERTS IN BOOK-KEEPERS JOURNAL. FROM 2(11)-
ISSUED AS A SEPARATE PUBLICATION WITH VOLUME
NUMBERING.
LO/N14. 4(22), 1973- ISSN 0011-6882

DATENVERARBEITUNG IM RECHT.
+ + *DATENVERARB. RECHT.*
[J. SCHWEITZER; W. DE GRUYTER]
BERLIN & NEW YORK 1, JE 1972-
SH/U-1.

DEFAZET. DEUTSCHE FARBEN-ZEITSCHRIFT.   XXX
[WISSENSCHAFTLICHE VERLAGSGESELLSCHAFT]
STUTTGART 27(4), 1973-
PREV: DEFAZET-AKTUELL FROM 25(10), 1971-
27(3), 1973.
LO/N14.

DEFEKTOLOGIJA.
AKADEMIJA PEDAGOGICHESKIKH NAUK RSFSR.
MOSCOW 1, 1969-
BH/U-1. 2, 1970-

DEJINY ROBOTNICKEHO HNUTA.   000
SEE: ZBORNIK: DEJINY ROBOTNICKEHO HNUTA.

DEMOGRAFICHESKIE TETRADI.
+ + *DEMOGR. TETRADI.*
AKADEMIJA NAUK UKRAJINS'KOJI RSR: INSTYTUT
EKONOMIKY.
KIEV 1, 1969-
ENGL. SUMM.
GL/U-1.

DEMOHRAFICHNI DOSLIDZHENNJA.
+ + *DEMOHR. DOSL.*
AKADEMIJA NAUK UKRAJINS'KOJI RSR: INSTYTUT
EKONOMIKY.
KIEV 1, 1970-
GL/U-1. CC/U-1. 2, 1971- LO/U15. 2, 1971.

DENTO-MAXILLOFACIAL RADIOLOGY.
+ + *DENTO-MAXILLOFAC. RADIOL.*
INTERNATIONAL ASSOCIATION OF MAXILLOFACIAL
RADIOLOGY.
ERLANGEN 1, 1972-
LD/U-1.

DENVER LAW JOURNAL. XXX
+ +*DENVER LAW J.* XXX
UNIVERSITY OF DENVER: COLLEGE OF LAW.
DENVER 43, 1966-
PREV: JOURNAL, DENVER LAW CENTER FROM 40(1),
JA/F 1963- 42, 1965.
OX/U15. ISSN 0011-8834

DESARROLLO.
CONGRESSO PARA EL DESARROLLO CIENTIFICO, CULT-
URAL Y ECONOMICO DE IBEROAMERICA.
BUENOS AIRES NO.1, 1968-
OX/U16. ISSN 0419-8999

DESARROLLO INDOAMERICANO.
+ +*DESARROLLO INDOAM.*
BARRANQUILLA, COLOMB. 1, 1966-
2M.
OX/U16. NO.18, MY 1972- ISSN 0418-7547

DESARROLLO DEL TROPICO AMERICANO.
+ +*DESARROLLO TROP. AM.*
FACULDADE DE CIENCIAS AGRARIAS DO PARA.
BELEM 1, JL/S 1972-
LO/R-6.

DEUTSCHES MEDIZINISCHES JOURNAL. XXX
+ +*DTSCH. MED. J.*
DEUTSCHER KONGRESS FUR AERZTLICHE FORTBILDUNG.
[MEDICUS VERLAG GMBH]
BERLIN 2(17/18), 1951- 23(12), 1972.//
PREV: BERLINER MEDIZINISCHE ZEITSCHRIFT FROM
1, 1949- 2(15/16), AG 1951.
LO/M17. LO/M32. ISSN 0012-1320

DEUTSCHE STOMATOLOGIE. XXX
SUBS (1974): STOMATOLOGIE DER DDR.

DIALEKTNAJA LEKSIKA.
AKADEMIJA NAUK SSSR: INSTITUT RUSSKOGO JAZYKA.
LENINGRAD 1969(1971)-
LD/U-1.

DICTA. XXX
SUBS (1963): JOURNAL, DENVER LAW CENTER.

DIFFUSION & DEFECT DATA. XXX
+ +*DIFFUS. & DEFECT DATA.*
DIFFUSION INFORMATION CENTER.
CLEVELAND, OHIO & SOLOTHURN 8, 1974-
Q. PREV: DIFFUSION DATA FROM 1(1), 1967- 7,
1973.
CA/U-2. LO/U12. SW/U-1.

DIFFUSION & DEFECT MONOGRAPH SERIES. XXX
+ +*DIFFUS. & DEFECT MONOGR. SER.*
[TRANS TECH SA]
RIEHEN NO.2, 1973-
PREV: DIFFUSION MONOGRAPH SERIES FROM NO.1,
1972.
LO/N14.

DIMENSIONS NBS. XXX
NATIONAL BUREAU OF STANDARDS (US).
WASHINGTON, D.C. 57(8), 1973-
PREV: TECHNICAL NEWS BULLETIN, NATIONAL BUR-
EAU OF STANDARDS (US) FROM [1]1, D 1917- 57(7)
1973.
LO/N-4. LO/N14. LO/R-6. BL/U-1. 58, 1974-

DIRECT CURRENT & POWER ELECTRONICS. XXX
+ +*DIR. CURR. & POWER ELECTRON.*
[WYNN WILLIAMS (PUBL.) LTD.]
WREXHAM 2, 1971-
PREV: DIRECT CURRENT: NS. FROM 1(1), 1969-
1(4), 1970.
LO/N14.

DIRITTO DI FAMIGLIA E DELLE PERSONE.
+ +*DIR. FAMIGLIA & PERS.*
MILAN 1, 1972-
Q.
OX/U15.

**DISCUSSION PAPERS IN ECONOMICS, UNIVERSITY OF
GLASGOW.**
+ +*DISCUSS. PAP. ECON. UNIV. GLASGOW.*
GLASGOW NO.1, 1973-
GL/U-1.

DIVINE TIMES.
DIVINE LIGHT MISSION.
LONDON NO.1, 12/AG 1972-
WKLY. ALSO AN AMERICAN EDITION.
MA/P-1.**

**DIVULGACIONES, DIRECCION NACIONAL DEL ANTART-
ICO (BRAZIL).**
+ +*DIVULG. DIR. NAC. ANTART. (BRAZ.).*
BUENOS AIRES NO.1, 1971-
LO/N-2.

**DOCUMENT, LAURENTIAN FOREST RESEARCH CENTRE,
FORESTRY SERVICE (CANADA).**
+ +*DOC. LAURENTIAN FOR. RES. CENT. FOR. SERV.
(CAN.).*
SAINTE FOY, QUE. 1, 1973-
OX/U-3.

DOCUMENTS ON NEW ZEALAND EXTERNAL RELATIONS.
+ +*DOC. N.Z. EXTERNAL RELAT.*
WELLINGTON, N.Z. 1, 1972-
LO/U-1.

DOUBLE LIAISON. XXX
SUBS (1974): DOUBLE LIAISON - CHIMIE DES
PEINTURES.

DOUBLE LIAISON - CHIMIE DES PEINTURES. XXX
+ +*DOUBLE LIAISON - CHIM. PEINT.*
[PRESSES CONTINENTALES]
PARIS 21(221), 1974-
PREV: DOUBLE LIAISON FROM NO.1, 1954- 220,
1973.
LO/N13.

DOUGHTY STREET PAPERS.
+ +*DOUGHTY STREET PAP.*
CENTRE FOR STUDIES IN SOCIAL POLICY.
[BEDFORD SQ. P.]
LONDON NO.1, 1973-
AD/U-1.

**DRITTE WELT. VIERTELJAHRESSCHRIFT ZUM WIRT-
SCHAFTLICHEN, KULTURELLEN, SOZIALEN UND POLIT-
ISCHEN WANDEL.**
MEISENHEIM 1, 1972-
ENGL., FR. OR GER. WITH SUMM. ENGL. S/T:
QUARTERLY JOURNAL DEVOTED TO ECONOMIC, CULT-
URAL, SOCIAL & POLITICAL CHANGE.
LO/U-3.

DRUG INFORMATION NEWSLETTER. XXX
+ +*DRUG INF. NEWSL.*
UNIVERSITY OF TENNESSEE: DRUG & TOXICOLOGY
INFORMATION CENTER.
MEMPHIS 1(1-2), 1973.//
CENTRE SUBORD. TO: COLLEGE OF PHARMACY.
LO/N13.

DRUZHBA.
[NARODNA MLADEZH]
SOFIA 1, 1972-
S/T: BULGARO-SUVETSKI LITERATURNO-KHUDOZHEST-
VEN I OBSHTESTVENO-POLITICHESKI ALMANAKH.
OX/U-1.

**DUNDEE TAYSIDE. JOURNAL OF THE DUNDEE & TAY-
SIDE CHAMBER OF COMMERCE & INDUSTRY.**
DUNDEE 1(1), MR 1974-
Q.
SA/U-1. ISSN 0306-0241

**DUROBRIVAE. A REVIEW OF NENE VALLEY ARCH-
AEOLOGY.**
NENE VALLEY RESEARCH COMMITTEE.
WERRINGTON 1, 1973-
BL/U-1. LD/U-1. OX/U-1.

EANHS BULLETIN. XXX
+ +*EANHS BULL.*
EAST AFRICA NATURAL HISTORY SOCIETY.
NAIROBI JA 1971-
PREV: EANHS NEWSLETTER FROM N-D 1970.
CA/U-6. LO/S10. OX/U-8. MY 1971-

EANHS NEWSLETTER. XXX
+ +*EANHS NEWSL.*
EAST AFRICA NATURAL HISTORY SOCIETY.
NAIROBI N-D 1970.
SUBS: EANHS BULLETIN.
CA/U-6. LO/N-2. LO/S10.

EARLY NORRLAND.
UPPSALA 1, 1972-
LO/N-2.

EARTHQUAKE INFORMATION BULLETIN.
+ +*EARTHQUAKE INF. BULL.*
NATIONAL EARTHQUAKE INFORMATION CENTER (US).
ROCKVILLE, MD. [1, 1967]-
CA/U-2. 5(4), 1973- LO/N13. 2, 1970- LO/U-2. 5(4), 1973-

EAST ANGLIAN HISTORY & ARCHAEOLOGY: WORK IN
PROGRESS.
+ +EAST ANGLIAN HIST. & ARCHAEOL., WORK PROG.
UNIVERSITY OF EAST ANGLIA: CENTRE OF EAST
ANGLIAN STUDIES.
NORWICH NO.1, 1970-
SH/U-1.   SW/U-1.

EAST LONDON PAPERS.   XXX
+ +EAST LOND. PAP.
[UNIVERSITY HOUSE]
LONDON 1, 1958- 15(1), 1973.//
S/T: A JOURNAL OF HISTORY, SOCIAL STUDIES &
THE ARTS.
CA/U-1.   HL/U-1.   LO/U-3.   ISSN 0012-8465

EASTERN AFRICA JOURNAL OF RURAL DEVELOPMENT.   XXX
+ +EAST. AFR. J. RURAL DEV.
KAMPALA 6, 1973-
PREV: EAST AFRICAN JOURNAL OF RURAL DEVELOP-
MENT FROM 1(1), 1968- 5, 1972.
LO/R-6.   LO/U-4.   NO/U-1.   RE/U-1.

EASY LISTENING.
+ +EASY LISTEN.
[CARDFONT PUBL.]
LONDON NO.1, JA 1973-
ED/N-1.   OX/U-1.

ECHOS DU COMMONWEALTH.
+ +ECHOS COMMONW.
SOCIETE D'ETUDES DES PAYS DU COMMONWEALTH.
PAU NO.1, JA 1973-
LO/U-8.

ECOLOGICAL ABSTRACTS.   XXX
+ +ECOL. ABSTR.
[GEO ABSTRACTS LTD.]
NORWICH 1, 1974-
6/A. PREV: BIOGEOGRAPHY SECTION OF GEO ABST-
RACTS: B: BIOGEOGRAPHY & CLIMATOLOGY.
BH/U-3.   ED/N-1.   GL/U-1.   GL/U-2.   LO/U-2.   LO/U-3.
OX/U-8.   RE/U-1.   SA/U-1.   SW/U-1.   ISSN 0305-196X

ECONOMIA ARGENTINA. + THE ARGENTINE ECONOMY.
+ +ECON. ARGENT.
CONSEJO TECNICO DE INVERSIONES S.A. (BUENOS
AIRES).
BUENOS AIRES 1962-
ANNU. PARALLEL SPAN. & ENGL. TEXTS.
LO/N10.   SO/U-1. 1965-1967.   ISSN 0424-2378

ECONOMIC BULLETIN, BANK OF TANZANIA.
+ +ECON. BULL. BANK TANZANIA.
DAR ES SALAAM 1, D 1966-
3/A.
LO/U14. 3(3), 1971-   ISSN 0045-1479

ECONOMIC INQUIRY.   XXX
+ +ECON. INQ.
WESTERN ECONOMIC ASSOCIATION.
LONG BEACH, CALIF. 12, 1974-
PREV: WESTERN ECONOMIC JOURNAL FROM 1, 1962-
11, 1973.
BL/U-1.   HL/U-1.   LO/U-2.   LO/U-3.   LO/U12.   NO/U-1.

ECONOMIC TITLES.
+ +ECON. TITLES.
(NETHERLANDS) MINISTRY OF ECONOMIC AFFAIRS:
ECONOMIC INFORMATION SERVICE.
[NIJHOFF]
THE HAGUE 1(1), 1974-
LO/N10.   LO/R-6.   NO/U-1.

EDGE (CHRISTCHURCH, N.Z.).
[EDGE P.]
CHRISTCHURCH, N.Z. 1, 1971-
3/A.
OX/U-1.   ISSN 0046-1253

EDICIA PROBLEMY A UVAHY: RAD PRAVNY.
+ +ED. PROBL. UVAHY, PRAVNY.
SLOVENSKA AKADEMIA VIED: USTAV STATU A PRAVA.
BRATISLAVA 1, 1966-
OX/U-1.

EDUCATION & COMMUNITY RELATIONS.
+ +EDUC. & COMMUNITY RELAT.
COMMUNITY RELATIONS COMMISSION (GB).
LONDON MY 1971-
LO/N-1.   LO/U-3.   CA/U-1. 1972-

EDUCATION RESEARCH & PERSPECTIVES.   XXX
+ +EDUC. RES. & PERSPECT.
UNIVERSITY OF WESTERN AUSTRALIA: DEPARTMENT OF
EDUCATION.
NEDLANDS 1, 1974-
PREV: AUSTRALIAN JOURNAL OF HIGHER EDUCATION
FROM 1, N 1961- 5(1), 1973.
AD/U-1.   GL/U-1.   LO/U-1.   SA/U-1.

EDUCATION YEARBOOK.
+ +EDUC. YEARB.
[MACMILLAN]
NEW YORK 1972/73-
SW/U-1.

EDUCATIONAL ADMINISTRATION & HISTORY MONO-
GRAPHS.
+ +EDUC. ADMIN. & HIST. MONOGR.
UNIVERSITY OF LEEDS: MUSEUM OF THE HISTORY OF
EDUCATION.
LEEDS NO.1, 1973-
LO/N-1.

EDUCATIONAL ADMINISTRATION QUARTERLY.
+ +EDUC. ADMIN. Q.
UNIVERSITY COUNCIL FOR EDUCATIONAL ADMINISTRAT-
ION.
COLUMBUS, OHIO 1, 1965-
3/A.
LV/U-2. 6, 1970-   SW/U-1. 10, 1974-   ISSN 0013-161X

EDUCATIONAL DEVELOPMENT INTERNATIONAL.
+ +EDUC. DEV. INT.
CENTRE FOR EDUCATIONAL DEVELOPMENT OVERSEAS.
[P. PEREGRINIUS LTD.]
STEVENAGE 1(1), MY 1973-
Q.
HL/U-2.   ISSN 0305-7461

EDUCATIONAL MEDIA YEARBOOK.
+ +EDUC. MEDIA YEARB.
[BOWKER]
NEW YORK 1973-
CA/U-1.   OX/U-1.   ISSN 0000-037X

EDUCATIONAL PRIORITY.
+ +EDUC. PRIORITY.
(GREAT BRITAIN) DEPARTMENT OF EDUCATION &
SCIENCE.
LONDON 1, 1972-
SPONS. BODY ALSO: SOCIAL SCIENCE RESEARCH
COUNCIL (GB).
LO/N-1.

EDUCATIONAL RESEARCH IN BRITAIN.
+ +EDUC. RES. BR.
[UNIV. LONDON P.]
LONDON 1968-
CA/U-1.   LO/U17.   AD/U-1. 3, 1973-

EDUCATIONAL TECHNOLOGY SYSTEMS.   000
SEE: JOURNAL OF EDUCATIONAL TECHNOLOGY
SYSTEMS.

EESTI NSV AJALOO KUSIMUSI.
TARTU RIIKLIK ULIKOOL.
TARTU 1, 1960-
TITLE ALSO IN RUSS.: VOPROSY ISTORII ESTONSKOJ
SSR. ALSO NUMBERED AS PART OF MAIN SERIES:
TARTU RIIKLIKU ULIKOOLI TOIMETISED.
OX/U-1. 3, 1964.

EGYPTIAN JOURNAL OF BOTANY (1972).   XXX
+ +EGYPT. J. BOT. (1972).
NATIONAL INFORMATION & DOCUMENTATION CENTRE
(EGYPT).   XXX
CAIRO 15(1), 1972-
PREV: JOURNAL OF BOTANY OF THE UNITED ARAB
REPUBLIC FROM 3(1), 1960- 14(2), 1971.
LO/R-6.

EGYPTIAN JOURNAL OF PHARMACEUTICAL SCIENCES
(1972).   XXX
+ +EGYPT. J. PHARM. SCI. (1972).
NATIONAL INFORMATION & DOCUMENTATION CENTRE
(EGYPT).   XXX
CAIRO 13(1), 1972-
PREV: UNITED ARAB REPUBLIC JOURNAL OF PHARM-
ACEUTICAL SCIENCES FROM 11(1), 1970- 12(2),
1971.
LO/R-6.   OX/U-8.

EKONOMICHESKAJA GAZETA.   XXX
++*EKON. GAZ.*
KOMMUNISTICHESKAJA PARTIJA SOVETSKOGO SOJUZA.
MOSCOW 1/JE 1960-
PREV: PROMYSHLENNO-EKONOMICHESKAJA GAZETA FROM
1, F 1956- 1960.
OX/U-1. 1966-

EKONOMICHESKAJA GEOGRAFIJA.
++*EKON. GEOGR.*
(UKRAINE) MINISTERSTVO VYSSHOJI I SEREDN'OJI
SPETSIAL'NOJI OS'VITY.
KHAR'KOV 1, 1964-
S/T: RESPUBLIKANSKIJ MEZHVEDOMSTVENNYJ
NAUCHNYJ SBORNIK.
LO/U-3.   BH/U-1. 2, 1964.

EKONOMICHNA HEOHRAFIJA.
++*EKON. HEOHRAFIJA.*
KYJIVS'KYJ DERZHAVNYJ UNIVERSYTET [IM. T.G.
SHEVEHENKIA.
KIEV 1, 1966-
RUSS. SUMM.   S/T: MIZHVIDOMCHYJ NAUKOVYJ
ZBIRNYK.
BH/U-1. 6-7, 1969.

EKONOMIKA I ORGANIZATSIJA PROMYSHLENNOGO PRO-
IZVODSTVA SIBIRI I DAL'NEGO VOSTOKA.
++*EKON. & ORGAN. PROM. PROIZVOD. SIB. & DAL'NEGO
VOSTOKA.*
AKADEMIJA NAUK SSSR (SIBIRSKOE OTDELENIE).
NOVOSIBIRSK 1, 1964-
SPONS. BODY ALSO: GOSUDARSTVENNAJA PUBLICHNAJA
NAUCHNO-TEKHNICHESKAJA BIBLIOTEKA SSSR:
NAUCHNO-BIBLIOGRAFICHESKIJ OTDEL.
OX/U-1. 1966-   SH/U-1. 1972-

EKONOMIKA I PRAVO. SBORNIK STATEJ ASPIRANTOV
I SOISKATELEJ.
++*EKON. & PRAVO.*
(KAZAKH SSR) MINISTERSTVO VYSSHEGO I SREDNEGO
SPETSIAL'NOGO OBRAZOVANIJA.
ALMA-ATA NO.1, 1966-
LO/U-3. NO.3, 1968-

EKONOMSKE STUDIJE.
++*EKON. STUD. (ZAGREB).*
EKONOMSKI INSTITUT.
ZAGREB 1, 1962-
ENGL. & RUSS. SUMM.
GL/U-1.

EKSPERIMENTAL'NAJA I KLINICHESKAJA FARMAKO-
TERAPIJA.
++*EKSP. & KLIN. FARMAKOTER.*
LATVIJAS PSR ZINATNU AKADEMIJA: ORGANISKAS
SINTEZES INSTITUTAS.
RIGA 1, 1970-
LO/N13.

EKSPERIMENTALNA MEDITSINA I MORFOLOGIJA.
++*EKSP. MED. & MORFOL.*
(BULGARIA) MINISTERSTVO NA NARODNOTO ZDRAVE I
SOTSIALNITE GRIZHI.
SOFIA 1, 1962-
SPONS. BODIES ALSO: NAUCHNO DRUZHESTVO ZA
FIZIOLOGICHESKI NAUKI; & NAUCHNO DRUZHESTVO NA
ANATOMITE, KHISTOLOZITE I PATOLOZITE.
LO/N13. 2, 1963-

ELECTRIC VEHICLE NEWS.
++*ELECTR. VEH. NEWS.*
[PORTER CORP.]
WESTPORT, CONN. 1, 1972-
Q. S/T: THE MAGAZINE COMMITTED TO BETTER
TRANSPORTATION.
SF/U-1. 3(1), 1974-

ELECTRICAL & NUCLEAR TECHNOLOGY.
++*ELECTR. & NUCL. TECHNOL.*
VALTION TEKNILLINEN TUTKIMUSKESKUS.
HELSINKI [NO.]1, 1973-
CA/U-2.   LO/N14.

ELECTRICAL RETAILER.
++*ELECTR. RETAILER.*
ELECTRICAL & ELECTRONIC RETAILERS' ASSOCIATION.
LONDON [NO.1], S 1973-
MON.
ED/N-1. NO.10, 1974-

ELECTRICIEN.   XXX
SUBS (1974): ELECTRICIEN INDUSTRIEL.

ELECTRICIEN INDUSTRIEL.   XXX
++*ELECTR. IND.*
[DUNOD]
PARIS 87(2157), 1974-
PREV: ELECTRICIEN FROM 2S. 1, 1891- 86(2156),
1973.
LO/N14.

ELECTROCHEMISTRY IN INDUSTRIAL PROCESSING &
BIOLOGY.   XXX
++*ELECTROCHEM. IND. PROCESS. & BIOL.*
[SCIENTIFIC INFORMATION CONSULTANTS]
LONDON JA/F 1971-
PREV: APPLIED ELECTRICAL PHENOMENA FROM JA/F
1965- 1970. ENGL. TRANSL. OF: ELEKTRONNAJA
OBRABOTKA MATERIALOV.
CA/U-1.   LO/N14.   ED/N-1. JL/AG 1971-   ISSN 0306-4832

ELECTRON MICROSCOPY ABSTRACTS.
++*ELECTRON MICROSC. ABSTR.*
[SCIENCE & TECHNOLOGY AGENCY]
LONDON 1(1), JL/S 1972-
Q.
CA/U-1. 2, 1973-   XS/R10. 1(3), 1973-

ELECTRONICS MANAGEMENT.
++*ELECTRON. MANAGE.*
[TRADE NEWS LTD.]
LONDON 1(1), AP 1973-
MON.
LO/N35.   CA/U-1. 2, 1974-   ED/N-1. 2, 1974-

ELEKTRONNAJA OBRABOTKA MATERIALOV (ENGL.
TRANSL. [1971]).   000
SEE: ELECTROCHEMISTRY IN INDUSTRIAL PROCESSING
& BIOLOGY.

ELELMISZERTUDOMANY.   XXX
KOZPONTI ELELMISZERIPARI KUTATO INTEZET.
BUDAPEST 1, 1967- 4(1-2), 1970.
PREV: KOZPONTI ELELMISZERIPARI KUTATO
INTEZETKOZLEMENYEI.
*LO/N-6. ***

ELYSIAN.
WORCESTER [JL 1972]-
6/A. INCORP: INTREPID.
OX/U-1.   ED/N-1. 1974-

EMIGRANTE. BOLETIN DEL TRABAJADOR ESPANOL EN
GRAN BRETANA.
LONDON NO.1, D 1973-
MON. PRELIM. ISSUE NO.0 PUBL. OC 1973.
LO/U-3.   ISSN 0306-1701

ENERGETICHESKOE MASHINOSTROENIE.
++*ENERGET. MASHINOSTR.*
KHAR'KOVSKIJ GOSUDARSTVENNYJ UNIVERSITET.
KHAR'KOV 1, 1966-
LO/N13. 10, 1970-

ENERGY PIPELINES & SYSTEMS.   XXX
++*ENERGY PIPELINES & SYST.*
[CHILTON]
HOUSTON, TEX. 1, JA 1974-
MON. PREV: GAS (HOUSTON, TEX.) FROM 12(5), MY
1936- 49(12), D 1973.
SF/U-1.

ENERGY PROCESSING CANADA.   XXX
++*ENERGY PROCESS. CAN.*
[SANFORD EVANS PUBL. (ALTA.) LTD.]
CALGARY 65(6), 1973-
PREV: GAS PROCESSING CANADA.
LO/N13.

ENERGY REPORT.
++*ENERGY REP.*
[MICROINFO LTD.]
ALTON, HANTS. 1(1), MR 1974-
S/T: ENERGY POLICY & TECHNOLOGY NEWS BULLETIN.
ED/N-1.   OX/U-8.   XS/R10.   LO/N14. CURRENT BOX ONLY.

ENERGY TRENDS. A STATISTICAL BULLETIN.
(GREAT BRITAIN) DEPARTMENT OF ENERGY.
LONDON JL 1974-
MON.
BN/U-1.   LO/U-3.   MA/U-1.   OX/U16. AG 1974-

ENGINEERING INDUSTRIES REVIEW.
++*ENG. IND. REV.*
[GOWER ECONOMIC PUBL.]
EPPING, ESSEX 1973/1974(1973)-
CA/U-1.

ENGINEERING OPTIMIZATION.
++ ENG. OPTIM.
[GORDON & BREACH]
 LONDON 1, 1974-
 BL/U-1.   BR/U-1.   CA/U-4.   ISSN 0305-215X

ENGLISH IN AFRICA.
++ ENGL. AFR.
 GRAHAMSTOWN 1, 1974-
 OX/U-1.

ENGLISH HARPSICHORD MAGAZINE, & EARLY KEYBOARD
INSTRUMENT REVIEW.   XXX
++ ENGL. HARPSICHORD MAG. & EARLY KEYBOARD
 INSTRUM. REV.
[EDGAR HUNT]
 AMERSHAM, BUCKS. 1(2), AP 1974-
 2/A. PREV: HARPSICHORD MAGAZINE FROM 1(1), OC
 1973.
 CA/U-1.   ED/N-1.   SH/U-1.   ISSN 0306-4395

ENTOMOLOGICAL PROBLEMS (BRATISLAVA).   000
 SEE: ENTOMOLOGICKE PROBLEMY.

ENTOMOLOGICHESKIE PROBLEMY (BRATISLAVA).   000
 SEE: ENTOMOLOGICKE PROBLEMY.

ENTOMOLOGICKE PROBLEMY.
++ ENTOMOL. PROBL.
SLOVENSKA AKADEMIA VIED.
 BRATISLAVA 1, 1961-
 GER. & SLOVAK. WITH ENGL. & RUSS. SUMM.
 NO.1-4, 1961 PUBL. IN BIOLOGICKE PRACE. TITLE
 ALSO IN RUSS.: ENTOMOLOGICHESKIE PROBLEMY, &
 IN ENGL.: ENTOMOLOGICAL PROBLEMS. SPONS. BODY
 ALSO: SLOVENSKA ENTOMOLOGICKA.
 LO/N13. 8, 1970-

ENTOMOLOGY LEAFLET, BRITISH MUSEUM (NATURAL
HISTORY).
++ ENTOMOL. LEAFL. BR. MUS. (NAT. HIST.).
 LONDON NO.1, 1974-
 LO/N-2.   ISSN 0305-3520

ENVIRONMENT ABSTRACTS.   XXX
++ ENVIRON. ABSTR.
ENVIRONMENT INFORMATION CENTER.
 NEW YORK 4, 1974-
 PREV: ENVIRONMENT INFORMATION ACCESS FROM 1,
 29/JA 1971- 3, 1973.
 GL/U-2.   LO/N13.

ENVIRONMENT & CHANGE.   XXX
++ ENVIRON. & CHANGE.
[MADDOX EDITORIAL LTD.]
 LONDON 2(1), S 1973- 2(6), F 1974. //
 PREV: ENVIRONMENT THIS MONTH FROM 1(1-2),
 1972.
 ED/N-1.   HL/U-1.   LO/N-2.   LO/N14.   SH/P-1.   SH/U-1.
 ISSN 0301-3715

ENVIRONMENTAL CONSERVATION.
++ ENVIRON. CONSERV.
FOUNDATION FOR ENVIRONMENTAL CONSERVATION.
 LAUSANNE 1, 1974-
 Q.
 GL/U-2.   LO/R-5.   LO/U-2.

ENVIRONMENTAL HEALTH PERSPECTIVES.
++ ENVIRON. HEALTH PERSPECT.
NATIONAL INSTITUTE OF ENVIRONMENTAL HEALTH
SCIENCES (US).
 RESEARCH TRIANGLE PARK, N.C. NO.1, AP 1972-
 LO/M10.*   LD/U-1. NO.3, 1973-

ENVIRONMENTAL PERIODICALS. INDEXED ARTICLE
TITLES.   000
 SEE: ENVIRONMENTAL PERIODICALS BIBLIOGRAPHY.

ENVIRONMENTAL PERIODICALS BIBLIOGRAPHY.
++ ENVIRON. PERIOD. BIBLIOGR.
INTERNATIONAL ACADEMY AT SANTA BARBARA:
ENVIRONMENTAL STUDIES INSTITUTE.
 SANTA BARBARA, CALIF. 1, MR 1972-
 V.1 ENTITLED: ENVIRONMENTAL PERIODICALS. IND-
 EXED ARTICLE TITLES.
 HL/U-1.   LO/N14.   LO/R-5.   ISSN 0046-2306

ENVIRONMENTAL PHYSIOLOGY & BIOCHEMISTRY.   XXX
++ ENVIRON. PHYSIOL. & BIOCHEM.
[MUNKSGAARD]
 COPENHAGEN 2(1), 1972-
 PREV: ENVIRONMENTAL PHYSIOLOGY FROM 1, 1971.
 AD/U-1.   BL/U-1.   CA/U-1.   GL/U-2.   LO/N13.   LO/R-5.
 SO/U-1.

ENVIRONMENTAL RESOURCE.
++ ENVIRON. RESOUR.
INTERNATIONAL ASSOCIATION FOR THE ADVANCEMENT
OF EARTH & ENVIRONMENTAL SCIENCES.
[MID-CONTINENT SCIENTIFIC]
 DES PLAINES, ILL. 1, S 1973-
 LO/N13.

ENZYME REGULATION.
++ ENZYME REGUL.
UNIVERSITY OF SHEFFIELD: BIOMEDICAL INFORMATION
PROJECT.
 SHEFFIELD 1, 1971-
 MON. PROJECT SUBORD. TO: DEPARTMENT OF
 PHYSIOLOGY.
 ED/N-1. 4(2), 1974.

ENZYME TECHNOLOGY DIGEST.
++ ENZYME TECHNOL. DIG.
[NEUS, INC.]
 SANTA MONICA, CALIF. 1, JL 1972-
 3/A.
 LO/N14.   OX/U-1.   XS/R10. 2(2), 1973-

EPIGRAPHIA TAMILICA. A JOURNAL OF TAMIL EPI-
GRAPHY.
++ EPIGR. TAMILICA.
JAFFNA ARCHAEOLOGICAL SOCIETY.
 JAFFNA 1, JE 1971-
 LO/N12.

ERBIL. LITERARY JOURNAL.
 LONDON NO.1, MR 1974-
 CA/U-1.   ED/N-1.   LO/U-2.   OX/U-1.

ERDA. ENGINEERING RESEARCH & DEVELOPMENT IN
AGRICULTURE.
(CANADA) DEPARTMENT OF AGRICULTURE: ENGINEERING
RESEARCH SERVICE.
 OTTAWA ISSUE 1, 1968-
 Q.
 LO/N14.   LO/N-6. 7, 1969-   ISSN 0012-7892

ERFAHRUNGSBERICHTE, ALLIANZ VERSICHERUNGS.   XXX
++ ERFAHRUNGSBER. ALLIANZ VERSICHER.
 MUNICH 1-2, 1965 ...
 SUBS: ALLIANZ BERICHTE FUR BETRIEBSTECHNIK UND
 SCHADENVERHUTUNG.
 LO/N14.

EROZIJA POCHV I RUSLOVYE PROTSESSY.
++ EROZIJA POCHV & RUSL. PROTSESSY.
MOSKOVSKIJ GOSUDARSTVENNYJ UNIVERSITET.
 MOSCOW 1, 1970-
 LO/N13.

ESPERANTO CONTACT.   XXX
BRITISH ESPERANTO ASSOCIATION.
 THORNTON HEATH, SURREY 1(1), 1971- 2(7), S
              1972.//
 MON.
 ED/N-1. 1(7), 1971-   OX/U-1. 1(7), 1971-   ISSN 0046-2519

ESSAYS IN FUNDAMENTAL IMMUNOLOGY.
++ ESSAYS FUNDAM. IMMUNOL.
[BLACKWELL SCIENTIFIC PUBL.]
 OXFORD 1, 1973-
 GL/U-1.   ISSN 0301-4703

ESTUDIOS DE ARQUELOGIA ALAVESA.
++ ESTUD. ARQUEL. ALAVESA.
DIPUTACION FORAL DE ALAVA.
 VITORIA 1, 1966-
 OX/U-2.   ISSN 0425-3507.

ESTUDIOS SOCIALES. REVISTA DE CIENCIAS
SOCIALES.
++ ESTUD. SOC. (GUATEMALA).
UNIVERSIDAD RAFAEL LANDIVAR: INSTITUTO DE
CIENCIAS POLITICO-SOCIALES.
 GUATEMALA CITY NO.1, JL 1970-
 Q.
 LO/S10. NO.6, 1972-

ESTUDIOS SOCIALES. REVISTA DE INFORMACION Y
ORIENTACION SOCIAL.
++ ESTUD. SOC. (SANTO DOMINGO).
CENTRO DE INVESTIGACION Y ACCION SOCIAL DE LA
COMPANIA DE JESUS (SANTO DOMINGO).
 SANTO DOMINGO 1968-
 Q.
 LO/U-3. ‡W. AP/JE 1968A

ESTUDIOS SOCIALES CENTROAMERICANOS.
++ESTUD. SOC. CENTROAM.
CONSEJO SUPERIOR UNIVERSITARIO CENTRO-
AMERICANO: PROGRAMA CENTROAMERICANO DE DESARR-
OLLO DE LAS CIENCIAS SOCIALES.
SAN JOSE 1, JA/AP 1972-
3/A.
LO/U-3.

ESTUDIOS DE URBANISMO, ARQUITECTURA Y OTRAS
ARTES.
++ESTUD. URBAN. ARQUIT. & OTRAS ARTES.
[EDITORIAL CASTALIA]
MADRID 1967-
CA/U-1.   ISSN 0425-3663

ESTUDIOS VIZCAINOS.
++ESTUD. VIZCAINOS.
CENTRO DE ESTUDIOS HISTORICOS DE VIZCAYA.
BILBAO 1, JA/JE 1970-
OX/U-1.

ETHIOPIAN FORESTRY REVIEW.   XXX
++ETHIOP. FOR. REV.
ETHIOPIAN FORESTRY ASSOCIATION.
ADDIS ABABA 1, JE 1961- 3/4, 1962.//
LO/R-6.   ISSN 0423-5290

ETHNICITY.
NEW YORK & LONDON 1, 1974-
BL/U-1.   LO/U-4.

ETHNOGRAPHY MONOGRAPH, ROYAL ONTARIO MUSEUM.
++ETHNOGR. MONOGR. R. ONT. MUS.
TORONTO [NO.]1, S 1973-
GL/U-1.   LO/U-1.   OX/U-1.   ISSN 0316-1277

ETHNOLOGIA AMERICANA.
++ETHNOL. AM.
DUSSELDORFER INSTITUT FUR AMERIKANISCHE VOELK-
ERKUNDE.
DUSSELDORF 1, MY/JE 1964-
LO/S10. 8, 1971-   ISSN 0531-7282

ETHOS.
[UNIV. OF CALIFORNIA P.]
BERKELEY, CALIF. 1, 1973-
BN/U-1.

ETUDES MONGOLES.
++ETUD. MONGOLES.
CENTRE DE DOCUMENTATION ET D'ETUDES MONGOLES.
PARIS 1, 1970-
ISSUE FOR 1970 PREPARED BY THE GROUP DE DOC-
UMENTATION ET D'ETUDES MONGOLES.
LO/U14.   OX/U-1.

ETUDES DE SOCIOLOGIE TUNISIENNE.
++ETUD. SOCIOL. TUNIS.
BUREAU DE RECHERCHES SOCIOLOGIQUES (TUNIS).
TUNIS 1, 1968-
LO/U14.   ISSN 0531-8769

ETUDES TOGOLAISES: NOUVELLE SERIE.
++ETUD. TOGOLAISES, NS.
INSTITUT NATIONAL DE LA RECHERCHE SCIENTIFIQUE
(TOGO).
LOME 1, 1971-
3/A. S/T: REVUE TOGOLAISES DES SCIENCES.
PREV. SERIES FROM 1, D 1965.
LO/U14.

EUROMEAT.
[IPC CONSUMER INDUSTRIES P. LTD.]
LONDON NO.1, [1973]-
GER. S/T: MAGAZINE FUR DIE EUROPAISCHE FLEISCH
INDUSTRIE. FR. S/T: REVUE DE L'EUROVIANDE.
ED/N-1. NO.2, 1973-

EUROPAISCHE HOCHSCHULSCHRIFTEN: REIHE 3:
GESCHICHTE UND IHRE HILFSWISSENSCHAFTEN.
++EUR. HOCHSCHULSCH., 3.
[VERLAG HERBERT LANG & CIE]
BERN 1, 1967-
CA/U-1. 2, 1968-   ISSN 0531-7320

EUROPAISCHE RUNDSCHAU.
++EUR. RUNDSCH.
[EUROPA VERLAG-AG]
VIENNA NO.1, JL 1973-
Q.
LO/S14.

EUROPARECHT.
WISSENSCHAFTLICHE GESELLSCHAFT FUR EUROPARECHT.
[BECK'SCHE VERLAGSBUCHHANDLUNG]
MUNICH 1, 1966-
ANNU.
LD/U-1.   LO/N10.   CB/U-1. 5, 1970-
ISSN 0531-2485

EUROPE DU SUD EST.   000
SEE: SOUTHEASTERN EUROPE.

EUROPEAN COMMUNITIES COMMENTARY.
++EUR. COMMUNITIES COMMENT.
[H.M.S.O.]
LONDON 1, 1973-
ISSUED AS SUPPL. TO: TRADE & INDUSTRY.
BL/U-1.

EUROPEAN INDUSTRIAL RELATIONS REVIEW.
++EUR. IND. RELAT. REV.
LONDON NO.1, JA 1974-
MON.
CA/U-1.   CA/U13.   ED/N-1.   LO/U-1.   OX/U-1.   SH/U-1.

EUROPEAN JOURNAL OF APPLIED PHYSIOLOGY & OCCU-
PATIONAL PHYSIOLOGY.   XXX
++EUR. J. APPL. PHYSIOL. & OCCUP. PHYSIOL.
[SPRINGER]
BERLIN &C. 32, 1973-
PREV: INTERNATIONALE ZEITSCHRIFT FUR ANGE-
WANDTE PHYSIOLOGIE EINSCHLIESSLICH ARBEITS-
PHYSIOLOGIE FROM 16, 1955- 31, 1973.
LD/U-1.   LO/N14.

EUROPEAN JOURNAL OF CARDIOLOGY.
++EUR. J. CARDIOL.
EXCERPTA MEDICA FOUNDATION.
AMSTERDAM 1, 1973-
Q.
LO/N13.   SH/U-1.

EUROPEAN PLASTICS NEWS.   XXX
++EUR. PLAST. NEWS.
LONDON 1(1), MY 1974-
PREV: EUROPLASTICS MONTHLY: BRITISH PLASTICS
EDITION FROM 45(4), 1972- 47(4), AP 1974.
ED/N-1.   GL/U-2.   LD/U-1.   LO/N14.   SF/U-1.   XS/T-4.

EUROPEAN REVIEW OF AGRICULTURAL ECONOMICS.
++EUR. REV. AGRIC. ECON.
THE HAGUE 1, 1973-
AD/U-1.   LO/R-6.   SA/U-1.   SW/U-1.

EUROPEAN SHIPBUILDING.   XXX
SUBS (1973): NORWEGIAN MARITIME RESEARCH.

EUROPLASTICS YEAR BOOK.   XXX
++EUROPLAST. YEAR BOOK.
[IPC INDUSTRIAL P.]
LONDON 1973-
PREV: BRITISH PLASTICS YEAR BOOK FROM 1931-
1972.
LD/U-1.   LO/N14.

EVENSONGS.
TAIPEI 1, 1970-
OX/U-1.

EVENT.
DOUGLAS COLLEGE: DEPARTMENT OF ENGLISH.
NEW WESMINSTER, B.C. 1, 1971-
3/A.
OX/U-1.

EVOLUTIONARY THEORY.
++EVOL. THEORY.
UNIVERSITY OF CHICAGO: DEPARTMENT OF BIOLOGY.
CHICAGO 1, JL 1973-
LO/N-2.   LO/U-2.   OX/U-8.

EXCEPTIONAL CHILD EDUCATION ABSTRACTS.
++EXCEPT. CHILD EDUC. ABSTR.
COUNCIL FOR EXCEPTIONAL CHILDREN.
ARLINGTON, VA. 1, 1969-
Q.
LV/U-2.   DB/U-2. 3, 1971-   SW/U-1. 5, 1973-

EXCHANGE OF INFORMATION ON RESEARCH IN EUROP-
EAN LAW.
++EXCH. INF. RES. EUR. LAW.
COUNCIL OF EUROPE: DIRECTORATE OF LEGAL
AFFAIRS.
STRASBOURG 1, D 1971-
ENGL. & FR.
LO/U-3.   NW/U-1.   OX/U17.   HL/U-1. ‡W. NO.3, 1973A

EXCITED STATES.
[ACADEMIC P.]
NEW YORK & LONDON 1, 1974-
CA/U-1.   LO/N14.

EXERCISE & SPORT SCIENCES REVIEWS.
++*EXERCISE & SPORT SCI. REV.*
[ACADEMIC P.]
NEW YORK & LONDON 1, 1973-
LO/N13.   ISSN 0091-6331

EXILE. A LITERARY QUARTERLY.
YORK UNIVERSITY (TORONTO): ATKINSON COLLEGE.
TORONTO 1, 1972-
OX/U-1.

EXPERIMENTAL EMBRYOLOGY & TERATOLOGY.   XXX
++*EXP. EMBRYOL. & TERATOL.*
[ELEK SCIENCE]
LONDON 1, 1974-
PREV: ADVANCES IN TERATOLOGY FROM 1, JE 1966-
5, 1972.
BL/U-1.   LD/U-1.   LO/N13.   LO/U-2.   SO/U-1.

EXPERIMENTAL HEMATOLOGY (COPENHAGEN).
++*EXP. HEMATOL. (COPENH.).*
INTERNATIONAL SOCIETY FOR EXPERIMENTAL
HEMATOLOGY.
COPENHAGEN 1, 1973-
2M.
SH/U-1.

EXPLORATIONS IN ECONOMIC HISTORY.   XXX
++*EXPLOR. ECON. HIST.*
[KENT STATE UNIV. P.]
KENT, OHIO 7, 1970-
Q. PREV: EXPLORATIONS IN ENTREPRENEURIAL
HISTORY: 2S. FROM 1, 1963- 6, 1969.
CA/U-1.   BN/U-1. 11(1), 1973-   ISSN 0014-4983

EXPLOSIVES & PYROTECHNICS.
++*EXPLOS. & PYROTECH.*
FRANKLIN INSTITUTE RESEARCH LABORATORIES.
PHILADELPHIA 1968-
MON.
LO/N14. ‡CURRENT BOX ONLY‡   ISSN 0014-505X

FACHSCHRIFT FUR TEXTILREINIGUNG.   XXX
++*FACHSCHR. TEXTILREINIG.*
[ZEITSCHRIFTENVERLAG STAFA]
STAFA 69, 1974-
PREV: SCHWEIZERISCHE WASCHEREI-ZEITUNG FROM
60, 1965- 68, 1973.
LO/N13.

FACTS (LONDON).
EUROPEAN MOVEMENT.
LONDON N 1973-
MON.
LO/U-3.   ED/N-1. F 1974-   ISSN 0306-0772

F.A.I.R. REVIEW.
++*F.A.I.R. REV.*
FEDERATION OF AFRO-ASIAN INSURERS & REINSURERS.
CAIRO NO.1, S 1971-
LO/S24. ‡W. NO.3, 4 & 6‡

**FAKTORY VNESHNEJ SREDY I IKH ZNACHENIE DLJA
ZDOROV'JA NASELENIJA.**
++*FAKT. VNESHN. SREDY & IKH ZNACHENIE ZDOROV'JA
NASELENIJA.*
L'VIVS'KYJ NAUKOVO-DOSLIDNYJ INSTYTUT EPIDEM-
IOLOHIJI I MIKROBIOLOHIJI.
KIEV 1, 1969-
SPONS. BODY ALSO: MINISTERSTVO ZDRAVOOKHRAN-
ENIJA USSR (UKRAINE). S/T: RESPUBLIKANSKIJ
MEZHVEDOMSTVENNYJ SBORNIK.
BH/U-1.

FARMING IN SOUTH AFRICA.   XXX
++*FARM. S. AFR.*
(SOUTH AFRICA) DEPARTMENT OF AGRICULTURE.
PRETORIA 1(1), 1926- 48(12), 1973.//
LO/R-6.   LO/N13. 24(274), 1949- ‡W. 39(3), 1963.‡

FARMLAND MARKET.
++*FARML. MARK.*
UNIVERSITY OF OXFORD: INSTITUTE OF AGRICULTURAL
ECONOMICS.
[ESTATES GAZETTE; FARMERS WEEKLY]
LONDON NO.1, F 1974-
2/A.
CA/U-1.   ED/N-1.   LO/N-6.   OX/U-1.   ISSN 0305-0157

FASTENING & JOINING.   000
SEE: TEIKETSU TO SETSUGO.

FEDERALIST (LONDON).
YOUNG UNITED FEDERALISTS.
LONDON NO.1, MY 1973-
ED/N-1.

**FERTILIZER INDUSTRY SERIES, UNITED NATIONS
INDUSTRIAL DEVELOPMENT ORGANIZATION.**
++*FERT. IND. SER. U.N. IND. DEV. ORGAN.*
NEW YORK NO.1, 1968-
MONOGR.
LO/N14.

FERTILIZER TRENDS.
++*FERT. TRENDS.*
NATIONAL FERTILIZER DEVELOPMENT CENTER (US).
MUSCLE SHOALS, ALA. 1967-
2A.
LO/N13.   ISSN 0071-4631

FICTION INTERNATIONAL.
++*FICTION INT.*
CANTON, N.Y. NO.1, 1973-
2A.
OX/U-1.   ISSN 0092-1912

FIELDFARE.
DUBLIN NATURALISTS' FIELD CLUB.
DUBLIN [NO.1, S 1973]-
2/A.
ED/N-1.

FIGARO AGRICOLE.   XXX
SUBS (1974): AGRICOLE.

**FINANCEMENT DES SYSTEMS EDUCATIFS: ETUDES CAS
SPECIFIQUES.**
SEE: FINANCING EDUCATIONAL SYSTEMS: SPECIFIC
CASE STUDIES.

FINANCIAL MAIL OF ZAMBIA.   XXX
SUBS (1967): BUSINESS & ECONOMY OF CENTRAL &
EAST AFRICA.

FINANCIAL TIMES WORLD COMMODITY SERVICE.   XXX
++*FINANC. TIMES WORLD COMMOD. SERV.*
[FINANCIAL TIMES LTD.]
LONDON 24/AP 1973- 29/OC 1974.
S/T: A WEEKLY DIGEST OF COMMODITY INFORMATION.
SUBS: WORLD COMMODITY REPORT.
CA/U-1.   ED/N-1. 18/S 1973-

**FINANCING EDUCATIONAL SYSTEMS: COUNTRY CASE
STUDIES.**
++*FINANC. EDUC. SYST., CTY. CASE STUD.*
INTERNATIONAL INSTITUTE FOR EDUCATIONAL
PLANNING.
PARIS NO.1, 1972-
LO/N-1.

**FINANCING EDUCATIONAL SYSTEMS: SPECIFIC CASE
STUDIES.**
++*FINANC. EDUC. SYST., SPECIFIC CASE STUD.*
INTERNATIONAL INSTITUTE FOR EDUCATIONAL
PLANNING.
PARIS NO.1, 1972-
FR. TITLE: FINANCEMENT DES SYSTEMS EDUCATIFS:
ETUDES CAS SPECIFIQUES.
LO/N-1.

FINISTERRA. REVISTA PORTUGUESA DE GEOGRAFIA.
UNIVERSIDADE DE LISBOA: CENTRO DE ESTUDOS
GEOGRAFICOS.
LISBON 1, 1966-
2/A.
LD/U-1. 1(2), 1966-   OX/U-1. 4(7), 1969-   ISSN 0430-5027

FIRE ENGINEERS JOURNAL.   XXX
++*FIRE ENG. J.*
INSTITUTION OF FIRE ENGINEERS.
[FRASER PEARCE]
CAMBRIDGE 33(89), MR 1973-
PREV: QUARTERLY, INSTITUTION OF FIRE ENGINEERS
FROM NS.1(1), 1941- 32(88), 1972.
LO/N14.   XS/R10. 33(90), JE 1973-

FIRE PREVENTION GUIDE.
++*FIRE PREV. GUIDE.*
(GREAT BRITAIN) HOME OFFICE: SCOTTISH HOME &
HEALTH DEPARTMENT.
LONDON NO.1, 1972-
CA/U-1.

FIZIKA I FIZIKO-KHIMIJA ZHIDKOSTEJ.
++*FIZ. & FIZ.-KHIM. ZHIDK.*
MOSKOVSKIJ GOSUDARSTVENNYJ UNIVERSITET.
MOSCOW 1, 1972-
LO/N13.

FIZIKA KONDENSIROVANNOGO SOSTOJANIJA.
++*FIZ. KONDENS. SOSTOJANIJA.*
AKADEMIJA NAUK UKRAJINS'KOJI RSR: FIZYKO-
TEKHNICHNYJ INSTYTUT.
KHAR'KOV 1, 1968-
LO/N13.

FIZIKA TVERDOGO TELA.
++*FIZ. TVERD. TELA.*
KHAR'KOVSKIJ GOSUDARSTVENNYJ UNIVERSITET.
KHAR'KOV 1, 1970-
LO/N13.

**FLAMBEAU. REVUE BELGE DES QUESTIONS POLITIQUES
ET LITTERAIRES.**   XXX
[EMILE DE BECO]
BRUSSELS 1, AP 1918- 55(2), 1972.//
2/M.
*CA/U-1.** LO/N-1. NO.8, 1919-*
ISSN 0015-3427

FLAME RETARDANCY OF POLYMERIC MATERIALS.
++*FLAME RETARD. POLYM. MATER.*
[DEKKER]
NEW YORK 1, 1973-
LO/N14.

**FLORA, RASTITEL'NOST' I RASTITEL'NYE RESURSY
ARMYANSKOJ SSR.**
++*FLORA RASTIT. & RASTIT. RESUR. ARM. SSR.*
AKADEMIJA NAUK ARMJANSKOJ SSR.
EREVAN 5, 1970-
SPONS. BODY ALSO: VSESOJUZNOE BOTANICHESKOE
OBSHCHESTVO (ARMJANSKOE OTDELENIE). NO DATA
AVAILABLE REGARDING VOLS. 1-4.
LO/N13. 5, 1970-

FLUID FLOW MEASUREMENT ABSTRACTS.
++*FLUID FLOW MEAS. ABSTR.*
BRITISH HYDROMECHANICS RESEARCH ASSOCIATION.
CRANFIELD 1(1), JA/F 1974-
6/A.
CA/U-1. ED/N-1. GL/U-2. LO/N14. SO/U-1.

FLUID INCLUSION RESEARCH.   000
SEE: PROCEEDINGS, COMMISSION ON ORE-FORMING
FLUIDS IN INCLUSIONS.

FOLIA HISTORIAE ARTIUM.
++*FOLIA HIST. ARTIUM.*
POLSKA AKADEMIA NAUK: KOMISJA TEORII I HISTORII
SZTUKI.
CRACOW 1, 1964-
POL. & FR.
OX/U-1. 3, 1966-

FOLIA MEDICA BIALOSTOCENSIA.
++*FOLIA MED. BIALOSTOC.*
BIALOSTOCKIE TOWARZYSTWO NAUKOWE: WYDZIAL NAUK
MEDYCZNYCH.
BIALYSTOK 1, 1972-
ENGL. SUMM.
OX/U-8.

FOLIA VETERINARIA LATINA.
++*FOLIA VET. LAT.*
MILAN 1(1), JA/MR 1971-
ENGL. & ONE OF THE LATIN LANGUAGES, WITH ENGL.
FR., GER., ITAL. & SPAN. SUMM.
LO/M18.

**FOLK OG KULTUR. ARBOG FOR DANSK ETNOLOGI OG
FOLKEMINDEVIDENSKAB.**   XXX
++*FOLK & KULT.*
FORENINGEN DANMARKS FOLKEMINDER.
[AKADEMISK FORLAG]
COPENHAGEN 1972-
ENGL. SUMM. PREV: FOLKEMINDER.
CA/U-1. LO/S30.

FOLKEMINDER.   XXX
SUBS (1972): FOLK OG KULTUR.

FOLKLORE ANNUAL.
++*FOLKLORE ANNU.*
UNIVERSITY FOLKLORE ASSOCIATION.
[UNIVERSITY OF TEXAS P.]
AUSTIN NO.1, 1969-
SPONS. BODY ALSO: CENTER FOR INTERCULTURAL
STUDIES IN FOLKLORE & ORAL HISTORY, UNIVERSITY
OF TEXAS.
SH/U-1. NO.3, 1971- ISSN 0071-6782

FOLKLORE FORUM.
INDIANA UNIVERSITY: FOLKLORE INSTITUTE.
BLOOMINGTON, INDIANA 1, 1968-
INCLUDES TWO BIBLIOGRAPHIC & SPECIAL SERIES.
SH/U-1. 7, 1974- ISSN 0015-5926

**FONTI E DOCUMENTI, CENTRO STUDI PER LA STORIA
DEL MODERNISMO, UNIVERSITA DI URBINA.**
++*FONTI & DOC. CENT. STUDI STOR. MOD. UNIV.
URBINO.*
URBINO 1, 1972-
OX/U-1.

FOOD PRESERVATION QUARTERLY.   XXX
SUBS (1971): CSIRO FOOD RESEARCH QUARTERLY.

FOREIGN NEWSPAPER REPORT.
++*FOREIGN NEWSPAP. REP.*
LIBRARY OF CONGRESS (US): REFERENCE DEPARTMENT.
WASHINGTON, D.C. NO.1, 1973-
3/A.
LO/N12. LO/U14. OX/U-1. ISSN 0090-225X

FORESTRY RESEARCH NOTE (CAMAS, WASH.).
++*FOR. RES. NOTE (CAMAS, WASH.).*
CROWN ZELLERBACH.
CAMAS, WASH. 1, 1972-
OX/U-3.

**FORESTRY RESEARCH REPORT, DEPARTMENT OF FOR-
ESTRY, AGRICULTURAL EXPERIMENT STATION
(ILLINOIS).**
++*FOR. RES. REP. DEP. FOR. AGRIC. EXP. STN.
(ILL.).*
URBANA NO.70-1, 1970-
LO/N13.

FORPRIDE DIGEST.
++*FORPRIDE DIG.*
FOREST PRODUCT RESEARCH & INDUSTRIES DEVELOP-
MENT COMMISSION (PHILIPPINES).
LAGUNA, PHILIPPINES 1(1), JA/MR 1972-
Q.
LO/R-6.

FORTSCHRITTE IM ACKER- UND PFLANZENBAU.
++*FORTSCHR. ACKER- & PFLANZENBAU.*
[P. PAREY]
BERLIN &C. 1, 1973-
ENGL. TITLE: ADVANCES IN AGRONOMY & CROP SCI-
ENCE. ISSUED AS SUPPL. TO: ZEITSCHRIFT FUR
ACKER- UND PFLANZENBAU.
AB/U-2. LO/N14.

FORUM (DON MILLS, ONT.).   XXX
LIFE UNDERWRITERS ASSOCIATION OF CANADA.
DON MILLS, ONT. 1, MY 1971-
10/A. ENGL. & FR. PREV: LIFE UNDERWRITERS
NEWS FROM 1, 1914- 57, 1971.
LO/S24.

FORUM MONTHLY BRIEFING.
++*FORUM MON. BRIEF.*
[FORUM WORLD FEATURES]
LONDON 1972-
S/T: THE FACTS & ISSUES BEHIND THE NEWS.
CA/U-1. OX/U-1. ED/N-1. 1974- ISSN 0305-3377

**FOSSIL FAUNA & FLORA OF THE FAR EAST
(VLADIVOSTOK).**   000
SEE: ISKOPAEMAJA FAUNA I FLORA DAL'NEGO
VOSTOKA.

FOUNDRY YEAR BOOK.
[FOUNDRY TRADE JOURNAL]
LONDON 1971/1972[1972]-
LO/N14. SW/U-1. 1974.

FRAMEWORK.
SCHOOLS COUNCIL (GB): CAREERS EDUCATION & GUID-
ANCE PROJECT.
CAMBRIDGE NO.1, 1972-
ED/N-1.

**FRANCIA. FORSCHUNGEN ZUR WESTEUROPAISCHEN
GESCHICHTE.**
DEUTSCHES HISTORISCHES INSTITUT IN PARIS.
[FINK]
MUNCHEN 1, 1973-
CA/U-1. EX/U-1. LD/U-1.

FRANCOPHONIE EDITION.
++*FRANCOPH. ED.*
PARIS NO.1, 1972-
Q. S/T: REVUE BIBLIOGRAPHIQUE DE L'EDITION DE
LANGUE FRANCAISE DANS LE MONDE.
CA/U-1. SF/U-1.

FRENCH TECHNIQUES: BUILDING, CIVIL ENGINEERING
& TOWN-PLANNING.
+ + FR. TECH., BUILD. CIV. ENG. & TOWN-PLANN.
 PARIS 1972 (1)-
 ED/N-1.   LO/N14.

FRENCH TECHNIQUES: CHEMICALS, GAS & PETROLEUM.
+ + FR. TECH., CHEM. GAS & PET.
 PARIS 1972 (1)-
 ED/N-1.   LO/N14.

FRENCH TECHNIQUES: THE ELECTRICAL ENGINEERING
& ELECTRONICS INDUSTRIES.
+ + FR. TECH., ELECTR. ENG. & ELECTRON. IND.
 PARIS 1971 (1)-
 ED/N-1.

FRENCH TECHNIQUES: THE MECHANICAL, HYDRAULIC
& CONSULTANT ENGINEERING INDUSTRIES.
+ + FR. TECH., MECH. HYDRAUL. & CONSULT. ENG. IND.
 PARIS 1971 (1)-
 ED/N-1.   LO/N14.

FRENCH TECHNIQUES: THE METAL INDUSTRIES.
+ + FR. TECH., MET. IND.
 PARIS 1972 (1)-
 ED/N-1.   LO/N14.

FRENCH TECHNIQUES: MISCELLANEOUS INDUSTRIES,
CONSUMER GOODS.
+ + FR. TECH., MISC. IND. CONS. GOODS.
 PARIS 1971 (1)-
 ED/N-1.   LO/N-6.   LO/N14. ‡W. 1971 (3)Ä

FRENCH TECHNIQUES: NUCLEAR INDUSTRIES.
+ + FR. TECH., NUCL. IND.
 PARIS 1971 (1)-
 ED/N-1.

FRENCH TECHNIQUES: TRANSPORTATION.
+ + FR. TECH., TRANSP.
 PARIS 1972 (1)-
 ED/N-1.

GAELTACHT.
 LETTERKENNY 1(1), F 1973-
 2W.
 ED/N-1.

GALLIA MONASTICA.
 PARIS 1, 1974-
 OX/U-1.

GARCIA DE ORTA: SERIE DE BOTANICA.   XXX
+ + GARCIA ORTA, BOT.
 JUNTA DE INVESTIGACOES DO ULTRAMAR (PORTUGAL).
 LISBON 1, 1973-
 PREV: TRABALHOS DO CENTRO DE BOTANICA DA JUNTA
 DE INVESTIGACOES DO ULTRAMAR (PORTUGAL) FROM
 NO.1, 1961- 33, 1970.
 LD/U-1.   LO/N-2.

GARCIA DE ORTA: SERIE DE FARMACOGNOSIA.
+ + GARCIA ORTA, FARMACOGN.
 JUNTA DE INVESTIGACOES DO ULTRAMAR (PORTUGAL).
 LISBON 1, 1972-
 LD/U-1.   LO/N-2.

GARCIA DE ORTA: SERIE DE GEOGRAFIA.
+ + GARCIA ORTA, GEOGR.
 JUNTA DE INVESTIGACOES DO ULTRAMAR (PORTUGAL).
 LISBON 1, 1973-
 LD/U-1.   LO/N-2.   LO/S13.

GARCIA DE ORTA: SERIE DE GEOLOGIA.
+ + GARCIA ORTA, GEOL.
 JUNTA DE INVESTIGACOES DO ULTRAMAR (PORTUGAL).
 LISBON 1, 1973-
 LD/U-1.

GARCIA DE ORTA: SERIE DE ZOOLOGIA.
+ + GARCIA ORTA, ZOOL.
 JUNTA DE INVESTIGACOES DO ULTRAMAR (PORTUGAL).
 LISBON 1, 1972-
 LO/N-2.   LD/U-1. ‡W. 1(2), 1972Ä

GARDENER.
 [SCOTTISH FARMER PUBL. LTD.]
 GLASGOW NO.1, F 1973-
 OX/U-8.

GARP NEWSLETTER.
+ + GARP NEWSL.
 INTERNATIONAL COUNCIL OF SCIENTIFIC UNIONS.
 GENEVA NO.1, F 1972-
 SPONS. BODY ALSO: WORLD METEOROLOGICAL ORGAN-
 IZATION.
 XS/R10.

GAS (HOUSTON, TEX.).   XXX
 SUBS (1974): ENERGY PIPELINES & SYSTEMS.

GAS ENGINEERING & MANAGEMENT.   XXX
+ + GAS ENG. & MANAGE.
 INSTITUTION OF GAS ENGINEERS.
 LONDON 14, 1974-
 PREV: JOURNAL, INSTITUTION OF GAS ENGINEERS
 FROM 1, 1961- 13(12), D 1973.
 ED/N-1.   GL/U-1.   LD/U-1.   LO/N14.

GATE REPORT.
+ + GATE REP.
 INTERNATIONAL COUNCIL OF SCIENTIFIC UNIONS.
 GENEVA NO.1, 1972-
 SPONS. BODY ALSO: WORLD METEOROLOGICAL ORGAN-
 IZATION.
 XS/N-1.   NO.1, 1972.

GAZZETTINO LIBRARIO.
+ + GAZZ. LIBR.
 ASSOCIAZIONE LIBRAI ANTIQUARI D'ITALIA.
 FLORENCE NO.1/2, 1972-
 ED/N-1.

GENERAL TECHNICAL REPORT, NORTH CENTRAL FOR-
EST EXPERIMENT STATION (US).
+ + GEN. TECH. REP. NORTH CENT. FOR. EXP. STN.(US)
 ST. PAUL, MINN. NC-1, 1972-
 STATION PART OF U.S. FOREST SERVICE.
 OX/U-3.

GENERAL TECHNICAL REPORT, PACIFIC SOUTHWEST
FOREST & RANGE EXPERIMENT STATION (US).
+ + GEN. TECH. REP. PAC. SOUTHWEST FOR. & RANGE
 EXP. STN. (US).
 BERKELEY, CALIF. PSW-1, 1972-
 STATION PART OF U.S. FOREST SERVICE.
 OX/U-3.

GENERAL TECHNICAL REPORT, SOUTHEASTERN FOREST
EXPERIMENT STATION (US).
+ + GEN. TECH. REP. SOUTHEAST. FOR. EXP. STN. (US)
 ASHEVILLE, N.C. SE-1, 1972-
 STATION PART OF U.S. FOREST SERVICE.
 OX/U-3.

GENERAL TECHNICAL REPORT, SOUTHERN FOREST EXP-
ERIMENT STATION (US).
+ + GEN. TECH. REP. SOUTH. FOR. EXP. STN. (US).
 NEW ORLEANS SO-1, 1973-
 STATION PART OF U.S. FOREST SERVICE.
 OX/U-3.

GEO ABSTRACTS: B: CLIMATOLOGY & HYDROLOGY.   XXX
+ + GEO ABSTR., B. (1974).
 NORWICH 1974-
 PREV: GEO ABSTRACTS: B: BIOGEOGRAPHY &
 CLIMATOLOGY FROM 1972- 1973. BIOGRAPHY SECT-
 ION CONTINUED AS ECOLOGICAL ABSTRACTS. EDITED
 AT THE UNIVERSITY OF EAST ANGLIA.
 AD/U-2.   GL/U-2.   LO/N13.   LO/U12.   RE/U-1.

GEO ABSTRACTS: D: SOCIAL & HISTORICAL   XXX
GEOGRAPHY.
+ + GEO ABSTR., D. (1974).
 NORWICH 1974-
 PREV: GEO ABSTRACTS: D: SOCIAL GEOGRAPHY &
 CARTOGRAPHY FROM 1972- 1973. EDITED AT THE
 UNIVERSITY OF EAST ANGLIA.
 AD/U-1.   LO/U12.   ISSN 0305-1927

GEO ABSTRACTS: G: REMOTE SENSING & CARTOGRAPHY.
+ + GEO ABSTR., G. (1974).
 NORWICH 1974-
 EDITED AT THE UNIVERSITY OF EAST ANGLIA.
 AD/U-1.   EX/U-1.   GL/U-2.   HL/U-1.   LO/R-5.   LO/U12.
 MA/U-1.   RE/U-1.   ISSN 0305-1951

GEOFIZICHESKIE ISSLEDOVANIJA.
+ + GEOFIZ. ISSLED.
 MOSKOVSKIJ GOSUDARSTVENNYJ UNIVERSITET: KAFEDRA
 GEOFIZICHESKIKH METODOV ISSLEDOVANIJA
 ZEMNOJKORY.
 MOSCOW 1, 1964-
 KAFEDRA SUBORD. TO: GEOLOGICHESKIJ FAKUL'TET.
 LO/N13.   SH/U-3.

GEOLOGIJA GAZOVYKH MESTOROZHDENIJ.
+ + GEOL. GAZOV. MESTOROZHD.
SREDNEAZIATSKIJ NAUCHNO-ISSLEDOVATEL'SKIJ
INSTITUT PRIRODNOGO GAZA.
  LENINGRAD 1, 1970-
  LO/N13.

GEOLOGY.
GEOLOGICAL SOCIETY OF AMERICA.
  BOULDER, COLO. 1, 1973-
  BH/U-3.   BL/U-1.   BR/U-1.   CA/U14.   GL/U-2.   LO/N-2.
  LO/N13.   LO/U-2.   OX/U-8.   RE/U-1.

GEOMECHANICS ABSTRACTS.   XXX
+ + GEOMECH. ABSTR.
[PERGAMON]
  OXFORD & NEW YORK 4, MR 1973-
  2/M. PREV: ROCK MECHANICS ABSTRACTS FROM 1,
  1970- 3, 1972. CONSTITUTES PART 2 OF INTER-
  NATIONAL JOURNAL OF ROCK MECHANICS & MINING
  SCIENCES.
  BL/U-1.   ED/N-1.   LO/N-4.   SH/U-1.

GEOPHYSICAL ABSTRACTS. ABSTRACTS OF CURRENT
LITERATURE PERTAINING TO THE PHYSICS OF THE
SOLID EARTH & TO GEOPHYSICAL EXPLORATION.   XXX
+ + GEOPHYS. ABSTR.
(UNITED STATES) GEOLOGICAL SURVEY.
  WASHINGTON, D.C. NO.1, 1929- 299, 1971.//
  BR/U-1.   LO/U-6.   BN/U-2. NO.204, 1964-
  LO/U-2. NO.192, 1963-   OX/U-8. NO.192, 1963-

GEOS. A QUARTERLY CONCERNED WITH THE EARTH'S
RESOURCES.
(CANADA) DEPARTMENT OF ENERGY, MINES &
RESOURCES.
  OTTAWA SUMMER 1972-
  LO/N-2.

GEOSCIENCE CANADA.   XXX
+ + GEOSCI. CAN.
GEOLOGICAL ASSOCIATION OF CANADA.
  TORONTO 1, 1974-
  PREV: PROCEEDINGS, GEOLOGICAL ASSOCIATION OF
  CANADA FROM 1, 1947/48- 25, 1973.
  GL/U-1.   LD/U-1.   LO/N13.

GEOTHERMAL ENERGY.
+ + GEOTHERM. ENERGY.
  WEST COVINA, CALIF. 1, 1973-
  ALSO ENTITLED: GEOTHERMAL ENERGY MAGAZINE.
  LO/N13.   LO/N14.

GIAI PHONG.
[GIAI PHONG PICTORIAL]
  HANOI NO.1, 1973-
  ENGL. ED.
  LO/U14.

GINGER.
[GINGERBREAD]
  LONDON NO.1, D 1973-
  MON. S/T: MAGAZINE FOR ONE PARENT FAMILIES.
  CA/U-1.   ED/N-1.   OX/U-1.

GLEDISTA. CASOPIS ZA DRUSTVENU KRITIKU I
TEORIJU.
BEOGRADSKI UNIVERZITET.
  BELGRADE 1, 1960-
  ENGL. SUMM.
  BD/U-1. 14, 1973-   GL/U-1. 7, 1966-   OX/U-1. 11, 1970-

GLEDITSCHIA. BEITRAGE ZUR BOTANISCHEN TAXONOMIE
UND DEREN GRENZGEBIETE.
[WALTER VENT]
  BERLIN 1, 1973-
  LO/N-2.

GLYNNS. JOURNAL OF THE GLENS OF ANTRIM HIST-
ORICAL SOCIETY.
  BELFAST 1, 1973-
  BL/U-1.   CA/U-1.   ED/N-1.   OX/U-1.

GOVERNMENT ECONOMIC SERVICE OCCASIONAL PAPERS.
+ + GOV. ECON. SERV. OCCAS. PAP.
(GREAT BRITAIN) TREASURY.
[H.M.S.O.]
  LONDON NO.1, 1971-
  GL/U-1.

GOVERNMENT PUBLICATIONS REVIEW.
+ + GOV. PUBL. REV.
[MICROFORMS INT. MARKETING CORP.]
  ELMSFORD, N.Y. 1, 1973-
  Q.
  ED/N-1.   ISSN 0093-061X

GOVERNMENT REFERENCE BOOKS. A BIENNIAL GUIDE
TO U.S. GOVERNMENT PUBLICATIONS.
+ + GOV. REF. BOOKS.
[LIBRARIES UNLIMITED]
  LITTLETON, COLO. 1968/69(1970)-
  LO/N14.   ISSN 0072-5188

GRADUATE TEXTS IN MATHEMATICS.
+ + GRAD. TEXTS MATH.
[SPRINGER-VERLAG]
  BERLIN &C. 1, 1971-
  CA/U-1.   ISSN 0072-5285

GRAECOLATINA ET ORIENTALIA.
+ + GRAECOLAT. & ORIENT.
UNIVERZITA KOMENSKEHO (BRATISLAVA): FILOZOFICKA
FACULTA.
  BRATISLAVA 1, 1969-
  FR., GER., ENGL. OR LAT. S/T: SBORNIK FILOZO-
  FICKEJ FAKULTY UNIVERZITY KOMENSKEHO.
  GL/U-1.   LO/U14.   CA/U-1. 1971-

GRASS CURTAIN.
SOUTHERN SUDAN ASSOCIATION.
  LONDON 1, MY 1970-
  Q.
  LO/U14. 2(1), 1971.   ISSN 0017-3509

GRAVITATSIJA I TEORIJA OTNOSITEL'NOSTI.
+ + GRAVITATS. & TEOR. OTNOSITEL'NOSTI.
KAZANSKIJ GOSUDARSTVENNYJ UNIVERSITET.
  KAZAN 3, 1967-
  NO DATA AVAILABLE REGARDING VOLS. 1 & 2.
  LO/N13. 3, 1967-

GRAZER BEITRAGE. ZEITSCHRIFT FUR DIE KLASSISCHE
ALTERTUMSWISSENSCHAFT.
+ + GRAZER BEITR.
[RODOPI]
  AMSTERDAM 1, 1973-
  BL/U-1.   CA/U-1.   LD/U-1.   OX/U-1.   SO/U-1.

GREAT WORKS.
[GREAT WORKS P.]
  STOKE-ON-TRENT NO.1, 1973-
  LO/U-2.

GREEN CANDLE.   XXX
  OXFORD NO.1, 1973.//
  ED/N-1.   OX/U-1.

GRIP. NEW MAGAZINE OF THE GLASSFIBRE WORLD.
[CENTIME LTD.]
  KINGSTON UPON THAMES NO.1, F 1974-
  MON.
  OX/U-1.   ED/N-1. NO.7, 1974-   ISSN 0305-4195

GTC NEWS.
GENERAL TEACHING COUNCIL FOR SCOTLAND.
  EDINBURGH NO.1, MY 1973-
  CA/U-1.   ED/N-1.   OX/U-1.

GUIDES TO COMMON MARKET LAW.
+ + GUIDES COMMON MARK. LAW.
BRITISH INSTITUTE OF INTERNATIONAL & COMPAR-
ATIVE LAW.
  LONDON NO.1, 1972-
  MONOGR.
  CA/U-1.   GL/U-1.

GUIDES TO WICKEN FEN.
NATIONAL TRUST: WICKEN FEN LOCAL COMMITTEE.
  IPSWICH NO.1, 1966-
  LO/N-2.   LO/N13.

GUILDHALL MISCELLANY.   XXX
  SUBS (1973): GUILDHALL STUDIES IN LONDON
  HISTORY.

GUILDHALL STUDIES IN LONDON HISTORY.   XXX
+ + GUILDHALL STUD. LOND. HIST.
GUILDHALL LIBRARY.
  LONDON 1(1), OC 1973-
  2/A. PREV: GUILDHALL MISCELLANY FROM 1(1),
  JA 1952- 4(4), AP 1973.
  AD/U-1.   CA/U-1.   ED/N-1.   GL/U-1.   LD/U-1.   LO/M13.
  MA/U-1.   OX/U-1.   SA/U-1.   ISSN 0306-3194

GYMNASION. INTERNATIONAL JOURNAL OF PHYSICAL
EDUCATION.
INTERNATIONAL COUNCIL OF HEALTH, PHYSICAL
EDUCATION & RECREATION.
[VERLAG KARL HOFMANN]
  SCHONDORF 1, 1963-
  Q.
  BN/U-1. 10, 1973-   ISSN 0533-7038

HADITH.
HISTORICAL ASSOCIATION OF KENYA.
[EAST AFRICAN PUBL. HOUSE]
NAIROBI 1, 1968-
ANNU. NO.1- ISSUED AS PROCEEDINGS OF THE
ANNUAL CONFERENCE OF THE HISTORICAL ASSOCIAT-
ION OF KENYA.
OX/U-9.

HALTWHISTLE QUARTERLY.
++*HALTWHISTLE Q.*
HALTWHISTLE NO.1, 1973-
CA/U-1. ED/N-1. LO/N-1. OX/U-1. OX/U16.

HAMMER OR ANVIL.   XXX
ACTION CENTRE FOR MARXIST-LENINIST UNITY.   XXX
LONDON 1(1), N 1965- 3(1), JL/AG 1967.
SUBS: RED FRONT.
LO/U-3. LO/N-1. 2(1), 1966.

**HAND-IN-HAND. INTERNATIONAL JOURNAL OF THE
COMMERCIAL UNION ASSURANCE COMPANY.**
LONDON 1, 1973-
ED/N-1.

HARANGUE. A POLITICAL & SOCIAL REVIEW.
BELFAST NO.1, F/MR 1974-
PUBL. AT QUEEN'S UNIVERSITY BELFAST.
LO/U-3. ISSN 0305-8484

HARD CHEESE. A JOURNAL OF EDUCATION.
LONDON [NO.1, 1973]
CA/U-1. ED/N-1. OX/U-1. ISSN 0305-9839

HARPSICHORD MAGAZINE.   XXX
++*HARPSICHORD MAG.*
[EDGAR HUNT]
AMERSHAM, BUCKS. 1(1), OC 1973 ...
SUBS: ENGLISH HARPSICHORD MAGAZINE, & EARLY
KEYBOARD INSTRUMENT REVIEW.
CA/U-1. ED/N-1. OX/U-1. ISSN 0301-7206

**HARVARD CIVIL RIGHTS - CIVIL LIBERTIES LAW
REVIEW.**
++*HARV. CIV. RIGHTS - CIV. LIBERTIES LAW REV.*
HARVARD UNIVERSITY: LAW SCHOOL.
CAMBRIDGE, MASS. 1(1), 1966-
PUBL. BY THE SCHOOL'S CIVIL RIGHTS COMMITTEE
& THE CIVIL LIBERTIES RESEARCH SERVICE IN
CONJ. WITH THE LAW STUDENTS CIVIL RIGHTS
RESEARCH COUNCIL.
LO/U-3. CR/U-1. 6, 1971- SO/U-1. 9, 1974-

HARVARD SEMITIC MONOGRAPHS.
++*HARV. SEMITIC MONOGR.*
[HARVARD UNIV. P.]
CAMBRIDGE, MASS. 1, 1968-
CA/U-1. ISSN 0073-0637

HAWAII ECONOMIC REVIEW.
++*HAWAII ECON. REV.*
(HAWAII) DEPARTMENT OF PLANNING & ECONOMICS
DEVELOPMENT.
HONOLULU [1], 1963-
LO/U-3. 8(2), S/OC 1970- ‡W. 8(4), JA/F 1971Å

HEALTH EDUCATION INDEX.
++*HEALTH EDUC. INDEX.*
HEALTH VISITORS' ASSOCIATION.
LONDON 1970-
ANNU.
OX/U-8.

HEALTH & SOCIAL SERVICE JOURNAL.   XXX
++*HEALTH & SOC. SERV. J.*
[LAW & LOCAL GOVERNMENT PUBL. LTD.]
LONDON 83, JA 1973-
PREV: BRITISH HOSPITAL JOURNAL & SOCIAL
SERVICE REVIEW FROM 75(3907), MR 1965-
82, 1972. INCORP: COMMUNITY MEDICINE.
LO/N-6. LO/N35. LO/U-3. SO/U-1.
ISSN 0300-8347

HEALTH TEAM.
NATIONAL ASSOCIATION OF HEALTH STUDENTS (GB).
LONDON 1(1), OC/N 1973-
Q.
ED/N-1. OX/U-8.

HEALTH & WELFARE LIBRARIES QUARTERLY.   XXX
++*HEALTH & WELFARE LIBR. Q.*
LIBRARY ASSOCIATION: HOSPITAL LIBRARIES &
HANDICAPPED READERS GROUP.
LONDON 1(1), MR 1974-
PREV: BOOK TROLLEY FROM 1(1), MR 1965- 3(12),
D 1973.
ED/N-1. GL/U-2. OX/U-1. SO/U-1.

HEAT TREATMENT OF METALS.
++*HEAT TREAT. MET.*
UNIVERSITY OF ASTON IN BIRMINGHAM: DEPARTMENT
OF METALLURGY.
BIRMINGHAM 1(1), MR 1974-
Q. SPONS. BODY ALSO: WOLFSON HEAT TREATMENT
CENTRE.
CA/U-1. LO/N14. OX/U-8. CA/U-4. 1(2), 1974-
ISSN 0305-4829

HEATING & AIR CONDITIONING JOURNAL.   XXX
++*HEAT. & AIR COND. J.*
[TROUP PUBL. LTD.]
LONDON 43(509), AP 1974-
MON. PREV: STEAM & HEATING ENGINEER FROM 33,
OC 1963- 43(508), MR 1974. S/T: ENVIRONMENTAL
SERVICES FOR INDUSTRIAL, COMMERCIAL & PUBLIC
BUILDINGS.
ED/N-1. LO/U-2. OX/U-8. XS/T-4. XS/T10.

HEBREW UNIVERSITY STUDIES IN LITERATURE.
++*HEB. UNIV. STUD. LIT.*
JERUSALEM 1, 1973-
OX/U-1.

**HELIX. THE MAGAZINE FOR ABERDEEN HEALTH
STUDENTS.**
ABERDEEN 1, 1974-
AD/U-1. ED/N-1. OX/U-1.

**HEPHAISTOS. A QUARTERLY DEVOTED TO COMPUTER
RESEARCH IN THE HUMANITIES.**
PHILADELPHIA 1, 1970-
MA/U-1. ISSN 0018-0440

HERALD OF GRACE.
APOSTOLIC FAITH CHURCH: GENERAL COUNCIL.
BELFAST 1(1), JA 1974-
ED/N-1. OX/U-1.

HERTFORDSHIRE ARCHAEOLOGICAL REVIEW.
++*HERTS. ARCHAEOL. REV.*
HERTFORDSHIRE ARCHAEOLOGICAL COUNCIL.
WELWYN GARDEN CITY SPRING 1970-
LO/U-2. OX/U-2. LO/N-1. AUTUMN 1970-

HI-FI SOUND ANNUAL.
++*HI-FI SOUND ANNU.*
[HAYMARKET PUBL.]
LONDON 1969-
CA/U-1. ISSN 0073-2044

**HIGH-SPEED GROUND TRANSPORTATION & URBAN RAPID
TRANSIT SYSTEMS BIBLIOGRAPHY SERVICE.**
++*HIGH-SPEED GROUND TRANSP. & URBAN RAPID
TRANSIT SYST. BIBLIOGR. SERV.*
[ROBERT TRILLO LTD.]
*BROCKENHURST, HANTS. 1(1), JL/AG 1973-
6/A.*
CA/U-1. ED/N-1. LO/N14. ISSN 0306-0586

HIMALAYAN GEOLOGY.
++*HIMALAYAN GEOL.*
WADIA INSTITUTE OF HIMALAYAN GEOLOGY.
DELHI 1, 1971-
LO/N-2.

HISTOIRE RUSSE.   000
SEE: RUSSIAN HISTORY.

HISTORIA MATHEMATICA.
++*HIST. MATH.*
INTERNATIONAL COMMISSION ON THE HISTORY OF
MATHEMATICS.
TORONTO 1, 1974-
S/T: INTERNATIONAL JOURNAL OF HISTORY OF MATH-
EMATICS.
AD/U-1. BL/U-1. LO/U-2. SW/U-1.

HISTORIA Y VIDA.
++*HIST. & VIDA.*
BARCELONA 1, 1968-
MON.
OX/U-1. ISSN 0018-2354

HISTORICA CARPATICA.
++*HIST. CARPATICA.*
VYCHODOSLOVENSKE MUZEUM.
KOSICE 1, 1969-
ANNU.
CA/U-1. OX/U-1.

**HISTORICAL BIBLIOGRAPHY SERIES, CAMBRIDGE
UNIVERSITY LIBRARY.**
++*HIST. BIBLIOGR. SER. CAMB. UNIV. LIBR.*
CAMBRIDGE 1, 1972-
CA/U-1.

HISTORICAL GEOGRAPHY NEWSLETTER.
++HIST. GEOGR. NEWSL.
SAN FERNANDO VALLEY STATE COLLEGE: DEPARTMENT
OF GEOGRAPHY.
NORTHRIDGE, CALIF. 1, D 1971-
CA/U-5.   SH/U-1. 3, 1973-

HISTORY IN MALAWI BULLETIN.
++HIST. MALAWI BULL.
UNIVERSITY OF MALAWI: HISTORY DEPARTMENT.
LIMBE NO.1, JL 1971-
LO/U-8.

HISTORY IN SCHOOL.
++HIST. SCH.
LEEDS NO.1, 1973-
LO/N14.   SW/U-1.

HISTORY, TECHNOLOGY & ART MONOGRAPH, ROYAL
ONTARIO MUSEUM.
++HIST. TECHNOL. & ART MONOGR. R. ONT. MUS.
TORONTO [NO.1], N 1973-
LO/U-1.   OX/U-1.   ISSN 0316-1269

HORISON. MADJALAH SASTRA.
DJAKARTA NO.1, JL 1966-
INDONES.
LO/U14. 7(11), 1972-   ISSN 0441-2168

HORIZONS U.S.A.   XXX
++HORIZ. U.S.A.
UNITED STATES INFORMATION AGENCY.
WASHINGTON, D.C. [NO.]1, JA 1974-
2M. PREV: INSIGHT U.S.A. FROM NO.1-6, 1973.
CA/U-1.   ED/N-1.

HORSE & RIDER REVIEW.
++HORSE & RIDER REV.
[ALLAN]
LONDON 1973-
CA/U-1.   OX/U-1.

HOSIERY TRADE JOURNAL.   XXX
SUBS (1974): KNITTING INTERNATIONAL.

HOSPITAL CAREER.
++HOSP. CAREER.
[DOMINION P. LTD.]
LONDON 1(1), N/D 1969-
8/A.
OX/U-8.   ED/N-1. 1(2), 1970-

HOVERFOIL NEWS.   XXX
[HORIZON PUBL. LTD.]
MONTACUTE, SOMERSET 4(1), JA 1973-
2W. PREV: AIR CUSHION VEHICLES.
BH/P-1.   ED/N-1.   LO/N35.   SF/U-1.   SO/U-1.   XS/R10.

HOVERSPORT.
[HORIZON PUBL.]
MONTACUTE, SOMERSET 1(1), S/OC 1973-
8/A.
CA/U-1.   OX/U-1.   ISSN 0306-1485

HRC GAZETTE.
++HRC GAZ.
HUNTINGDON RESEARCH CENTRE.
HUNTINGDON 1(1), 1970-
CA/U11.   ED/N-1.   OX/U-8. 2(1), 1971-

HTFS DIGEST. THE INFORMATION BULLETIN OF THE
HEAT TRANSFER & FLUID FLOW SERVICE.
++HTFS DIG.
ATOMIC ENERGY RESEARCH ESTABLISHMENT.
HARWELL [1(1)], JE 1968-
XS/R10.   EX/U-1. 6(1), 1973-   LO/U12. 5(12), 1972-
XS/T-4. 2 YEARS.

HUMAN BEHAVIOR & SOCIAL INSTITUTIONS.
++HUM. BEHAV. & SOC. INST.
NATIONAL BUREAU OF ECONOMIC RESEARCH (US).
[COLUMBIA UNIV. P.]
NEW YORK 1, 1972-
GL/U-1.

HUMAN EXPERIMENTATION ABSTRACTS.
++HUM. EXP. ABSTR.
[WASHINGTON PUBL. HOUSE]
RIPON, YORKS. 1, 1974-
LO/N13.   ISSN 0302-3338

HUMANIDADES.
PONTIFICIA UNIVERSIDAD CATOLICA DEL PERU:
DEPARTAMENTO DE HUMANIDADES.
LIMA NO.1, 1967-
DEPARTAMENTO SUBORD. TO: FACULTAD DE LETRAS.
OX/U-1.

HUMANITIES INDEX.   XXX
++HUMANIT. INDEX.
[H.W. WILSON]
NEW YORK 1(1), JE 1974-
Q. WITH ANNU. CUMMULATION. PREV. PART OF:
SOCIAL SCIENCES & HUMANITIES INDEX FROM
53(1), JE 1965- 61, 1973/74.
BN/U-1.   ED/N-1.   GL/U-1.   GL/U-2.   HL/U-1.   LO/U-3.
NO/U-1.   OX/U-1.   SH/U-1.   ISSN 0095-5981

HUMBERSIDE STATISTICAL BULLETIN.
++HUMBERSIDE STATIST. BULL.
UNIVERSITY OF HULL.
HULL NO.1, MR 1974-
2/A.
CA/U-1.   ED/N-1.   HL/U-1.   LO/U-3.   NO/U-1.   OX/U-1.

HUNGARIAN ECONOMY.
++HUNG. ECON.
[HIRLAPKIADO VALLALAT]
BUDAPEST 1, D 1972-
Q.
OX/U-1.

HUNGARIAN JOURNAL OF INDUSTRIAL CHEMISTRY.
++HUNG. J. IND. CHEM.
VESZPREM 1, 1973-
ENGL., FR., RUSS. OR GER.
LO/N14.   LO/S-3.

HUNGARIAN LIBRARY & INFORMATION SCIENCE
ABSTRACTS.
CENTRE FOR LIBRARY SCIENCE & METHODOLOGY
(BUDAPEST).
BUDAPEST 1, 1972-
2/A. ENGL.
OX/U-1.   ISSN 0046-8304

HYDRO NEWS.
NORTH OF SCOTLAND HYDRO-ELECTRIC BOARD.
EDINBURGH NO.1, JA 1973-
MON.
CA/U-1.   ED/N-1.

HYGIEN OCH MILJO.   XXX
++HYG. MILJO.
STOCKHOLM 63, 1974-
PREV: HYGIENSK REVY FROM 1, 1912- 62, 1973.
LO/N14.

HYGIENSK REVY.   XXX
SUBS (1974): HYGIEN OCH MILJO.

IBCAM. JOURNAL OF THE INSTITUTE OF BRITISH
CARRIAGE & AUTOMOBILE MANUFACTURERS.   XXX
OXFORD 1(1), JA 1974-
MON. PREV: INSTITUTE BULLETIN, INSTITUTE OF
BRITISH CARRIAGE & AUTOMOBILE MANUFACTURERS
FROM 26(302), 1937- 37(706), D 1973.
ED/N-1.   LO/N14.   ISSN 0306-2910

I C DIARY.
IMPERIAL COLLEGE OF SCIENCE & TECHNOLOGY.
LONDON [NO.1], 30/S 1974-
ED/N-1.

1.C.E. ABSTRACTS.
++I.C.E. ABSTR.
INSTITUTION OF CIVIL ENGINEERS.
LONDON 1974 (1)-
10/A. PUBL. WITH THE COOPERATION OF THE AMER-
ICAN SOCIETY OF CIVIL ENGINEERS & CITIS LTD.,
DUBLIN.
BH/U-3.   CA/U-1.   ED/N-1.   LO/N14.   MA/P-1.

ICHCA MONTHLY JOURNAL.   XXX
+++ICHCA MON. J.
INTERNATIONAL CARGO HANDLING COORDINATION
ASSOCIATION.
LONDON JA 1967- S/OC 1973.
PREV: ICHCA QUARTERLY JOURNAL FROM NO.1, 1963-
16, 1966. SUBS: CARGO SYSTEMS.
ED/N-1.

ICSSR RESEARCH ABSTRACTS QUARTERLY.
++ICSSR RES. ABSTR. Q.
INDIAN COUNCIL OF SOCIAL SCIENCE RESEARCH.
[ORIENT LONGMAN]
NEW DELHI 1(1), OC 1971-
LO/U14.

IDS BRIEF.
[INCOMES DATA SERVICES]
LONDON NO.1, N 1972-
EX/U-1.   SF/U-1.

IEEE TRANSACTIONS ON ACOUSTICS, SPEECH & SIG-   XXX
NAL PROCESSING.
+ +IEEE TRANS. ACOUST. SPEECH & SIGNAL PROCESS.
INSTITUTE OF ELECTRICAL & ELECTRONICS ENGINEERS
NEW YORK ASSP-22, 1974-
PREV: IEEE TRANSACTIONS ON AUDIO & ELECTRO-
ACOUSTICS FROM AU-14, 1966- 21, 1973.
HL/U-1.   LD/U-1.   LO/N14.   LO/U-2.

IEEE TRANSACTIONS ON AUDIO & ELECTROACOUSTICS.XX
+ +IEEE TRANS. AUDIO & ELECTROACOUST.
INSTITUTE OF ELECTRICAL & ELECTRONICS ENGINEERS
NEW YORK AU-14, 1966- 21, 1973 ...
PREV: IEEE TRANSACTIONS ON AUDIO FROM AU-11,
1963- 13, 1965. SUBS: IEEE TRANSACTIONS ON
ACOUSTICS, SPEECH & SIGNAL PROCESSING.
CA/U-2.   CB/U-1.   HL/U-1.   LO/N14.
ISSN 0018-9278

IEEE TRANSACTIONS ON CIRCUITS & SYSTEMS.   XXX
+ +IEEE TRANS. CIRCUITS & SYST.
INSTITUTION OF ELECTRICAL & ELECTRONICS ENG-
INEERS: CIRCUITS & SYSTEMS SOCIETY.
NEW YORK CAS-21, 1974-
PREV: IEEE TRANSACTIONS ON CIRCUIT THEORY FROM
CT-10, 1963- 20, 1973.
CA/U-2.   LD/U-1.   LO/U-2.

IFS NEWSLETTER.
+ +IFS NEWSL.
INSTITUTE FOR FISCAL STUDIES.
LONDON NO.1, 1973-
CA/U-1.   ED/N-1.   ISSN 0306-0500

IIC ABSTRACTS.   XXX
SUBS (1966): ART & ARCHAEOLOGICAL TECHNICAL
ABSTRACTS.

ILLUSTRATED WEEKLY OF INDIA ANNUAL.
+ +ILLUS. WKLY INDIA ANNU.
BOMBAY 1972-
LO/N12.

IMMIGRANTS IN AUSTRALIA.
+ +IMMIGR. AUST.
ACADEMY OF THE SOCIAL SCIENCES IN AUSTRALIA.
[AUSTRALIAN NATIONAL UNIV. P.]
CANBERRA 1, 1972-
CA/U-1.   OX/U-9.

IMS MONITOR. QUARTERLY REVIEW OF THE LABOUR
MARKET.
+ +IMS MONIT.
INSTITUTE OF MANPOWER STUDIES.
[CHAPMAN & HALL]
LONDON 1(1), AP 1972-
Q.
LO/U-2.   AD/U-1. 3, 1974-   CA/U-1. 2, 1973-
EX/U-1. 2(1), 1973-   OX/U-8. 2(1), 1973-   SH/P-1. 1974-

INDEX OF BIOCHEMICAL REVIEWS.
+ +INDEX BIOCHEM. REV.
FEDERATION OF EUROPEAN BIOCHEMICAL SOCIETIES.
AMSTERDAM 1, 1971/1972(1973)-
ISSUED AS A SUPPL. TO: FEBS LETTERS.
BL/U-1.   LO/U-2.   SO/U-1.

INDEX ON CENSORSHIP.
WRITERS & SCHOLARS INTERNATIONAL.
LONDON 1(1), 1972-
Q.
LO/U-3.

INDEX TO IEEE PERIODICALS.
+ +INDEX IEEE PERIOD.
INSTITUTION OF ELECTRICAL & ELECTRONICS
ENGINEERS.
NEW YORK 1971(1972)-
HL/U-1.   LO/N14.   NW/U-1.   SW/U-1.   GL/U-1. 1972-

INDEX TO THE LITERATURE OF MAGNETISM.
+ +INDEX LIT. MAGN.
AMERICAN INSTITUTE OF PHYSICS.
NEW YORK 1, 1961-
2/A. VOL.1-2 ARE REPRINTS OF AN INDEX PUBL-
ISHED BY BELL TELEPHONE LABORATORIES FOR INT-
ERNAL USE, & REPRINTED FOR DISTRIBUTION AT THE
1962 CONFERENCE ON MAGNETISM & MAGNETIC
MATERIALS.
LO/N14.*   ISSN 0019-4115

INDEX MEDICUS KOREA.
+ +INDEX MED. KOREA.
RESEARCH INSTITUTE OF MEDICAL SCIENCE
OF KOREA.
SEOUL 1, JL 1973-
LO/N13.

INDEX TO NIGERIANA IN SELECTED PERIODICALS.   XXX
+ +INDEX NIGER. SEL. PERIOD.
NATIONAL LIBRARY OF NIGERIA.
LAGOS 1967-
ANNU. 1967 VOL. ENTITLED INDEX TO SELECTED
NIGERIAN PERIODICALS.
LO/U-3.

INDEX TO SELECTED NIGERIAN PERIODICALS.   000
SEE: INDEX TO NIGERIANA IN SELECTED PERIOD-
ICALS.

INDIAN JOURNAL OF ANIMAL HEALTH.   XXX
+ +INDIAN J. ANIM. HEALTH.
WEST BENGAL VETERINARY ASSOCIATION.
CALCUTTA 4, 1965-
PREV: ANIMAL HEALTH FROM 1, 1960- 3, 1962.
LO/M26.   LO/N13. 5, 1966-   ISSN 0019-5057

INDIAN PRESS.
INDIAN & EASTERN NEWSPAPER SOCIETY.
NEW DELHI 1(1), 1962-
Q.
LD/U-1. 2(2) & (4), AP & OC 1963.

INDIAN PRESS INDEX.
DELHI LIBRARY ASSOCIATION.
DELHI 1(1), AP 1968-
MON. VOL.1(1) PRECEDED BY MR 1968 ISSUE
CALLED PILOT FASCICULE.
LO/N12.   ISSN 0019-6177

INDIAN WRITING TODAY.   XXX
+ +INDIAN WRIT. TODAY.
CENTRE FOR INDIAN WRITERS.
[NIRMALA SADANAND PUBL.]
BOMBAY 1, JL/S 1967- 5, 1972.//
S/T: A QUARTERLY DEVOTED TO SIGNIFICANT WRIT-
ING IN INDIA. ALSO NUMBERED NO.1- 18.
LO/N12.   LD/U-1. 1(2), OC/D 1967; 2(1- 4), 1968.

INDICADORES ECONOMICOS.
+ +INDIC. ECON. (MEX.).
BANCO DE MEXICO: GERENCIA DE INVESTIGACION
ECONOMICA.
MEXICO, D.F. 1(1), D 1972-
MON.
LO/U-3.

INDOLOGICAL STUDIES.   XXX
+ +INDOL. STUD.
UNIVERSITY OF DELHI: DEPARTMENT OF SANSKRIT.
DELHI 2(1), 1973-
PREV: JOURNAL, DEPARTMENT OF SANSKRIT, UNIVER-
SITY OF DELHI FROM 1, 1971/72.
LO/N12.

INDONESIA CIRCLE.
+ +INDONES. CIRCLE.
UNIVERSITY OF LONDON: SCHOOL OF ORIENTAL &
AFRICAN STUDIES.
LONDON NO.1, 1973-
PRODUCED BY THE SCHOOL'S INDONESIA CIRCLE.
LO/U14.   CA/U-1. 2, 1973-   ED/N-1. 2, 1973-

INDUSTRIA ALIMENTICIA.
+ +IND. ALIMENT.
(CUBA) MINISTERIO DE LA INDUSTRIA ALIMENTICIA.
HAVANA 1(1), JA 1968-
Q. SPAN. WITH ENGL., FR. & SPAN. SUMM.
LO/R-6.   ISSN 0019-7459

INDUSTRIAL AIR POWER.
+ +IND. AIR POWER.
[TRADE & TECHNICAL P.]
MORDEN, SURREY 1, JE 1972-
LO/N14.   CA/U-1. 1(4), 1973-   ED/N-1. 1(6), 1973-
OX/U-1. 1(2-6), 1972/73.

INDUSTRIAL TUTOR.
+ +IND. TUTOR.
SOCIETY OF INDUSTRIAL TUTORS.
[LONDON] 1, 1969-
SO/U-1.

INDUSTRIAL WASTES INFORMATION BULLETIN.
+ +IND. WASTES INF. BULL.
ATOMIC ENERGY RESEARCH ESTABLISHMENT.
HARWELL 1(1), OC 1973-
ED/N-1.   EX/U-1.   LO/N14.   MA/U-1.   OX/U-8.   XS/R10.
ISSN 0306-0780

INDUSTRY TREND SERIES, BUSINESS & DEFENSE
SERVICES ADMINISTRATION (US).   000
SEE: BDSA INDUSTRY TREND SERIES.

INFECTION, INFLAMMATION & IMMUNITY.
SEE: KANSEN ENSHO MENEKI.   000

INFECTIOUS DISEASE REVIEWS.
++INFECT. DIS. REV.
[FUTURA PUBL. CO.]
MOUNT KISCO, N.Y. 1, 1972-
VOLS. 1- ARE PROCEEDINGS OF THE 7TH/8TH IN-
FECTIOUS DISEASE SYMPOSIUM.
BL/U-1.   OX/U-8.

INFOCAST.
UNITED KINGDOM CHEMICAL INFORMATION SERVICE.
NOTTINGHAM NO.1, AG 1973-
CA/U-1.   ED/N-1.   XS/U-1.

INFORMATION BULLETIN, INTERNATIONAL MAIZE &
WHEAT IMPROVEMENT CENTER.
++INF. BULL. INT. MAIZE & WHEAT IMPROV. CENT.
MEXICO, D.F. NO.1, JA 1972-
LD/U-1.

INFORMATION BULLETIN, SOCIETY FOR LATIN AMER-
ICAN STUDIES.   XXX
++INF. BULL. SOC. LAT. AM. STUD.
LONDON NO.1, 1964- 7, 1967 ...
SUBS: BULLETIN OF THE SOCIETY FOR LATIN AMER-
ICAN STUDIES.
ED/N-1.   LO/U23.   GL/U-1. NO.6, 1966-

INFORMATION BULLETIN, WESTERN ASSOCIATION OF
MAP LIBRARIES.   XXX
++INF. BULL. WEST. ASSOC. MAP LIBR.
SACRAMENTO, CALIF. NO.1, 1970-
2M. PREV: NEWSLETTER, WESTERN ASSOCIATION OF
MAP LIBRARIES FROM NO.1-2, 1969.
AD/U-1.   CA/U-1.   LO/N-2.   ISSN 0049-7282

INFORMATION DIGEST, EUROPEAN PARLIAMENT.
++INF. DIG. EUR. PARLIAMENT.
EUROPEAN PARLIAMENT: INFORMATION OFFICES.
LUXEMBOURG 1, JA 1971-
LO/U-3.   OX/U-1.   ISSN 0014-3049

INFORMATION NORTH.   XXX
++INF. NORTH.
ARCTIC INSTITUTE OF NORTH AMERICA.
MONTREAL SPRING 1973-
PREV: NEWSLETTER, ARCTIC INSTITUTE OF NORTH
AMERICA FROM NO.1, 1968- 4, 1972.
BL/U-1.   LO/N13.

INFORMATION PAPER, CHEMICAL & ALLIED PRODUCTS
INDUSTRY TRAINING BOARD (GB).
++INF. PAP. CHEM. & ALLIED PROD. IND. TRAIN.
BOARD (GB).
STAINES NO.1, JA 1969-
LO/N-1.

INFORMATION REPORT, FOREST FIRE RESEARCH INST-
ITUTE (CANADA).
++INF. REP. FOR. FIRE RES. INST. (CAN.).
OTTAWA FF-X-1, MR 1966-
OX/U-3.   ISSN 0068-757X

INFORMATION REPORT, FOREST MANAGEMENT INST-
ITUTE (CANADA).   XXX
++INF. REP. FOR. MANAGE. INST. (CAN.).
OTTAWA FMR-X-1, 1966-
EARLY NUMBERS ISSUED BY THE BODY UNDER ITS
FORMER NAME: FOREST MANAGEMENT & RESEARCH
SERVICES INSTITUTE.
OX/U-3.   ISSN 0532-1573

INFORMATION REPORT, FOREST PRODUCTS LABORAT-
ORY (VANCOUVER).
++INF. REP. FOR. PROD. LAB. (VANCOUVER).
VANCOUVER VP-X-1, 1965-
OX/U-3.

INFORMATION REVIEW ON CRIME & DELINQUENCY.   XXX
++INF. REV. CRIME & DELINQ.
NATIONAL COUNCIL ON CRIME & DELINQUENCY (US).
NEW YORK 1(1-9), 1968- 1969.
6/A. SUBS. PART OF: CRIME & DELINQUENCY LIT-
ERATURE.
ISSN 0579-501X

INFORMATION SERIES, ROYAL SCOTTISH MUSEUM:
NATURAL HISTORY.
++INF. SER. R. SCOTT. MUS., NAT. HIST.
EDINBURGH NO.1, 1973-
MONOGR.
LO/N-2.   LO/U-1.

INFORMATION FOR SURVIVAL DIGEST.
++INF. SURVIVAL DIG.
STOWMARKET, SUFFOLK, NO.1, OC 1972-
Q.
ED/N-1.   OX/U-1.

INHABIT.
[LINK HOUSE PUBL.]
CROYDON N 1973-
MON.
ED/N-1.   OX/U-1.

INORGANIC CHEMISTRY OF THE MAIN-GROUP
ELEMENTS.
++INORG. CHEM. MAIN-GROUP ELEM.
CHEMICAL SOCIETY.
LONDON 1, 1973-
BH/U-3.   CA/U-1.   ED/N-1.   GL/U-2.   HL/U-1.   LO/S-3.
SF/U-1.   ISSN 0305-697X

INSIDEOUT. MONTHLY MAGAZINE FOR SCOTLAND.
DUNDEE NO.1, S/OC 1973-
ED/N-1.

INSIGHT U.S.A.   XXX
(UNITED STATES) INFORMATION SERVICE (GB).
LONDON NO.1-6, 1973.
SUBS: HORIZONS U.S.A.
CA/U-1.   RE/U-1.   ED/N-1. NO.2, 1973-

INSTITUTE BULLETIN, INSTITUTE OF BRITISH
CARRIAGE & AUTOMOBILE MANUFACTURERS.   XXX
SUBS (1974): IBCAM.

INSURANCE.
[FINANCIAL TIMES BUSINESS ENTERPRISES]
LONDON 1(1), JA 1974-
MON.
CA/U-1. 1(7), 1974-   ED/N-1. 1(7), 1974-

INSURANCE FACTS & FIGURES.
++INSUR. FACTS & FIG.
BRITISH INSURANCE ASSOCIATION.
LONDON 1969[1970]-
ANNU.
BL/U-1.   LO/U-3.   RE/U-1.   AD/U-1. 1970-

INSURGENT SOCIOLOGIST.
++INSURGENT SOCIOL.
UNIVERSITY OF OREGON: DEPARTMENT OF SOCIOLOGY.
EUGENE, OREG. 1, 1971-
Q.
AD/U-1. 3, 1973-   ISSN 0047-0384

INTEGRATED STUDIES BULLETIN.
++INTEGR. STUD. BULL.
[OXFORD UNIV. P.]
OXFORD NO.1, F 1973-
2/A. S/T: DEVELOPING THE SCHOOLS COUNCIL
INTEGRATED STUDIES PROJECT.
ED/N-1.   OX/U-1.

INTEGRATION & MEASURE.
++INTEGR. & MEAS.
[CAMBRIDGE UNIV. P.]
CAMBRIDGE 1, 1973-
CA/U-1.

INTERIM. BULLETIN OF THE YORK ARCHAEOLOGICAL
TRUST.
YORK 1(1), MR 1973-
6/A.
CA/U-1.   ED/N-1.   OX/U-1.

INTERMEDIA (LONDON).
INTERNATIONAL BROADCAST INSTITUTE.
LONDON NO.1, MR/AP 1973-
CA/U-1.   OX/U-1.

INTERNATIONAL CERAMIC INDUSTRIES MANUAL.
++INT. CERAM. IND. MAN.
[TURRET P.]
LONDON 1, 1971-
LO/N14. CURRENT ISSUE ONLY.

INTERNATIONAL CLASSIFICATION.
++INT. CLASSIF.
[VERLAG DOKUMENTATION]
MUNICH 1, 1974-
SH/U-1.

INTERNATIONAL ELECTROCHEMICAL PROGRESS.
++INT. ELECTROCHEM. PROG.
INTERNATIONAL ELECTROCHEMICAL INSTITUTE.
MILLBURN, N.J. 1972-
MON.
LO/N14.

INTERNATIONAL FICTION REVIEW.
+ +INT. FICT. REV.
INTERNATIONAL FICTION ASSOCIATION.
FREDERICTON, N.B. 1, 1974-
2/A.
SH/U-1.

INTERNATIONAL GAS TECHNOLOGY HIGHLIGHTS.
+ +INT. GAS TECHNOL. HIGHLIGHTS.
INSTITUTE OF GAS TECHNOLOGY.
CHICAGO 1, AP 1971-
2W.
SF/U-1. 3, 1973-

INTERNATIONAL HISTOLOGICAL CLASSIFICATION OF
TUMOURS.
+ +INT. HISTOL. CLASSIF. TUMOURS.
WORLD HEALTH ORGANIZATION.
GENEVA NO.1, 1967-
GL/U-1.

INTERNATIONAL INDEX TO FILM PERIODICALS.
+ +INT. INDEX FILM PERIOD.
INTERNATIONAL FEDERATION OF FILM ARCHIVES.
[BOWKER]
NEW YORK 1972(1973)-
EX/U-1. GL/U-1. MA/P-1. OX/U-1.

INTERNATIONAL JOURNAL OF AFRICAN HISTORICAL
STUDIES.   XXX
+ +INT. J. AFR. HIST. STUD.
BOSTON UNIVERSITY: AFRICAN STUDIES CENTER.
[AFRICANA PUBL. CO.]
NEW YORK 5(1), JA 1972-
4/A. ENGL. & FR. PREV: AFRICAN HISTORICAL
STUDIES FROM 1(1), 1968- 4(3), D 1971.
EX/U-1. LO/U-8.

INTERNATIONAL JOURNAL OF AGING & HUMAN DEV-
ELOPMENT.   XXX
+ +INT. J. AGING & HUM. DEV.
[BAYWOOD PUBL. CO.]
FARMINGDALE, N.Y. 4, 1973-
PREV: AGING & HUMAN DEVELOPMENT FROM 1, 1970-
3, 1973.
SO/U-1.

INTERNATIONAL JOURNAL OF CHILD PSYCHOTHERAPY.
+ +INT. J. CHILD PSYCHOTHER.
[INTERNATIONAL JOURNAL P.]
NEW YORK 1(1), JA 1972-
Q.
OX/U-8. 1(3), 1972-

INTERNATIONAL JOURNAL OF FORENSIC DENTISTRY.
+ +INT. J. FORENSIC DENT.
[FORENSIC DENTISTRY]
BOGNOR REGIS 1(1), JL 1973-
Q.
CA/U-1. ED/N-1. LO/N13. OX/U-8.

INTERNATIONAL JOURNAL OF GENERAL SYSTEMS.
+ +INT. J. GEN. SYST.
[GORDON & BREACH]
LONDON & NEW YORK 1(1), JA 1974-
S/T: METHODOLOGY, APPLICATIONS, EDUCATION.
CA/U-1. ED/N-1. OX/U-1. SH/U-1. SW/U-1.

INTERNATIONAL JOURNAL OF MECHANICAL ENGINEER-
ING EDUCATION.   XXX
+ +INT. J. MECH. ENG. EDUC.
UNIVERSITY OF MANCHESTER: INSTITUTE OF SCIENCE
& TECHNOLOGY.   XXX
LONDON 1, 1973-
PREV: BULLETIN OF MECHANICAL ENGINEERING EDUC-
ATION: NS FROM 1, 1962- 11(1), 1972.
AD/U-2. BR/U-1. ED/N-1. GL/U-1. LD/U-1. LO/U-2.
SF/U-1. SW/U-1. ISSN 0306-4190

INTERNATIONAL JOURNAL OF MINERAL PROCESSING.
+ +INT. J. MINER. PROCESS.
[ELSEVIER]
AMSTERDAM 1, 1974-
LD/U-1. LO/N14. OX/U-8. SW/U-1.

INTERNATIONAL JOURNAL OF MULTIPHASE FLOW.
+ +INT. J. MULTIPHASE FLOW.
[PERGAMON]
OXFORD & NEW YORK 1(1), OC 1973-
2M. FR., GER. & RUSS. SUMM.
EX/U-1. LO/U-2. OX/U-8. SF/U-1. SW/U-1.

INTERNATIONAL JOURNAL OF PSYCHOLINGUISTICS.
+ +INT. J. PSYCHOLINGUIST.
[MOUTON]
THE HAGUE & PARIS NO.1, 1972-
LD/U-1. OX/U-1. SH/U-1.

INTERNATIONAL JOURNAL OF SOCIAL ECONOMICS.
+ +INT. J. SOC. ECON.
[MCB (SOCIAL ECONOMICS) LTD.]
BRADFORD 1(1), 1974-
AD/U-1. BH/U-3. CA/U-1. CA/U38. ED/N-1. EX/U-1.
HL/U-1. LO/U-3. LO/U12. OX/U-1. OX/U16. SH/U-1.
SW/U-1. XS/R10.

INTERNATIONAL JOURNAL OF TRANSPORT ECONOMICS.   000
SEE: RIVISTA INTERNAZIONALE DI ECONOMIA
DEI TRANSPORTI.

INTERNATIONAL MEDIEVAL BIBLIOGRAPHY.
+ +INT. MEDIEVAL BIBLIOGR.
[INTERNATIONAL MEDIEVAL BIBLIOGRAPHY]
LEEDS 1967(1968)-
ANNU. VARIOUS LANG.
BH/U-1. BL/U-1. CA/U-1. CB/U-1. ED/N-1. GL/U-1.
LO/U-4. LO/U19. LV/U-1. MA/U-1. OX/U-1. RE/U-1.
SO/U-1. ISSN 0020-7950

INTERNATIONAL MONOGRAPH SERIES ON EARLY CHILD
CARE.
+ +INT. MONOGR. SER. EARLY CHILD CARE.
[GORDON & BREACH]
LONDON 1, 1972-
CA/U-1.

INTERNATIONAL NURSING INDEX.
+ +INT. NURS. INDEX.
[AMERICAN JOURNAL OF NURSING CO.]
NEW YORK 1, 1966-
Q.
SO/U-1. BL/U-1. 9, 1974- ISSN 0020-8124

INTERNATIONAL PERFUMER.   XXX
SUBS (1974): COSMETIC WORLD NEWS.

INTERNATIONAL POLLUTION CONTROL MAGAZINE.
+ +INT. POLLUT. CONTROL MAG.
[SCRANTON PUBL. CO.]
CHICAGO 1, N 1972-
Q.
LO/N14.

INTERNATIONAL POLYMER SCIENCE & TECHNOLOGY.
RUBBER & PLASTICS RESEARCH ASSOCIATION OF GREAT
BRITAIN.
SHREWSBURY 1, 1974-
SPONS. BODY ALSO: BRITISH LIBRARY: LENDING
DIVISION.
BH/U-3. ED/N-1. LO/N14. OX/U-8.

INTERNATIONAL REGISTER OF RESEARCH IN ACCOUNT-
ING & FINANCE.
+ +INT. REGIST. RES. ACCOUNT. & FINANCE.
LANCASTER 1, 1974-
BH/U-3. CB/U-1. SH/U-1. SH/U-1. SO/U-1.

INTERNATIONAL REVIEW OF NEUROBIOLOGY: SUPPLEMENT
+ +INT. REV. NEUROBIOL., SUPPL.
[ACADEMIC P.]
NEW YORK & LONDON 1, 1972-
GL/U-1.

INTERNATIONAL REVIEW OF PSYCHO-ANALYSIS.
+ +INT. REV. PSYCHO-ANAL.
INSTITUTE OF PSYCHO-ANALYSIS.
[BAILLIERE TINDALL]
LONDON 1, MY 1974-
PUBL. IN CONJUNCTION WITH THE INTERNATIONAL
JOURNAL OF PSYCHO-ANALYSIS.
LO/S18. LO/U-2. OX/U-1. ISSN 0306-2643

INTERNATIONAL WILDLIFE.
+ +INT. WILDL.
NATIONAL WILDLIFE FEDERATION (US).
WASHINGTON, D.C. 1, 1971-
2M. S/T: DEDICATED TO THE WISE USE OF THE
WORLD'S NATURAL RESOURCES.
LO/R-5. 4, 1974- ISSN 0029-9112

INTERNATIONALE ZEITSCHRIFT FUR ANGEWANDTE PHYS-
IOLOGIE EINSCHLIESSLICH ARBEITSPHYSIOLOGIE.   XXX
SUBS (1973): EUROPEAN JOURNAL OF APPLIED PHYS-
IOLOGY & OCCUPATIONAL PHYSIOLOGY.

INTERVENTION. REVOLUTIONARY MARXIST JOURNAL.
CARLTON, VICTORIA NO.1, AP 1972-
4/A.
LO/U-3.

**INTRODUKTSIJA TA AKLIMATYZATSIJA ROSLYN NA
UKRAJINI.**   XXX
++*INTROD. AKLIM. ROSL. UKR.*
AKADEMIJA NAUK UKRAJINS'KOJI RSR.
KIEV [1], 1966-
1-2 ENTITLED INTRODUKTSIJA TA AKLIMATYZATSIJA
ROSLYN. NUMBERING COMMENCED WITH 3, 1968.
LO/N-2.   LO/N13. 3, 1968-

**INTRODUKTSIJA TA EKSPERYMENTAL'NA EKOLOHIJA
ROSLYN.**
++*INTROD. EKSP. EKOL. ROSL.*
DONETS'KYJ BOTANICHNYJ SAD.
KIEV 1, 1972-
LO/N-2.

IPC PAPERS.
++*IPC PAP.*
INSTITUTE OF PHILIPPINE CULTURE.
[MANILA UNIV. P.]
QUEZON CITY 1, 1960-
ENGL.
LO/N-1. NO.2, ‡1970A-   ISSN 0073-9545

IRANIAN JOURNAL OF AGRICULTURAL RESEARCH.
++*IRAN. J. AGRIC. RES.*
PAHLAVI UNIVERSITY: COLLEGE OF AGRICULTURE.
SHIRAZ, IRAN 1(1), OC 1971-
Q.
LO/R-6.

IRANIAN JOURNAL OF SCIENCE & TECHNOLOGY.
++*IRAN. J. SCI. & TECHNOL.*
PAHLAVI UNIVERSITY.
SHIRAZ 1, 1971-
LO/N-2.

IRIAN. BULLETIN OF WEST IRIAN DEVELOPMENT.   XXX
UNIVERSITY OF TJENDERAWASIH: INSTITUTE OF
ANTHROPOLOGY.
ABEPURA-DJAJAPURA 1, 1972-
3/A.
LO/S10. 1(2), 1972-

IRISH ANGUS HERD BOOK.
++*IR. ANGUS HERD BOOK.*
IRISH ANGUS CATTLE SOCIETY.
DUBLIN 1, 1968-
DB/U-2.   LO/N13.

IRISH ARCHAEOLOGICAL RESEARCH FORUM.
++*IR. ARCHAEOL. RES. FORUM.*
BELFAST 1, 1974-
BL/U-1.   LO/U-2.

IRISH CHAROLAIS HERD BOOK.
++*IR. CHAROLAIS HERD BOOK.*
IRISH CHAROLAIS CATTLE SOCIETY.
DUBLIN 1, 1967-
DB/U-2.   LO/N13.

IRONMAKING & STEELMAKING.   XXX
METALS SOCIETY.
LONDON 1, 1974-
PREV. PART OF: JOURNAL OF THE IRON & STEEL
INSTITUTE FROM 1, 1871- 211, D 1973. SPONS.
BODY ALSO: AMERICAN SOCIETY FOR METALS.
AD/U-1.   BH/U-3.   ED/N-1.   GL/U-2.   LO/N14.   OX/U-1.

IRRIGATION FARMER DIGEST.   XXX
++*IRRIG. FARMER DIG.*
[GARDNER PRINT. & PUBL.]
NUNAWADING, AUST. 1, 1973-
PREV: IRRIGATION FARMER FROM 5, 1969- 8, 1973.
LO/N14.

ISKOPAEMAJA FAUNA I FLORA DAL'NEGO VOSTOKA.
++*ISKOP. FAUNA & FLORA DAL'NEGO VOSTOKA.*
AKADEMIJA NAUK SSSR: LABORATORIJA PALEONTOLOGII
I STRATIGRAFII.
VLADIVOSTOK 1, 1969-
LABORATORIJA SUBORD. TO: DAL'NEVOSTOCHNYJ
GEOLOGICHESKIJ INSTITUT. ENGL. SUMM. & TITLE:
FOSSIL FAUNA & FLORA OF THE FAR EAST.
LO/N-2.

ISKUSSTVO I BYT. SBORNIK STATEJ.
[SOVETSKIJ KHUDOZHNIK]
MOSCOW 1, 1963-
LO/U15. 2, 1964-

ISLAMIC STUDIES (DENVER).
++*ISLAMIC STUD. (DENVER).*
AMERICAN INSTITUTE OF ISLAMIC STUDIES.
DENVER, COLO. 1, 1973-
5/A.
CA/U-1.   LO/N12.

ISLAND.
YOUNG EXPLORERS' TRUST.
AMBLESIDE NO.1, 1972-
LO/N-2.

**ISSLEDOVANIJA PO ELEKTROKHIMII, MAGNETOKHIMII
I ELEKTROKHIMICHESKIM METODAM ANALIZA.**
++*ISSLED. ELEKTROKHIM. MAGNETOKHIM. & ELEKTRO-
KHIM. METODAM ANAL.*
KAZANSKIJ GOSUDARSTVENNYJ UNIVERSITET.
KAZAN' 1, 1965-
LO/N13. 3, 1970-

ISSUES & RESEARCH. (CHINESE ED., TAIPEI).   000
SEE: WEN-T'I YU YEN-CHIU.

ISSUES & STUDIES. (CHINESE ED., TAIPEI).   000
SEE: WEN-T'I YU YEN-CHIU.

**ISTORIJA I ISTORIKI. ISTORIOGRAFICHESKIJ
EZHEGODNIK.**
++*ISTOR. & ISTOR.*
AKADEMIJA NAUK SSSR: NAUCHNYJ SOVET £ISTORIJA
ISTORICHESKOJ NAUKI£.
MOSCOW 1965-
SPONS. BODY ALSO: INSTITUT ISTORII SSSR.
CC/U-1.   LD/U-1.   OX/U-1.

ISTORIJA RABOCHEGO KLASSA UZBEKISTANA.
++*ISTOR. RAB. KL. UZB.*
AKADEMIJA NAUK UZBEKSKOJ SSR.
TASHKENT 1, 1964-
GL/U-1.

ISTORIJA RADNICKOG POKRETA, ZBORNIK RADOVA.
++*ISTOR. RADNICKOG POKRETA ZB. RAD.*
INSTITUT ZA IZUCAVANJE RADNICKOG POKRETA.
BELGRADE 1, 1965-
OX/U-1.

**ISTORIJA, SOJUZ NA ISTORISKITE DRUSTVA NA SR
MAKEDONIJA.**
++*ISTOR. SOJUZ ISTOR. DRUS. SR MAKEDONIJA.*
SKOPJE 1(1), 1965-
OX/U-1.

ISTORIOGRAFICHESKIJ SBORNIK.
++*ISTORIOGR. SB.*
SARATOVSKIJ GOSUDARSTVENNYJ UNIVERSITET.
SARATOV [1], 1962-
VOL.1 UNNUMBERED.
GL/U-1. 1965-

**ISTORIOGRAFIJA I ISTOCHNIKOVEDENIE ISTORII
STRAN AZII.**
++*ISTOR. & ISTOCHNIKOVED. ISTOR. STRAN AZII.*
LENINGRADSKIJ GOSUDARSTVENNYJ UNIVERSITET.
LENINGRAD 1, 1965-
CC/U-1.

ISTORYCHNI DZHERELA TA JIKH VYKORYSTANNJA.
++*ISTOR. DZHERELA JIKH VYKORYSTANNJA.*
AKADEMIJA NAUK UKRAJINS'KOJI RSR: INSTYTUT
ISTORIJI.
KIEV 1, 1964-
LO/U15. 2, 1966-   OX/U-1. 3, 1968-

ITALIA NEL MONDO.
++*ITAL. MONDO.*
LONDON SUMMER 1972-
S/T: BILINGUAL ANGLO-ITALIAN MONTHLY.
ED/N-1.

I.W.C. NEWS.   XXX
IRISH WILDBIRD CONSERVANCY.
DUBLIN NO.1, 1974-
PREV: NEWSLETTER, IRISH WILDBIRD CONSERVANCY
FROM NO.1, 1969- 19, 1974.
LO/R-5.

IZ ISTORII RUSSKOGO ROMANTIZMA.
++*IZ ISTOR. RUSS. ROMANTIZMA.*
KEMEROVSKIJ GOSUDARSTVENNYJ PEDAGOGICHESKIJ
INSTITUT.
KEMEROVO 1, 1971-
LO/U15.

**IZ OPYTA PREPODAVANIJA RUSSKOGO JAZYKA NERUS-
SKIM. SBORNIK NAUCHNOMETODICHESKIKH STATEJ.**
++*IZ OPYTA PREPOD. RUSS. JAZYKA NERUSS.*
VYSSHAJA PARTIJNAJA SHKOLA PRI TSK KPSS:
KAFEDRA RUSSKOGO JAZYKA.
MOSCOW 1, 1961-
LD/U-1.   BD/U-1. 7, 1972.   LO/U15. 4, 1968.

IZVESTIJA AKADEMII NAUK BSSR: SERIJA FIZIKO-
MATEMATICHESKIKH NAUK (MINSK).   000
  SEE: VESTI AKADEMII NAVUK BELARUSKAJ SSR:
  SERYJA FIZIKA-MATEMATYCHNYKH NAVUK.

IZVESTIJA, ALTAJSKIJ OTDEL, GEOGRAFICHESKOE
OBSHCHESTVO SSSR.
  ++IZV. ALTAJ. OTD. GEOGR. O-OV. SSSR.
  BARNAUL 1, 1961-
  LO/N13. 9, 1969-

IZVESTIJA, ZABAJKAL'SKIJ FILIAL GEOGRAFICH-
ESKOGO OBSHCHESTVA SSSR.   XXX
  ++IZV. ZABAJK. FIL. GEOGR. O-VA. SSSR.
  IRKUTSK 1, 1965-
  VOL.1 PUBL. AS: IZVESTIJA, ZABAJKAL'SKIJ OTDEL
  GEOGRAFICHESKO OBSHCHESTVO SSSR.
  LO/N13. 2, 1966-

JABBERWOCKY.
  LEWIS CARROLL SOCIETY.
  LONDON 1, 1969-
  ED/N-1. 3(2), 1974-   LO/U-2. 2(3), 1973.

JACT NYUSU.   XXX
  CHUZO GIJUTSO FUKYU KYOKU.
  TOKYO NO.185, 1972-
  PREV: SHERU MORUDO NYUSU FROM NO.1, 1962-
  184, 1972.
  LO/N13.

JAHRBUCH FUR AMERIKASTUDIEN.   XXX
  SUBS (1974): AMERIKASTUDIEN.

JAHRBUCH FUR AMERIKASTUDIEN: BEIHEFT.   XXX
  SUBS (1974): AMERIKASTUDIEN: BEIHEFT.

JAHRBUCH FUR EISENBAHNGESCHICHTE.
  ++JAHRB. EISENBAHNGESCH.
  DEUTSCHE GESELLSCHAFT FUR EISENBAHNGESCHICHTE.
  KARLSRUHE 1, 1968-
  LO/N-4.

JAHRBUCH DER INTERNATIONALEN POLITIK UND
WIRTSCHAFT.
  ++JAHRB. INT. POLIT. & WIRTSCH.
  BERLIN 1, 1973-
  OX/U-1.

JAHRBUCH FUR OSTERREICHISCHE KULTURGESCHICHTE.
  ++JAHRB. OSTERR. KULTURGESCH.
  INSTITUT FUR OSTERREICHISCHE KULTURGESCHICHTE.
  EISENSTADT 1, 1971-
  OX/U-1.

JAHRBUCH DER SCHWEIZERISCHEN GESELLSCHAFT FUR
UR- UND FRUHGESCHICHTE.   XXX
  ++JAHRB. SCHWEIZ. GES. UR- & FRUHGESCH.
  BASLE 53, 1966/7-
  PREV: JAHRBUCH DER SCHWEIZERISCHEN GESELL-
  SCHAFT FUR URGESCHICHTE FROM 30, 1938- 52,
  1965.
  LO/S10.

JAHRBUCH DER SCHWEIZERISCHEN GESELLSCHAFT FUR
URGESCHICHTE.   XXX
  SUBS (1966): JAHRBUCH DER SCHWEIZERISCHEN
  GESELLSCHAFT FUR UR- UND FRUHGESCHICHTE.

JAPAN ILLUSTRATED (1963).
  ++JAP. ILLUS. (1963).
  [JAPAN TIMES LTD.]
  TOKYO 1, OC 1963-
  Q.
  ED/N-1. 12(2), 1974-   ISSN 0021-4418

JAPANESE JOURNAL OF RELIGIOUS STUDIES.   XXX
  ++JAP. J. RELIG. STUD.
  INTERNATIONAL INSTITUTE FOR THE STUDY OF
  RELIGIONS.
  TOKYO 1, 1974-
  PREV: CONTEMPORARY RELIGIONS IN JAPAN FROM
  1, 1960- 11, 1970.
  LO/U14.   MA/U-1.   OX/U-1.   ISSN 0021-4361

JCU. JOURNAL OF CLINICAL ULTRASOUND.
  [REAM HOUSE]
  DENVER, COLO. 1, MR 1973-
  Q.
  LO/N13.   ISSN 0091-2751

JENGA.
  NATIONAL DEVELOPMENT CORPORATION (TANZANIA).
  DAR ES SALAAM NO.1, 1968-
  LO/U14. NO.2, 1968-   OX/U-9. NO.6, 1970-

JOB FINDER - BUILDING & CONSTRUCTION.
  ++JOB FINDER - BUILD. & CONSTR.
  UNION OF CONSTRUCTION, ALLIED TRADES &
  TECHNICIANS.
  [IPC BUILDING & CONTRACT JOURNALS LTD.]
  LONDON NO.1, MY 1974-
  WKLY.
  ED/N-1. NO.2, 1974-

JOURNAL OF THE AICHI MEDICAL UNIVERSITY ASSOC-
IATION.   000
  SEE: AICHI IKA DAIGAKU IGAKKAI ZASSI.

JOURNAL OF ANTHROPOLOGICAL RESEARCH.   XXX
  ++J. ANTHROPOL. RES.
  UNIVERSITY OF NEW MEXICO.
  ALBUQUERQUE 29, 1973-
  PREV: SOUTHWESTERN JOURNAL OF ANTHROPOLOGY
  FROM 1, 1945- 28, 1972.
  CA/U-3.   GL/U-1.   HL/U-1.   LO/N-2.   LO/U-1.

JOURNAL OF ARCHAEOLOGICAL SCIENCE.
  ++J. ARCHAEOL. SCI.
  [ACADEMIC P.]
  LONDON & NEW YORK 1(1), MR 1974-
  BN/U-1.   CA/U-1. 1(3), 1974-   CA/U-3.   LO/U-2.   SH/U-1.
  ED/N-1. 1(3), 1974-

JOURNAL OF ARCHITECTURAL RESEARCH.   XXX
  ROYAL INSTITUTE OF BRITISH ARCHITECTS.
  LONDON 3(1), JA 1974-
  PREV: ARCHITECTURAL RESEARCH & TEACHING FROM
  1, MY 1970- 2(3), JE 1973. SPONS. BODY ALSO:
  AMERICAN INSTITUTE OF ARCHITECTS.
  RE/U-1.   SH/P-1.

JOURNAL OF ASIAN INTEGRATION STUDIES.
  ++J. ASIAN INTEGRAT. STUD.
  LONDON SCHOOL OF ECONOMICS & POLITICAL SCIENCE:
  ASIAN CLUB.
  LONDON NO.1, 1973-
  LO/U14.

JOURNAL, ASSOCIATION FOR THE ADVANCEMENT
OF MEDICAL INSTRUMENTATION.   XXX
  ++J. ASSOC. ADV. MED. INSTRUM.
  BALTIMORE 1, JL/AG 1966- 6, 1972...
  SUBS: MEDICAL INSTRUMENTATION JOURNAL. PUBL.
  SUSPENDED S 1967- 1968.
  OX/U-8. 6(1), 1972-   ISSN 0004-5446

JOURNAL OF THE ASSOCIATION OF WORKERS FOR
MALADJUSTED CHILDREN: NS.
  ++J. ASSOC. WORKERS MALADJUSTED CHILD., NS.
  CAERLEON, MON. NO.1, 1973-
  CA/U-1.   ED/N-1.   HL/U-1.   LD/U-2.   OX/U-1.   SW/U-1.

JOURNAL, AUSTRALIAN CERAMIC SOCIETY.
  ++J. AUST. CERAM. SOC.
  KENSINGTON, N.S.W. 1(1), 1965-
  2/A.
  LO/N14. ‡W. 1(2), 1965‡   ISSN 0004-881X

JOURNAL OF BALTIC STUDIES.   XXX
  ++J. BALTIC STUD.
  ASSOCIATION FOR THE ADVANCEMENT OF BALTIC
  STUDIES.
  NEW YORK 3(1), 1972-
  PREV: BULLETIN OF BALTIC STUDIES FROM 1, 1970-
  2, 1971.
  CA/U-1.   OX/U-1.   AD/U-1. 4, 1973-

JOURNAL OF BELIZEAN AFFAIRS.
  ++J. BELIZEAN AFF.
  BELIZE CITY NO.1, JE 1973-
  2/A.
  LO/U-3. NO.2, 1973-

JOURNAL OF BIOGEOGRAPHY.
  ++J. BIOGEOGR.
  [BLACKWELL SCI. PUBL.]
  OXFORD 1, MR 1974-
  AD/U-1.   CA/U-1.   CA/U-6.   ED/N-1.   HL/U-1.   LO/N-2.
  LO/U-1.   LO/U-4.   LO/U12.   MA/U-1.   NO/U-1.   OX/U-8.
  ISSN 0305-0270

JOURNAL OF BIOLOGICAL PHYSICS.
  ++J. BIOL. PHYS.
  [PHYSICAL BIOLOGICAL SCIENCES, LTD.]
  BLACKSBURG, VA. 1, 1973-
  Q.
  LO/N14.

JOURNAL DE BIOLOGIE BUCCALE.
++J. BIOL. BUCCALE.
[EDITIONS S.N.P.M.D.]
PARIS 1, 1973-
LO/U-2. MA/U-1.

JOURNAL, BRITISH SPELEOLOGICAL ASSOCIATION. XXX
++J. BR. SPELEOL. ASSOC.
SETTLE, YORKS. 6(41), 1967- 6,(47), 1971...
PREV: CAVE SCIENCE FROM NO.1, 1947- 40, 1967.
SUBS: CAVE SCIENCE.
LO/N13.

JOURNAL OF BUSINESS FINANCE & ACCOUNTING. XXX
++J. BUS. FINANC. & ACCOUNT.
OXFORD 1, SPRING 1974-
PREV: JOURNAL OF BUSINESS FINANCE FROM
1, 1969- 5(2) SUMMER 1973.
BL/U-1. BN/U-1. CB/U-1. EX/U-1. GL/U-2. HL/U-1.
SA/U-1. SO/U-1

JOURNAL CANADIEN D'OTOLARYNGOLOGIE. 000
SEE: CANADIAN JOURNAL OF OTOLARYNGOLOGY.

JOURNAL CANADIEN DES SCIENCES NEUROLOGIQUES. 000
SEE: CANADIAN JOURNAL OF NEUROLOGICAL SCIENCES

**JOURNAL OF THE CENTRE FOR ADVANCED TELEVISION
STUDIES.**
++J. CENT. ADV. TELEV. STUD.
LONDON 1(1), 1973-
CA/U-1. OX/U-1. RE/U-1.

JOURNAL OF CHILD LANGUAGE.
++J. CHILD LANG.
[CAMBRIDGE UNIV. P.]
LONDON 1, 1974-
AD/U-1. ED/N-1. OX/U-1. SH/U-1.

JOURNAL OF CHINESE LINGUISTICS.
++J. CHIN. LINGUIST.
UNIVERSITY OF CALIFORNIA: PROJECT ON LINGUISTIC
ANALYSIS.
BERKELEY, CALIF. 1, JA 1973-
CA/U-1. LD/U-1. LO/U14.

JOURNAL OF CHINESE PHILOSOPHY.
++J. CHIN. PHILOS.
[REIDEL]
DORDRECHT 1(1), D 1973-
4/A.
OX/U-1.

JOURNAL OF CLINICAL PERIODONTOLOGY.
++J. CLIN. PERIODONTOL.
BRITISH SOCIETY OF PERIODONTOLOGY.
[MUNKSGAARD]
COPENHAGEN 1, 1974-
SPONS. BODIES ALSO: FRENCH, GERMAN, SWISS
& SCANDINAVIAN SOCIETIES OF PERIODONTOLOGY.
AD/U-1. LD/U-1. OX/U-8.

JOURNAL OF COATED FABRICS. XXX
++J. COAT. FABRICS.
[TECHNOMIC PUBL. CO.]
WESTPORT, CONN. 3, 1973-
PREV: JOURNAL OF COATED FIBROUS MATERIALS FROM
1, 1971- 2, 1973.
LO/N14.

JOURNAL OF COFFEE RESEARCH.
++J. COFFEE RES.
CENTRAL COFFEE RESEARCH INSTITUTE (INDIA).
BALEHONNUR 1, OC 1971-
LO/N13. LO/R-6.

**JOURNAL OF COMMONWEALTH & COMPARATIVE
POLITICS.** XXX
++J. COMMONW. & COMP. POLIT.
INSTITUTE OF COMMONWEALTH STUDIES.
[CASS]
LONDON 12, 1974-
PREV: JOURNAL OF COMMONWEALTH POLITICAL
STUDIES FROM 1, 1961- 11(2), JL 1973.
GL/U-1. HL/U-1. LO/U-3. LO/U14. SO/U-1.

JOURNAL OF COMMUNITY PSYCHOLOGY.
++J. COMMUNITY PSYCHOL.
[CLINICAL PSYCHOLOGY PUBL. CO.]
BRANDON, VT. 1, JA 1973-
Q.
BL/U-1. OX/U-8. SH/U-1. ISSN 0090-4392

JOURNAL OF CONTEMPORARY BUSINESS. XXX
++J. CONTEMP. BUS.
UNIVERSITY OF WASHINGTON: GRADUATE SCHOOL OF
BUSINESS ADMINISTRATION.
SEATLE 1, 1972-
Q. PREV: UNIVERSITY OF WASHINGTON BUSINESS
REVIEW FROM 17(5), F 1958- 31(1), 1971.
SH/U-1. GL/U-2. 1(3), 1974-

JOURNAL OF CRIMINAL LAW & CRIMINOLOGY. XXX
++J. CRIM. LAW & CRIMINOL.
NORTHWESTERN UNIVERSITY: SCHOOL OF LAW.
[WILLIAMS & WILKINS]
BALTIMORE 64, MR 1973-
Q. PREV: PART OF JOURNAL OF CRIMINAL LAW,
CRIMINOLOGY & POLICE SCIENCE FROM 22, 1932-
63(4), 1973.
RE/U-1.

**JOURNAL OF CRIMINAL LAW, CRIMINOLOGY & POLICE
SCIENCE.** XXX
SUBS (1973): PART OF JOURNAL OF POLICE SCIENCE
& ADMINISTRATION; & JOURNAL OF CRIMINAL LAW &
CRIMINOLOGY.

JOURNAL OF CUTANEOUS PATHOLOGY.
++J. CUTANEOUS PATHOL.
[MUNKSGAARD]
COPENHAGEN 1, 1974-
2M.
LO/N13.

JOURNAL, DENVER LAW CENTER. XXX
++J. DENVER LAW CENT. XXX
UNIVERSITY OF DENVER: LAW CENTER.
DENVER 40(1), JA/F 1963- 42, 1965 ...
PREV: DICTA FROM 6, 1928- 39, 1962. SUBS:
DENVER LAW JOURNAL.
OX/U15.

**JOURNAL, DEPARTMENT OF SANSKRIT, UNIVERSITY
OF DELHI.** XXX
++J. DEP. SANSKRIT UNIV. DELHI.
DELHI 1, 1971/72 ...
SUBS: INDOLOGICAL STUDIES.
LO/N12.

JOURNAL OF DEVELOPMENT ECONOMICS.
++J. DEV. ECON.
[NORTH-HOLLAND]
AMSTERDAM 1, 1974-
CB/U-1. EX/U-1. LO/U-2. LO/U-3. LO/U12. MA/U-1.

JOURNAL OF EAST & WEST STUDIES.
++J. EAST & WEST STUD.
YONSEI TAEHAKKYO (SEOUL): TONGSO MUNJE YON'-
GUNON.
SEOUL 1, 1973-
2/A.
LO/U14.

JOURNAL, EDINBURGH NATURAL HISTORY SOCIETY. XXX
++J. EDINB. NAT. HIST. SOC.
EDINBURGH 1972-
PREV: NEWSLETTER, EDINBURGH NATURAL HISTORY
SOCIETY FROM 1965- 1971.
ED/N-1.

JOURNAL OF EDUCATIONAL TECHNOLOGY SYSTEMS.
++J. EDUC. TECHNOL. SYST.
[BAYWOOD PUBL. CO.]
FARMINGDALE, N.Y. 1, JE 1972-
Q. SPINE TITLE: EDUCATIONAL TECHNOLOGY
SYSTEMS.
LO/N14.

JOURNAL OF ELASTOMERS & PLASTICS. XXX
++J. ELASTOMERS & PLAST.
[TECHNOMIC PUBL. CO.]
WESTPORT, CONN. 6, 1974-
PREV: JOURNAL OF ELASTOPLASTICS FROM 1, 1969-
5, 1973.
LO/N14.

**JOURNAL OF ENVIRONMENTAL ECONOMICS &
MANAGEMENT.**
++J. ENVIRON. ECON. & MANAGE.
[ACADEMIC P.]
NEW YORK & LONDON 1, 1974-
LO/U-2.

JOURNAL OF FINANCIAL ECONOMICS.
++J. FINANC. ECON.
[NORTH-HOLLAND]
 AMSTERDAM 1(1), MY 1974-
 Q. PUBL. IN COLLAB. WITH THE GRADUATE SCHOOL
 OF MANAGEMENT, UNIVERSITY OF ROCHESTER.
 BN/U-1. EX/U-1.

JOURNAL OF GENERAL MANAGEMENT. XXX
++J. GEN. MANAGE.
[MERCURY HOUSE BUSINESS PUBL.]
 LONDON 1, 1973-
 PREV: JOURNAL OF BUSINESS FINANCE FROM 1,
 1969- 5(2), 1973; INCORP: JOURNAL OF BUSINESS
 POLICY FROM 1(1), 1970- 3(1), 1973.
 AD/U-1. BL/U-1. BN/U-1. CA/U-1. ED/N-1. GL/U-2.
 LD/U-1. OX/U-1. OX/U17. SF/U-1.

JOURNAL OF THE HISTORICAL BREECHLOADING SMALL-
ARMS ASSOCIATION.
++J. HIST. BREECHLOAD. SMALLARMS ASSOC.
 LONDON 1(1), S 1973-
 2/A.
 ED/N-1. OX/U-1.

JOURNAL OF HUMAN ERGOLOGY.
++J. HUM. ERGOL.
 HUMAN ERGOLOGY RESEARCH ASSOCIATION.
 TOKYO 1, S 1972-
 2/A.
 BH/U-3. 2, 1973-

JOURNAL OF IMMUNOGENETICS.
++J. IMMUNOGENET.
 OXFORD 1, 1974-
 AD/U-1. CA/U-1. ED/N-1. LO/N-2. LO/U-2. SO/U-1.

JOURNAL OF THE INDIAN ACADEMY OF GEOSCIENCE. XXX
++J. INDIAN ACAD. GEOSCI.
 HYDERBAD 14, 1972-
 PREV: JOURNAL OF THE INDIAN GEOSCIENCE ASSOC-
 IATION.
 LO/N-2.

JOURNAL OF THE INDIAN GEOSCIENCE ASSOCIATION. XXX
 SUBS (1972): JOURNAL OF THE INDIAN ACADEMY
 OF GEOSCIENCE.

JOURNAL OF THE INDIAN MUSICOLOGICAL SOCIETY. XXX
++J. INDIAN MUSICOL. SOC.
 BARODA 2, 1971-
 Q. PREV: SANGEET KALA VIHAR: ENGLISH SUPP-
 LEMENT.
 ED/N-1. OX/U13.

JOURNAL OF INDIAN WRITING IN ENGLISH.
++J. INDIAN WRIT. ENGL.
 GULBARGA, INDIA 1, JA 1973-
 2/A.
 LO/N12. SH/U-1. 2, 1974-

JOURNAL OF THE INLAND FISHERIES SOCIETY OF
INDIA.
++J. INLAND FISH. SOC. INDIA.
 BARRACKPORE 1, 1969-
 ANNU.
 LO/N-2.

JOURNAL, INSTITUTE OF ASPHALT TECHNOLOGY.
++J. INST. ASPHALT TECHNOL.
 LONDON NO.1, AP 1966-
 LO/N14. NO.5, 1968- ‡W. NO.6 & 14Å

JOURNAL OF THE INSTITUTION OF ELECTRONICS &
TELECOMMUNICATION ENGINEERS. XXX
++J. INST. ELECTRON. & TELECOMMUN. ENG.
 NEW DELHI 19(7), JL 1973-
 PREV: JOURNAL OF THE INSTITUTION OF TELECOMM-
 UNICATION ENGINEERS FROM 1, MR 1955- 19(6),
 JE 1973.
 CA/U-2. LO/N14.

JOURNAL OF THE INSTITUTE OF METALS. XXX
 SUBS (1974) PART OF: METALS TECHNOLOGY.

JOURNAL, INSTITUTE OF PETROLEUM. XXX
 SUBS (1974): [REPORT] INSTITUTE OF PETROLEUM.

JOURNAL OF THE INSTITUTION OF TELECOMMUNICAT-
ION ENGINEERS. XXX
 SUBS (1973): JOURNAL OF THE INSTITUTION OF
 ELECTRONICS & TELECOMMUNICATION ENGINEERS.

JOURNAL, INTERNATIONAL ASSOCIATION OF
DENTISTRY FOR CHILDREN.
++J. INT. ASSOC. DENT. CHILD.
 LONDON 1, S 1970-
 CA/U-1. 5, 1974- ED/N-1. 5, JL 1974- LD/U-1. 2, 1971-

JOURNAL OF THE INTERNATIONAL FOLK MUSIC
COUNCIL. XXX
 SUBS (1969): YEARBOOK OF THE INTERNATIONAL
 FOLK MUSIC COUNCIL.

JOURNAL, INTERNATIONAL LAW SOCIETY, UNIVER-
SITY, OF TEXAS. XXX
++J. INT. LAW SOC. UNIV. TEX.
 AUSTIN, TEX. 1, JA 1965 ...
 SUBS: TEXAS INTERNATIONAL LAW FORUM. SOCIETY
 SUBORD. TO: SCHOOL OF LAW.
 CA/U13. LO/U24.

JOURNAL OF IRISH LITERATURE.
++J. IR. LIT.
[PROSCENIUM P.]
 NEWARK, N.J. 1(1), 1972-
 3/A.
 OX/U-1. ISSN 0047-2514

JOURNAL OF THE IRON & STEEL INSTITUTE. XXX
 SUBS (1974) PART OF: METALS TECHNOLOGY; &
 IRONMAKING & STEELMAKING.

JOURNAL OF THE KRIO LITERARY SOCIETY.
++J. KRIO LIT. SOC.
 NEW YORK 1(1), 1972-
 LO/U14.

JOURNAL OF LAW REFORM. XXX
++J. LAW REFORM.
 UNIVERSITY OF MICHIGAN: LAW SCHOOL.
 ANN ARBOR 4(1), 1970-
 PREV: PROSPECTUS FROM 1(1), AP 1968- 3, 1970.
 OX/U15. ISSN 0033-1546

JOURNAL OF MATHEMATICAL BIOLOGY.
++J. MATH. BIOL.
 VIENNA 1, 1974-
 Q.
 LO/R-5. OX/U-8.

JOURNAL OF MATHEMATICAL ECONOMICS.
++J. MATH. ECON.
[NORTH-HOLLAND]
 AMSTERDAM 1, 1974-
 AD/U-1. LO/U-2. MA/U-1. RE/U-1. SO/U-1.

JOURNAL MONDIAL DE PHARMACIE. XXX
++J. MOND. PHARM.
 FEDERATION INTERNATIONALE PHARMACEUTIQUE.
 BRUSSELS &C. 1, N 1957- 15, D 1972.//
 Q. ENGL., FR. & GER. PREV: BULLETIN DE LA
 FEDERATION INTERNATIONALE PHARMACEUTIQUE FROM
 1, 1912- 29, 1956.
 XY/N-1.* LO/N13. 7, 1964- ISSN 0449-2099

JOURNAL OF MULTIVARIATE EXPERIMENTAL PERSONALITY
& CLINICAL PSYCHOLOGY.
++J. MULTIVAR. EXP. PERS. & CLIN. PSYCHOL.
 BANDON, OREG. 1, 1974-
 Q.
 SH/U-1.

JOURNAL OF NEURAL TRANSMISSION. XXX
++J. NEURAL TRANSM.
 INTERNATIONAL SOCIETY FOR NEUROVEGETATIVE
 RESEARCH.
 VIENNA & NEW YORK 33, N 1972-
 ENGL., FR. & GER. PREV: JOURNAL OF NEURO-
 VISCERAL RELATIONS FROM 31, 1968- 32, 1972.
 LO/U-2.

JOURNAL OF NEURO-VISCERAL RELATIONS. XXX
++J. NEURO-VISC. RELAT.
[SPRINGER]
 VIENNA 31, 1968- 32, 1972 ...
 PREV: ACTA NEUROVEGETATIVA FROM 1, 1950- 30,
 1967. SUBS: JOURNAL OF NEURAL TRANSMISSION.
 S/T: A MULTIDISCIPLINARY JOURNAL FOR THE STUDY
 OF THE AUTONOMIC NERVOUS SYSTEM & OF NEURO-
 ENDOCRINOLOGY.
 LO/U-2. ISSN 0022-3026

JOURNAL, NEWARK BETH ISRAEL HOSPITAL. XXX
 SUBS (1969): JOURNAL, NEWARK BETH ISRAEL
 MEDICAL CENTER.

JOURNAL, NEWARK BETH ISRAEL MEDICAL CENTER. XXX
++*J. NEWARK BETH ISR. MED. CENT.*
NEWARK, N.J. 20(1), 1969-
Q. PREV: JOURNAL, NEWARK BETH ISRAEL HOSPITAL
FROM 1, JA 1950- 19, 1968.
BL/U-1. LO/U-1. ISSN 0028-8845

JOURNAL OF NORTHERN LUZON.
++*J. NORTH. LUZON.*
SAINT MARY'S COLLEGE, BAYOMBONG.
BAYOMBONG, NUEVA VIZCAYA 1, JL 1970-
S/T: A SEMI-ANNUAL RESEARCH FORUM.
LO/U14.

JOURNAL OF ORAL REHABILITATION.
++*J. ORAL REHABIL.*
[BLACKWELL]
OXFORD &C. 1, 1974-
CA/U-1. ED/N-1. LD/U-1. OX/U-8. ISSN 0305-182X

JOURNAL OF PEASANT STUDIES.
++*J. PEASANT STUD.*
[CASS]
LONDON 1(1), 1973-
AD/U-1. BN/U-1. CA/U-1. CA/U-3. ED/N-1. GL/U-1.
LO/S10. LO/U-3. LO/U14. MA/U-1. OX/U-1.
RE/U-1. SW/U-1. XS/U-1.

JOURNAL OF PERINATAL MEDICINE.
++*J. PERINATAL MED.*
[DE GRUYTER]
BERLIN &C. 1(1), 1973-
AD/U-1. BL/U-1. LO/N13. OX/U-8.

JOURNAL OF PHARMACOKINETICS & BIOPHARMACEUTICS.
++*J. PHARMACOKINET. & BIOPHARM.*
[PLENUM P.]
NEW YORK & LONDON 1, 1973-
LO/N13. CA/U-1. 2(2), 1974- ED/N-1. 2(2), 1974-

JOURNAL DE PHARMACOLOGIE CLINIQUE.
++*J. PHARM. CLIN.*
[EDIFOR]
PARIS 1, 1973-
LO/N13.

JOURNAL OF PLANNING & ENVIRONMENT LAW. XXX
++*J. PLANN. & ENVIRON. LAW.*
[SWEET & MAXWELL]
LONDON JA 1973
PREV: JOURNAL OF PLANNING & PROPERTY LAW FROM
JA 1954- D 1972.
ED/N-1. HL/U-1. LO/U-1. NW/U-1. RE/U-1.

JOURNAL OF PLANNING & PROPERTY LAW. XXX
SUBS (1973): JOURNAL OF PLANNING & ENVIRONMENT
LAW.

JOURNAL OF POLICE SCIENCE & ADMINISTRATION. XXX
++*J. POLICE SCI. & ADMIN.*
INTERNATIONAL ASSOCIATION OF CHIEFS OF POLICE.
GAITHERSBURG, MD. 1, MR 1973-
Q. PREV: PART OF JOURNAL OF CRIMINAL LAW,
CRIMINOLOGY & POLICE SCIENCE FROM 22, 1932-
63(4), 1973. SPONS. BODY ALSO: NORTHWESTERN
UNIVERSITY: SCHOOL OF LAW.
CA/U37. HL/U-1. MA/U-1. RE/U-1. SO/U-1.

JOURNAL, QUEENSLAND LAW SOCIETY.
++*J. QUEENSL. LAW SOC.*
BRISBANE 1, JL 1971-
Q. PREV. ISSUED AS THE QUEENSLAND SECTION OF
THE JOURNAL OF THE LAW INSTITUTE OF VICTORIA.
OX/U15.

**JOURNAL OF THE RADICAL ECONOMICS GROUP,
LONDON SCHOOL OF ECONOMICS.**
++*J. RADICAL ECON. GROUP LOND. SCH. ECON.*
LONDON SCHOOL OF ECONOMICS & POLITICAL SCIENCE:
RADICAL ECONOMICS DISCUSSION GROUP.
LONDON 1, 1974-
2/A.
LO/U-3.

JOURNAL OF REHABILITATION OF THE DEAF.
++*J. REHABIL. DEAF.*
PROFESSIONAL REHABILITATION WORKERS WITH THE
ADULT DEAF.
URBANA, ILL. 1, AP 1967-
Q.
MA/U-1. 7, 1973- ISSN 0022-4170

**JOURNAL, SAUDI ARABIAN NATURAL HISTORY
SOCIETY.** XXX
++*J. SAUDI ARABIAN NAT. HIST. SOC.*
JEDDAH 1(2), 1971-
PREV: REPORT, SAUDI ARABIAN NATURAL HISTORY
SOCIETY FROM 1(1), 1971.
LO/N-2.

JOURNAL, SOUTH AFRICAN VETERINARY ASSOCIATION.XX
++*J. SOUTH AFR. VET. ASSOC.*
PRETORIA 43, 1972-
AFR. & ENGL. PREV: JOURNAL, SOUTH AFRICAN
VETERINARY MEDICAL ASSOCIATION FROM 1, AG
1927- 42, 1971. AFR. TITLE: TYDSKRIF, SUID-
AFRIKAANSE VETERINERE VERENIGING.
LO/N13.

**JOURNAL, SOUTH AFRICAN VETERINARY MEDICAL
ASSOCIATION.** XXX
SUBS (1972): JOURNAL, SOUTH AFRICAN VETERIN-
ARY ASSOCIATION.

JOURNAL OF SPANISH STUDIES: TWENTIETH CENTURY.
++*J. SPAN. STUD., 20TH CENTURY.*
KANSAS STATE UNIVERSITY: DEPARTMENT OF
MODERN LANGUAGES.
MANHATTAN, KANS. 1(1), 1973-
3/A.
LO/U-2. 1(2), 1973-

JOURNAL OF SYMBOLIC ANTHROPOLOGY.
++*J. SYMB. ANTHROPOL.*
[MOUTON]
THE HAGUE 1, 1973-
CA/U-3. MA/U-1. SW/U-1.

JOURNAL OF TRANSPERSONAL PSYCHOLOGY.
++*J. TRANSPERS. PSYCHOL.*
TRANSPERSONAL ASSOCIATION.
PALO ALTO, CALIF 1, 1969-
2/A.
HL/U-1. 1973- ISSN 0022-524X

JOURNAL OF THE TREVITHICK SOCIETY.
++*J. TREVITHICK SOC.*
REDRUTH NO.1, 1973-
ANNU.
CA/U-1. ED/N-1. OX/U-1.

JOURNAL OF URBAN ECONOMICS.
++*J. URBAN ECON.*
LONDON 1, 1974-
Q.
CB/U-1. LO/U-3. SA/U-1.

JOURNAL OF WORLD HISTORY. XXX
SUBS (1973): CULTURES.

JOURNEYMAN BAKER: NS. XXX
SUBS (1969): BAKERY WORKER.

**JUSTINIEN. REVUE ANNUELLE DES INSTITUTIONS
JURIDIQUES DU QUEBEC.** XXX
UNIVERSITY OF OTTAWA: FACULTY OF LAW.
OTTAWA 1964- 1969.
Q. ISSUED IN THE FACULTY'S COLLECTION DES
TRAVAUX. SUBS: REVUE GENERALE DE DROIT.
OX/U15. ISSN 0449-4504

KALIKASAN. PHILIPPINE JOURNAL OF BIOLOGY.
UNIVERSITY OF THE PHILIPPINES: NATURAL SCIENCE
RESEARCH CENTER.
[KALIKASAN P.]
LAGUNA 1, 1972-
3/A. ENGL. & PHILLIP. WITH ENGL. SUMM.
LO/N-2.

**KANSAI UNIVERSITY REVIEW OF ECONOMICS &
BUSINESS.**
++*KANSAI UNIV. REV. ECON. & BUS.*
KANSAI DAIGAKU.
OSAKA 1(1), 1972-
LO/U-3.

KANSEN ENSHO MENEKI.
[IYAKU NO MON-SHA]
TOKYO 1[NO.]1, 1971-
ENGL. TITLE: INFECTION, INFLAMMATION & IMMUN-
ITY.
LO/N14.

KAZAKHSKAJA DIALEKTOLOGIJA.
+ +KAZ. DIALEKTOL.
AKADEMIJA NAUK KAZAKHSKOJ SSR: INSTITUT
JAZIKOZNANIJA.
ALMA-ATA 1, 1965-
KAZ. & RUSS.
OX/U-1.

KENTRON EPISTEMONIKON EREUMON. TEXTS & STUDIES
OF THE HISTORY OF CYPRUS.
NICOSIA 1, 1965-
SA/U-1. 4, 1973-   ISSN 0453-5197

KEY TO GEOPHYSICAL RECORDS DOCUMENTATION.
+ +KEY GEOPHYS. REC. DOC.
NATIONAL GEOPHYSICAL & SOLAR-TERRESTRIAL DATA
CENTER (US).
BOULDER, COLO. NO.1, 1972-
LO/N13.

KEY-WORD-INDEX OF WILDLIFE RESEARCH.
+ +KEY-WORD-INDEX WILDL. RES.
SWISS WILDLIFE INFORMATION SERVICE.
ZURICH 1, 1974-
ANNU.
LO/R-5.

KHRONIKA TEKUSHCHIKH SOBYTIJ.
+ +KHRON. TEKUSHCHIKH SOBYTIJ.
[POSSEV-VERLAG]
FRANKFURT AM MAIN 1, 1968(1969)-
NO.1-20 INCLUDED IN POSEV SPETSIAL'NYJ VYPUSK
1-9. PUBLISHED SEPARATELY FROM VYP. 21, 1972.
EX/U-1. GL/U-1. HL/U-1. LD/U-1.

KLIMA-KALTE-TECHNIK.   XXX
DEUTSCHER KALTETCHNISCHER VEREIN.
STUTTGART 15, 1973-
MON. PREV: KLIMA-TECHNIK FROM 1, 1959- 15,
1972.
LO/N13.

KLIMA-TECHNIK.   XXX
SUBS (1973): KLIMA-KALTE-TECHNIK.

KLIMATIZACIJA, GREJANJE, HLADENJE.
+ +KLIM. GREJANJE HLADENJE.
SAVEZ MASINSKIH I ELEKTROTEHNICIH INZENJERA I
TEHNICARA SRBIJE: DRUSTVO ZA GREJANJE, HLADENJE
I KLIMATIZACIJU.
BELGRADE 1(1), 1972-
XS/T10.

KNITTING INTERNATIONAL.   XXX
+ +KNITT. INT.
LEICESTER 81(961), 1974-
PREV: HOSIERY TRADE JOURNAL FROM 17(193),
1910- 80(960), 1973.
LO/N14.

KNIZNICE A VEDECKE INFORMACIE.
+ +KNIZNICE VED. INF.
MATICA SLOVENSKA V MARTINE.
TURCIANSKY SV. MARTIN 1(1), 1969-
CZECH. OR SLOVAK.
OX/U-1.

KODAK COLOUR LAB NOTES.
KODAK LTD.
[HEMEL HEMPSTEAD] NO.1, 1973-
ED/N-1. OX/U-1.

KONTROL I TEKHNOLOGIJA PROTSESSOV OBOGASH-
CHENIJA POLEZNYKH ISKOPAEMYKH.
+ +KONTROL & TEKHNOL. PROTSESSOV OBOGASHCH.
POLEZN. ISKOP.
UKRAINSKIJ ZAOCHNYJ POLITEKHNICHESKIJ INSTITUT.
MOSCOW 1, 1971-
LO/N13.

KOREA JOURNAL.
+ +KOREA J.
KOREAN NATIONAL COMMISSION FOR UNESCO.
SEOUL 1, S 1961-
MON.
LO/S74. **   ED/N-1. 12(4), 1972-   SH/U-1. 8, 1968-

KOSMICHESKAJA BIOLOGIJA I AVIAKOSMICHESKAJA
MEDITSINA.   XXX
+ +KOSM. BIOL. & AVIAKOSM. MED.
(RUSSIA SSSR) MINISTERSTVO ZDRAVOOKHRANENIJA.
MOSCOW 8, 1974-
PREV: KOSMICHESKAJA BIOLOGIJA I MEDITSINA FROM
1, 1967- 7, 1973. CONTINUES PREV. NUMBERING.
LO/N13. OX/U-8.

KOTSU ANZEN KOGAI KENKYUJO HOKOKU.
TOKYO NO.1, 1973-
LO/N13.

KOZPONTI ELELMISZERIPARI KUTATO INTEZET   XXX
KOZLEMENYEI.
SUBS (1967): ELELMISZERTUDOMANY.

KRKONOSE, PODKRKONOSI.
MUZEUM TRUTNOV.
HRADEC KRALOVE 1, 1963-
GER. SUMM. S/T: VLASTIVEDNY SBORNIK MUZEUM
TRUTNOV.
OX/U-1.

K.S.U. ECONOMIC & BUSINESS REVIEW.
+ +K.S.U. ECON. & BUS. REV.
KYOTO SANGYO UNIVERSITY: SOCIETY OF ECONOMICS
& BUSINESS ADMINISTRATION.
KYOTO 1, 1974-
BL/U-1.   OX/U-1.

KULFOLDI MAGYAR NYELVU FOLYOIRATOK REPERT-
ORIUMA.
+ +KULFOLDI MAGY. NYELVU FOLY. REPERT.
ORSZAGOS SZECHENY1 KONYVTAR.
BUDAPEST 1, JA/JE 1972-
Q.
CA/U-1. 1(3), 1972-

KVANTOVAJA ELEKTRONIKA (KIEV).
+ +KVANTOVAJA ELEKTRON.
AKADEMIJA NAUK UKRAJINS'KOJI RSR: INSTITUT
POLUPROVODNIKOV.
KIEV [1], 1966-
S/T: TRUDY RESPUBLIKANSKOGO SEMINARA PO
KVANTOVOJ ELEKTRONIKE. VOL.1 IS UNNUMBERED.
LO/N13. 3, 1969-

KVANTOVAJA ELEKTRONIKA: SBORNIK STATEJ (MOSKVA).
+ +KVANTOVAJA ELEKTRON., SB. STATEJ (MOSK.).
MOSCOW 1(1), 1971-
LO/N13.

LABORATORY WEEKLY.   XXX
+ +LAB. WKLY.
[MILTON PUBL. CO. LTD.]
LONDON NO.1, 4/OC 1973-
PREV: LAB FROM 1(1), S/OC 1971- 3(15), MY/JE
1973.
OX/U-8. ED/N-1. NO.3, 1973-

LAND (OXFORD).
OXFORD UNIVERSITY FORESTRY SOCIETY.
OXFORD 1, 1974-
LO/R-5. ISSN 0305-5116

LANDMASCHINEN-MARKT.   XXX
SUBS (1974): AGRARTECHNIK INTERNATIONAL.

LANDS TRIBUNAL CASES.
+ +LANDS TRIB. CASES.
[BARRY ROSE]
CHICHESTER 1, 1974-
RE/U-1.

LATIN AMERICAN LITERARY REVIEW.
+ +LAT. AM. LIT. REV.
CARNEGIE-MELLON UNIVERSITY: DEPARTMENT OF MOD-
ERN LANGUAGES.
PITTSBURGH 1, 1972-
2/A.
NO/U-1. LO/U-2. 2(3), 1973-   ISSN 0047-4134

LATIN AMERICAN PERSPECTIVES.
+ +LAT. AM. PERSPECT.
RIVERSIDE, CALIF. 1, 1974-
3/A. S/T: A JOURNAL ON CAPITALISM &
SOCIALISM.
OX/U-1.

LATIN AMERICAN YEARLY REVIEW.
+ +LAT. AM. YRLY. REV.
PARIS 1, 1973-
OX/U-1.

LAW BOOK GUIDE.
[LAW BOOK GUIDE LTD.]
NEW YORK 1, 1973-
10/A. SUBSERIES OF COMPUTEXT BIBLIOGRAPHY
SERIES.
SH/U-1. ISSN 0000-0353

LAW TEACHER.   XXX
ASSOCIATION OF LAW TEACHERS.
[SWEET & MAXWELL]
LONDON 5, 1971-
PREV: JOURNAL OF THE ASSOCIATION OF LAW TEACH-
ERS FROM 1, 1967- 4, 1970.
DB/U-2.   LO/U24.   SO/U-1.

**LEAFLET, PHYSICAL EDUCATION ASSOCIATION OF
GREAT BRITAIN & NORTHERN IRELAND.**   XXX
**SUBS (1970) PART OF: BRITISH JOURNAL OF
PHYSICAL EDUCATION.**

LECTURE NOTES IN COMPUTER SCIENCE.
++LECT. NOTES COMPUT. SCI.
[SPRINGER-VERLAG]
BERLIN &C. NO.1, 1973-
ENGL. OR GER.
LO/N14.   MA/U-1.

**LECTURES, HAROLD L. LYON ARBORETUM, UNIVER-
SITY OF HAWAII.**
++LECT. HAROLD L. LYON ARBOR. UNIV. HAWAII.
HONOLULU NO.1, 1970-
ANNU.
LO/N-2.

**LEG NEWS. NEWSLETTER OF THE LIBRARY EDUCATION
GROUP OF THE LIBRARY ASSOCIATION.**
LONDON NO.1, OC 1972-
BL/U-1. NO.2, 1973-   CA/U-1. NO.4, 1973-

**LEGAL DEPOSIT ACCESSIONS, LIBRARY, UNIVERSITY
OF THE SOUTH PACIFIC.**
++LEG. DEPOSIT ACCESS. LIBR. UNIV. SOUTH PAC.
SUVA 1, 1972-
LO/U14.   OX/U-1.

LEKTSII PO ISTORII KPSS.
++LEKTSII ISTOR. KPSS.
AKADEMIJA OBSHCHESTVENNYKH NAUK PRI TSK KPSS:
KAFEDRA ISTORII KPSS.
MOSCOW 1961/1962(1963)-
LO/U15.   OX/U-1.

LEOPARD. THE GRAMPIAN MAGAZINE.
[LEOPARD PUBL. LTD.]
ABERDEEN NO.1, AG 1974-
NO.1 ENTITLED: ABERDEEN LEOPARD.
AD/U-1.   ED/N-1.

LESNICKE STUDIE.
++LESN. STUD.
VYSKUMNY USTAV LESNEHO HOSPODARSTVA.
ZVOLEN 1, 1969-
ENGL., FR., GER. & RUSS. SUMM.
OX/U-3.

LESOVODSTVO, LESNYE KUL'TURY I POCHVOVEDENIE.
++LESOVOD. LESN. KUL'T. & POCHVOVED.
LENINGRADSKIJ GOSUDARSTVENNYJ UNIVERSITET.
LENINGRAD 1, 1973-
SPONS. BODY ALSO: MINISTERSTVO VYSSHEGO
I SREDNEGO SPETSIAL'NOGO OBRAZOVANIJA.
LO/N13.

LEY HUNTER.
HARTLEPOOL NO.1, N 1969-
ED/N-1. NO.27, 1972-   OX/U-1. NO.27, 1972-

LIBERACION Y DERECHO.
UNIVERSIDAD NACIONAL Y POPULAR DE BUENOS AIRES:
FACULTAD DE DERECHO Y CIENCIAS SOCIALES.
BUENOS AIRES 1, 1974-
3/A.
LO/U-3.

LIBERATION STRUGGLE.
++LIBERAT. STRUGGLE.
CENTRE FOR WRITERS & JOURNALISTS FROM THE
EXPLOITED WORLD.
LONDON NO.1, JA 1972-
ED/N-1. 3/4, 1972-   LO/U-8. 9/10, 1972-

**LIBERATOR. A NEWSPAPER OF THE YOUNG LIBERAL
MOVEMENT.**
[LIBERATOR PUBL.]
LONDON S 1970-
MON.
CA/U-1. 1974-   ED/N-1. 1974-   LO/U-3. S 1971-*

LIBRARY OF ANALYTICAL PSYCHOLOGY.
++LIBR. ANAL. PSYCHOL.
SOCIETY OF ANALYTICAL PSYCHOLOGY.
[WILLIAM HEINEMANN MEDICAL BOOKS]
LONDON 1, 1973-
SELECTED ARTICLES FROM THE JOURNAL OF ANALYT-
ICAL PSYCHOLOGY.
CA/U-1.   LO/N-1.

**LIBRARY INFORMATION SERIES, DEPARTMENT OF
EDUCATION & SCIENCE (GB).**
++LIBR. INF. SER. DEP. EDUC. & SCI (GB).
LONDON NO.1, 1972-
MONOGR.
CA/U-1.   ISSN 0306-4387

LIETUVOS ISTORIJOS METRASTIS.
++LIET. ISTOR. METRASTIS.
LIETUVOS TSR MOKSLU AKADEMIJA: ISTORIJOS
INSTITUTAS.
VILNIUS 1971-
RUSS. SUMM.
OX/U-1.   CA/U-1. 1972-

LIFE UNDERWRITERS NEWS.   XXX
SUBS (1971): FORUM (DON MILLS, ONT.).

LINCOLNSHIRE INDUSTRIAL ARCHAEOLOGY.   XXX
++LINCS. IND. ARCHAEOL.
LINCOLNSHIRE LOCAL HISTORY SOCIETY:
INDUSTRIAL ARCHAEOLOGY GROUP.
LINCOLN 4, 1969-
PREV: NEWSLETTER, INDUSTRIAL ARCHAEOLOGY
GROUP, LINCOLNSHIRE LOCAL HISTORY SOCIETY
FROM 1, 1966- 3, 1968.
NO/U-1.   CA/U-1. 8, 1973-

LINGUIST.   XXX
SUBS (1973): NEW LINGUIST.

LINGUISTICA (TARTU).
TARTU R11KLIK ULIKOOL.
TARTU, EST. 1, 1969-
ENGL., EST. OR GER. EDITED BY THE FOREIGN
LANGUAGES DEPARTMENTS OF THE UNIVERSITY.
SA/U-1. 3, 1971-

LINGUISTISCHE ARBEITEN.
++LINGUIST. ARB.
TUBINGEN 1, 1973-
OX/U-1.

LINGUISTISCHE REIHE.
++LINGUIST. REIHE.
[MAX HUEBER VERLAG]
MUNCHEN 1, 1970-
LO/N-1.

LINK. COMMUNIST PARTY WOMEN'S JOURNAL.
COMMUNIST PARTY OF GREAT BRITAIN.
LONDON NO.1, SPRING 1973-
Q.
LO/U-3.

LINKS. SOZIALISTISCHE ZEITUNG.
[VERLAG 2000 GMBH]
OFFENBACH NO.1, 1969-
MON.
LO/U-3. NO.27, N 1971- ‡W. NO.30 & 34A   ISSN 0024-404X

LITERACY DOCUMENTATION.
++LITERACY DOC.
INTERNATIONAL INSTITUTE FOR ADULT LITERACY
METHODS.
TEHRAN 1, 1972-
S/T: AN INTERNATIONAL BULLETIN FOR LIBRARIES &
INFORMATION CENTRES.
ED/N-1.   ISSN 0047-4789

LITERARY SUPPLEMENT.
++LIT. SUPPL.
[NOTHING DOING]
LONDON NO.1, 8/S 1972-
CA/U-1.   ED/N-1.   OX/U-1.

LITERATURA STRAN AFRIKI.
++LIT. STRAN AFR.
AKADEMIJA NAUK SSSR: INSTITUT AFRIKI.
MOSCOW 1, 1964-
OX/U-1.

LITTERATURE CHINOISE.   000
SEE: CHINESE LITERATURE.

LITTERATURE POLONAISE.   000
SEE: POLISH LITERATURE.

LLOYD'S MARITIME & COMMERCIAL LAW QUARTERLY.
+ +*LLOYD'S MAR. & COMMER. LAW Q.*
[LLOYD'S OF LONDON P. LTD.]
LONDON [NO.1], MY 1974-
CA/U-1.   CA/U13.   CB/U-1.   ED/N-1.   HL/U-1.   LO/U12.

LOCAL GOVERNMENT COMPANION.
+ +*LOCAL GOV. COMPANION.*
[PARLIAMENTARY RESEARCH SERVICES]
CHICHESTER, SUSSEX NO.1, 1974-
2/A.
SO/U-1.   NO/U-1. 2, 1974-   ISSN 0305-0130

LOCAL GOVERNMENT FINANCE.   XXX
SUBS (1973): PUBLIC FINANCE & ACCOUNTANCY.

LOCAL GOVERNMENT TRENDS.
+ +*LOCAL GOV. TRENDS.*
CHARTERED INSTITUTE OF PUBLIC FINANCE
& ACCOUNTANCY.
LONDON 1973-
ANNU.
CA/U-1.   LO/U-3.   SO/U-1.

**LOCAL INFORMATION PAPER, DEPARTMENT OF
GEOGRAPHY & GEOLOGY, HUDDERSFIELD POLYTECHNIC.**
+ +*LOCAL INF. PAP. DEP. GEOGR. & GEOL. HUDDERS-
HUDDERSFIELD 1, 1973-*
CA/U-1.   ISSN 0306-1558

LONDON DRAMA.   XXX
+ +*LOND. DRAMA.*
[STACY]
BROMLEY 5(1), JL 1973-
2/A. PREV: BROADSHEET.
CA/U-1.   ED/N-1.   OX/U-1.

**LONG ROOM. BULLETIN OF THE FRIENDS OF THE
LIBRARY, TRINITY COLLEGE, DUBLIN.**   XXX
DUBLIN NO.1, 1970-
PREV: ANNUAL BULLETIN OF THE FRIENDS OF THE
LIBRARY OF TRINITY COLLEGE, DUBLIN FROM 1946-
1958.
BL/U-1.   DB/S-1.   ED/N-1.   LD/U-1.   LO/U-1.

LUGHA.
KENYA LANGUAGE ASSOCIATION.
NAIROBI 1(1), 1969-
LO/U14. 1(1), 1969; 1(2), 1971.

LUGHA YETU.
(TANZANIA) MINISTRY OF NATIONAL EDUCATION.
DAR ES DALAAM 1(1), MR 1969-
6/A. SWAHILI.
LO/U14. 1969- 1971.*   ISSN 0047-5165

MAATSKAPLIKE WERK.   000
SEE: SOCIAL WORK. MAATSKAPLIKE WERK.

MAINTENANCE MANAGEMENT.   XXX
+ +*MAINT. MANAGE.*
MAINTENANCE ADVISORY SERVICE.
[A.E. MORGAN PUBL. LTD.]
EPSOM, SURREY 12(1), JA 1974-
MON. PREV: MAINTENANCE FROM 5(7), 1967-
11(12), D 1973. S/T: THE MAINTENANCE, SERVIC-
ING & CLEANING OF THE FABRIC & CONTENTS OF
INDUSTRIAL, COMMERCIAL & PUBLIC BUILDINGS.
BL/U-1.   ED/N-1.   LO/N14. CURRENT BOX ONLY.

MAKEDONSKI ARHIVIST.
+ +*MAKEDON. ARH.*
DRUSTVO NA ARHIVSKITE RABOTNICI I ARHIVITE
VO SR MAKEDONIJA.
SKOPJE 1, 1972-
OX/U-1.

MAKER-UP.   XXX
SUBS (1967): MAKER-UP OF WOMEN'S & GIRLS'
CLOTHING.

MAKER-UP OF WOMEN'S & GIRLS' CLOTHING.   XXX
+ +*MAKER-UP WOMEN'S & GIRLS' CLOTH.*
[UNITED TRADE P.]
LONDON 57, 1967- 67, 1972 ...
PREV: MAKER-UP FROM 1, 1939- 56, 1967. SUBS:
MAKER-UP & WOMEN'S WEAR MANUFACTURER.
LO/N14.

MAKER-UP & WOMEN'S WEAR MANUFACTURER.   XXX
+ +*MAKER-UP & WOMEN'S WEAR MANUF.*
[UNITED TRADE P.]
LONDON 68, 1973-
PREV: MAKER-UP OF WOMEN'S & GIRLS' CLOTHING
FROM 57, 1967- 67, 1972.
LO/N14.

MAKTABA.
KENYA LIBRARY ASSOCIATION.
NAIROBI 1(1), 1974-
OX/U-1.

MALTESE NATURALIST.
+ +*MALTESE NAT.*
SLIEMA NO.1, 1970-
LO/N-2.

MAN-MADE TEXTILES IN INDIA.   XXX
+ +*MAN-MADE TEXT. INDIA.*
SILK & ART SILK MILLS' RESEARCH ASSOCIATION.
BOMBAY 16(8), 1973-
PREV: SILK & RAYON INDUSTRIES OF INDIA FROM 1,
1958- 16(6/7), 1972.
LO/N13.

MAN IN THE NORTHEAST.
FRANKLIN PIERCE COLLEGE: ANTHROPOLOGICAL RES-
EARCH CENTER OF NORTHERN NEW ENGLAND.
RINDGE, N.H. NO.1, MR 1971-
LO/S10.

**MANAGEMENT CONSULTANT. JOURNAL OF THE INST-
ITUTE OF MANAGEMENT CONSULTANTS.**
+ +*MANAGE. CONSULT.*
LONDON NO.1, MR 1974-
Q.
ED/N-1.

MANAGEMENT REVIEW & DIGEST.
+ +*MANAGE. REV. & DIG.*
BRITISH INSTITUTE OF MANAGEMENT.
LONDON 1(1), 1974-
INCORP: MANAGEMENT ABSTRACTS.
ED/N-1.   LO/R-5.   LO/S-1.   MA/P-1.   OX/U-1.   SH/P-1.
XS/U-1.

MANJAK.
BLACK ROCK, BARBADOS NO.1, 11/N 1973-
LO/U-8.

MANNA. A REVIEW OF CONTEMPORARY POETRY.
OTTAWA NO.1, MR 1972-
2/A.
LO/N-1.

**MANTATOPHOROS. BULLETIN OF MODERN GREEK
STUDIES.**
UNIVERSITY OF BIRMINGHAM: DEPARTMENT OF GREEK.
BIRMINGHAM NO.1, N 1972-
CA/U-1. NO.2, 1973-   ED/N-1. NO.2, 1973-

MANTEIA.
MARSEILLE NO.1, 1967-
Q.
LO/U-2. NO.1, 1967.   ISSN 0025-2492

MAP BULLETIN, GEOLOGICAL SURVEY (MALAYSIA).
+ +*MAP BULL. GEOL. SURV. (MALAYSIA).*
(MALAYSIA) MINISTRY OF LANDS & MINES: GEOL-
OGICAL SURVEY.
IPOH 1, 1970-
SA/U-1.

MARDI RESEARCH BULLETIN.
+ +*MARDI RES. BULL.*
MALAYSIAN AGRICULTURAL RESEARCH & DEVELOPMENT
INSTITUTE.
SELANGOR, WEST MALAYSIA 1(1), 1973-
LO/R-6.

MARINE POLLUTION RESEARCH TITLES.
+ +*MAR. POLLUT. RES. TITLES.*
MARINE BIOLOGICAL ASSOCIATION OF THE UNITED
KINGDOM.
PLYMOUTH 1(1), AG 1974-
WKLY.
LO/N-2.   LO/R-5.   XS/R10.

MARINE WEEK.   XXX
+ +*MAR. WEEK.*
[IPC INDUSTRIAL P.]
LONDON 1(1), 5/AP 1974-
WKLY. INCORP: SHIPBUILDING & SHIPPING RECORD
FROM 1, 3/AP 1913- 123, 1974.
ED/N-1.   GL/U-1.   LO/N14.   OX/U-1.   ISSN 0306-347X

MASKE UND KOTHURN: BEIHEFT.
UNIVERSITAT WIEN: INSTITUT FUR THEATERWISSEN-
SCHAFT.
VIENNA NO.1, 1970-
S/T: VIERTELJAHRESSCHRIFT FUR THEATERWISSEN-
SCHAFT.
GL/U-1.

MATEMATICHESKIE METODY RESHENIJA EKONOMICHESKIKH ZADACH.
++MAT. METODY RESHENIJA EKON. ZADACH.
AKADEMIJA NAUK SSSR: TSENTRAL'NYJ
EKONOMIKO- MATEMATICHESKIJ INSTITUT.
MOSCOW 1, 1969-
CC/U-1.

MATEMATIKA V SHKOLE.
++MAT. SHK.
(RUSSIA RSFSR) MINISTERSTVO PROSVESHCHENIJA.
MOSCOW 1, JA 1963-
SW/U-1. 1964 (3).

MATERIALEN ZU METRIK UND STILISTIK.
++MATER. METRIK & STILISTIK.
TUBINGEN 1, 1973-
OX/U-1.

MATERIALS PERFORMANCE.   XXX
++MATER. PERFORM.
NATIONAL ASSOCIATION OF CORROSION ENGINEERS.
HOUSTON, TEX. 13, 1974-
PREV: MATERIALS PROTECTION & PERFORMANCE FROM
9(7), 1970- 12, 1973.
GL/U-2. LO/N14. LO/S-3. SF/U-1. SH/P-1. XS/R10.

MATICNE CITANIE.
MATICA SLOVENSKA V MARTINE.
TURCIANSKY SV. MARTIN 1, OC 1968-
LA/U-1. OX/U-1.

MAURI ORA.
UNIVERSITY OF CANTERBURY: BIOLOGICAL SOCIETY.
CHRISTCHURCH, N.Z. 1, 1973-
LO/N-2. OX/U-8.

MAZDA LIGHT.
A.E.I. LAMP & LIGHTING., LTD.
LEICESTER NO.1, 1966-
LO/N14.

MCILVAINEA.
NORTH AMERICAN MYCOLOGICAL ASSOCIATION.
PORTSMOUTH, OHIO 1, 1972-
LO/N13.

ME JUDICE.   XXX
SUBS (1969): PART OF SINGAPORE LAW REVIEW.

MEASUREMENT FOCUS. BRITISH CALIBRATION SERVICE NEWSLETTER.
++MEAS. FOCUS.
LONDON NO.1, SPRING 1974-
3/A.
CA/U-1. ED/N-1. OX/U-8.

MEDIEVAL MONOGRAPH SERIES, UNIVERSITY OF YORK.
++MEDIEVAL MONOGR. SER. UNIV. YORK.
UNIVERSITY OF YORK: CENTRE FOR MEDIEVAL STUDIES
YORK [NO.]1, 1972-
CA/U-1.

MEDIAEVALIA BOHEMICA.
++MEDIAEVALIA BOHEM.
CESKOSLOVENSKA AKADEMIE VED: HISTORICKY USTAV.
PRAGUE 1, 1969-
BH/U-1. OX/U-1.

MEDIAEVALIA LOVANIENSIA: SERIES 1: STUDIA.
++MEDIAEVALIA LOUV., 1.
UNIVERSITE CATHOLIQUE DE LOUVAIN: INSTITUT
INTERFACULTE D'ETUDES MEDIEVALES.
LOUVAIN &C. 1, 1972-
OX/U-1.

MEDICAL INSTRUMENTATION JOURNAL.   XXX
++MED. INSTRUM. J.
ASSOCIATION FOR THE ADVANCEMENT OF MEDICAL
INSTRUMENTATION.
ARLINGTON, VA. 7, JA/F 1973-
PREV: JOURNAL, ASSOCIATION FOR THE ADVANCE-
MENT OF MEDICAL INSTRUMENTATION FROM 1, JL/AG
1966- 6, 1972.
OX/U-8.

MEDICAL JOURNAL OF AUSTRALIA: SPECIAL SUPPLE-MENT.
++MED. J. AUST., SPEC. SUPPL.
[AUSTRALIAN MEDICAL PUBL. CO.]
GLEBE 1, 1973-
BL/U-1.

MEDICAL UNION REVIEW.
++MED. UNION REV.
MEDICAL UNION.
[UNIVERSAL PUBL. CO.]
DUBLIN 1(1), JE 1972-
ED/N-1.

MEDICAL WEEK.
++MED. WEEK.
[UPDATE PUBL. LTD.]
LONDON NO.1, F 1974-
CA/U-1. ISSN 0305-0114

MEDITSINSKI PROBLEMI.   XXX
++MED. PROBL.
VISSH MEDITSINSKI INSTITUT (PLOVDIV).
PLOVDIV 19, 1967-
PREV: SBORNIK TRUDOVE NA VISSHIJA MEDIT-
SINSKI INSTITUT (PLOVDIV) FROM 8, 1956-
18, 1964. NOT PUBL. IN 1965 & 1966.
GL/U-1.

MEDIZIN UND ERNAHRUNG.   XXX
++MED. & ERNAHR.
[GEORG THIEME VERLAG]
STUTTGART 1, OC 1959- 13, 1972.//
MON.
LO/N13. ISSN 0025-8407

MEMO - MIDDLE EAST MONEY.
LONDON 1(1), 19/JE 1974-
S/T: A WEEKLY BULLETIN OF NEWS & EXPERT VIEWS
FROM THE OIL STATES.
ED/N-1.

MEMOIRS, CANADIAN SOCIETY OF PETROLEUM GEOL-OGISTS.
++MEM. CAN. SOC. PET. GEOL.
CALGARY NO.1, 1973-
LO/N-2. OX/U-8.

MEMOIRS, ECOLOGICAL SOCIETY OF AUSTRALIA.
++MEM. ECOL. SOC. AUST.
CANBERRA 1, 1973-
GL/U-1. LO/N-2. LO/N13.

MEMOIRS, PACIFIC TROPICAL BOTANICAL GARDENS.
++MEM. PAC. TROP. BOT. GARD.
LAWAI, HAWAII NO.1, 1973-
LO/N-2.

MEMOIRES DE PHOTO-INTERPRETATION.
++MEM. PHOTO INTERPRET.
ECOLE PRATIQUE DES HAUTES ETUDES (PARIS):
SECTION DES SCIENCES ECONOMIQUES ET SOCIALES.
PARIS NO.1, 1963-
LO/N-1. ISSN 0076-6364

MEMOIRS, SHIRLEY INSTITUTE.   XXX
++MEM. SHIRLEY INST.
MANCHESTER 1, 1922- 42, 1969/70.//
LO/N14.

MENCKENIANA.
ENOCH PRATT FREE LIBRARY.
BALTIMORE NO.1, 1962-
Q.
CA/U-1. 40, 1971- ISSN 0025-9233

MERIDIAN. POETRY MAGAZINE.
[RONDO PUBL.]
LIVERPOOL 1, 1973-
CA/U-1. ED/N-1. MA/U-1. OX/U-1. ISSN 0306-3461

MEROITIC NEWSLETTER. BULLETIN D'INFORMATIONS MEROITIQUES.
++MEROITIC NEWSL.
CENTRE DE RECHERCHES EGYPTOLOGIQUES (PARIS).
PARIS NO.1, 1968-
LO/U-2. OX/U-2.

MEROITICA.
BERLIN 1, 1973-
CA/U-1. OX/U-1.

MESOPOTAMIA AGRICULTURE.   XXX
++MESOPOTAMIA AGRIC.
UNIVERSITY OF MOSUL: FACULTY OF AGRICULTURE &
VETERINARY SCIENCE.
MOSUL 3, 1968- 4, 1969 ...
PREV: MESOPOTAMIA. JOURNAL OF AGRICULTURE &
FORESTRY RESEARCH FROM 1(1), JE 1966- 2, 1967.
SUBS: MESOPOTAMIA JOURNAL OF AGRICULTURE.
LO/N-2. ISSN 0543-5501

MESOPOTAMIA JOURNAL OF AGRICULTURE.   XXX
++MESOPOTAMIA J. AGRIC.
MOSUL 5, 1970-
PREV: MESOPOTAMIA AGRICULTURE FROM 3, 1968-
4, 1969.
LO/N-2.

METAL SCIENCE.   XXX
++MET. SCI.
METALS SOCIETY.
LONDON 8, 1974-
PREV: METAL SCIENCE JOURNAL FROM 1, 1967- 7,
1973.
ED/N-1.   LO/N14.   LO/U-2.   LO/U12.   ISSN 0306-3453

METALS TECHNOLOGY.   XXX
++MET. TECHNOL.
METALS SOCIETY.
LONDON 1(1), JA 1974-
MON. PREV. PART OF: JOURNAL OF THE INSTITUTE
OF METALS FROM 1, 1909- 101, 1973; & JOURNAL
OF THE IRON & STEEL INSTITUTE FROM 1, 1871-
211, D 1973.
AD/U-1.   CA/U-1.   CA/U-2.   GL/U-2.   LO/N14.   LO/U-2.
OX/U-8.   SF/U-1.   SO/U-1.

METHODS IN CELL BIOLOGY.   XXX
++METHODS CELL BIOL.
[ACADEMIC P.]
NEW YORK; LONDON 6, 1973-
PREV: METHODS IN CELL PHYSIOLOGY FROM 1, 1964-
5, 1972.
LO/N13.   SO/U-1.

METHODS IN INVESTIGATIVE & DIAGNOSTIC ENDO-
CRINOLOGY.
++METHODS INVEST. & DIAGN. ENDCRINOL.
[NORTH-HOLLAND]
AMSTERDAM & LONDON 1, 1972-
DB/U-2.   GL/U-1.

METHODS IN MEMBRANE BIOLOGY.
++METHODS MEMBR. BIOL.
[PLENUM P.]
NEW YORK 1, 1974-
LO/U-2.

METODICHESKIE UKAZANIJA PO GEOLOGICHESKOJ
SŁEMKE MASSHTABA 1: 50000.
++METOD. UKAZANIJA GEOL. SŁEMKE MASSHTABA 1:
50000.
VSESOJUZNYJ NAUCHNO-ISSLEDOVATEL'SKIJ GEOLOGI-
CHESKIJ INSTITUT (VSEGEI).
LENINGRAD 1, 1969-
LO/N-4.

METODOLOGICZESKIE VOPROSY OBSHCHESTVENNYKH
NAUK.
++METODOL. VOPR. OBSHCHESTV.
LENINGRADSKIJ GOSUDARSTVENNYJ UNIVERSITET.
LENINGRAD [1] 1968-
OX/U-1.   2, 1971-

MEZHDUNARODNI OTNOSHENIJA.
++MEZHDUNAR. OTNOSHENIJA.
INSTITUT ZA VUNSHNA POLITIKA IVAN BASHEV.
SOFIA 1, 1972-
OX/U-1.

MICROBIOLOGIA, PARAZITOLOGIA, EPIDEMIOLOGIA.   XXX
SUBS (1974): BACTERIOLOGIA, VIRUSOLOGIA,
PARAZITOLOGIA, EPIDEMIOLOGIA.

MIDDLE EAST.
LONDON NO.1, MY/JE 1974-
CA/U-1.   ED/N-1.   ISSN 0305-0734

MIDWEST JOURNAL OF POLITICAL SCIENCE.   XXX
SUBS (1973): AMERICAN JOURNAL OF POLITICAL
SCIENCE.

MIKROELEKTRONIKA. SBORNIK STATEJ.
[SOVETSKOE RADIO]
MOSCOW 1, 1967-
LO/N13.

MILITANT INTERNATIONAL REVIEW.
++MILITANT INT. REV.
[CAMBRIDGE HEATH P.]
LONDON NO.1, AUTUMN 1969-
LO/U-3.   HL/U-1.   NO.7, 1973-

MIMS MAGAZINE.
++MIMS MAG.
[HAYMARKET PUBL.]
LONDON NO.1, JA 1974-
MON.
CA/U-1.   ED/N-1.   OX/U-8.

MINUIT. REVUE PERIODIQUE.
PARIS NO.1, N 1972-
2M.
ED/N-1.   LO/U12.   NO.7, 1974-

MISCELANEA DE TEXTOS MEDIEVALES.
++MISC. TEXTOS MEDIEVALES.
BARCELONA 1, 1972-
AD/U-1.   EX/U-1.   OX/U-1.

MISCELLANEOUS PUBLICATION, COMMONWEALTH INST-
ITUTE OF BIOLOGICAL CONTROL.
++MISC. PUBL. COMMONW. INST. BIOL. CONTROL.
FARNHAM ROYAL NO.1, 1970-
CA/U11.   LO/N-2.   CA/U-1.   3, 1972-   ISSN 0305-3008

MISSIOLOGY. AN INTERNATIONAL REVIEW.   XXX
AMERICAN SOCIETY OF MISSIOLOGY.
SOUTH PASADENA, CALIF. 1, JA 1973-
Q. PREV: PRACTICAL ANTHROPOLOGY FROM 1, JA/F
1953- 19(6), 1972.
AD/U-1.   LO/S10.   MA/U-1.   OX/U-1.

MISSISSIPPI FOLKLORE REGISTER.
++MISS. FOLKLORE REGIST.
MISSISSIPPI FOLKLORE SOCIETY.
HATTIESBURG 1, 1967-
SH/U-1.   7, 1973-   ISSN 0026-6248

MITTEILUNGEN DER BERLINER GESELLSCHAFT FUR
ANTHROPOLOGIE, ETHNOLOGIE UND URGESCHICHTE.
++MITT. BERL. GES. ANTHROPOL. ETHNOL. & URGESCH.
BERLIN 1, 1965-
LO/S10.

MITTEILUNGEN, INSTITUT FUR ORIENTFORSCHUNG,
DEUTSCHE AKADEMIE DER WISSENSCHAFTEN ZU
BERLIN.   XXX
++MITT. INST. ORIENTFORSCH. DTSCH. AKAD. WISS.
BERL.
BERLIN 1, 1953- 17, 1971.//
BH/U-1.   CA/U-1.   OX/U-1.   ISSN 0020-2304

MODEL SHIPWRIGHT.
LONDON 1(1), 1972-
CR/N-1.   LO/N-4.   OX/U-1.   ED/N-1.   1(3), 1973-

MODERN TRAMWAY & RAPID TRANSIT REVIEW.   XXX
++MOD. TRAMWAY & RAPID TRANSIT REV.
LIGHT RAILWAY TRANSPORT LEAGUE.
[IAN ALLAN]
SHEPPERTON 37(433), 1974-
PREV: MODERN TRAMWAY & LIGHT RAILWAY REVIEW
FROM 25(289), 1962- 36(432), 1973.
LO/N14.

MODERN WOOD.   XXX
SUBS (1973): TREATED WOOD PERSPECTIVES.

MOLECULAR & CELLULAR ENDOCRINOLOGY.
[NORTH-HOLLAND]
AMSTERDAM 1, 1974-
2M.
BH/U-3.   LO/N13.   LO/U-2.   SH/U-1.

MOLECULAR SIEVE ABSTRACTS.
++MOL. SIEVE ABSTR.
UNION CARBIDE CORPORATION.
NEW YORK 1, 1971-
2/A.
LO/N13.   ISSN 0047-7826

MOLECULAR STRUCTURE BY DIFFRACTION METHODS.
++MOL. STRUCT. DIFFR. METHODS.
CHEMICAL SOCIETY.
LONDON 1, 1973-
BH/U-3.   ED/N-1.   GL/U-2.   HL/U-1.   LO/S-3.   LO/U12.
SF/U-1.   ISSN 0305-9790

MONDE ALPIN ET RHODANIEN.
LYONS 1, 1973-
OX/U-1.

MONDE INTERNATIONAL DE L'ENSEIGNEMENT DE
L'INFORMATIQUE.
++MONDE INT. ENSEIGN. INF.
EDINBURGH 1, D 1973-
ED/N-1.

MONETARY STUDIES SERIES.
+ +*MONETARY STUD. SER.*
OECD: SECRETARIAT.
PARIS NO.1, 1972-
GL/U-1. LO/N-1.

MONOGRAFIAS ARQUEOLOGICAS.
+ +*MONOGR. ARQUEOL.*
SARAGOSSA UNIVERSIDAD: SEMINARIO DE PREHISTORIA
Y PROTOHISTORIA.
SARAGOSSA 1, 1966-
CA/U-1. ISSN 0544-7941

MONOGRAPHS ON ATHEROSCLEROSIS.
+ +*MONOGR. ATHEROSCLER.*
[KARGER]
BASLE &C. 1, 1969-
OX/U-8. ISSN 0077-099X

MONOGRAPHS IN CLINICAL CYTOLOGY.
+ +*MONOGR. CLIN. CYTOL.*
[KARGER]
BASLE &C. NO.1, 1965-
NO.1 ENTITLED CLINICAL CYTOLOGY.
OX/U-8. 2, 1969- ISSN 0077-0809

MONOGRAPHS IN DEVELOPMENTAL BIOLOGY.
+ +*MONOGR. DEV. BIOL.*
[KARGER]
BASLE &C. 1, 1969-
OX/U-8. ISSN 0077-0825

MONOGRAFIE FAUNY POLSKI.
+ +*MONOGR. FAUNY POL.*
POLSKA AKADEMIA NAUK: ZAKLAD ZOOLOGII
SYSTEMATYCZNEJ.
CRACOW 1, 1973-
LO/N-2.

MONOGRAPHIEN ZUR HUMANETHOLOGIE.
+ +*MONOGR. HUMANETHOL.*
[R. PIPER & CO. VERLAG]
MUNCHEN 1, [1972]
LO/N-1.

MONOGRAPHS IN NEURAL SCIENCES.
+ +*MONOGR. NEURAL SCI.*
BASLE &C. 1, 1973-
OX/U-8.

MONOGRAPHS IN PATHOLOGY.
+ +*MONOGR. PATHOL.*
INTERNATIONAL ACADEMY OF PATHOLOGY.
NEW YORK NO.1, 1960-
OX/U-8. ISSN 0077-0922

**MONOGRAPHS, PERCY FITZPATRICK INSTITUTE OF
AFRICAN ORNITHOLOGY.**
+ +*MONOGR. PERCY FITZPATRICK INST. AFR. ORNITHOL.*
CAPE TOWN NO.1, 1972.//
LO/N13.

MONOGRAPHS IN POLITICAL SCIENCE.
+ +*MONOGR. POLIT. SCI.*
UNIVERSITY OF RHODESIA.   XXX
SALISBURY NO.1, 1968-
EARLY ISSUES PUBL. BY UNIVERSITY COLLEGE OF
RHODESIA.
OX/U-9.

**MONOGRAPH SERIES, PUBLIC HEALTH LABORATORY
SERVICE BOARD (GB).**
+ +*MONOGR. SER. PUBLIC HEALTH LAB. SERV. BOARD
(GB).*
LONDON NO.1, 1972-
LO/N-1.

MONOGRAPH SERIES, TENNYSON SOCIETY.   XXX
+ +*MONOGR. SER. TENNYSON SOC.*
LINCOLN NO.1, 1969-
PREV: THE SOCIETY'S PUBLICATIONS.
LO/U-1. ISSN 0082-285X

**MONOGRAFIAS, UNIVERSIDAD DE SANTIAGO DE
COMPOSTELA.**
+ +*MONOGR. UNIV. SANTIAGO COMPOSTELA.*
SANTIAGO DE COMPOSTELA NO.1, 1971-
LO/U-1. *

MONTALBAN.
UNIVERSIDAD CATOLICA ANDRES BELLO: FACULTAD DE
HUMANIDADES Y EDUCACION.
CARACAS NO.1, 1972-
FACULTAD SUBORD. TO: INSTITUTOS HUMANISTICOS
DE INVESTIGACION.
OX/U-1.

MONUMENTA HISTORICA CARMELI TERESIANI.
+ +*MONUMENTA HIST. CARMELI TERESIANI.*
ROME 1, 1973-
OX/U-1.

**MONUMENTA IURIS CANONICI: SERIES B: CORPUS
COLLECTIONUM.**
+ +*MONUMENTA IURIS CANONICI, B.*
VATICAN CITY 1, 1973-
OX/U-1.

MOOT. THIRKILL & THRELKELD FAMILY HISTORY.
LONDON NO.1, AP 1973-
3/A.
CA/U-1. ED/N-1. OX/U-1.

MORSKAJA GEOLOGIJA I GEOFIZIKA.
+ +*MORSK. GEOL. & GEOFIZ.*
VSESOJUZNYJ NAUCHNO-ISSLEDOVATEL'SKIJ INSTITUT
MORSKOJ GEOLOGII I GEOFIZIKI.
RIGA 1, 1970-
ENGL. SUMM.
LO/N-2. LO/N13.

MOST BEAUTIFUL BOOKS OF CZECHOSLOVAKIA.   000
SEE: CESKOSLOVENSKE NEJKRASNEJSI KNIHY.

MOUSAION 11.
UNIVERSITY OF SOUTH AFRICA.
PRETORIA NO.1, AG 1973-
PREV. SER. FROM NO.1, 1955- 100, 1972.
S/T: CONTRIBUTIONS IN LIBRARY SCIENCE
OF THE DEPARTMENT OF LIBRARY SCIENCE & THE
LIBRARY OF THE UNIVERSITY OF SOUTH AFRICA.
LO/U-2.

MOUSE & HAMSTER IN RESEARCH.   XXX
+ +*MOUSE & HAMSTER RES.*
[LITERATURE SEARCHERS]
KETTERING, OHIO NO.12, 1967-
PREV: MOUSE IN RESEARCH FROM NO.1, 1966- 11,
1967.
LO/N13.

MOUSE IN RESEARCH.   XXX
+ +*MOUSE RES.*
[LITERATURE SEARCHERS]
KETTERING, OHIO NO.1, 1966- 11, 1967 ...
SUBS: MOUSE & HAMSTER IN RESEARCH.
LO/N13.

MULTIDISCIPLINARY RESEARCH.
+ +*MULTIDISCIP. RES.*
INTERNATIONAL MULTIDISCIPLINARY RESEARCH
ASSOCIATION.
EUGENE, OREG. 1, 1973-
LO/U-2. SA/U-1. 2, 1974-

**MUSIC & MAN. AN INTERDISCIPLINARY JOURNAL OF
STUDIES ON MUSIC.**
[GORDON & BREACH]
LONDON & NEW YORK 1(1), 1973-
4/A.
ED/N-1. SH/U-1. CA/U-1. 1(2), 1974- ISSN 0306-2082

MUSIC YEARBOOK.
+ +*MUSIC YEARB.*
[MACMILLAN]
LONDON 1972/73(1972)-
ED/N-1. SW/U-1. 1973/74.

MUSICAL INSTRUMENT TECHNOLOGY.
+ +*MUSICAL INSTRUM. TECHNOL.*
INSTITUTE OF MUSICAL INSTRUMENT TECHNOLOGY.
LONDON 1, 1969-
LO/N14. ED/N-1. 2, 1973- ISSN 0305-0335

MUSICALIA. RIVISTA INTERNAZIONALE DI MUSICA.   XXX
GENOA 1, 1970- 2, 1971.//
LO/U-1.

**MUSICANADA. NEWSLETTER OF THE CANADIAN MUSIC
CENTRE.**   XXX
TORONTO NO.1, MY 1967- 29, 1970.//
PREV: NEWSLETTER, CANADIAN MUSIC CENTRE FROM
NO.1, 1964- 14, D 1965.
ED/N-1. ISSN 0580-3144

**MUSIIKKI. SUOMEN MUSIKKITIETEELLINEN SEURA
RY:N JULKAISU.**
HELSINKI 1(1), 1971-
LO/N-1.

MUSIKETHNOLOGISCHE JAHRESBIBLIOGRAPHIE
EUROPAS. ANNUAL BIBLIOGRAPHY OF EUROPEAN
ETHNOMUSICOLOGY.
++MUSIKETHNOL. JAHRESBIBLIOGR. EUR.
SLOVENSKE NARODNE MUZEUM V BRATISLAVA.
BRATISLAVA 1, 1967-
PRODUCED BY THE MUSEUM'S DEPARTMENT OF MUSIC.
CA/U-1. LO/U-1. ISSN 0077-2534

MUZIKOLOSKI ZBORNIK.
++MUZIKOL. ZB.
UNIVERZA V LJUBLJANI: ODDELEK ZA
MUZIKOLOGIJO FILOSOFSKE FAKULTE.
LJUBLJANA 1, 1965-
OX/U-1.

MYTHLORE.
MYTHOPOETIC SOCIETY.
MAYWOOD, CALIF. 1(1), 1969-
OX/U-1. 2(1), 1970-

NACHRICHTENTECHNIK.   XXX
SUBS (1973): NACHRICHTENTECHNIK - ELEKTRONIK.

NACHRICHTENTECHNIK - ELEKTRONIK.   XXX
++NACHRICHTENTECH. - ELEKTRON.
[VEB VERLAG TECHNI]
BERLIN 23, 1973-
MON. ENGL., FR. & RUSS. SUMM. PREV: NACH-
RICHTENTECHNIK FROM 1, OC 1951- 22, 1972.
S/T: TECHNISCHE-WISSENSCHAFTLICHE ZEITSCHRIFT
FUR DIE GESAMIE ELECTRONISCHE NACHRICHTENTECH-
NIK.
LO/N14.   ISSN 0092-668X

NAGASAKI-KEN SOGO NORIN SHIKENJO KENKYU
HOKOKU: NOGYO BUMON.
ISAHAYA NO.1, 1973-
ENGL. TITLE: BULLETIN OF THE NAGASAKI AGRI-
CULTURAL & FORESTRY EXPERIMENT STATION:
SECTION OF AGRICULTURE.
LO/N13.

NAMUIN AM'DRAL. PARTY LIFE.
ULAN-BATOR NO.1, 1972-
LO/U14.

NARODNOE KHOZJAISTVO SOTSIALISTICHESKIKH
STRAN.
++NAR. KHOZ. SOTS. STRAN.
AKADEMIJA NAUK SSSR: INSTITUT EKONOMIKI MIROVOJ
SOTSIALISTICHESKOJ SISTEMY.
MOSCOW 1961(1962)-
S/T: SOOBSHCHENIJA STATISTICHESKIKH UPRAVLENIJ
GL/U-1.   CC/U-1. 1970(1971)-   LO/U15. 1963(1964)-

NARODOPISNE AKTUALITY.
++NARODOP. AKTUAL.
KRAJSKE STREDISKO LIDOVEHO UMENI VE STRAZNICI.
STRAZNICE 1, 1964-
ED/N-1. 1966-   LO/S30. 2, 1965-   OX/U-1. 2, 1965-

NARODOPISNE ZBIERKY.
++NARODOP. ZBIERKY.
SLOVENSKE NARODNE MUZEUM: NARODOPISNY
ODBOR.
TURCIANSKY SV. MARTIN 1, 1962-
OX/U-1.

NATIONAL HAIRDRESSER.
++NATL. HAIRDRESSER.
NATIONAL HAIRDRESSERS' FEDERATION.
LONDON 1(1), 1973-
Q.
CA/U-1. 1(2), 1973-   ED/N-1. 1(2), 1973-

NATIONAL PARK SERIES OF STUDIES IN LAND USE   000
HISTORY & LANDSCAPE CHANGE.
SEE: STUDIES IN LAND USE HISTORY & LANDSCAPE
CHANGE: NATIONAL PARK SERIES.

NATIONALITIES PAPERS.
++NATL. PAP.
ASSOCIATION FOR THE STUDY OF NATIONALITIES
(USSR & EAST EUROPE).
CHARLESTON, ILL. 1, 1972-
2/A.
SH/U-1.   ISSN 0090-5992

NAUCHNI TRUDOVE, NAUCHNOIZSLEDOVATELSKI INST-
ITUT PO RADIOLOGIJA I RADIATSIONNA KHIGIENA.
++NAUCHNI TR. NAUCHNOIZSLED. INST. RADIOL. &
RADIATS. KHIG.
SOFIA 1, 1965-
ENGL. SUMM. IN SOME ISSUES.
LO/N13. 2, 1968-

NAUCHNI TRUDOVE, VISSH LESOTEKHNICHESKI INST-   XXX
ITUT: SERIJA OZELENJAVANE.
++NAUCHNI TR. VISSH LESOTEK. INST., OZELENJAVANE
SOFIA 15, 1967-
PREV: PART OF ABOVE MAIN TITLE FROM 1, 1952-
14, 1966. CONT. IT'S VOL. NUMBERING.
LO/N13. 16, 1968-

NAUCHNO-ISSLEDOVATEL'SKIE TRUDY, LATVIJSKIJ
NAUCHNO-ISSLEDOVATEL'SKIJ INSTITUT LEGKOJ
PROMYSHLENNOSTI.
++NAUCHNO-ISSLED. TR. LATV. NAUCHNO-ISSLED.
INST. LEGK. PROM-ST.
RIGA 2, 1968-
NO DATA AVAILABLE REGARDING VOL.1.
LO/N13.

NAUCHNYE TRUDY, INSTITUT MEKHANKIKI MOSKOV-
SKOGO GOSUDARSTVENNOGO UNIVERSITETA.
++NAUCHN. TR. INST. MEKH. MOSK. GOS. UNIV.
MOSCOW 1, 1970-
LO/N13.

NAUCHNYE TRUDY, NAUCHNO-ISSLEDOVATEL'SKIJ   XXX
INSTITUT STROITEL'NOJ FIZIKI.
++NAUCHN. TR. NAUCHNO-ISSLED. INST. STROIT. FIZ.
MOSCOW 1(9), 1969-
ALSO ENTITLED: USPEKHI STROITEL'NOJ FIZIKI.
PREV: TRUDY INSTITUTA STROITEL'NOJ FIZIKI,
AKADEMIJA STROITEL'STVA I ARKHITEKTURY SSSR
FROM 1, 1962- 8, 1968.
LO/N13.

NAUCHNYJ KOMMUNIZM.
++NAUCHN. KOMMUNIZM.
(RUSSIA SSSR) MINISTERSTVO VYSSHEGO I SREDNEGO
SPETSIAL'NOGO OBRAZOVANIJA SSSR.
MOSCOW 1, 1973-
6/A.
LO/U-3. 2, 1974-

NAWPA PACHA.
INSTITUTE OF ANDEAN STUDIES.
BERKELEY, CALIF. 1, 1963-
ANNU.
LO/S10.   ISSN 0077-6297

NEOHELICAN. ACTA COMPARATIONIS LITTERARUM
UNIVERSARUM.
BUDAPEST 1, 1973-
OX/U-1.

NETWORK. INTERNATIONAL COMMUNICATIONS IN
LIBRARY AUTOMATION.
[L.A.R.C. PRESS]
PEORIA, ILL. 1, 1974-
GL/U-2.   LO/N-2.   LO/N14.   SO/U-1.

NEUE HEIDELBERGER STUDIEN ZUR MUSIKWISSENSCHAFT.
++NEUE HEIDELB. STUD. MUSIKWISS.
[FRANCKE VERLAG]
BERN & MUNCHEN 1, 1969-
LO/N-1.

NEW EARNINGS SURVEY.
++NEW EARN. SURV.
(GREAT BRITAIN) DEPARTMENT OF EMPLOYMENT &
PRODUCTIVITY.
[H.M.S.O.]
LONDON 1968(1970)-
ANNU.
NW/U-1.

NEW FRONTIERS IN EDUCATION.
++NEW FRONT. EDUC.
ALL INDIA ASSOCIATION FOR CHRISTIAN HIGHER
EDUCATION.
DELHI 1, MY 1971-
3/A.
BH/C-3.   ISSN 0047-9705

NEW GUINEA WRITING.   XXX
(PAPUA & NEW GUINEA) DEPARTMENT OF INFORMATION
& EXTENSION SERVICES: BUREAU OF LITERATURE.
[NEW GUINEA NEWS SERVICE]
PORT MORESBY NO.1, AG 1970- 4, 1971 ...
SUBS: PAPUA NEW GUINEA WRITING.
LD/U-1.   ISSN 0085-3941

NEW INDUSTRIAL PRODUCTS FOR EUROPE.
++NEW IND. PROD. EUR.
[IPC INDUSTRIAL P.]
LONDON [NO.1], S 1973-
6/A. ENGL., FR., GER. & ITAL.
CA/U-1.   ED/N-1.   OX/U-8.

NEW LINGUIST.   XXX
[RICHARD GAINSBOROUGH PERIODICALS LTD.]
LONDON 1(1), F 1973-
PREV: LINGUIST FROM 1, MR 1938- 29, 1967.
GL/U-2.   CA/U-1. 1(5), 1973-   ED/N-1. 1(5), 1973-
ISSN 0300-3752

NEW LOCATIONS.
[CONSYL PUBL.]
LONDON 1, 1973-
6/A.
CA/U-1.   ED/N-1.   OX/U-1.   SH/U-1.

**NEW PUBLICATIONS IN THE DAG HAMMARSKJOLD
LIBRARY.**   XXX
SUBS (1971): PART OF CURRENT BIBLIOGRAPH-
ICAL INFORMATION.

NEW REVIEW.   XXX
+ +*NEW REV.*
[NEW REVIEW LTD.]
LONDON 1, 1974-
PREV: REVIEW FROM 1, 1962- 29/30, 1972.
AD/U-1.   BL/U-1.   BN/U-1.   ED/N-1.   EX/U-1.   HL/U-1.
LO/U-1.   LO/U-2.   NO/U-1.   OX/U-1.   RE/U-1.   SA/U-1.
SH/U-1.   SW/U-1.   ISSN 0305-8344

NEW TECHNIQUES IN BIOPHYSICS & CELL BIOLOGY.
+ +*NEW TECH. BIOPHYS. & CELL BIOL.*
[WILEY-INTERSCIENCE]
LONDON &C. 1, 1973-
LO/N13.   ISSN 0301-374X

**NEW ZEALAND JOURNAL OF EXPERIMENTAL AGRICULT-
URE.**
+ +*N.Z. J. EXP. AGRIC.*
(NEW ZEALAND) DEPARTMENT OF SCIENTIFIC &
INDUSTRIAL RESEARCH.
WELLINGTON, N.Z. 1, 1973-
AB/U-2.   LD/U-1.   LO/N-2.

NEW ZEALAND JOURNAL OF ZOOLOGY.
+ +*N.Z. J. ZOOL.*
(NEW ZEALAND) DEPARTMENT OF SCIENTIFIC &
INDUSTRIAL RESEARCH.
WELLINGTON, N.Z. 1, 1974-
Q.
CA/U12.   ED/N-1.   LO/N-6.   LO/N14.   OX/U-8.

**NEW ZEALAND TIMBER JOURNAL & WOOD PRODUCTS
REVIEW.**   XXX
SUBS (1973): NEW ZEALAND WOOD INDUSTRIES.

NEW ZEALAND WOOD INDUSTRIES.   XXX
+ +*N.Z. WOOD IND.*
[TIDMARSH PUBL.]
AUCKLAND 19(9), 1973-
PREV: NEW ZEALAND TIMBER JOURNAL & WOOD PROD-
UCTS REVIEW FROM 4(7), MR 1958- 19(8), 1973.
LO/N13.

NEWS. A MISCELLANY OF FORTEAN CURIOSITIES.
BIRMINGHAM 1(1), N 1973-
6/A.
ED/N-1.   OX/U-1.   ISSN 0306-0764

NEWS, AFRICAN BIBLIOGRAPHIC CENTER.
+ +*NEWS AFR. BIBLIOGR. CENT.*
WASHINGTON, D.C. 1(1), 1972-
LO/U14.   ISSN 0044-6521

NEWS FROM FRANCE.   XXX
+ +*NEWS FR.*
(FRANCE) EMBASSY, LONDON: PRESS & INFORMATION
SERVICE.
LONDON 1, 1974-
MON. PREV: BULLETIN MENSUEL D'INFORMATION,
AMBASSADE DE FRANCE A LONDRES FROM 1, 1959-
10, 1973.
BL/U-1.   ED/N-1.   OX/U-1.   SH/P-1.
LO/U12. ‡CURRENT YEAR ONLY‡

NEWS, PETROLEUM INDUSTRY TRAINING BOARD.
+ +*NEWS PET. IND. TRAIN. BOARD.*
WEMBLEY NO.1, JE 1968-
3/A.
ED/N-1.   OX/U-1.   LO/U-3. ‡CURRENT ISSUES ONLY‡

NEWS & VIEWS, AMERICAN FERN SOCIETY.
+ +*NEWS & VIEWS AM. FERN SOC.*
EAST ORANGE, N.J. NO.1, 1971-
LO/N-2.

**NEWS & VIEWS OF THE BRITISH NATIONAL COMMIT-
TEE ON LARGE DAMS.**
+ +*NEWS & VIEWS BR. NATL. COMM. LARGE DAMS.*
LONDON NO.1, MY 1967-
2/A.
LO/U12.   BL/U-1. NO.2, 1967-   ED/N-1. NO.9, 1971-

NEWSLETTER, ANTHROPOLOGICAL SURVEY (INDIA).
+ +*NEWSL. ANTHROPOL. SURV. (INDIA).*
CALCUTTA 1, 1972-
6/A.
LO/N12.

**NEWSLETTER, ASSOCIATION OF CARIBBEAN UNIV-
ERSITY & RESEARCH LIBRARIES.**
+ +*NEWSL. ASSOC. CARIBB. UNIV. & RES. LIBR.*
SAN JUAN 1(1), AU 1973-
LO/U-8.

**NEWSLETTER, ASSOCIATION FOR THE STUDY OF MED-
ICAL EDUCATION.**
+ +*NEWSL. ASSOC. STUDY MED. EDUC.*
LONDON NO.1, 1972-
MA/U-1.

**NEWSLETTER, AUSTRALIAN ASSOCIATION OF SOCIAL
ANTHROPOLOGISTS.**   XXX
+ +*NEWSL. AUST. ASSOC. SOC. ANTHROPOL.*
NEDLANDS 9, 1970-
PREV: NEWSLETTER, AUSTRALIAN BRANCH OF THE
ASSOCIATION OF SOCIAL ANTHROPOLOGISTS OF THE
BRITISH COMMONWEALTH FROM 1, 1957- 8, 1968.
LO/S10.

**NEWSLETTER, AUSTRALIAN BRANCH OF THE ASSOC-
IATION OF SOCIAL ANTHROPOLOGISTS OF THE BRIT-
ISH COMMONWEALTH.**   XXX
SUBS (1970): NEWSLETTER, AUSTRALIAN ASSOC-
IATION OF SOCIAL ANTHROPOLOGISTS.

NEWSLETTER, BRITISH PTERIDOLOGICAL SOCIETY.   XXX
+ +*NEWSL. BR. PTERIDOL. SOC.*
LOUGHTON, ESSEX NO.1, 1963- 10, 1972.
SUBS: BULLETIN, BRITISH PTERIDOLOGICAL SOCIETY
LO/N-2.   LO/N13.   HL/U-1. NO.6, 1968-
RE/U-1. NO.6, 1968-

NEWSLETTER, CAMDEN HISTORY SOCIETY.
+ +*NEWSL. CAMDEN HIST. SOC.*
LONDON NO.1, 1970-
LO/U-2.

NEWSLETTER, CANADIAN MUSIC CENTRE.   XXX
+ +*NEWSL. CAN. MUSIC CENT.*
TORONTO NO.1, 1964- 14, D 1965.
MON. SUBS: MUSICANADA.

**NEWSLETTER, CAVE RESEARCH GROUP OF GREAT
BRITAIN.**   XXX
SUBS (1973): BULLETIN, BRITISH CAVE RESEARCH
ASSOCIATION.

NEWSLETTER, DELAWARR LABORATORIES LIMITED.
+ +*NEWSL. DELAWARR LAB. LTD.*
OXFORD [NO.1], SPRING 1973-
Q.
ED/N-1.

NEWSLETTER, ENTOMOLOGICAL SOCIETY OF NIGERIA.
+ +*NEWSL. ENTOMOL. SOC. NIGER.*
ILE-IFE NO.1, 1973-
LO/N-2.

**NEWSLETTER OF THE EUROPEAN ASSOCIATION FOR
JAPANESE STUDIES.**   XXX
+ +*NEWSL. EUR. ASSOC. JAP. STUD.*
VIENNA NO.1-2, 1973...
SUBS: BULLETIN OF THE EUROPEAN ASSOCIATION FOR
JAPANESE STUDIES.
LO/U14.

**NEWSLETTER, HISTORY GROUP, COMMUNIST PARTY OF
GREAT BRITAIN.**
+ +*NEWSL. HIST. GROUP COMMUNIST PARTY G.B.*
LONDON NO.1, OC 1973-
Q.
LO/U-3.

NEWSLETTER, INDIA OFFICE LIBRARY & RECORDS.
+ +*NEWSL. INDIA OFF. LIBR. & REC.*
(GREAT BRITAIN) INDIA OFFICE LIBRARY.
LONDON NO.1, 1974-
LO/N12.   LO/U-8.   OX/U-1.

NEWSLETTER, INDUSTRIAL ARCHAEOLOGY GROUP,   XXX
LINCOLNSHIRE LOCAL HISTORY SOCIETY.
++NEWSL. IND. ARCHAEOL. GROUP LINCS. LOCAL
HIST. SOC.
LINCOLN 1, 1966- 3, 1968...
SUBS: LINCOLNSHIRE INDUSTRIAL ARCHAEOLOGY.
NO/U-1

NEWSLETTER, IRISH COMPUTER SOCIETY.
++NEWSL. IR. COMPUT. SOC.
DUBLIN NO.1, JL 1973-
ED/N-1.   OX/U-8.

NEWSLETTER, NATIONAL COUNCIL FOR SPECIAL
EDUCATION (GB).
++NEWSL. NATL. COUNC. SPEC. EDUC. (GB).
CHELMSFORD 1, 1973-
CA/U-1.   ED/N-1.

NEWSLETTER, NUFFIELD FOUNDATION GROUP ON RES-
EARCH & INNOVATION IN HIGHER EDUCATION.
++NEWSL. NUFFIELD FOUND. GROUP RES. & INNOVAT.
HIGHER EDUC.
LONDON NO.1, 1973-
ED/U-1.   LD/U-1.

NEWSLETTER, PEACE PLEDGE UNION.
++NEWSL. PEACE PLEDGE UNION.
LONDON MY 1973-
6/A.
CA/U-1.   ED/N-1.   OX/U-1.   LO/U-3. JA 1974-

NEWSLETTER, PEREGRINE FUND.
++NEWSL. PEREGRINE FUND.
CORNELL UNIVERSITY: LABORATORY OF ORNITHOLOGY.
ITHACA, N.Y. NO.1, 1973-
LO/N13.

NEWSLETTER, RARE BOOKS GROUP, LIBRARY ASSOC-
IATION.
++NEWSL. RARE BOOKS GROUP LIB. ASSOC.
LONDON 1, MR 1974-
CA/U-1.   ED/N-1.   LO/U-1.   NO/U-1.   OX/U-1.   SA/U-1.

NEWSLETTER, SALFORD LOCAL HISTORY SOCIETY.
++NEWSL. SALFORD LOCAL HIST. SOC.
SALFORD 1, 1973-
SF/U-1.

NEWSLETTER, STUDY GROUP ON EIGHTEENTH-CENTURY
RUSSIA.
++NEWSL. STUDY GROUP EIGHTEENTH-CENTURY RUSS.
UNIVERSITY OF EAST ANGLIA: STUDY GROUP ON
EIGHTEENTH-CENTURY RUSSIA.
NORWICH NO.1, S 1973-
BN/U-1.   CA/U-1.   ED/N-1.   EX/U-1.   HL/U-1.   LD/U-1.
SA/U-1.   SH/U-1.

NEWSLETTER FOR TARGUM STUDIES.
++NEWSL. TARGUM STUD.
TORONTO 1, 1974-
OX/U-1.

NEWSLETTER, WESTERN ASSOCIATION OF MAP   XXX
LIBRARIES.
++NEWSL. WEST. ASSOC. MAP. LIBR.
SACRAMENTO, CALIF. NO.1- 2, 1969.
SUBS: INFORMATION BULLETIN, WESTERN ASSOCIAT-
ION OF MAP LIBRARIES.
AD/U-1.   CA/U-1.   ED/N-1.

NEWTON MANUSCRIPT SERIES, CAMBRIDGE UNIVER-
SITY LIBRARY.
++NEWTON MANUSCR. SER. CAMB. UNIV. LIBR.
CAMBRIDGE 1, 1973-
CA/U-1.

NIF NEWSLETTER.
NORDISK INSTITUT FOR FOLKED'GTNING.
TURKU 1, 1972-
ISSUED BY THE INSTITUTE UNDER ITS ENGLISH FORM
OF NAME: NORDIC INSTITUTE OF FOLKLORE.
HL/U-1.   LO/N-1.   LO/S10.   OX/U-1.

NIIGATA DAIGAKU RIGAKUBU CHISHITSU KOBUTSU-
GAKU KYOSHITSU KENKYU HOKOKU. CONTRIBUTIONS,
DEPARTMENT OF GEOLOGY & MINERALOGY, NIIGATA
UNIVERSITY.
NIIGATA NO.1, 1966-
ANNU. JAP. WITH EUR. SUMM. DEPT. SUBORD: TO
FACULTY OF SCIENCE.
LO/N-2.

NINETEENTH-CENTURY FRENCH STUDIES.
++NINETEENTH-CENTURY FR. STUD.
STATE UNIVERSITY COLLEGE OF NEW FREDONIA:
DEPARTMENT OF FOREIGN LANGUAGES.
NEW YORK 1, 1972-
Q.
AD/U-1.   CA/U-1.   EX/U-1.   GL/U-1.   SH/P-1.   SW/U-1.

NINETEENTH CENTURY STUDIES.
++NINETEENTH CENTURY STUD.
BIBLIOGRAPHICAL RESEARCH CENTRE (INDIA).
CALCUTTA NO.1, 1973-
Q.
LO/N12.

NORWEGIAN MARITIME RESEARCH.   XXX
++NORW. MARIT. RES.
NORGES TEKNISK-NATURVITENSKAPELIGE FORSKNING-
SRAD.
[SELVIGS]
OSLO 1, 1973-
Q. PREV: EUROPEAN SHIPBUILDING FROM 1, 1952-
21(5/6), 1972.
NW/U-1.

NOTAS DE MATEMATICAS.
++NOTAS MAT. (LIMA).
INSTITUTO DE MATEMATICAS PURAS Y APLICADAS
(LIMA).
LIMA 1, 1962-
LO/N14.

NOTE, RESEARCH SERVICE, DEPARTMENT OF LANDS &
FORESTS (QUEBEC).
++NOTE RES. SERV. DEP. LANDS & FOR. (QUE.).
QUEBEC 1, 1972-
OX/U-3.

NOTIZIARIO, ISTITUTO DI AUTOMATICA, UNIV-
ERSITA DI ROMA.
++NOT. ISTIT. AUTOM. UNIV. ROMA.
ROME 1, 1970-
LO/N14.

NOUVEAU COMMERCE DE LA LECTURE.
++NOUV. COMMER. LECT.
ASSOCIATION DES AMIS DES CAHIERS DU NOUVEAU
COMMERCE.
PARIS NO.1, 1971-
Q. S/T: CARNETS TRIMESTRIELS DE CRITIQUES ET
DE LECTURES. SUPPL. TO: NOUVEAU COMMERCE.
MA/U-1.

NOVA HEDWIGIA: BEIHEFTE.
++NOVA HEDWIGIA, BEIH.
[J. CRAMER]
WEINHEIM 1, 1962-
AT HEAD OF TITLE: BEIHEFTE ZUR NOVA HEDWIGIA.
LO/N13.   ISSN 0078-2238

NOVAJA SOVETSKAJA LITERATURA PO ISKUSSTVU.
BIBLIOGRAFICHESKIJ UKAZATEL'.
++NOV. SOV. LIT. ISKUSSTVU.
GOSUDARSTVENNAJA BIBLIOTEKA SSSR IM. V.I.
LENINA: INFORMATSIONNYJ TSENTR PO PROBLEMAM
KUL'TURY I ISKUSSTVA.
MOSCOW 7, 1973-
NO DATA AVAILABLE REGARDING VOLS. 1-6.
OX/U-1.

NSS BULLETIN. QUARTERLY JOURNAL OF THE NAT-
IONAL SPELEOLOGICAL SOCIETY.   XXX
++NSS BULL.
HUNTSVILLE, ALA. 36, 1974-
PREV: BULLETIN, NATIONAL SPELEOLOGICAL SOCIETY
FROM 1, 1940- 35, 1973.
LO/N-2.   ISSN 0028-0216

NUCLEAR ACTIVE.
++NUCL. ACT.
(SOUTH AFRICA) ATOMIC ENERGY BOARD.
PRETORIA 1969-
2/A. ENGL. WITH FR., RUSS., GER., SPAN. &
JAP. SUMM.
LO/N14. 1970-   XS/R10. JL 1969-   ISSN 0048-1025

NUCLEIC ACIDS RESEARCH.
++NUCL. ACIDS RES.
[INFORMATION RETRIEVAL LTD.]
LONDON 1(1), JA 1974-
MON.
GL/U-1.   OX/U-8.   SH/U-1.   ED/N-1. 1(2), 1974-

NUEVO FILM.
MONTEVIDEO NO.1, 1967-
CC/U-1.

NUMBER 1.
CAMBRIDGESHIRE COLLEGE OF ARTS & TECHNOLOGY.
CAMBRIDGE 1(1), JA 1973-
ANNU.
ED/N-1.   OX/U-1.

**NUSANTARA. JOURNAL OF THE ARTS & SOCIAL
SCIENCES OF SOUTHEAST ASIA.**
[DEWAN BAHASA DAN PUSTAKA]
KUALA LUMPUR NO.1, JA 1972-
2/A. ENGL. OR MALAY.
HL/U-1.   CA/U-1. NO.2, 1972-

OBSHCHAJA I PRIKLADNAJA KHIMIJA.
++*OBSHCH. & PRIKL. KHIM.*
(BELORUSSIA) MINISTERSTVO VYSSHEGO 1
SREDNEGO SPETSIAL'NOGO OBRAZOVANIJA.
MINSK   2, 1970-
SPONS. BODY ALSO: BELORUSSKIJ TEKHNOLO-
GICHESKIJ INSTITUT.
LO/N13.

**OCCASIONAL BULLETIN, CLIMATIC RESEARCH UNIT,
UNIVERSITY OF EAST ANGLIA.**   000
SEE: CLIMATIC RESEARCH UNIT OCCASIONAL
BULLETIN.

**OCCASIONAL PAPERS, AUSTRALIAN ACADEMY OF THE
HUMANITIES.**
SYDNEY &C. 1, 1972-
OX/U-1.

**OCCASIONAL PAPERS, CENTRE FOR CONTINUING
EDUCATION, UNIVERSITY OF SUSSEX.**
++*OCCAS. PAP. CENT. CONTIN. EDUC. UNIV. SUSSEX.*
BRIGHTON NO.1, 1973-
CA/U-1.   ISSN 0306-1108

**OCCASIONAL PAPERS, CENTRE FOR THE STUDY OF
DEVELOPING SOCIETIES (NEW DELHI).**
++*OCCAS. PAP. CENT. STUDY DEV. SOC. (NEW DELHI).*
[ALLIED PUBL.]
BOMBAY NO.1, 1967-
LO/N-1.   ISSN 0069-195X

**OCCASIONAL PAPERS, DACORUM COLLEGE OF FURTHER
EDUCATION.**
++*OCCAS. PAP. DACORUM COLL. FURTHER EDUC.*
HEMEL HEMPSTEAD NO.1, 1973-
CA/U-1.

**OCCASIONAL PAPER, DIVISION OF ART & ARCHAEOL-
OGY, ROYAL ONTARIO MUSEUM.**   XXX
++*OCCAS. PAP. DIV. ART & ARCHAEOL. R. ONT. MUS.*
TORONTO NO.1, 1959- 25, 1971.//
BL/U-1.   CA/U-3.   OX/U-1.   ISSN 0082-5077

**OCCASIONAL PAPERS OF THE FARLOW HERBARIUM OF
CRYPTOGAMIC BOTANY.**
++*OCCAS. PAP. FARLOW HERB. CRYPTOGRAM. BOT.*
CAMBRIDGE, MASS. NO.1, 1969-
LO/N-2.   ISSN 0532-9744

OCCASIONAL PAPERS, GARDEN HISTORY SOCIETY.
++*OCCAS. PAP. GARD. HIST. SOC.*
READING NO.1, 1969-
LO/N-2.

OCCASIONAL PAPERS, HATFIELD POLYTECHNIC.
++*OCCAS. PAP. HATFIELD POLYTECH.*
HATFIELD NO.1, 1973-
CA/U-1.

**OCCASIONAL PAPERS SERIES, CENTRE FOR MIDDLE
EASTERN & ISLAMIC STUDIES, UNIVERSITY OF
DURHAM.**
++*OCCAS. PAP. SER. CENT. MIDDLE EAST. & ISLAMIC
STUD. UNIV. DURHAM.*
DURHAM NO.1, 1972-
LO/N-1.   OX/U-1.

**OCCASIONAL PAPERS, SOCIETY FOR RENAISSANCE
STUDIES.**
++*OCCAS. PAP. SOC. RENAISSANCE STUD.*
LONDON NO.1, 1973-
CA/U-1.

**OCCASIONAL PAPERS, WARWICKSHIRE NATURE CON-
SERVATION TRUST.**
WARWICK NO.1, 1974-
LO/N-2.

**OCCASIONAL PUBLICATIONS, ABERDEEN COLLEGE OF
EDUCATION.**
++*OCCAS. PUBL. ABERDEEN COLL. EDUC.*
ABERDEEN NO.1, 1973-
CA/U-1.

**OCCASIONAL PUBLICATIONS, INSTITUTE OF BRITISH
GEOGRAPHERS.**
++*OCCAS. PUBL. INST. BR. GEOGR.*
LONDON 1, 1972-
GL/U-1.   MA/U-1.

OCCUPATIONAL THERAPY (LONDON).   XXX
SUBS (1974): BRITISH JOURNAL OF OCCUPATIONAL
THERAPY.

**OCEANOGRAPHICAL CRUISE REPORT. OCEANOGRAPHIC
OBSERVATIONS IN INDONESIAN & ADJACENT SEAS.**
++*OCEANOGR. CRUISE REP. (DJAKARTA).*
LEMBAGA PENELITIAN LAUT.
DJAKARTA NO.1, 1971-
HL/U-1.

OCEANOLOGIA.
POLSKA AKADEMIA NAUK: KOMITET BADAN MORZA.
WROCLAW & WARSAW 1, 1971-
ENGL. SUMM. & ADDED T/P.
LO/N13.

OCHERKI FIZIKO-KHIMICHESKOJ PETROLOGII.
++*OCHERKI FIZ.-KHIM. PETROL.*
AKADEMIJA NAUK SSSR: INSTITUT FIZIKI TVERDOGO
TELA.
MOSCOW 1, 1969-
ENGL. CONT. LISTS & TITLE: CONTRIBUTIONS TO
PHYSICO-CHEMICAL PETROLOGY.
LO/N13.

**OCHERKI ISTORII NARODOV POVOLZH'JA I PRIU-
RAL'JA.**   000
SEE: OCHERKI ISTORII POVOLZH'JA I PRIURAL'JA.

OCHERKI ISTORII POVOLZH'JA I PRIURAL'JA.
++*OCHERKI ISTOR. POVOLZH'JA & PRIURAL'JA.*
KAZANSKIJ GOSUDARSTVENNYJ UNIVERSITET.
KAZAN' 1, 1967-
TITLE VARIES. VOL. 1 PUBLISHED AS: OCHERKI
ISTORII NARODOV POVOLZH'JA I PRIURAL'JA.
GL/U-1.   LO/U-3.

ODI. BILINGUAL QUARTERLY OF MALAWIAN WRITING.
UNIVERSITY OF MALAWI.
LIMBE 1(1), 1972-
LO/U14.

ODI REVIEW.
++*ODI REV.*
OVERSEAS DEVELOPMENT INSTITUTE.
LONDON NO.1, 1966- 6, 1973.
N.S. NO.1, 1974-
CA/U-1.   LO/R-6.   LO/U-3.   ED/N-1. NO.1, 1974-

ODINANI. THE JOURNAL OF THE ODINANI MUSEUM.
NRI, NIGERIA 1(1), 1972-
LO/U14.

OECD AGRICULTURAL REVIEW.   XXX
++*OECD AGRIC. REV.*
PARIS 15(1), 1968- 20(4), 1973.//
PREV: FATIS FROM 11, 1964- 14, 1967.
BN/U-2.   LO/N13.   LO/N17.   RE/U-1.   XS/U-1.
ISSN 0474-5566

OECD SOCIAL INDICATOR DEVELOPMENT PROGRAMME.
++*OECD SOC. INDIC. DEV. PROGRAMME.*
OECD: MANPOWER & SOCIAL AFFAIRS DIRECTORATE.
PARIS 1, [1973]
NW/U-1.

OECOLOGIA AQUATICA.
++*OECOL. AQUAT.*
BARCELONA NO.1, 1973-
LO/N-2.

OFFSHORE ABSTRACTS.
++*OFFSHORE ABSTR.*
[OFFSHORE INFORMATION LITERATURE]
LONDON 1(1), JA/F 1974-
6/A.
CA/U-1.   ED/N-1.   LO/N14.   LO/R-5.   ISSN 0305-0513

OFFSHORE ENGINEER.
++*OFFSHORE ENG.*
[THOMAS TELFORD LTD.]
LONDON JA 1975-
MON.
ISSN 0305-876X

OIL & GAS.   XXX
[PRINCE-TECPRESS]
  SYDNEY 19(2), 1972-
  PREV: AUSTRALASIAN OIL & GAS REVIEW FROM
  14(5), 1968- 19(1), 1972.
  LO/N13.

**OKHRANA PRIRODY I VOSPROIZVODSTVO ESTESTVENN-
YKH RESURSOV.**
+ + *OKHR. PRIR. & VOSPROIZVOD. ESTESTV. RESUR.*
VSESOJUZNOE BOTANICHESKOE OBSHCHESTVO: ZABAJ-
KAL'SKOE OTDELENIE.
  CHITA 1, 1967-
  LO/N13.

OKIKE. A NIGERIAN JOURNAL OF NEW WRITING.
[NWANKWO-IFEJIKA & CO.]
  ENUGU NO.1, AP 1971-
  2/A.
  LO/U14.   SO/U-1.   OX/U-1. 1(3), 1972-

ON THE BIAS.   XXX
SUBS (1970): WRIT.

ON CONTINUING PRACTICE.
+ + *ON CONTIN. PRACT.*
ONTARIO COLLEGE OF PHARMACY.
  TORONTO 1, 1973-
  LO/N13.

OPEN LETTER.
+ + *OPEN LETT.*
[COACH HOUSE P.]
  VICTORIA, B.C. NO.1, 1966-
  3/A.
  LD/U-1. NO.1, 1966- 8, 1968.   ISSN 0048-1939

OPERATIONAL HYDROLOGY REPORT.
+ + *OPER. HYDROL. REP.*
WORLD METEOROLOGICAL ORGANIZATION.
  GENEVA NO.1, 1973-
  LO/N13.

ORIENTAL INSECTS: SUPPLEMENT.
+ + *ORIENT. INSECTS, SUPPL.*
ASSOCIATION FOR THE STUDY OF ORIENTAL INSECTS.
  DELHI NO.1, 1971-
  LO/N13.

ORIGINS OF LIFE.   XXX
+ + *ORIG. LIFE.*
[D.REIDEL]
  DORDRECHT & BOSTON 5, JA/AP 1975-
  Q. PREV: SPACE LIFE SCIENCES FROM
  1(1), 1968- 4(3/4), 1973.
  LO/N-2.   OX/U-1.

OROT. JOURNAL OF HEBREW LITERATURE.
WORLD ZIONIST ORGANIZATION: DEPARTMENT FOR
EDUCATION & CULTURE IN THE DIASPORA.
  JERUSALEM NO.1, 1966-
  Q. ENGL. & HEB.
  SO/U-1.   ISSN 0030-5766

ORTHODOX WORD.
BROTHERHOOD OF SAINT HERMAN OF ALASKA.
[ORTHODOX CHRISTIAN BOOKS & ICONS]
  SAN FRANCISCO 1, JA/F 1965-
  2/M.
  HL/U-1. 4(1), 1968-   LO/U11. 7(6), 1971-   ISSN 0030-5839

OSIRIS (NEW YORK).
[OSIRIS]
  NEW YORK NO.1, 1972-
  LO/U-2.

**OSIRIS. STUDIES ON THE HISTORY & PHILOSOPHY
OF SCIENCE, & ON THE HISTORY OF LEARNING &
CULTURE.**   XXX
[SAINT CATHERINE P.]
  BRUGES 1, 1936- 15, 1968.//
  LO/U-1.   LO/U-2.   CB/U-1. 15, 1968.

OSTERREICHISCHE KUNSTMONOGRAPHIE.
+ + *OSTERR. KUNSTMONOGR.*
[VERLAG ST. PETER]
  SALZBURG 1. 1969-
  LO/N-1.

OSVOBODITEL'NOE DVIZHENIE V ROSSII.
+ + *OSVOBOD. DVIZHENIE ROSS.*
SARATOVSKIJ GOSUDARSTVENNYJ UNIVERSITET.
  SARATOV 1, 1971-
  GL/U-1.   LA/U-1.   OX/U-1.

OTEMON ECONOMIC STUDIES.
+ + *OTEMON ECON. STUD.*
OTEMON GAKUIN DAIGAKU KEIZAIGAKUBU.
  IBARAKI 1, 1968-
  ANNU.
  LO/U-3.   OX/U16.

OTOLARYNGOLOGIC CLINICS OF NORTH AMERICA.
+ + *OTOLARYNGOL. CLIN. NORTH AM.*
[W.B. SAUNDERS CO.]
  PHILADELPHIA 1, JE 1968-
  3/A.
  LO/U12.   OX/U-1.   XY/N-1.   BL/U-1. 3, 1970-
  ISSN 0030-6665

OVERSEAS REVIEW (LONDON, 1946).   XXX
SUBS (1968): BARCLAYS OVERSEAS REVIEW.

OVERSEAS REVIEW (LONDON, 1969).   XXX
CONSERVATIVE POLITICAL CENTRE.
  LONDON NO.37, 1969-
  PREV: COMMONWEALTH, EUROPEAN & OVERSEAS
  REVIEW FROM NO.1, AG/S 1965- 36, D 1968.
  BH/U-1.   HL/U-1.   SO/U-1. NO.41, 1969- ‡W. 42, 44 & 46Å

OXFORD BULLETIN OF ECONOMICS & STATISTICS.   XXX
+ + *OXF. BULL. ECON. & STAT.*
UNIVERSITY OF OXFORD: INSTITUTE OF ECONOMICS &
STATISTICS.   XXX
  OXFORD 35(1), F 1973-
  PREV: BULLETIN OF THE OXFORD UNIVERSITY INST-
  ITUTE OF ECONOMICS & STATISTICS FROM 25, 1963-
  34, 1972.
  LO/U-2.   LO/U-3.   LO/U12.   OX/U16.   ISSN 0305-9049

OXFORD MAGAZINE. A WEEKLY NEWSPAPER & REVIEW.XX
+ + *OXF. MAG.*
  OXFORD 1, 1883- 91(4), 15/JE 1973.//
  LO/N-1.   OX/U-1.

OXFORD POETRY MAGAZINE.
+ + *OXF. POETRY MAG.*
OXFORD UNIVERSITY POETRY SOCIETY.
  OXFORD NO.1, MR 1973-
  3/A.
  CA/U-1.   ED/N-1.   OX/U-1.

PACIFIC ANTHROPOLOGISTS.
+ + *PAC. ANTHROPOL.*
BISHOP MUSEUM: PACIFIC SCIENTIFIC INFORMATION
CENTER.
  HONOLULU 1962-
  LO/S10.   ISSN 0078-7418

PACKAGING INDIA.
+ + *PACKAG. INDIA.*
INDIAN INSTITUTE OF PACKAGING.
  BOMBAY 1, 1968-
  Q.
  LO/N14.   ISSN 0030-9125

PAINT JOURNAL OF AUSTRALIA & NEW ZEALAND.   XXX
SUBS (1960): AUSTRALIAN PAINT JOURNAL.

PAINT TITLES.
PAINT RESEARCH ASSOCIATION.
  TEDDINGTON 1, 1973-
  WKLY.
  LO/N14. ‡CURRENT BOX ONLYÅ

PAKHA SANJAM.
PUNJABI UNIVERSITY: DEPARTMENT OF LINGUISTICS.
  PATIALA 1(1), 1968-
  2/A. ENGL. OR PUNJABI.
  LO/U14.   ISSN 0556-4417

PAKISTAN ANNUAL LAW DIGEST.
+ + *PAK. ANNU. LAW DIG.*
  LAHORE 1967[1968]-
  OX/U15.   ISSN 0078-785X

PAKISTAN JOURNAL OF BOTANY.
+ + *PAK. J. BOT. [PJBO-B]*
BOTANICAL SOCIETY OF PAKISTAN.
  JAMSHORO 1, JE/D 1969-
  2/A.
  LO/N-2.

PAKISTAN LABOUR CASES.
+ + *PAK. LABOUR CASES.*
[PUNJAB EDUCATIONAL P.]
  LAHORE 1, 1960-
  MON.
  LO/U14.   ISSN 0479-994X

PAKISTAN PICTORIAL. XXX
+ +PAK. PICT.
  KARACHI 1, 1973-
  PREV: PAKISTAN QUARTERLY FROM 1, 1952- 18,
  1972.
  ED/N-1. LO/N12.

PAKISTAN QUARTERLY. XXX
  SUBS (1973): PAKISTAN PICTORIAL.

**PALEORIENT. REVUE INTERDISCIPLINAIRE DE PRE-
HISTOIRE ET DE PROTOHISTOIRE DE L'ASIE DU SUD-
OUEST.**
  [PERROT/VANDERMEERSCH]
  PARIS 1, 1973-
  2/A. ENGL. S/T: INTERDISCIPLINARY REVIEW OF
  PREHISTORY & PROTOHISTORY OF SOUTHWEST ASIA.
  CA/U-3. LO/S10.

PANORAMA. EZHEGODNIK.
  MOSCOW 1, 1967-
  CC/U-1. LO/U15.

**PANTOI JOURNAL OF THE BRITISH PANTOMIME
ASSOCIATION.**
  LONDON NO.1, 1972-
  ED/N-1. OX/U-1.

PAPERS. TRABAJOS DE SOCIOLOGIA.
  UNIVERSIDAD DE BARCELONA: DEPARTMENTO DE
  SOCIOLOGICOS.
  [BARRAL]
  BARCELONA 1, 1973-
  CATALAN & SPAN.
  OX/U-1.

**PAPERS, ASSOCIATION OF CARIBBEAN UNIVERSITY &
RESEARCH LIBRARIES.**
  + +PAP. ASSOC. CARIBB. UNIV. & RES. LIBR.
  CHICAGO 1/2, 1973-
  OX/U-1.

PAPERS, ROYAL ONTARIO MUSEUM: ARCHAEOLOGY.
  + +PAP. R. ONT. MUS., ARCHAEOL.
  TORONTO 1, 1973-
  ED/N-1. GL/U-1. OX/U-9.

PAPUA NEW GUINEA WRITING. XXX
  + +PAPUA NEW GUINEA WRIT.
  (PAPUA & NEW GUINEA) DEPARTMENT OF INFORMATION
  & EXTENSION SERVICES: BUREAU OF LITERATURE.
  PORT MORESBY NO.5, 1972-
  PREV: NEW GUINEA WRITING.
  LD/U-1.

PARLAMENTE UND PARTEIEN.
  [ATHENAUM VERLAG]
  BAD HOMBURG 1, [1970]-
  MONOGR.
  LO/N-1.

PARTY LIFE (ULAN-BATOR) 000
  SEE: NAMUIN AM'DRAL.

PAVLOVIAN JOURNAL OF BIOLOGICAL SCIENCE. XXX
  + +PAVLOVIAN J. BIOL. SCI.
  [J.B. LIPPINCOTT CO.]
  PHILADELPHIA & TORONTO 9, 1974-
  PREV: CONDITIONAL REFLEX FROM 1, JA/MR 1966-
  8, 1973.
  LO/N13. LO/U-2. ISSN 0093-2213

PEASANT STUDIES NEWSLETTER.
  + +PEASANT STUD. NEWSL.
  UNIVERSITY OF PITTSBURGH: DEPARTMENT OF HISTORY
  PITTSBURGH 1(1), JA 1972-
  MA/U-1. 1(2), 1972-

PEOPLE.
  INTERNATIONAL PLANNED PARENTHOOD FEDERATION.
  LONDON 1(1), 1973-
  Q.
  BL/U-1. ED/N-1. LO/U-3. OX/U-1. RE/U-1. SH/U-1.
  ISSN 0301-5645

PERFORMANCE.
  NEW YORK SHAKESPEARE FESTIVAL PUBLIC THEATER.
  NEW YORK 1(1), D 1971-
  Q.
  EX/U-1. ISSN 0006-1883

PERSPECTIVES IN PEDIATRIC PATHOLOGY.
  + +PERSPECT. PEDIATR. PATHOL.
  [YEAR BOOK MEDICAL PUBL.]
  CHICAGO 1, 1973-
  LO/N13. ISSN 0091-2921

PESQUISA E PLANEJAMENTO ECONOMICO.
  + +PESQUI. & PLANEJAMENTO ECON.
  INSTITUTO DE PLANEJAMENTO ECONOMICO E SOCIAL
  (BRAZIL).
  RIO DE JANEIRO 1(1), JE 1971-
  2/A.
  LO/U-3.

PETROLEUM ECONOMIST. XXX
  + +PET. ECON.
  LONDON 41, 1974-
  PREV: PETROLEUM PRESS SERVICE FROM 1, JA 1934-
  40(12), D 1973.
  SH/P-1. ISSN 0306-395X

PETROLEUM INTERNATIONAL. XXX
  + +PET. INT.
  [PETROLEUM PUBL. CO.]
  LONDON 14, 1974-
  PREV: PETROLEUM & PETROCHEMICAL INTERNATIONAL
  FROM 11(11), 1971- 13, 1973.
  CA/U-1. LO/N14. ISSN 0301-6242

PETROLEUM PRESS SERVICE. XXX
  SUBS (1974): PETROLEUM ECONOMIST.

PETRONIAN SOCIETY NEWSLETTER.
  + +PETRONIAN SOC. NEWSL.
  GAINSVILLE, FLA. 1(1), JE 1970-
  LO/N-1.

PHARMACOLOGY, BIOCHEMISTRY & BEHAVIOR.
  + +PHARMACOL. BIOCHEM. & BEHAV.
  [ANKHO INTERNATIONAL INC.]
  NEW YORK 1, JA/F 1973-
  BL/U-1. CA/M-3. OX/U-8. SH/U-1. LD/U-1. 2, 1974-

PHILIPPINE ECONOMY BULLETIN.
  + +PHILIPP. ECON. BULL.
  (PHILIPPINES) NATIONAL ECONOMIC COUNCIL.
  MANILA 1(1), S/OC 1962-
  LO/U-3. HL/U-1. 3(2-4); 4(1; 3-6); 5(3-4); 8(2; 4).
  ISSN 0031-7519

**PHILIPPINE FINANCIAL STATISTICS. QUARTERLY
BULLETIN.**
  + +PHILIPP. FINANC. STAT.
  CENTRAL BANK OF THE PHILIPPINES: DEPARTMENT OF
  ECONOMIC RESEARCH.
  MANILA 1(1), MR 1970-
  LO/U14. ISSN 0008-9303

**PHILOLOGISCHE BEITRAGE ZUR SUDOST- UND
OSTEUROPA-FORSCHUNG.**
  + +PHILOL. BEITR. SUDOST- & OSTEUR.-FORSCH.
  [WILHELM BRAUMULLER]
  VIENNA & STUTTGART 1, 1972-
  MONOGR.
  CA/U-1. LO/N-1.

PHILOSOPHICAL CURRENTS.
  + +PHILOS. CURR.
  [B.R. GRUNER]
  AMSTERDAM 1, 1971-
  MONOGR.
  LO/N-1.

PHOTO TRADE WORLD. XXX
  SUBS (1973): PHOTO TRADER.

PHOTO TRADER. XXX
  [GREENWOOD]
  LONDON 1, 12/S 1973-
  2W. PREV: PHOTO TRADE WORLD FROM MY 1954- AG
  1973.
  ED/N-1. CA/U-1. NO.2, 1973-

PHOTOELECTRIC SPECTROMETRY GROUP BULLETIN. XXX
  SUBS (1973): UV SPECTROMETRY GROUP BULLETIN.

PHOTOGRAPHIC TECHNIQUES IN SCIENTIFIC RESEARCH.
  + +PHOTOGR. TECH. SCI. RES.
  [ACADEMIC P.]
  LONDON &C. 1, 1973-
  GL/U-1. LO/N14. LO/U-2. ISSN 0302-4210

PHRONENSIS: SUPPLEMENT.
  ASSEN 1, 1973-
  OX/U-1.

PHYSICAL EDUCATION. XXX
  SUBS (1970) PART OF: BRITISH JOURNAL OF
  PHYSICAL EDUCATION.

PHYSICS OF CONDENSED MATTER.   XXX
++*PHYS. CONDENS. MATTER.*
[SPRINGER]
BERLIN 17(1), 1973-
ENGL., FR., OR GER. WITH ENGL. SUMM. PREV:
PHYSIK DER KONDENSIERTEN MATERIE FROM BAND 1,
1963- 16, 1973.
LO/N14.   XS/R10.

PHYTOPARASITICA.
AGRICULTURAL RESEARCH ORGANIZATION (ISRAEL):
VOLCANI CENTER.
BET DAGAN 1(1), JE 1973-
AB/U-2.   BL/U-1.   LO/N-2.   LO/N13.   LO/R-6.

PICKLE PAK SCIENCE.
++*PICKLE PAK SCI.*
PICKLE PACKERS INTERNATIONAL, INC.
ST. CHARLES, ILL. 1, JL 1971-
LO/N14.

**PIONEER. JOURNAL OF THE RHODESIA PIONEERS' &
EARLY SETTLERS' SOCIETY.**
BULAWAYO 1, N 1968-
LO/N-1.

PITCH PINE NATURALIST.
++*PITCH PINE NAT.*
CENTRAL ISLIP, N.Y. NO.1, 1972-
LO/N-2.

**PLANNER. JOURNAL OF THE ROYAL TOWN PLANNING
INSTITUTE.**   XXX
LONDON 59(7), JL/AG 1973-
PREV: JOURNAL OF THE ROYAL TOWN PLANNING INST-
ITUTE FROM 57(6), 1971- 59(6), 1973.
ED/N-1.   HL/U-1.   LO/R-5.

PLANNING & TRANSPORTATION ABSTRACTS.   XXX
++*PLANN. & TRANSP. ABSTR.*
GREATER LONDON COUNCIL: DEPARTMENT OF PLANNING
& TRANSPORTATION.
LONDON NO.1, JL 1969- 50, F/MR 1974.
SUBS: URBAN ABSTRACTS.
SO/U-1. NO.9, 1970-   HL/U-1. NO.45, 1973-
NO/U-1. NO.34, 1972-   SH/P-1. N 1973-

PLANT FOODS FOR MAN.
[NEWMAN BOOKS LTD.]
LONDON 1(1), 1973-
Q.
ED/N-1.   LO/N13.   LO/R-6.   OX/U-8.   OX/U-8.

PLASTY A KAUCUK.   XXX
++*PLASTY KAUC.*
(CZECHOSLOVAKIA) MINISTERSTVO CHEMICKEHO
PRUMYSLU.
PRAGUE 11, 1974-
PREV: PLASTICKE HMOTY A KAUCUK FROM 1, 1964-
10, 1973. CONTINUES PREV. NUMBERING.
LO/N14.

PLEBS.
YOUNG FABIAN GROUP.
LONDON NO.1, MR 1973-
2M.
LO/U-3.

POETRY NATION.
[CARCANET P.]
CHEADLE HULME, CHES. NO.1, N 1973-
2/A.
AD/U-1.   BN/U-1.   CA/U-1.   ED/N-1.   HL/U-1.   HL/U-2.
LO/U-2.   MA/P-1.   MA/U-1.   OX/U-1.   SH/U-1.

POETRY NEWS.
BIRMINGHAM POETRY CENTRE.
BIRMINGHAM NO.1, 1971-
CA/U-1.   ED/N-1. NO.7, 1973-   OX/U-1. NO.7, 1973-

POLACY. FOTO-PLOTKI.
[FIGARO-PRESS]
LONDON NO.1, 1974-
Q.
ED/N-1.   LO/N-1.

**POLICY ABSTRACTS & RESEARCH NEWSLETTER, MAK-
ERERE INSTITUTE OF SOCIAL RESEARCH.**   XXX
++*POLICY ABSTR. & RES. NEWSL. MAKERERE INST.
SOC. RES.*
KAMPALA 1(1), 1970- 1(2), 1971 ...
TITLE VARIES: POLICY ABSTRACTS & MISR NEWS-
LETTER. S/T: A JOURNAL OF POLICY COMMUNICAT-
ION. SUBS: RESEARCH ABSTRACTS & NEWSLETTER,
MAKERERE INSTITUTE OF SOCIAL RESEARCH.
LD/U-1. 1(2), 1971.

POLICY STUDIES JOURNAL.
++*POLICY STUD. J.*
POLICY STUDIES ORGANISATION.
URBANA, ILL. 1, 1972-
Q.
GL/U-2.

POLISH LITERATURE. LITTERATURE POLONAISE.
++*POL. LIT.*
WARSAW 1, JL/S 1968-
Q. ENGL. & FR.
ED/N-1. 7(1- 2), 1974-   ISSN 0032-289X

POLISH MEDICAL SCIENCES & HISTORY BULLETIN.   XXX
SUBS (1973): POLISH MEDICAL SCIENCES &
HISTORY BULLETIN & ABSTRACTS.

**POLISH MEDICAL SCIENCES & HISTORY BULLETIN &
ABSTRACTS.**   XXX
++*POL. MED. SCI. & HIST. BULL. & ABSTR.*
[POLISH MEDICAL PUBL.]
WARSAW 1, 1973-
PREV: POLISH MEDICAL SCIENCES & HISTORY BULL-
ETIN FROM 3, JL 1960- 14, 1971.
LD/U-1.   MA/U-1.

POLITICAL SCIENCE REVIEWER.
++*POLIT. SCI. REV.*
HAMPDEN-SYDNEY COLLEGE.
HAMPDEN-SYDNEY, VA. 1, 1971-
ANNU.
MA/U-1. 3, 1973-

POLITIK UND WAHLER.
++*POLIT. & WAHLER.*
[VERLAG ANTON HAIN]
MEISENHEIM AM GLAN 1, 1970-
MONOGR.
LO/N-1.

POLYSAR PROGRESS.
++*POLYSAR PROGR.*
DAVIDSON POLYSAR LTD.
SARNIA, ONT. 1965-
2M.
LO/N14. CURRENT BOX ONLY.   ISSN 0032-4027

POPULAR ELECTRONICS.   XXX
++*POP. ELECTRON.*
[ZIFF-DAVIS PUBL. CO.]
NEW YORK 5, 1974-
PREV: POPULAR ELECTRONICS INCLUDING ELECTRON-
ICS WORLD FROM 1, 1972- 4, 1973.
LO/N14.   ISSN 0032-4485

**POPULATION REPORT: SERIES B: INTERUTERINE
DEVICES.**
++*POPUL. REP., B.*
GEORGE WASHINGTON UNIVERSITY: DEPARTMENT OF
MEDICAL & PUBLIC AFFAIRS.
WASHINGTON, D.C. 1, D 1973-
DEPARTMENT SUBORD. TO: MEDICAL CENTER.
BL/U-1.   LO/S74.

POPULATION REPORT: SERIES C-D: STERILIZATION.
++*POPUL. REP., C-D.*
GEORGE WASHINGTON UNIVERSITY: DEPARTMENT OF
MEDICAL & PUBLIC AFFAIRS.
WASHINGTON, D.C. 1, 1973-
SEE NOTE FOR SERIES B.
BL/U-1.   LO/S74.

**POPULATION REPORT: SERIES F: PREGNANCY TERM-
INATION.**
++*POPUL. REP., F.*
GEORGE WASHINGTON UNIVERSITY: DEPARTMENT OF
MEDICAL & PUBLIC AFFAIRS.
WASHINGTON, D.C. 1, 1973-
SEE NOTE FOR SERIES B.
BL/U-1.   LO/S74.

POPULATION REPORT: SERIES G: PROSTAGLANDINS.
++*POPUL. REP., G.*
GEORGE WASHINGTON UNIVERSITY: DEPARTMENT OF
MEDICAL & PUBLIC AFFAIRS.
WASHINGTON, D.C. 1, 1973-
SEE NOTE FOR SERIES B.
BL/U-1.   LO/S74.

POPULATION REPORT: SERIES J: FAMILY PLANNING.
++*POPUL. REP., J.*
GEORGE WASHINGTON UNIVERSITY: DEPARTMENT OF
MEDICAL & PUBLIC AFFAIRS.
WASHINGTON, D.C. 1, 1973-
SEE NOTE FOR SERIES B.
BL/U-1.   LO/S74.

POROMAN.
PORT MORESBY NO.1, AP 1973-
LO/U-8.

POSTGRADUATE NEWS.
++POSTGRAD. NEWS.
SCOTTISH COUNCIL FOR POSTGRADUATE MEDICAL
EDUCATION.
EDINBURGH 1(1), 1973-
LO/N-1.

POVERTY RESEARCH SERIES.
++POVERTY RES. SER.
CHILD POVERTY ACTION GROUP.
LONDON NO.1, 1972[1973]
MONOGR.
SO/U-1.

POWER OF WOMEN.
POWER OF WOMEN COLLECTIVE.
LONDON 1(1), MR/AP 1974-
2/M.
LO/U-3.

POWLOKI OCHRONNE.   XXX
++POWLOKI OCHRON.
INSTYTUT MECHANIKI PRECYZYJNEJ.
[AGENCJA AUTORSKA]
WARSAW 1, AP 1973-
PREV: PRACE INSTYTUTU MECHANIKI PRECYZYJNEJ
FROM 1, 1952- 20, 1972.
LO/N13.

PRACE INSTYTUTU MECHANIKI PRECYZYJNEJ.   XXX
SUBS (1973): POWLOKI OCHRONNE.

**PRACE NAUKOWE INSTYTUTU TECHNOLOGII BUDOWY
MASZYN POLITECHNIKI WROCLAWSKIEJ: STUDIA I
MATERIALY.**
++PR. NAUK. INST. TECHNOL. BUDOWY MASZ.
POLITECH. WROCLAW., STUD. & MATER.
WROCLAW 1, 1970-
ENGL. SUMM.
LO/N13.

PRACTICAL ANTHROPOLOGY.   XXX
SUBS (1973): MISSIOLOGY.

PRAKTISCHE FORSTWIRT FUR DIE SCHWEIZ.   XXX
SUBS (1974): SCHWEIZER FORSTER.

PRAMANA. A JOURNAL OF PHYSICS.
INDIAN ACADEMY OF SCIENCES.
BANGALORE 1, 1973-
SPONS. BODIES ALSO: INDIAN PHYSICS ASSOCIATION
& INDIAN NATIONAL SCIENCE ACADEMY.
CA/U-2.   LO/N14.   OX/U-8. 1(2), 1973-

PRATO. STORIA E ARTE.
ASSOCIAZIONE TURISTICA PRATESE.
PRATO NO.1, AP 1960-
Q.
LO/U17.   ISSN 0032-6925

PRAZHEKTAR. LITARATURNA-MASTATSKI AL'MANAKH.
CLEVELAND 1, 1967-
WHITE RUSS. ENGL. TITLE: PROJECTOR. LITERARY-
ARTISTIC ALMANAC.
LO/U15.

**PRIBORY I SISTEMY UPRAVLENIJA (ENGL. TRANSL.
[1971-]).**
SEE: SOVIET INSTRUMENTATION & CONTROL JOURNAL.

PRIESTLICHE DIENST.
FREIBURG &C. 1, 1970-
OX/U-1.

**PRIO STUDIES FROM THE INTERNATIONAL PEACE
RESEARCH INSTITUTE.**
++PRIO STUD. INT. PEACE RES. INST.
[UNIVERSITETFORLAGET; ALLEN & UNWIN]
OSLO; LONDON NO.1, [1973]
MONOGR.
LO/N-1.

PRIRODA I KHOZJAISTVO SEVERA.
++PRIR. & KHOZ. SEV.
GEOGRAFICHESKOE OBSHCHESTVO SSSR: SEVERNYJ
FILIAL.
APATITY 1, 1969-
CA/U12.   LO/N13.

PRIRODNYJ GAZ SIBIRI.
++PRIR. GAZ SIB.
VSESOJUZNYJ NAUCHNO-ISSLEDOVATEL'SKIJ INSTITUT
PRIRODNYKH GAZOV: TJUMENSKIJ FILIAL.
TJUMEN 1, 1969-
LO/N13.

PROBLEMS OF EVOLUTION (NOVOSIBIRSK).   000
SEE: PROBLEMY EVOLJUTSII.

PROBLEMY BOR'BY S PRESTUPNOST'JU.
++PROBL. BOR'BY PRESTUPNOST'JU.
IRKUTSKIJ GOSUDARSTVENNYJ UNIVERSITET:
JURIDICHESKIJ FAKUL'TET.
IRKUTSK 1, 1970-
SPONS. BODY ALSO: OMSKAJA VYSSHAJA SHKOLA
MILITSII.
GL/U-1.

PROBLEMY BOR'BY PROTIV BURZHUAZNOJ IDEOLOGII.
++PROBL. BOR'BY PROTIV BURZHUAZNOJ IDEOL.
LENINGRADSKIJ GOSUDARSTVENNYJ UNIVERSITET.
LENINGRAD 1, 1971-
CC/U-1.   GL/U-1.   OX/U-1.

PROBLEMY EVOLJUTSII.
++PROBL. EVOL.
AKADEMIJA NAUK SSSR (SIBIRSKOE OTDELENIE):
OTDELENIE OBSHCHEJ BIOLOGII.
NOVOSIBIRSK 1, 1968-
ENGL. SUMM. & TITLE: PROBLEMS OF EVOLUTION.
LO/N-2.   LO/N13.

PROBLEMY ISTORICHESKOGO MATERIALIZMA.
++PROBL. ISTOR. MATER.
LENINGRADSKIJ GOSUDARSTVENNYJ UNIVERSITET.
LENINGRAD 1, 1971-
CC/U-1.   LO/U15.   OX/U-1.

**PROBLEMY ISTORIOGRAFII I ISTOCHNIKOVEDENIJA
ISTORII KPSS.**
LENINGRADSKIJ GOSUDARSTVENNYJ UNIVERSITET:
INSTITUT POVYSHENIJA KVALIFIKATSII
PREPODAVATELEJ OBSHCHESTVENNYKH NAUK.
LENINGRAD 1, 1971-
CA/U-1.   CC/U-1.   LO/U15.

PROBLEMY OSADOCHNOJ GEOLOGII DOKEMBRIJA.
(RUSSIA SSSR) MINISTERSTVO GEOLOGII.
MOSCOW 1, 1966-
SPONS. BODY ALSO: PETROZAVODSKIJ INSTITUT
GEOLOGII.
LO/N-4.   LO/N13.

PROBLEMY PALINOLOGII.
++PROBL. PALINOL.
AKADEMIJA NAUK UKRAJINS'KOJI RSR: INSTYTUT
BOTANIKY.
KIEV 1, 1971-
LO/N13.

PROBLEMY ROMANTIZMA. SBORNIK STATEJ.
++PROBL. ROMANTIZMA.
[IZDATEL'STVO ISKUSSTVO]
MOSCOW 1, 1967-
CC/U-1.

PROBLEMY TECHNIKI W MEDYCYNIE.
++PROBL. TECH. MED.
CENTRALNY OSRODEK TECHNIKI MEDYCZNEJ.
WARSAW 1, 1970-
ENGL., GER. & RUSS. SUMM.
LO/N13.

**PROCEEDINGS, COMMISSION ON ORE-FORMING FLUIDS
IN INCLUSIONS.**
++PROC. COMM. ORE-FORM. FLUIDS INCLUS.
WASHINGTON, D.C. 1968-
ANNU. COVER TITLE: FLUID INCLUSION RESEARCH;
PROCEEDINGS OF COFFI.
LO/N14.   OX/U-8.

**PROCEEDINGS, GEOLOGICAL ASSOCIATION OF
CANADA.**   XXX
SUBS (1974): GEOSCIENCE CANADA.

**PROCEEDINGS OF THE SOCIETY FOR GENERAL MICRO-
BIOLOGY.**   XXX
++PROC. SOC. GEN. MICROBIOL.
READING 1(1), 1973-
PREV: PUBL. AS PART OF JOURNAL OF GENERAL
MICROBIOLOGY.
AD/M-1.   GL/U-1.   GL/U-2.   HL/U-1.   LD/U-1.   LO/R-5.
LO/U-2.   SH/U-1.   SO/U-1.   ISSN 0306-2708

**PROCESSING. THE PLANT, EQUIPMENT & SYSTEMS
JOURNAL FOR THE PROCESSING INDUSTRIES.** XXX
[IPC IND. P.]
LONDON 20(10), OC 1974-
MON. PREV: CHEMICAL PROCESSING (LONDON)
FROM 1, 1955- 20(9), 1974.
LO/N14. LO/R-6. LO/U-2. XS/R10. ISSN 0305-439X

PROCUREMENT. XXX
INSTITUTE OF PURCHASING & SUPPLY.
LONDON NO.1, S 1973-
PREV: PURCHASING JOURNAL FROM 1947- AG 1973.
ED/N-1. SH/P-1. ISSN 0305-9073

PROCUREMENT WEEKLY. XXX
++*PROCURE. WKLY.*
INSTITUTE OF PURCHASING & SUPPLY.
LONDON 1(1), S 1973-
PREV: PURCHASING BULLETIN FROM 1, 1950- 24(35)
AG 1973.
ED/N-1. XS/R10. ISSN 0306-1922

PROGRES DE LA BIBLIOTHEQUE CANADIENNE. 000
SEE: CANADIAN LIBRARY PROGRESS.

PROGRESS IN BIOMETEOROLOGY: DIVISION A.
++*PROG. BIOMETEOROL., A.*
[SWETTS-ZEITLINGER]
AMSTERDAM 1, 1972-
LO/N-2. OX/U-1.

PROGRESS IN CLINICAL CANCER.
++*PROG. CLIN. CANCER.*
[GRUNE & STATTON, INC.]
NEW YORK 1, 1965-
CA/U-1. ISSN 0079-6166

PROGRESS IN EXPANDING NORTHAMPTON.
++*PROG. EXPAND. NORTHAMPTON.*
NORTHAMPTON DEVELOPMENT CORPORATION.
NORTHAMPTON 1, 1972-
ED/N-1. OX/U-1.

PROGRESS INTERNATIONAL.
++*PROG. INT.*
[NEW PROGRESS (PUBL.) LTD.]
LONDON 1, JA 1974-
MON.
ED/N-1. OX/U-1. LO/U-8. F 1974-

**PROGRESS REPORT, INTERNATIONAL DECADE OF
OCEAN EXPLORATION.**
++*PROG. REP. INT. DECADE OCEAN EXPLOR.*
(UNITED STATES) NATIONAL OCEANIC & ATMOSPHERIC
ADMINISTRATION.
WASHINGTON, D.C. [1], 1970/72(1973)-
LO/N14.

**PROJECT TECHNOLOGY BULLETIN, SCHOOLS COUNCIL
(GB).** XXX
SUBS (1971): SCHOOL TECHNOLOGY.

PROJECTOR. LITERARY-ARTISTIC ALMANAC. 000
SEE: PRAZHEKTAR. LITARATURNA-MASTATSKI
AL'MANAKH.

PROMYSHLENNO-EKONOMICHESKAJA GAZETA. XXX
SUBS (1960): EKONOMICHESKAJA GAZETA.

PROSPICE. A REVIEW OF THE ARTS.
[AQUILA PUBL. CO. LTD.]
SOLIHULL, WARKS. 1, 1973-
3/A.
BL/U-1. ED/N-1. OX/U-1.

PROTESTI FOR RADICAL CHANGE WITHOUT VIOLENCE.
[GRAHAM JAY]
LONDON 1(1), 1973-
MON.
ED/N-1.

PSYCHIATRIA CLINICA. XXX
++*PSYCHIATR. CLIN.*
[S. KARGER]
BASLE & C. 1(1), 1968-
ENGL., FR. & GER. WITH ENGL. SUMM. PREV:
SECTION A OF PSYCHIATRIA ET NEUROLOGIA.
LV/U-1. OX/U-8. ISSN 0033-264X

PSYCHIC RESEARCHER & SPIRITUALIST GAZETTE. XXX
++*PSYCH. RES. & SPIRITUALIST GAZ.*
SPIRITUALIST ASSOCIATION OF GREAT BRITAIN.
[LENNARD & ERSKINE LTD.]
GERRARDS CROSS NO.12, JE 1973-
PREV: SPIRITUALIST GAZETTE FROM NO.1, JE 1972-
11, MY 1973.
LO/N-1.

**[PUBBLICAZIONI] ISTITUTO DI CHIMICA FARMAC-
EUTICA E TOSSICOLOGICA, UNIVERSITA DI TRIESTE.XX**
TRIESTE N.5, 1968- 17, 1971.
PREV: [PUBBLICAZIONI] ISTITUTO DI CHIMICA
FARMACEUTICA, UNIVERSITA DI TRIESTE FROM N.1,
1959- 4, 1960.
LO/N14.

**[PUBBLICAZIONI] ISTITUTO DI CHIMICA FARMAC-
EUTICA, UNIVERSITA DI TRIESTE.** XXX
SUBS (1968): [PUBBLICAZIONI] ISTITUTO DI
CHIMICA FARMACEUTICA E TOSSICOLOGICA, UNIV-
ERSITA DI TRIESTE.

**[PUBBLICAZIONI] ISTITUTO DI TECNICA FARMAC-
EUTICA, UNIVERSITA DI TRIESTE.** XXX
TRIESTE N.1, 1972-
PREV: [PUBBLICAZIONI] ISTITUTO DI CHIMICA
FARMACEUTICA E TOSSICOLOGICA, UNIVERSITA DI
TRIESTE FROM N.5, 1968- 17, 1971.
LO/N14.

PUBLIC AFFAIRS. LEARGAS. XXX
INSTITUTE OF PUBLIC ADMINISTRATION (EIRE).
DUBLIN 1(1), OC 1968-
PREV: LEARGAS FROM NO.1, 1965- 16, S 1968.
CB/U-1. DB/U-2. ED/N-1. BL/U-1. 5, 1972-

PUBLIC CLEANSING. XXX
SUBS (1973): SOLID WASTES MANAGEMENT.

PUBLIC FINANCE & ACCOUNTANCY. XXX
++*PUBLIC FINANC. & ACCOUNT.*
CHARTERED INSTITUTE OF PUBLIC FINANCE &
ACCOUNTANCY.
LONDON 1, 1974-
MON. PREV: LOCAL GOVERNMENT FINANCE FROM 39,
1935- 77, 1973.
CA/U-1. ED/N-1. GL/U-1. LO/U-3. OX/U-1. OX/U17.
SH/U-1. SO/U-1. ISSN 0305-9014

PUBLIC HEALTH IN EUROPE.
++*PUBLIC HEALTH EUR.*
WORLD HEALTH ORGANIZATION: REGIONAL OFFICE FOR
EUROPE.
COPENHAGEN 1, 1972-
ANNU.
LO/U-3.

PUBLIC HEALTH REVIEWS.
++*PUBLIC HEALTH REV.*
[INTERNATIONAL HEALTH PUBL.]
TEL AVIV 1, 1972-
Q.
LO/N13.

**PUBLICACIONES, ARCHIVO GENERAL DE LA NACION
(MEXICO): SERIE II.**
++*PUBL. ARCH. GEN. NAC. (MEX.). SII.*
MEXICO, D.F. NO.1, 1971-
PREV: SERIES FROM 1910- 1936.
CA/U-1.

**PUBLICATIONS, ASSOCIATION FOR 18TH-CENTURY
STUDIES, MCMASTER UNIVERSITY.**
++*PUBL. ASSOC. 18TH-CENTURY STUD. MCMASTER UNIV.*
[A.M. HAKKERT LTD.]
TORONTO 1, 1971-
OX/U-1.

**PUBLICATIONS, ASSOCIATION FOR SCOTTISH LIT-
ERARY STUDIES.**
++*PUBL. ASSOC. SCOTT. LIT. STUD.*
[SCOTTISH ACADEMIC P.]
EDINBURGH NO.1, 1972-
GL/U-1.

**PUBLICATIONS DE L'ASSOCIATION SUISSE DE POLIT-
IQUE ETRANGERE.**
++*PUBL. ASSOC. SUISSE POLIT. ETRANG.*
[EDITIONS PAUL HAUPT]
BERNE & STUTTGART NO.1, [1972]-
MONOGR.
LO/N-1.

**PUBLICATIONS, DEPARTMENT OF FISHERIES & FAUNA
CONSERVATION (SOUTH AUSTRALIA).**
++*PUBL. DEP. FISH. & FAUNA CONSERV.(SOUTH AUST.)*
ADELAIDE NO.1, [1971]-
LO/N-2.

**PUBLICATION, INSTITUTE OF BIOMETRY & COMMUN-
ITY MEDICINE, UNIVERSITY OF EXETER.**
++*PUBL. INST. BIOM. & COMMUNITY MED. UNIV.*
EXETER.
EXETER NO.1, 1973-
CA/U-1.

PUBLICATIONS, INSTITUTE FOR FISCAL STUDIES.
++PUBL. INST. FISCAL STUD.
LONDON NO.1, F 1971-
CA/U-1. NO.7, 1973-

**[PUBLICATIONS] INSTITUTE OF MUSICAL INST-
RUMENT TECHNOLOGY.**   XXX
LONDON NO.1, 1938- 59, 1965.//
LO/N14.

**PUBLICATIONS IN SALVAGE ARCHEOLOGY, RIVER
BASIN SURVEYS, SMITHSONIAN INSTITUTION.**   XXX
++PUBL. SALVAGE ARCHEOL. RIVER BASIN SURV.
SMITHSON. INST.
LINCOLN, NEBR. NO.1, 1966- 13, 1969.//
LO/N-2.

PUBLIZISTIK-HISTORISCHE BEITRAGE.
++PUBL.-HIST. BEITR.
[VERLAG DOKUMENTATION]
BERLIN 1, 1971-
LO/N-1. OX/U-1.

PURATATTVA.
INDIAN ARCHAEOLOGICAL SOCIETY.
VARANASI NO.1, 1967-
CA/U-1.

PURCHASING BULLETIN.   XXX
SUBS (1973): PROCUREMENT WEEKLY.

PURCHASING BULLETIN ANNUAL REVIEW.
++PURCH. BULL. ANNU. REV.
INSTITUTE OF PURCHASING & SUPPLY.
LONDON 1973-
CA/U-1.

PURCHASING JOURNAL.   XXX
SUBS (1973): PROCUREMENT.

PYTANNJA MOVNOJI KUL'TURY.   XXX
++PYTANNJA MOVNOJI KUL'T.
AKADEMIJA NAUK UKRAJINS'KOJI RSR: INSTYTUT
MOVOZNAVSTVA.
KIEV 1, 1967- 4, 1970 ...
SUBS: RIDNE SLOVO.
LO/U15.

**PYTANNJA SOTSIALISTYCHNOHO REALIZMU. ZBIRNYK
STATEJ PRO SUCHASNU UKRAJINS'KU LITERATURA.**
++PYTANNJA SOTS. REALIZMU.
KIEV 1, 1961-
LO/U15.

PYTANNJA TEKSTOLOHIJI
++PYTANNJA TEKSTOL.
AKADEMIJA NAUK UKRAJINS'KOJI RSR: INSTYTUT
LITERATURY.
KIEV 1, 1968-
LO/U15.

**QUADERNI DELLA BIBLIOTECA CENTRALE, UNIV-
ERSITA DI LECCE.**
++QUAD. BIBL. CENT. UNIV. LECCE.
LECCE NO.1, 1972-
LO/N-1.

**QUADERNI DELL'ISTITUTO DI ARCHITETTURA DELL'
UNIVERSITA DI GENOVA.**
++QUAD. IST. ARCHIT. UNIV. GENOVA.
GENOA 1, 1968-
LO/U17.

QUADERNI VERONESI DI VARIA LETTERATURA.
++QUAD. VERONESI VARIA LETT.
[FIORINI & GHIDINI]
VERONA NO.1, 1967-
MONOGR.
LO/N-1.

QUARRY MANAGEMENT & PRODUCTS.   XXX
++QUARRY MANAGE. & PROD.
LONDON 1, 1974-
MON. PREV. PART OF: CEMENT, LIME & GRAVEL
FROM 4, 1929- 49, 1974; & QUARRY MANAGERS'
JOURNAL FROM 1, 1918- 58, 1974. CONTAINS A
SECTION ENTITLED: TRANSACTIONS, INSTITUTE OF
QUARRYING WHICH PREV. APPEARED AS PART OF
QUARRY MANAGERS' JOURNAL.
GL/U-2. LO/N14. ISSN 0305-9421

QUARRY MANAGERS' JOURNAL.   XXX
SUBS (1974): PART OF QUARRY MANAGEMENT & PRO-
DUCTS.

**QUARTERLY, INSTITUTION OF FIRE ENGINEERS: NEW
SERIES.**   XXX
SUBS (1973): FIRE ENGINEERS JOURNAL.

**QUARTERLY LIST OF ADDITIONS IN RUSSIAN & EAST
EUROPEAN LANGUAGES, BRITISH LIBRARY OF POLIT-
ICAL & ECONOMIC SCIENCE.**
++Q. LIST ADDIT. RUSS. & EAST EUROP. LANG. BR.
LIBR. POLIT. & ECON. SCI.
LONDON SCHOOL OF ECONOMICS & POLITICAL SCIENCE:
BRITISH LIBRARY OF POLITICAL & ECONOMIC SCIENCE
LONDON NO.1, MR 1973-
DB/U-2. OX/U-1. SH/U-1.

**QUEENSLAND JUSTICE OF THE PEACE & LOCAL AUTH-
ORITIES' JOURNAL.**   XXX
SUBS (1973): QUEENSLAND LAWYER.

QUEENSLAND LAWYER.   XXX
++QUEENSL. LAWYER.
[LAW BOOK CO.]
BRISBANE 1, 1973-
2M. PREV: QUEENSLAND JUSTICE OF THE PEACE &
LOCAL AUTHORITIES' JOURNAL FROM 1, 1907- 66,
1972.
OX/U15.

RACING WORLD.
++RAC. WORLD.
JOCKEYS' ASSOCIATION OF GREAT BRITAIN.
LONDON 1(1), 1973-
CA/U-1. ED/N-1.

RADIALS BULLETIN.
++RADIALS BULL.
LIBRARY ASSOCIATION.
LONDON 1, 1974-
3/A. S/T: RESEARCH & DEVELOPMENT- INFORMATION
& LIBRARY SCIENCE.
CA/U-1. ED/N-1. GL/U-2. NO/U-1. OX/U-1. SF/U-1.
ISSN 0302-2706

RADIATION & ENVIRONMENTAL BIOPHYSICS.   XXX
++RADIAT. & ENVIRON. BIOPHYS.
[SPRINGER]
BERLIN &C. 11, 1974-
GER., ENGL. OR FR. PREV: BIOPHYSIK FROM 1,
1963- 10, 1973.
BL/U-1. LO/N14.

RADICAL SCIENCE JOURNAL.
++RADICAL SCI J.
LONDON NO.1, JA 1974-
3/A.
ED/N-1. LO/U-3. OX/U-8. ISSN 0305-0963

**RAIN. ROYAL ANTHROPOLOGICAL INSTITUTE NEWS-
LETTER.**
LONDON NO.1, MR 1974-
6/A.
CA/U-1. ED/N-1. LO/M24. OX/U-1.

RAPTOR RESEARCH.   XXX
++RAPTOR RES.
RAPTOR RESEARCH FOUNDATION, INC.
VERMILLION, S.D. 6, 1972-
PREV: RAPTOR RESEARCH NEWS FROM 1, JA 1967- 5,
1972.
LO/N13.

RAPTOR RESEARCH NEWS.   XXX
++RAPTOR RES. NEWS.
RAPTOR RESEARCH FOUNDATION, INC.
CENTERVILLE, S.D. 1, JA 1967- 5, 1972 ...
Q.
LO/N13.**

RASILIMALI. TANZANIA INVESTMENT OUTLOOK.
TANZANIA INVESTMENT BANK.
DAR ES SALAAM NO.1, 1972-
2A.
LO/U-3. LO/U14.

R.C. REVOLUCION Y CULTURA.   XXX
HAVANA NO.1, 1967- 3(21), 1970.
SUBS: REVOLUCION Y CULTURA.
OX/U-1.

RE. REVIEW OF ETHNOLOGY.
[E. STIGLMAYR]
VIENNA 1, AG 1968-
2/M.
LO/S10. ISSN 0048-6507

READINGS IN ECONOMICS.   000
SEE: ANNUAL EDITIONS: READINGS IN ECONOMICS.

RECENT PUBLICATIONS IN THE SOCIAL & BEHAVIORAL SCIENCES.
++RECENT PUBL. SOC. & BEHAV. SCI.
[SAGE PUBL.]
BEVERLEY HILLS, CALIF. 1966-
ISSUED AS AN ANNUAL SUPPL. TO: ABS GUIDE TO
RECENT PUBLICATIONS IN THE SOCIAL & BEHAVIORAL
SCIENCES.
LO/U-3.   BL/U-1.   ‡W. 1967A   ISSN 0079-998X

RECENT PUBLICATIONS IN THEOLOGY.
++RECENT PUBL. THEOL.
[HOPKINS INFORMATION SERVICES]
NORWICH NO.1, 1971-
CA/U-1.   ED/N-1.   OX/U-1.

RECHERCHE URBAINE.
++RECH. URBAINE.
THE HAGUE &C. 1, 1972-
OX/U-1.

RECLAMATION INDUSTRIES INTERNATIONAL.
++RECLAM. IND. INT.
[MACLAREN]
CROYDON NO.1, MY/JE 1973-
6/A. ENGL., FR. & GER. ABSTR.
ED/N-1.   OX/U-1.   XS/R10. NO.3, 1973-   ISSN 0306-3658

RECREATION NEWS.
++RECREAT. NEWS.
COUNTRYSIDE COMMISSION (GB).
LONDON NO.1, 4/N 1968-
PRODUCED BY THE COMMISSION FOR THE COUNTRYSIDE
RESEARCH ADVISORY GROUP.
LO/N-1.   LO/U-2.   BN/U-2. NO.3, 1969-   NO/U-1. 1970-
HL/U-1. NO.3-4; 9-10; 12-17; 20-23; 25-

RECREATION NEWS: SUPPLEMENT.
++RECREAT. NEWS, SUPPL.
COUNTRYSIDE COMMISSION (GB).
LONDON NO.1, JE 1970-
HL/U-1.   LO/N-1.   OX/U-3.   LO/U12. NO.10, D 1973-

RED FRONT. BULLETIN OF THE RED FRONT MOVEMENT.
LONDON NO.1, JA/F 1973-
MON.
ED/N-1.   OX/U-1.   OX/U17.

RED FRONT. FOR WORKING-CLASS POWER, FOR A SOCIALIST BRITAINI XXX
MARXIST-LENINIST ORGANISATION OF BRITAIN. XXX
LONDON 1(1), OC 1967- MY/JE 1972.
NS. NO.1, JA/F 1973.
PREV: HAMMER OR ANVIL FROM 1(1), N 1965- 3(1),
JL/AG 1967. SUBS: CLASS AGAINST CLASS.
LO/U-3.   ED/N-1. MR 1970-   OX/U-1. 1970-

REFORMED & PRESBYTERIAN WORLD. XXX
SUBS (1971): REFORMED WORLD.

REFORMED WORLD. XXX
WORLD ALLIANCE OF REFORMED CHURCHES (PRESBYTER-
IAN & CONGREGATIONAL).
GENEVA 31(5), 1971-
Q. PREV: REFORMED & PRESBYTERIAN WORLD FROM
24, 1956- 31(3/4), 1970.
OX/U-1.   ISSN 0034-3056

REFRACTAIRE.
ASSOCIATION DES AMIS DE LOUIS LECOIN.
PARIS NO.1, AP 1974-
MON.
LO/U-3.

REGIONAL SCIENCE PERSPECTIVES.
MID-CONTINENT REGIONAL SCIENCE ASSOCIATION.
MANHATTAN, KANSAS 1, 1971-
SPONS. BODY ALSO: DEPARTMENT OF ECONOMICS,
KANSAS STATE UNIVERSITY OF AGRICULTURE &
APPLIED SCIENCE.
CA/U-1.

REGIONAL & URBAN ECONOMICS.
++REG. & URBAN ECON.
[NORTH-HOLLAND]
AMSTERDAM 1, MY 1971-
Q.
BN/U-1.   GL/U-1.

REGULAE BENEDICTI STUDIA.
++REGULAE BENEDICTI STUD.
[VERLAG GERSTENBERG]
HILDESHEIM 1, 1972-
AD/U-1.   OX/U-1.

RELIGIONI E CIVILTA.
++RELIG. & CIVILTA.
UNIVERSITA DI ROMA: SCUOLA DI STUDI STORICO-
RELIGIOSI.
ROME 1, 1972-
OX/U-1.

RENAL PHYSIOLOGY.
++RENAL PHYSIOL.
UNIVERSITY OF SHEFFIELD: BIOMEDICAL INFORMATION
PROJECT.
SHEFFIELD 1, 1970-
MON. BIOMEDICAL INFORMATION PROJECT SUBORD.
TO: DEPARTMENT OF PHYSIOLOGY.
CA/U-1. 5(2), 1974-   ED/N-1. 5(2), 1974-
ISSN 0300-3434

RENEWABLE ENERGY BULLETIN.
++RENEWABLE ENERGY BULL.
[MULTI-SCIENCE PUBL. CO.]
LONDON 1(1), JA/MR 1974-
Q.
CA/U-1.   ED/N-1.   LO/N14.   OX/U-1.   ISSN 0306-364X

REPERTOIRE MONDIAL DES INSTITUTIONS DE SCIENCES SOCIALES. 000
SEE: WORLD INDEX OF SOCIAL SCIENCE INSTITUT-
IONS.

REPERTOIRE DES THESES DE DOCTORAT EUROPEENNES.
++REPERT. THESES DOCT. EUR.
UNIVERSITE DE LIEGE: BIBLIOTHEQUE GENERALE.
[EDITIONS ANDRE DEWALLENS]
LIEGE 1969/1970-
ANNU.
CA/U-1. 1971/72-   GL/U-1. 1970/71-   LO/U-1. 1971/72-
SW/U-1. 1971/72.

REPORT, ASTROPHYSICS RESEARCH UNIT, SCIENCE RESEARCH COUNCIL (GB).
++REP. ASTROPHYS. RES. UNIT SCI. RES. COUNC.(GB)
ABINGDON ARU-R1, 1969-
LO/N14.

REPORT, CENTRE FOR EUROPEAN AGRICULTURAL STUDIES, WYE COLLEGE.
++REP. CENT. EUR. AGRIC. STUD. WYE COLL.
WYE NO.1, [1973]-
MA/U-4.

REPORT, CHEMICAL ENGINEERING DEPARTMENT, MONASH UNIVERSITY.
++REP. CHEM. ENG. DEP. MONASH UNIV.
CLAYTON, VICTORIA CMER 72-1, 1972-
LO/N14.

[REPORT] INSTITUTE OF PETROLEUM. XXX
LONDON IP 74-001, 1974-
PREV: JOURNAL, INSTITUTE OF PETROLEUM FROM
25(183), 1939- 59(570), 1973.
LO/N14.

REPORT, INSTITUTE OF SEAWEED RESEARCH. XXX
++REP. INST. SEAWEED RES.
EDINBURGH 1951- 1968.//
LO/N-2.

REPORTS ON MATHEMATICAL LOGIC.
++REP. MATH. LOGIC.
WARSAW 1, 1973-
OX/U-1.

REPORT, NEWFOUNDLAND SOIL SURVEY.
++REP. NEWFOUNDLAND SOIL SURV.
(CANADA) DEPARTMENT OF AGRICULTURE: RESEARCH
BRANCH.
OTTAWA NO.1, 1972-
LO/N-1.

REPORT, SAUDI ARABIAN NATURAL HISTORY SOCIETY.XX
++REP. SAUDI ARABIAN NAT. HIST. SOC.
JEDDAH 1(1), 1971 ...
SUBS: JOURNAL, SAUDI ARABIAN NATURAL HISTORY
SOCIETY.
LO/N-2.

REPORT & STUDIES IN THE HISTORY OF ART, NAT-IONAL GALLERY OF ART (US). XXX
++REP. & STUD. HIST. ART NATL. GALLERY ART (US).
WASHINGTON, D.C. 1967- 1969.
SUBS: ANNUAL REPORT, NATIONAL GALLERY OF ART
(US).
GL/U-1.   LO/U17.   RE/U-1.   ISSN 0080-1240

REPORT OF TRAFFIC SAFETY & NUISANCE RESEARCH INSTITUTE (JAPAN). 000
SEE: KOTSU ANZEN KOGAI KENKYUJO HOKOKU.

REPROGRAPHICS QUARTERLY.   XXX
+ +REPROGRAPHICS Q.
NATIONAL REPROGRAPHIC CENTRE FOR DOCUMENTATION.
HATFIELD, HERTS. 7(1), 1973/74-
PREV: NRCD BULLETIN FROM 1, 1967- 6, 1972/73.
AD/U-1.   ED/N-1.   LO/N-2.   LO/N12.   MA/U-1.

**RESEARCH ABSTRACTS & NEWSLETTER, MAKERERE
INSTITUTE OF SOCIAL RESEARCH.**   XXX
+ +RES. ABSTR. & NEWSL. MAKERERE INST. SOC. RES.
KAMPALA 1(3), JL 1973-
PREV: POLICY ABSTRACTS & RESEARCH NEWSLETTER,
MAKERERE INSTITUTE OF SOCIAL RESEARCH FROM
1(1), 1970- 1(2), 1971. S/T: A JOURNAL OF
POLICY COMMUNICATION.
LO/U14.

**RESEARCH BULLETIN, DEPARTMENT OF FORESTS
(PAPUA & NEW GUINEA).**
+ +RES. BULL. DEP. FOR. (PAPUA & NEW GUINEA).
PORT MORESBY 1, 1973-
OX/U-3.

RESEARCH INTO HIGHER EDUCATION MONOGRAPHS.
+ +RES. HIGHER EDUC. MONOGR.
SOCIETY FOR RESEARCH INTO HIGHER EDUCATION.
LONDON NO.1, 1966-
LO/U-1.   ISSN 0486-5049

**RESEARCH NEWS, NIGERIAN INSTITUTE OF SOCIAL &
ECONOMIC RESEARCH.**
+ +RES. NEWS NIGER. INST. SOC. & ECON. RES.
IBADAN NO.1, 1972-
LO/U14.

RESEARCH IN NORWAY.
+ +RES. NORWAY.
OSLO 1, 1973-
BL/U-1.   ED/N-1.

RESEARCH OUTLOOK.   XXX
+ +RES. OUTLOOK.
BATTELLE MEMORIAL INSTITUTE.
COLUMBUS, OHIO 5(1), 1973-
3/A. PREV. BATTELLE RESEARCH OUTLOOK
FROM 1, 1969- 4, 1972.
XS/R10.   ISSN 0092-1122

**RESEARCH PAPERS, CENTRE FOR ENVIRONMENTAL
STUDIES.**
+ +RES. PAP. CENT. ENVIRON. STUD.
LONDON NO.1, 1973-
LO/U-2.   SA/U-1.   CA/U-1. NO.2, 1973   ISSN 0306-297X

**RESEARCH IN PROGRESS, AFRICAN STUDIES CENTER,
UNIVERSITY OF CALIFORNIA.**
+ +RES. PROG. AFR. STUD. CENT. UNIV. CALIF.
LOS ANGELES [NO.1], 1972-1973(1973)-
LO/U14.

**RESEARCH IN PROGRESS IN ENGLISH & HISTORICAL
STUDIES IN THE UNIVERSITIES OF THE BRITISH
ISLES.**
+ +RES. PROG. ENGL. & HIST. STUD. UNIV. BR. ISLES
[ST. JAMES P.]
LONDON 1971-
AD/U-1.   GL/U-1.` CURRENT & PRECURRENT EDITIONS ONLY.

**RESEARCH IN PROGRESS, SCHOOL OF LIBRARIANSHIP,
POLYTECHNIC OF NORTH LONDON.**
+ +RES. PROG. SCH. LIBR. POLYTECH. NORTH LOND.
LONDON NO.1, JE 1969-
Q.
SH/U-1. NO.12, 1973-

**RESEARCH & PUBLICATIONS, DEPARTMENT OF LAND
ECONOMY, UNIVERSITY OF CAMBRIDGE.**
+ +RES. & PUBL. DEP. LAND ECON. UNIV. CAMB.
CAMBRIDGE OC 1971/JL 1973(1973)-
CA/U-1.

**RESEARCH PUBLICATION, ONTARIO HISTORICAL
SOCIETY.**
+ +RES. PUBL. ONT. HIST. SOC.
TORONTO NO.1, 1972-
OX/U-9.

**RESEARCH REPORT, DERWENT ARCHAEOLOGICAL
SOCIETY.**
+ +RES. REP. DERWENT ARCHAEOL. SOC.
MATLOCK 1, 1973-
SH/P-1.

**RESEARCH REPORT, SAFETY IN MINES RESEARCH
ESTABLISHMENT.**   XXX
SUBS (1973): SMRE REPORT.

RESEARCH REPORTS, SMITHSONIAN INSTITUTION.
+ +RES. REP. SMITHSON. INST.
WASHINGTON, D.C. NO.1, 1972-
Q.
LO/N-2.   LO/N13.

**RESEARCH REVIEW, MINERALS RESEARCH LABORATOR-
IES, CSIRO (AUSTRALIA).**
+ +RES. REV. MINER. RES. LAB. CSIRO (AUST.).
CANBERRA NO.1, 1971-
LO/N14.

**RESEARCH USING TRANSPLANTED TUMOURS OF LABOR-
ATORY ANIMALS.**
+ +RES. USING TRANSPLANT. TUMOURS LAB. ANIM.
IMPERIAL CANCER RESEARCH FUND.
LONDON 1, 1964-
S/T: A CROSS-REFERENCED BIBLIOGRAPHY.
CR/M-1.   LO/N13.   MA/U-1.   ISSN 0080-1747

RESOURCES FOR AMERICAN LITERARY STUDY.
+ +RESOUR. AM. LIT. STUDY.
UNIVERSITY OF MARYLAND: DEPARTMENT OF ENGLISH.
COLLEGE PARK, MD. 1(1), 1971-
2/A. SPONS. BODY ALSO: VIRGINIA COMMONWEALTH
UNIVERSITY.
EX/U-1.   ISSN 0048-7384

RESOURCES POLICY.
+ +RESOUR. POLICY.
[IPC SCI. & TECHNOL. P.]
GUILDFORD 1(1), S 1974-
Q.
AD/U-1.   CA/U-4.   LO/S14.   MA/U-1.   XS/R10.   XS/T-4.

RESPIRATORY TECHNOLOGY.   XXX
+ +RESPIR. TECHNOL.
CANADIAN SOCIETY OF INHALATION THERAPY TECH-
NICIANS.
EDMONTON 7(2), 1971-
PREV: CANADIAN INHALATION THERAPY FROM 1,
1965- 7(1), 1971.
LO/N13.

RETAIL & DISTRIBUTION MANAGEMENT.
+ +RETAIL & DISTRIB. MANAGE.
LONDON [NO.]1, 1973-
CA/U-1.   GL/U-2.   MA/P-1.   OX/U-1.

**RETE. STRUKTURGESCHICHTE DER NATURWISSEN-
SCHAFTEN.**
[VERLAG GERSTENBERG]
HILDESHEIM 1(1), 1971-
ENGL. OR GER. WITH SUMM. IN THE OTHER LANGUAGE
LO/N-1.   LO/N-4.

**REVIEW OF EDUCATION. A JOURNAL OF THE INST-
ITUTE OF EDUCATION, UNIVERSITY OF NIGERIA.**
+ +REV. EDUC.
NSUKKA 1(1), 1971-
LO/U14. 1(1), 1971.

REVIEW OF ETHNOLOGY.   000
SEE: RE. REVIEW OF ETHNOLOGY.

REVIEWS OF PURE & APPLIED CHEMISTRY.   XXX
+ +REV. PURE & APPL. CHEM.
ROYAL AUSTRALIAN CHEMICAL INSTITUTE.
MELBOURNE 1, MR 1951- 22, 1972.//
XS/R10.   ED/N-1. 12, 1962-   SW/U-1. 13, 1963-
ISSN 0034-687X

REVIEW OF RADICAL POLITICAL ECONOMICS.
+ +REV. RADICAL POLIT. ECON.
UNION FOR RADICAL POLITICAL ECONOMICS.
ANN ARBOR, MICH. 1, MY 1969-
Q.
SH/U-1. 5, 1973-   LO/U-3. AG 1970; 3(1), 1971-

**REVIEW, TUSSOCK GRASSLANDS & MOUNTAIN LANDS
INSTITUTE.**
+ +REV. TUSSOCK GRASSL. & MT. LANDS INST.
CHRISTCHURCH, N.Z. NO.1, 1961-
3/A.
LO/R-5. NO.22, 1971-   ISSN 0577-9898

**REVISTA, ACADEMIA COLOMBIANA DE HISTORIA
ECLESIASTICA.**
+ +REV. ACAD. COLOMB. HIST. ECLESIASTICA.
MEDELLIN NO.1, 1966-
Q. ISSUED BY THE UNIVERSIDAD PONTIFICIA
BOLIVARIANA.
OX/U-1.   ISSN 0567-5669

REVISTA, ARCHIVO GENERAL (ARGENTINA).
+ + REV. ARCH. GEN. (ARGENT.).
BUENOS AIRES 1(1), 1971-
OX/U-1.

REVISTA BRASILEIRA DE FOLCLORE.
+ + REV. BRAS. FOLCLORE.
(BRAZIL) MINISTERIO DA EDUCACAO E
CULTURA: CAMPANHA DE DEFESA DO
FOLCLORE BRASILEIRO.
RIO DE JANEIRO 1(1), S/D 1961-
3/A.
LO/S30. 2(2-3), 1962; 7(19), 1967-   ISSN 0034-7213

REVISTA DO CENTRO DE ESTUDOS DE CABO VERDE:
SERIE DE CIENCIAS BIOLOGICAS.
+ + REV. CENT. ESTUD. CABO VERDE, CIENC. BIOL.
PRAIA 1, 1972-
LO/N-2.

REVISTA DE CIENCIAS MATEMATICAS: SERIE A.   XXX
+ + REV. CIENC. MAT., A.
UNIVERSIDADE DO LOURENCO MARQUES.
LOURENCO MARQUES 1, 1969-
PREV: PART OF REVISTA DOS ESTUDOS GERAIS UNIV-
ERSITARIOS DE MOCAMBIQUE: SERIE 1: CIENCIAS
MATEMATICAS FISICAS E QUIMICAS FROM 1, 1964.
LO/N13.

REVISTA CIVILIZACAO BRASILEIRA.
+ + REV. CIVILIZ. BRAS.
RIO DE JANEIRO 1(1), MR 1965-
LO/U-1. 1(2), 1965- 4(21/22), 1968.*

REVISTA CIVILIZACAO BRASILEIRA: CUADERNO
ESPECIAL.
+ + REV. CIVILIZ. BRAS., CUAD. ESPEC.
[EDITORA CIVILIZACAO BRASILEIRA]
RIO DE JANEIRO NO.1, N 1967-
LO/U-1. NO.2 & 3, 1968.

REVISTA DE ESTUDIOS DEL PACIFICO.
+ + REV. ESTUD. PAC.
CENTRO DE ESTUDIOS DEL PACIFICO (CHILE).
VALPARAISO NO.1, AP 1971-
3/A.
LO/U-1.

REVISTA, FACULTAD DE CIENCIAS VETERINARIAS,
UNIVERSIDAD NACIONAL DE LA PLATA: TERCERA
EPOCA.   XXX
SUBS (1969): ANALECTA VETERINARIA.

REVISTA DA FACULDADE DE LETRAS, UNIVERSIDADE
DO PORTO: SERIE DE HISTORIA.
+ + REV. FAC. LET. UNIV. PORTO, SER. HIST.
OPORTO 1, 1970-
LO/U17.

REVISTA DA FACULDADE DE MEDICINA VETERINARIA,
UNIVERSIDADE DE SAO PAULO.   XXX
SUBS (1972): REVISTA DA FACULDADE DE MED-
ICINA VETERINARIA E ZOOTECNIA, UNIVERSIDADE
DE SAO PAULO.

REVISTA DA FACULDADE DE MEDICINA VETERINARIA
E ZOOTECNIA, UNIVERSIDADE DE SAO PAULO.   XXX
+ + REV. FAC. MED. VET. & ZOOTEC. UNIV. SAO PAULO.
SAO PAULO 9, 1972-
PREV: REVISTA DA FACULDADE DE MEDICINA VET-
ERINARIA, UNIVERSIDADE DE SAO PAULO FROM 1,
1938- 8, 1971.
LO/N-2.

REVISTA, FACULDADE DE ODONTOLOGIA DE SAO JOSE
DOS CAMPOS.
+ + REV. FAC. ODONTOL. SAO JOSE CAMPOS.
SAO JOSE DOS CAMPOS 1, 1972-
LO/N13.

REVISTA IBEROAMERICANA DE LITERATURA: 2S.
+ + REV. IBEROAM. LIT., 2S.
UNIVERSIDAD DE LA REPUBLICA (URUGUAY):
DEPARTAMENTO DE LITERATURA IBEROAMERICANA.
MONTEVIDEO 1(1), 1966-
PREV. SERIES FROM 1, 1959- 4, 1962. PUBL.
SUSPENDED 1963- 1965.
SO/U-1.

REVISTA DE INSTITUTIONES EUROPEAS.
+ + REV. INST. EUR.
INSTITUTO DE ESTUDIOS POLITICOS (MADRID).
MADRID 1, 1974-
LO/U-2.

REVISTA DE LA INTEGRACION CENTROAMERICANA.
+ + REV. INTEGRAC. CENTROAM.
TEGUCIGALPA 1, 1971-
OX/U-1.

REVISTA INTERAMERICANA DE SOCIOLOGIA.
SOCIEDAD MEXICANA DE GEOGRAFIA Y
ESTADISTICA.
MEXICO, D.F. 1(1), JL/S 1966-
SPONS. BODIES ALSO: ASOCIACION MEXICANA
DE SOCIOLOGICA; & INTERNATIONAL SOCIO-
LOGICAL ASSOCIATION.
OX/U-1. 2(8), 1972-   ISSN 0557-8558

REVOLUCION Y CULTURA.   XXX
+ + REVOLUC. & CULT.
HAVANA MY 1972-
PREV: R.C. FROM NO.1, 1967- 3(21), 1970.
OX/U-1.

REVUE D'ANALYSE NUMERIQUE ET DE LA THEORIE DE
L'APPROXIMATION.
+ + REV. ANAL. NUMER. & THEOR. APPROXIM.
[EDITIONS DE L'ACADEMIE]
CLUJ 1, 1972-
CA/U-2.   LO/N13.

REVUE BULGARE D'HISTOIRE.   000
SEE: BULGARIAN HISTORICAL REVIEW.

REVUE CAMEROUNAISE DE DROIT. CAMEROON LAW
REVIEW.
+ + REV. CAMEROUNAISE DROIT.
YAOUNDE NO.1, 1972-
LO/U14.

REVUE FRANCAISE DES MALADIES RESPIRATOIRES.
+ + REV. FR. MAL. RESPIR.
PARIS 1(1), 1973-
OX/U-8.

REVUE GENERALE DE DROIT.   XXX
+ + REV. GEN. DROIT.
UNIVERSITY OF OTTAWA: FACULTY OF LAW.
OTTAWA 1, 1970-
2/A. PREV: JUSTINIEN FROM 1964- 1969. ISSUED
BY THE FACULTY'S CIVIL LAW SECTION. SUBSERIES
OF COLLECTION DES TRAVAUX DE LA FACULTE DE
DROIT DE L'UNIVERSITE D'OTTAWA.
OX/U15.   ISSN 0035-3086

REVUE HORTICOLE SUISSE.   XXX
+ + REV. HORTIC. SUISSE.
ECOLE CANTONALE D'HORTICULTURE: ASSOCIATION DES
ANCIENS ELEVES.
GENEVA 1, 1928- 46, 1973.//
LO/N13. 37, 1964-

REVUE ROUMAINE DE NEUROLOGIE ET DE PSYCH-
IATRIE.   XXX
+ + REV. ROUM. NEUROL. & PSYCHIATR.
ACADEMIA REPUBLICII POPULARE ROMINE.
[EDITIONS DE L'ACADEMIE]
BUCHAREST 1, 1974-
PREV: REVUE ROUMAINE DE NEUROLOGIE FROM 1,
1964- 10, 1973.
GL/U-1.   LO/N13.

RHODESIA RESEARCH INDEX.
+ + RHOD. RES. INDEX.
(RHODESIA) DEPARTMENT OF THE PRIME MINISTER:
SCIENTIFIC LIASION OFFICE.
SALISBURY 1970-
SPONS. BODY ALSO: UNIVERSITY OF RHODESIA
LIBRARY.
LO/N14. 1971-

RIBA LIBRARY BULLETIN.   XXX
SUBS (1973): PART OF ARCHITECTURAL PERIOD-
ICALS INDEX.

RICERCHE DI STORIA SOCIALE E RELIGIOSA.
+ + RIC. STOR. SOC. & RELIG.
CENTRO STUDI PER LE FONTI DELLA STORIA DELLA
CHIESA NEL VENTO.
[EDIZIONI DI STORIA E LETTERATURA]
ROME 1, JA/JE 1972-
SPONS. BODY ALSO: CENTRO STUDI DI STORIA SOC-
IALE E RELIGIOSA NEL MEZZOGIORNO.
OX/U-1.

RIDNE SLOVO.   xxx
AKADEMIJA NAUK UKRAJINS'KOJI RSR: INSTYTUT
MOVOZNAVSTVA.
KIEV 5, 1971-
PREV: PYTANNJA MOVNOJI KUL'TURY FROM 1, 1967-
4, 1970.
LO/U15.

RIVISTA INTERNAZIONALE DI ECONOMIA DEI TRAS-
PORTI. INTERNATIONAL JOURNAL OF TRANSPORT
ECONOMICS.
++*RIV. INT. ECON. TRASP.*
ROME 1, 1974-
LD/U-1.

ROEBUCK. JOURNAL OF THE NORTHUMBERLAND WILD-
LIFE TRUST.
NEWCASTLE UPON TYNE NO.1, 1973-
LO/N-2.

ROMANISTIK.
[SCHAUBLE VERLAG]
BENSBERG NO.1, [1971]
MONOGR. ENGL. & FR. SUMM.
LO/N-1.

ROS. JOURNAL OF KERRY LIFE.
KILLARNEY 1(1), 1971-
CA/U-1.   OX/U-1.

RUSSIAN HISTORY. HISTOIRE RUSSE.
++*RUSS. HIST.*
UNIVERSITY OF PITTSBURGH: UNIVERSITY CENTER FOR
INTERNATIONAL STUDIES.
PITTSBURGH 1, 1974-
AD/U-1.   LD/U-1.

RUSSKIJ JAZYK DLJA STUDENTOV-INOSTRANTSEV.
++*RUSS. JAZYK STUD.-INOSTR.*
[UCHEBNO-METODICHESKOE UPRAVLENIE PO VYSSHIM
UCHEBNYM ZAVEDENIJAMA
MOSCOW 1, 1961-
S/T: SBORNIK METODICHESKICH STATEJ.
LO/U15.

SAFETY SCIENCE ABSTRACTS.
++*SAF. SCI. ABSTR.*
NEW YORK UNIVERSITY: CENTER FOR SAFETY.
[CAMBRIDGE SCIENTIFIC ABSTRACTS]
RIVERDALE, MD. 1, 1973-
LO/N14.

SAFETY SURVEYOR.
++*SAF. SURV.*
[VICTOR GREEN LTD.]
LONDON 1(1), MY 1973-
LO/S24.

SAGE INTERNATIONAL YEARBOOK OF FOREIGN POLICY
STUDIES.
++*SAGE INT. YEARB. FOREIGN POLICY STUD.*
[SAGE PUBL.]
BEVERLY HILLS & LONDON 1973-
AD/U-1.   CA/U-1.   OX/U-1.

SAMBHAVANA.
KURUKSHETRA UNIVERSITY.
KURUKSHETRA, PUNJAB. 1(1), 1972-
2/A. HINDI.
LO/U14.

SANDOZ BULLETIN.
++*SANDOZ BULL.*
SANDOZ AG.
BASLE NO.1, 1965-
ALSO ISSUED IN FR., GER. & SPAN.
*LO/N-2.***

SANGEET KALA VIHAR: ENGLISH SUPPLEMENT.   xxx
INDIAN MUSICOLOGICAL SOCIETY.
BARODA 1(1-4), JA/MR- D 1970 ...
SUBS: JOURNAL OF THE INDIAN MUSICOLOGICAL
SOCIETY.
ED/N-1.   OX/U13.   ISSN 0036-4320

SAUGETIERSCHUTZ. ZEITSCHRIFT FUR THERIOPHYLAXE.
HOHENBUCHEN 1, 1970-
LO/N-2.

SBORNIK, KHIMIKO-TEKHNOLOGICHESKIJ INSTITUT
(PRAGUE): PROTSESSY I APPARATY, AVTOMATIZAT-
SIJA.   000
SEE: SBORNIK VYSOKE SKOLY CHEMICKO-TECHNOLOG-
ICKE V PRAZE: CHEMICKE INZENYRSTVI A AUTOMAT-
IZACE.

SBORNIK NAUCHNOJ FANTASTIKI.   xxx
++*SB. NAUCHN. FANTASTIKI.*
[IZDATEL'STVO £ZNANIE£]
MOSCOW 11, 1972-
PREV: AL'MANAKH NAUCHNOJ FANTASTIKI FROM 1,
1964- 10, 1971. CONT. PREV. NUMBERING.
GL/U-1.

SBORNIK NAUCHNYKH RABOT, NAUCHNO-ISSLED-
OVATEL'SKIJ SEKTOR, KIEVSKIJ UNIVERSITET.
++*SB. NAUCHN. RAB. NAUCHNO-ISSLED. SEKT. KIEV.*
UNIV.
KIEV NO.1, 1963-
*LO/N-2.***

SBORNIK NEOPUBLIKOVANNYKH MATERIALOV.
++*SB. NEOPUBL. MATER.*
TSENTRAL'NYJ GOSUDARSTVENNYJ ARKHIV LITERATURY
I ISKUSSTVA SSSR.
MOSCOW 1, 1970-
GL/U-1.

SBORNIK NORMATIVNYKH MATERIALOV PO
VOPROSAM VNESHNEJ TORGOVL1 SSSR.
++*SB. NORMATIVNYKH MATER. VOPR. VNESHN.*
TORG. SSSR.
(RUSSIA SSSR) MINISTERSTVO VNESHNEJ
TORGOVLI.
MOSCOW 1, 1961-
LO/U15. 1970-

SBORNIK PRIRODNE VEDY: OBORY GEOLOGIE, GEOG-
RAFIE, BIOLOGIE.   xxx
SUBS (1960): ACTA UNIVERSITATIS PALACKIANAE
OLOMUCENSIS: GEOGRAPHICA-GEOLOGICA.

SBORNIK TRUDOVE NA VISSHIJA MEDITSINSKI   xxx
INSTITUT (PLOVDIV).
SUBS (1967): MEDITSINSKI PROBLEMI.

SBORNIK VYSOKE SKOLY CHEMICKO-TECHNOLOGICKE
V PRAZE: CHEMICKE INZENYRSTVI A AUTOMATIZACE.
++*SB. VYS. SK. CHEM.-TECHNOL. PRAZE, CHEM. INZ.*
& AUTOM.
PRAGUE 1, 1967-
CZECH OR ENGL. WITH CZECH., ENGL., GER. OR
RUSS. SUMM. TITLE ALSO IN RUSS.: SBORNIK,
KHIMIKO-TEKHNOLOGICHESKIJ INSTITUT: PROTSEEY I
APPARATY, AVTOMATIZATSIJA; & ENGL.: SCIENT-
IFIC PAPERS, INSTITUTE OF CHEMICAL TECHNOLOGY:
CHEMICAL ENGINEERING & AUTOMATION.
LO/N14.

SCALE JOURNAL.   xxx
SUBS (1974): WEIGHING & MEASUREMENT.

SCANDINAVIAN ACTUARIAL JOURNAL.   xxx
DANISH SOCIETY OF ACTUARIES.
STOCKHOLM NO.1, 1974-
Q. PREV: SKANDINAVISK AKTUARIETIDSKRIFT FROM
1, 1918- 56, 1973. SPONS. BODIES ALSO: ACT-
UARIAL SOCIETY OF FINLAND; NORWEGIAN SOCIETY
OF ACTUARIES; & SWEDISH SOCIETY OF ACTUARIES.
CA/U-2.

SCANDINAVIAN AUDIOLOGY.
++*SCAND. AUDIOL.*
NORDISK AUDIOLOGISK SELSKAB.
COPENHAGEN 1, MR 1972-
LO/N13.   MA/U-1. 3, 1974-   ISSN 0048-9271

SCANDINAVIAN JOURNAL OF RHEUMATOLOGY: SUPPLEMENT
++*SCAND. J. RHEUMATOL., SUPPL.*
[ALMQVIST & WIKSELL]
STOCKHOLM 1, 1973-
BL/U-1.

SCANDIANAVIAN JOURNAL OF STATISTICS THEORY &
APPLICATIONS.
++*SCAND. J. STAT. THEOR. & APPL.*
SWEDISH STATISTICAL ASSOCIATION.
[ALMQVIST & WIKSELL]
STOCKHOLM 1(1), 1974-
SPONS. BODIES ALSO: DANISH SOCIETY FOR THEOR-
ETICAL STATISTICS; FINNISH STATISTICAL SOCIETY
& NORWEGIAN STATISTICAL SOCIETY.
ED/U-1.   LO/N10.

SCANNER. A FORTNIGHTLY DIGEST OF CURRENT
EVENTS IN THE SOUTH ASIAN SUBCONTINENT.
RESEARCH & DOCUMENTATION CENTRE.
LONDON 1(1), AP 1973-
LO/N12.   OX/U-1.

SCHOOL TECHNOLOGY.   XXX
++SCH. TECH.
SCHOOLS COUNCIL (GB): PROJECT TECHNOLOGY.
LOUGHBOROUGH 4, 1971-
PREV: PROJECT TECHNOLOGY BULLETIN, SCHOOLS
COUNCIL (GB) FROM 1, 1968.
ED/N-1. 4(2), 1971-   EX/U-1. 5(3), 1972-
SW/U-1. 6, 1972/73-

**SCHRIFTENREIHE, INSTITUT FUR VERKEHRSWESEN
(KARLSRUHE).**
++SCHRIFTENR. INST. VERKEHRSWESEN (KARLSRUHE).
KARLSRUHE 1, 1967-
LO/N14. ‡W. 2(6)Å.

**SCHRIFTENREIHE DER VEREINIGUNG ZUR ERFORSCHUNG
DER NEUEREN GESCHICHTE.**
++SCHRIFTENR. VER. ERFORSCH. NEUEREN GESCH.
[ASCHENDORFF]
MUNSTER 1, 1965-
CA/U-1.   GL/U-1.

SCHWEIZER FORSTER.   XXX
++SCHWEIZ. FOR.
[SAUERLANDER]
AARAU 110, 1974-
PREV: PRAKTISCHE FORSTWIRT FUR DIE SCHWEIZ
FROM 1, 1865- 109, 1973.
LO/N13.

SCHWEIZERISCHE WASCHEREI- UND FARBEREI-ZEITUNG.X
SUBS (1965): SCHWEIZERISCHE WASCHEREI-ZEITUNG.

SCHWEIZERISCHE WASCHEREI-ZEITUNG.   XXX
++SCHWEIZER. WASCHEREI-ZTG.
[BUCHDRUCKEREI STAFA]
STAFA 60, 1965- 68, 1973 ...
PREV: SCHWEIZERISCHE WASCHEREI- UND FARBEREI-
ZEITUNG FROM 1, 1906- 59, 1964. SUBS: FACH-
SCHRIFT FUR TEXTILREINIGUNG.
LO/N13.

SCIENCE FICTION MONTHLY.
++SCI. FICT. MON.
[NEW ENGLISH LIBRARY]
LONDON 1(1), JA 1974-
CA/U-1. 1(7), 1974-   ED/N-1. 1(7), 1974-

SCIENCE & PSYCHOANALYSIS.   XXX
++SCI. & PSYCHOANAL.
ACADEMY OF PSYCHOANALYSIS.
NEW YORK & LONDON 1, 1958- 21, 1972.//
EACH VOL. HAS A DISTINCTIVE TITLE.
LO/U-1.   ED/U-1. 3, 1960- 13, 1968 ‡W. 4;5;7;8;&10Å
ISSN 0080-7443

SCIENCE & PUBLIC POLICY.   XXX
++SCI. & PUBLIC POLICY.
SCIENCE POLICY FOUNDATION.
LONDON 1(1), JA 1974-
PREV: SCIENCE POLICY FROM 1, 1972- 2(6), N/D
1973.
BL/U-1.   ED/N-1.   LO/N-2.   LO/N13.   SH/P-1.   XS/T-4.

**SCIENTIFIC PAPERS, INSTITUTE OF CHEMICAL
TECHNOLOGY (PRAGUE): CHEMICAL ENGINEERING &
AUTOMATION.**   000
SEE: SBORNIK VYSOKE SKOLY CHEMICKO-TECHNOLOG-
ICKE V PRAZE: CHEMICKE INZENYRSTVI A AUTOMAT-
IZACE.

**SCIENTIFIC REPORTS ON INDUSTRIAL HYGIENE &
OCCUPATIONAL DISEASES IN CZECHOSLOVAKIA.**   XXX
SUBS (1971): CZECHOSLOVAK BIBLIOGRAPHY ON
INDUSTRIAL HYGIENE & OCCUPATIONAL DISEASES.

SCOTLAND.   XXX
SUBS (1974): BUSINESS SCOTLAND.

SCOTTISH CATERING NEWS.
++SCOTT. CATER. NEWS.
GLASGOW NO.1, 7/S 1973-
SUPPL. TO: SCOTTISH LICENSED TRADE NEWS.
ED/N-1.

SCOTTISH ECONOMIC HISTORY NEWSLETTER.
++SCOTT. ECON. HIST. NEWSL.
UNIVERSITY OF ABERDEEN: DEPARTMENT OF ECONOMIC
HISTORY.
ABERDEEN NO.1, 1972-
AD/U-1.   ED/N-1.   LO/U-2.   SO/U-1.

SCOTTISH LITERARY JOURNAL.
++SCOTT. LIT. J.
ASSOCIATION FOR SCOTTISH LITERARY STUDIES.
ABERDEEN 1, 1974-
AD/U-1.   BL/U-1.   OX/U-1.   ISSN 0305-0785

SCOTTISH LOCAL GOVERNMENT REVIEW.
++SCOTT. LOCAL GOV. REV.
KIRKNEWTON 1, JL 1971-
ED/N-1.

**SCOTTISH TENANT. NEWSPAPER OF THE SCOTTISH
COUNCIL OF TENANTS.**
++SCOTT. TENANT.
GLASGOW NO.1, AP 1973-
ED/N-1.   OX/U-1.

SCREEN PRINTING.   XXX
++SCREEN PRINT.
[SIGNS OF THE TIMES PUBL. CO.]
CINCINNATI 53, 1970-
PREV: SCREEN PRINTING MAGAZINE FROM 46(1), JA
1968- 52, 1970.
LO/N14.

SCREEN PRINTING MAGAZINE.   XXX
++SCREEN PRINT. MAG.
[SIGNS OF THE TIMES PUBL. CO.]
CINCINNATI 46(1), JA 1968- 52, 1970 ...
PREV: SCREEN PROCESS MAGAZINE. SUBS: SCREEN
PRINTING.
LO/N14.   ISSN 0036-9594

SCREEN PROCESS MAGAZINE.   XXX
SUBS (1968): SCREEN PRINTING MAGAZINE.

SEA GRANT 70'S.
TEXAS A & M UNIVERSITY.
COLLEGE STATION, TEX. 1, S 1970-
MON. SPONS. BODY ALSO: ENVIRONMENTAL DATA
SERVICE, NATIONAL OCEANIC & ATMOSPHERIC
ADMINISTRATION (US).
LO/N14. CURRENT BOX ONLY.   ISSN 0048-9867

SEAISI QUARTERLY.
++SEAISI Q.
SOUTH EAST ASIA IRON & STEEL INSTITUTE.
SINGAPORE 1(1), JA 1972-
LO/N14.

SEDIMENTA.
UNIVERSITY OF MIAMI: ROSENSTIEL SCHOOL OF
MARINE & ATMOSPHERIC SCIENCE.
MIAMI 1, 1972-
PRODUCED BY THE SCHOOL'S COMPARATIVE SEDIMENT-
OLOGY LABORATORY.
LO/N-2.   LO/N13.

**SELECTED HIGHLIGHTS ON CRIME & DELINQUENCY
LITERATURE.**   XXX
++SEL. HIGHLIGHTS CRIME & DELINQ. LIT.
NATIONAL COUNCIL ON CRIME & DELINQUENCY (US).
NEW YORK NO.1, OC 1968- 8, D 1969.
2M. SUBS. PART OF: CRIME & DELINQUENCY
LITERATURE.
ISSN 0582-494X

**SERIE BOTANICA E FISIOLOGIA VEGETAL, INSTIT-
UTO DE PESQUISAS E EXPERIMENTACAO AGROPECU-
ARIAS DO NORTE (BRAZIL).**   XXX
++SER. BOT. & FISIOL. VEG. INST. PESQUI. & EXP.
AGROPECU. NORTE (BRAZ.).
BELEM 1, 1970/1972.//
LO/N-2.

**SERIE DIVULGACION, INSTITUTO COLOMBIANO DE
PEDAGOGICA.**
++SER. DIVULG. INST. COLOMB. PEDAGOG.
BOGOTA 1, 1972-
OX/U-1.

**SERIE FAUNA, INSTITUTO DE INVESTIGACION DE
LOS RECURSOS NATURALES RENOVABLES.**
++SER. FAUNA INST. INVEST. RECURSOS NAT. RENOV.
SALTA, ARGENT. NO.1, 1972-
LO/N-2.

**SERIE FERTILIDADE DE SOLO, INSTITUTO DE PES-
QUISAS E EXPERIMENTACAO AGROPECUARIAS DO
NORTE (BRAZIL).**   XXX
++SER. FERT. SOLO INST. PESQUI. & EXP. AGROPECU.
NORTE (BRAZ.).
BELEM 1, 1971.//
LO/N-2.

**SERIE INVESTIGACIONES, INSTITUTO COLOMBIANO
DE PEDAGOGICA.**
++SER. INVEST. INST. COLOMB. PEDAGOG.
BOGOTA 1, 1971-
OX/U-1.

SERIE SOLOS DA AMAZONIA, INSTITUTO DE PES-
QUISAS E EXPERIMENTACAO AGROPECUARIAS DO
NORTE (BRAZIL).   XXX
++SER. SOLOS AMAZONIA INST. PESQUI. & EXP.
 AGROPECU. NORTE (BRAZ.).
 BELEM 1, 1967- 3, 1971.//
 LO/N-2.

SHELL MOLD NEWS.   000
 SEE: SHERU MORUDO NYUSU.

SHERU MORUDO NYUSU. SHELL MOLD NEWS.   XXX
 NIHON SHERU MORUDO KYOKAI.
 TOKYO NO.1, 1962- 184, 1972...
 MON. SUBS: JACT NYUSU.
 LO/N13.   ISSN 0582-9992

SHIPBUILDING & SHIPPING RECORD.   XXX
 SUBS (1974): PART OF MARINE WEEK.

SIGN LANGUAGE STUDIES.
++SIGN LANG. STUD.
 INDIANA UNIVERSITY: RESEARCH CENTER FOR THE
 LANGUAGE SCIENCES.
 [MOUTON]
 THE HAGUE 1, 1972-
 2/A.
 MA/U-1.   SH/U-1.

SILK & RAYON INDUSTRIES OF INDIA.   XXX
 SUBS (1973): MAN-MADE TEXTILES IN INDIA.

SINGAPORE BULLETIN.
++SINGAPORE BULL.
 (SINGAPORE) MINISTRY OF CULTURE.
 SINGAPORE 1, 1972-
 HL/U-1.*

SINGAPORE LAW REVIEW.   XXX
++SINGAPORE LAW REV.
 UNIVERSITY OF SINGAPORE LAW SOCIETY.
 SINGAPORE 1, 1969-
 ANNU. INCORP: ME JUDICE FROM 1, 1957- 8,
 1967.
 OX/U15.   ISSN 0080-9705

SIWA NEWS.
 SCOTTISH INLAND WATERWAYS ASSOCIATION.
 EDINBURGH [NO.1, JE] 1972-
 CA/U-1. NO.4, 1973-   ED/N-1. NO.2, 1972-

SKANDINAVISK AKTUARIETIDSKRIFT.   XXX
 SUBS (1974): SCANDINAVIAN ACTUARIAL JOURNAL.

SLOVAKIA. SLOVENSKO.
 [TATRAPRESS]
 BRATISLAVA 1, 1969-
 Q. ENGL. & SLOVAK.
 LA/U-1.

SMRE REPORT.   XXX
++SMRE REP.
 SAFETY IN MINES RESEARCH ESTABLISHMENT.
 SHEFFIELD R1, 1973-
 PREV: RESEARCH REPORT, SAFETY IN MINES RES-
 EARCH ESTABLISHMENT FROM NO.1, 1950- 284, 1973
 LO/N-4.   LO/N14.

SOCIAL INDICATORS RESEARCH.
++SOC. INDIC. RES.
 [REIDEL PUBL. CO.]
 DORDRECHT 1(1), MY 1974-
 4/A. S/T: AN INTERNATIONAL & INTERDISCIPLIN-
 ARY JOURNAL FOR QUALITY OF LIFE MEASUREMENT.

SOCIAL & LABOUR BULLETIN.
++SOC. & LABOUR BULL.
 INTERNATIONAL LABOUR OFFICE.
 GENEVA NO.1, 1974-
 Q.
 BL/U-1.   ED/N-1.   LO/U-3.   NW/U-1.   OX/U16.   RE/U-1.

SOCIAL SCIENCE SERIES (OTTAWA).   000
 SEE: SOCIAL SCIENCE SERIES, NORTHERN SCIENCE
 RESEARCH GROUP (CANADA).

SOCIAL SCIENCE SERIES, NORTHERN SCIENCE RES-
EARCH GROUP (CANADA).
++SOC. SCI. SER. NORTH. SCI. RES. GROUP (CAN.).
 [UNIV. OF OTTAWA P.]
 OTTAWA NO.1, 1971-
 LO/N-1.

SOCIAL SCIENCES CITATION INDEX.
++SOC. SCI. CIT. INDEX.
 INSTITUTE FOR SCIENTIFIC INFORMATION.
 PHILADELPHIA 1, 1973-
 OX/U-1.   CA/U-1.   GL/U-2.

SOCIAL SECURITY STATISTICS.
++SOC. SECUR. STAT. (GB).
 (GREAT BRITAIN) DEPARTMENT OF HEALTH & SOCIAL
 SECURITY.
 LONDON 1, 1972(1973)-
 AD/U-1.   CA/U-1.   LO/U-3.   RE/U-1.

SOCIAL SERVICES YEAR BOOK.
++SOC. SERV. YEAR BOOK.
 [COUNCILS & EDUCATION P.]
 LONDON 1973/74(1973)-
 LO/N-1.   LO/S18.   MA/U-1.   SO/U-1.

SOCIAL WORK. MAATSKAPLIKE WERK.
++SOC. WORK. (S. AFR.).
 STELLENBOSCH 1, 1965-
 Q. ENGL. & AFR.
 SO/U-1. 1, 1965- 9, 1973.   ISSN 0037-8054

SOCIAL WORK SERVICE.
++SOC. WORK SERV.
 (GREAT BRITAIN) DEPARTMENT OF HEALTH &
 SOCIAL SECURITY.
 LONDON NO.1, MR 1973-
 SO/U-1.

SOCIALISM: THEORY AND PRACTICE.
++SOCIAL., THEORY & PRACT.
 [NOVOSTI PRESS AGENCY]
 MOSCOW NO.1, 1965-
 ED/N-1.   OX/U-1.   CA/U-1. 1973-

SOCIALIST PERSPECTIVE.
++SOC. PERSPECT.
 COUNCIL FOR POLITICAL STUDIES (INDIA).
 CALCUTTA 1(1), JE 1973-
 S/T: A QUARTERLY JOURNAL OF SOCIAL SCIENCES.
 LO/N12.   LO/U-3.

SOCIALIST RECONSTRUCTION.   XXX
++SOC. RECONSTR.
 NEW YORK 1(1), AG 1971.
 2M. PREV: DE LEONIST FROM 1(1), MY/JE 1969-
 S/OC 1970. SUBS: SOCIALIST REPUBLIC.
 LO/U-3.

SOCIALIST REPUBLIC.   XXX
++SOC. REPUB.   XXX
 LEAGUE FOR SOCIALIST RECONSTRUCTION.
 NEW YORK 1(1), JA/F 1973-
 2M. PREV: SOCIALIST RECONSTRUCTION FROM 1(1),
 AG 1971.
 LO/U-3.

SOCIALIST WORKER (TRINIDAD).
++SOC. WORK. (TRINIDAD).
 TRANSPORT & INDUSTRIAL WORKERS' UNION
 (TRINIDAD).
 CUREPE NO.1, 1/N 1973-
 LO/U-8.

SOCIOLOGY. REVIEWS OF NEW BOOKS.
 HELEN DWIGHT REID EDUCATIONAL FOUNDATION.
 WASHINGTON, D.C. 1, OC 1973-
 MON.
 OX/U-1.

SOCIOLOSKI PREGLED.
++SOCIOL. PREGL.
 SRPSKO SOCIOLOSKO DRUSTVO.
 BELGRADE 1, 1961-
 OX/U-1.

SOCJOLOGICZNE PROBLEMY PRZEMYSLU I KLASY
ROBOTNICZEJ.
++SOCJOL. PROBL. PRZEM. & KLASY ROB.
 WYZSZA SZKOLA NAUK SPOLECZNYCH: ZAKLAD BADAN
 SPOLECZNYCH PRZEMYSLU I KLASY ROBOTNICZEJ.
 WARSAW 1, 1966-
 GL/U-1.

SOFTWARE. PRACTICE & EXPERIENCE.
 [WILEY INTERSCIENCE]
 LONDON 1, 1971-
 Q.
 SF/U-1.   MA/U-1. 3, 1973-   ISSN 0038-0644

SOLID FUEL & COAL MERCHANT & SHIPPER.　XXX
++*SOLID FUEL & COAL MERCH. & SHIPP.*
[HARPER TRADE JOURNALS]
LONDON NO.151, 1972-
PREV: SOLID FUEL FROM NO.1, 1966- 150, 1971.
LO/N14.

SOLID WASTES MANAGEMENT.　XXX
++*SOLID WASTES MANAGE.*
INSTITUTE OF SOLID WASTES MANAGEMENT.
LONDON 63(8), AG 1973-
PREV: PUBLIC CLEANSING FROM 49(587), 1959-
63(7), 1973.
ED/N-1.　XS/R10.

SOLIDARITY MOTOR BULLETIN.
++*SOLIDARITY MOT. BULL.*
LONDON NO.1, [1973]-
HL/U-1.　OX/U17.

SOLOMON ISLANDS RESEARCH REGISTER.
++*SOLOMON ISL. RES. REGIST.*
HONIARA 1, 1972-
OX/U-9.

SOLOMON ISLANDS STAMP MAGAZINE.
++*SOLOMON ISL. STAMP MAG.*
(BRITISH SOLOMON ISLANDS) POSTS & TELECOMMUN-
ICATIONS DEPARTMENT.
HONIARA NO.1, D 1966-
Q.
LO/N10.

SOLSTICE. POETRY MAGAZINE.
CAMBRIDGE 1, 1966-
Q.
ED/N-1.　GL/U-1.　ISSN 0038-1225

SOTHIS. A MAGAZINE OF THE NEW AEON.
ST. ALBANS 1(1), MR 1973-
2/A.
CA/U-1.　ED/N-1.　OX/U-1.

SOTSIOLOGICHESKI IZSLEDOVANIJA.　XXX
++*SOTSIOL. IZSLED.*
BULGARSKA AKADEMIJA NA NAUKITE: INSTITUT PO
SOTSIOLOGIJA.
SOFIA 1-4, 1968.
SUBS: SOTSIOLOGICHESKI PROBLEMI.
OX/U-1.

SOTSIOLOGICHESKI PROBLEMI.　XXX
++*SOTSIOL. PROBL.*
BULGARSKA AKADEMIJA NA NAUKITE: INSTITUT PO
SOTSIOLOGIJA.
SOFIA 1(1), 1969-
2/M. ENGL. & RUSS. SUMM. PREV: SOTSIOLOGICH-
ESKI IZSLEDOVANIJA FROM 1-4, 1968.
LO/N-1.　OX/U-1.

SOUNDING BRASS ø THE CONDUCTOR.　XXX
++*SOUND. BRASS ■ CONDUCTOR.*
NATIONAL ASSOCIATION OF BRASS BAND CONDUCTORS.
[NOVELLO]
LONDON 1, AP 1972-
CONDUCTOR PREV. PUBL. SEPARATELY FROM 1958.
CA/U-1.　ED/N-1.　OX/U-1.

SOUNDING ROCKET DATA IN JAPAN.
++*SOUND. ROCKET DATA JAP.*
TOKYO DAIGAKU: INSTITUTE OF SPACE & AERONAUT-
ICAL SCIENCE.
TOKYO 1, 1972-
VOL.1 COVERS 1958- 1972.
LO/N14.

**SOUNDINGS. AN ANNUAL ANTHOLOGY OF NEW IRISH
POETRY.**
[BLACKSTAFF P.]
BELFAST 1, 1972-
AD/U-1.　CA/U-1.

SOUTH AFRICA. A VISUAL HISTORY.
JOHANNESBURG 1, 1971-
NO/U-1.　SA/U-1.　CA/U-1. 1972-　LO/U14. 1973-

SOUTH AFRICAN ARCHIVES OF OPHTHALMOLOGY.
++*SOUTH AFR. ARCH. OPHTHALMOL.*
BLINDNESS RESEARCH FOUNDATION.
JOHANNESBURG 1(1), 1973-
LO/N14.　OX/U-8.

**SOUTH AFRICAN GEOGRAPHER. SUID-AFRIKAANSE
GEOGRAAF.**　XXX
++*SOUTH AFR. GEOGR.*
STELLENBOSCH 4, 1972/3-
2/A. ENGL. & AFR. PREV: TYDSKRIF VIR AARDY-
RYDSKUNDE FROM 1, 1957- 3, 1972.
AD/U-1.

SOUTHEASTERN EUROPE. L'EUROPE DU SUD EST.
++*SOUTHEAST. EUR.*
UNIVERSITY OF PITTSBURGH: UNIVERSITY
CENTER FOR INTERNATIONAL STUDIES.
PITTSBURGH 1, 1974-
AD/U-1.

SOUTHERN ECONOMIC REVIEW.
++*SOUTH. ECON. REV.*
ANNAMALAI UNIVERSITY.
ANNAMALAINAGAR 1, 1971-
Q.
LO/N12.

SOUTHWESTERN JOURNAL OF ANTHROPOLOGY.　XXX
SUBS (1973): JOURNAL OF ANTHROPOLOGICAL
RESEARCH.

SOVETSKIJ DAGESTAN .
++*SOV. DAGEST.*
KOMMUNISTICHESKAJA PARTIJA SOVETSKOGO SOJUZA:
DAGESTANSKIJ OBLASTNOJ KOMITET.
MAKHACHKALA 1, 1965-
2M. S/T: OBSHCHESTVENNO-POLITICHESKIJ I
LITERATURNYJ ZHURNAL.
GL/U-1. 1970-

SOVETSKIJ KOLLEKTSIONER.
++*SOV. KOLLEKT.*
MOSKOVSKOE GORODSKOE OBSHCHESTVO KOLLEKTSION-
EROV.
MOSCOW 1, 1963-
LO/U15.

SOVIET INSTRUMENTATION & CONTROL JOURNAL.　XXX
++*SOV. INSTRUM. & CONTROL J.*
[TRANSCRIPTS JOURNALS LTD.]
OXFORD & LONDON JA 1971-
MON. ENGL. TRANSL. OF PRIBORY I SISTEMY UPRA-
VLENIJA. PREV: SOVIET JOURNAL OF INSTRUMENT-
ATION & CONTROL FROM NO.1, JA 1967- 12, 1970.
BH/P-1.　LO/N-4.

**SOVREMENNIK. ZHURNAL RUSSKOJ KUL'TURY I NAT-
SIONAL'NOJ MYSLI.**
TORONTO 1, MR 1960-
HL/U-1. 5, 1962-

SOVREMENNYE PROBLEMY OTORINOLARINGOLOGII.
UKRAINSKOE NAUCHNOE OBSHCHESTVO VRACHEJ-
OTOLARINGOLOGOV.
KIEV 1, 1970-
SPONS. BODY ALSO: KIEVSKIJ NAUCHNO-ISSLE-
DOVATEL'SKIJ INSTITUT OTOLARINGOLOGII. S/T:
RESPUBLIKANSKIJ MEZHVEDOMSTVENNYJ SBORNIK.
LO/N13.

SOVREMENNYE PROBLEMY RADIOBIOLOGII.
++*SOVREM. PROBL. RADIOBIOL.*
[ATOMIZDAT]
MOSCOW 1, 1970-
LO/N13.

SPACE RESEARCH.
++*SPACE RES.*
COMMITTEE ON SPACE RESEARCH.
[NORTH-HOLLAND]
AMSTERDAM 1, 1960-
ENGL. & FR. WITH SUMM. PROCEEDINGS OF THE 1ST
1960- INTERNATIONAL SPACE SCIENCE SYMPOSIUM.
BH/U-1.　CB/U-1.　LO/U-2.　SO/U-1.　ISSN 0081-3273

**SPARK. DEVOTED TO A CORRECT INTERPRETATION
OF MARX.**
NATIONAL FRONT STUDENTS ASSOCIATION.
CROYDON NO.1, 1973-
ED/N-1.　LO/U-3.　OX/U-1.

**SPECIAL OCCASIONAL PUBLICATIONS, MUSEUM OF
COMPARATIVE ZOOLOGY, HARVARD UNIVERSITY.**
++*SPEC. OCCAS. PUBL. MUS. COMP. ZOOL. HARVARD
UNIV.*
CAMBRIDGE, MASS. NO.1, 1973-
PRODUCED BY THE MUSEUM'S DEPARTMENT OF MOLL-
USKS.
LO/N13.

SPECIAL OFFICE BRIEF.   XXX
++ SPEC. OFF. BRIEF.
[KILBRITTAIN NEWSPAPERS LTD.]
  DUBLIN NO.1, 25/JA 1973-
  PREV: BANKERS' DIGEST.
  DB/U-1.   ED/N-1.   OX/U-1.

SPECIAL PAPERS, CENTRE FOR PRECAMBRIAN RES-
EARCH, UNIVERSITY OF ADELAIDE.
++ SPEC. PAP. CENT. PRECAMBRIAN RES. UNIV.
  ADELAIDE.
  ADELAIDE NO.1, 1972-
  LO/N-2.   LO/N13.

SPECIAL PUBLICATION SERIES, INTERNATIONAL
ATLANTIC SALMON FOUNDATION.
++ SPEC. PUBL. SER. INT. ATL. SALMON FOUND.
  NEW YORK 1, 1970-
  LO/N13.

SPECIAL REPORT, MEAT RESEARCH INSTITUTE.
++ SPEC. REP. MEAT RES. INST.
  LANGFORD NO.1, 1972-
  OX/U-8.

SPEED. THE CURRENT INDEX TO THE DRUG ABUSE
LITERATURE.
  STUDENT ASSOCIATION FOR THE STUDY OF HALLUCIN-
  OGENS, INC.
  BELOIT, WIS. 1, 1973-
  2/M.
  LO/N13.

SPEED & POWER.
[IPC TRANSPORT PRESS]
  LONDON NO.1, 22/29 MR 1974-
  WKLY.
  CA/U-1.   ED/N-1.   OX/U-1.

SPEL. SELECTED PUBLICATIONS IN EUROPEAN
LANGUAGES.
  COLLEGE OF LIBRARIANSHIP, WALES.
  ABERYSTWYTH NO.1, F 1973-
  5/A.
  ED/N-1.   OX/U-1.   SH/U-1.

SPI-GLASS. HOUSE MAGAZINE OF THE SCOTTISH
PROVIDENT INSTITUTION.
  EDINBURGH NO.1, D 1972-
  ED/N-1.

SPICILEGIO MODERNO, ISTITUTO DI LINGUE E LETT-
ERATURE STRANIERE, UNIVERSITA DI BOLOGNA.
++ SPICILEGIO MOD. IST. LINGUE & LETT. STRAN.
  UNIV. BOLOGNA.
  PISA 1, 1972-
  ISTITUTO SUBORD. TO: FACOLTA DI MAGISTERO.
  NO/U-1.   OX/U-1.

SPIRITUALIST GAZETTE.   XXX
  SPIRITUALIST ASSOCIATION OF GREAT BRITAIN.
  LONDON NO.1, JE 1972- 11, MY 1973 ...
  SUBS: PSYCHIC RESEARCHER & SPIRITUALIST
  GAZETTE.
  LO/N-1.

SPORTS COUNCIL STUDIES.
++ SPORTS COUNC. STUD.
  LONDON NO.1, 1971-
  LO/N-1.

SPORTS DOCUMENTATION MONTHLY BULLETIN.   XXX
++ SPORTS DOC. MON. BULL.
  UNITED KINGDOM NATIONAL DOCUMENTATION CENTRE
  FOR SPORT, PHYSICAL EDUCATION & RECREATION.
  BIRMINGHAM 4, 1974-
  PREV: SPORTS INFORMATION MONTHLY BULLETIN FROM
  NO.1, JA 1972- 3(11/12), N/D 1973.
  ED/N-1.   LD/U-1.

SPORTS EQUIPMENT NEWS.   XXX
++ SPORTS EQUIP. NEWS.
[BENN BROTHERS LTD.]
  LONDON S 1964- F 1971.
  3/A. SUBS: SPORTS & RECREATION EQUIPMENT.
  LO/N14**

SPORTS & RECREATION EQUIPMENT.   XXX
++ SPORTS & RECREAT. EQUIP.
[BENN BROTHERS LTD.]
  LONDON MY 1971-
  MON. PREV: SPORTS EQUIPMENT NEWS FROM S 1964-
  F 1971.
  ED/N-1. S 1973-   LO/N14. CURRENT BOX ONLY.

SPORTS, RECREATION & LEISURE CENTRES.
++ SPORTS RECREAT. & LEISURE CENT.
[CLARKE & HUNTER (LONDON) LTD.]
  GUILDFORD 1(1), AP 1973-
  Q.
  CA/U-1.   ED/N-1.

SPRINGS MAGAZINE.
++ SPRINGS MAG.
  SPRING MANUFACTURERS INSTITUTE.
  BRISTOL, CONN. 1, MY 1962-
  MON. CAPTION TITLE: SPRINGS.
  LO/N14. 12, 1973-   ISSN 0584-9667

SRI LANKA FORESTER.   XXX
++ SRI LANKA FOR.
  COLOMBO 1972-
  PREV: CEYLON FORESTER: NS. FROM 1, 1952- 1971.
  LO/N-2.   LO/R-6.

STAINLESS STEEL INDUSTRY.
++ STAINLESS STEEL IND.
[MODERN METALS PUBL. LTD.]
  BETCHWORTH, SURREY 1(1), MY 1973-
  6/A. S/T: THE JOURNAL FOR STAINLESS STEEL
  MANUFACTURERS, STOCKHOLDERS & FABRICATORS.
  CA/U-1. 1(2), 1973-   ED/N-1. 1(2), 1973-
  ISSN 0306-2988

STARINE CRNE GORE.
  ZAVOD ZA ZASTITU SPOMENIKA KULTURE SR CRNE GORE
  CETINJE 1, 1963-
  OX/U-1.

STARINE KOSOVA I METOHIJE.
  OBLASNI ZAVOD ZA ZASTITU SPOMENIKA KULTURE.
  PRISTINA 1, 1961-
  TITLE ALSO IN ALBANIAN: ANTIKITETE TE KOSOVE E
  METOHIS; & FR.: ANTIQUITES DE KOSOVO ET METO-
  HIJA.
  OX/U-1.

STATION PAPERS, FOREST, WILDLIFE & RANGE
EXPERIMENT STATION, UNIVERSITY OF IDAHO.
++ STN. PAP. FOR. WILDL. & RANGE EXP. STN. UNIV.
  IDAHO.
  MOSCOW, IDAHO NO.1, D 1966-
  LO/N-2.

STATIONER & NEWSPAPER MAKER.
++ STATIONER & NEWSPAP. MAKER.
  WORSHIPFUL COMPANY OF STATIONERS & NEWSPAPER
  MAKERS.
  LONDON 1(1), 1970-
  OX/U-1.

STATISTICAL BULLETIN, SOUTH PACIFIC COMMISS-
ION.
++ STAT. BULL. SOUTH PAC. COMM.
  NOUMEA 1972(1)-
  ENGL. & FR. FR. TITLE: BULLETIN STATISTIQUE.
  LO/U-3.   CA/U-1. 1973-   LD/U-1. 1973(1)-

STEINBECK MONOGRAPH SERIES.
++ STEINBECK MONOGR SER.
  BALL STATE UNIVERSITY.
  MUNCIE, INDIANA NO.1, 1971-
  LO/U-1.   ISSN 0085-6746

STOCKHOLMIANA.
  SALLSKAPET BOKVANNERNA.
  STOCKHOLM NO.1, 1972-
  MONOGR.
  LO/N-1.

STOMATOLOGIE DER DDR.   XXX
++ STOMATOL. DDR.
[VEB VERLAG VOLK UND GESUNDHEIT]
  BERLIN 24, 1974-
  PREV: DEUTSCHE STOMATOLOGIE FROM 1, JL 1951-
  23, 1973.
  LO/N13.

STONE DRUM.
[STONE DRUM P.]
  HUNTSVILLE, TEX. 1, 1972-
  2/A.
  OX/U-1.

STRATH.
[RANNOCH GILLAMOOR POETS]
  TOWCESTER, NORTHANTS. NO.1, 1973-
  Q.
  OX/U-1.   LO/U-2. NO.3, 1974-

STRONG-MOTION EARTHQUAKE RECORDS IN JAPAN.
++STRONG-MOTION EARTHQUAKE REC. JAP.
TOKYO DAIGAKU JISHIN KENKYUJO.
TOKYO 1, 1960-
PRODUCED BY INSTITUTE'S STRONG-MOTION EARTH-
QUAKE OBSERVATION COMMITTEE.
OX/U-8.   ISSN 0563-7902

STUDENT (PRAGUE).   XXX
[CESKOSLOVENSKY SVAZ MLADEZE]
PRAGUE 1(1), 1965- 4(34), 1968.//
LA/U-1.

STUDIES IN ARABIC LITERATURE.
++STUD. ARABIC LIT.
LEIDEN 1, 1971-
ISSUED AS SUPPL. TO: JOURNAL OF ARABIC LIT-
ERATURE.
GL/U-1.   OX/U-1.

STUDIES IN BROWNING & HIS CIRCLE.   XXX
++STUD. BROWNING & CIRCLE.
WACO, TEX. 1, 1973-
2/A. PREV: BROWNING NEWSLETTER FROM NO.1,
1968- 9, 1972.
CA/U-1.   OX/U-1.   ISSN 0095-4489

STUDIES IN CANADIAN LITERATURE.
++STUD. CAN. LIT.
[COPP CLARK PUBL. CO.]
TORONTO NO.1, [1969]-
MONOGR.
LO/N-1.

STUDIEN ZUR DEUTSCHEN SPRACHE UND LITERATUR.
++STUD. DTSCH. SPRACHE & LIT.
[KLAUS SCHWARZ VERLAG]
FREIBURG IM BREISGAU 1, 1971-
LO/N-1.

STUDIES ON EDUCATION.
++STUD. EDUC. (AMST. &C.).
[ELSEVIER SCIENTIFIC PUBL. CO.]
AMSTERDAM &C. 1, 1973-
MONOGR.
LO/N-1.

STUDIA NAD EKONOMIKA REGIONU.
++STUD. EKON. REG.
SLASKI INSTYTUT NAUKOWY.
KATOWICE 1, 1971-
ENGL. & RUSS. SUMM.
LO/U-3.

STUDIA GEOGRAPHICA.
++STUD. GEOGR. (BRNO).
CESKOSLOVENSKA AKADEMIE VED: GEOGRAFICKY USTAV.
BRNO 1, 1969-
ENGL., FR. OR GER. SUMM.
LO/N13.   OX/U-1.

STUDIES IN GEOGRAPHY.   XXX
++STUD. GEOGR. (BUDAPEST).
MAGYAR TUDOMANYOS AKADEMIA: FOLDRAJZTUDOMANYI
KUTATOCSOPORT.
BUDAPEST NO.1, 1964- 3, 1966 ...
SUBS: STUDIES IN GEOGRAPHY IN HUNGARY.
CA/U-1.   BH/U-1. NO.3, 1966.
ISSN 0081-7961

STUDIES IN GEOGRAPHY IN HUNGARY.   XXX
++STUD. GEOGR. HUNG.
MAGYAR TUDOMANYOS AKADEMIA: FOLDRAJZTUDOMANYI
KUTATOCSOPORT.
BUDAPEST NO.4, 1967-
PREV: STUDIES IN GEOGRAPHY FROM NO.1, 1964- 3,
1966.
CA/U-1.

STUDIA HISTORICA GOTHOBURGENSIA.
++STUD. HIST. GOTHOB.
[AKADEMI-FORLAGET-GUMPERTS]
GOTEBORG 1, 1963-
CA/U-1. 1964-   ISSN 0081-6515

STUDIA HISTORICA SLAVO-GERMANICA.
++STUD. HIST. SLAVO-GER.
UNIWERSYTET IM. ADAMA MICKIEWICZA W POZNANIU.
POZNAN 1, 1972-
GER. SUMM.
CA/U-1.   OX/U-1.

STUDIES IN THE HISTORY OF ART, NATIONAL GALL-   XXX
ERY OF ART (US).
++STUD. HIST. ART NATL. GALLERY ART (US).
WASHINGTON, D.C. 1971/72-
PREV: ANNUAL REPORT, NATIONAL GALLERY OF ART
(US) FROM 1969/70.
GL/U-1.   LO/U17.   ISSN 0091-7338

STUDIA IRANICA.
++STUD. IRAN.
ASSOCIATION POUR L'AVANCEMENT DES ETUDES IRAN-
IENNES.
[P. GEUTHNER]
PARIS 1, 1972-
2/A.
CA/U-1.

STUDIES IN JUDAISM IN LATE ANTIQUITY.
++STUD. JUDAISM LATE ANTIQ.
LEIDEN 1, 1973-
CA/U-1.   GL/U-1.   OX/U-1.

STUDIEN ZUR KUNST DES NEUNZEHNTEN JAHRHUNDERTS.
++STUD. KUNST NEUNZEHNTEN JAHRHUNDERTS.
FRITZ THYSSEN-STIFTUNG: ARBEITSKREIS KUNSTGES-
CHICHTE.
[PRESTEL-VERLAG]
MUNCHEN 1, 1965-
LO/N-1.   OX/U-1.

STUDIES IN LAND USE HISTORY & LANDSCAPE
CHANGE: NATIONAL PARK SERIES.
++STUD. LAND USE HIST. & LANDSCAPE CHANGE, NATL.
PARK SER.
UNIVERSITY OF CALGARY.
CALGARY 1, 1968-
TITLE VARIES: NATIONAL PARK SERIES OF STUDIES
IN LAND USE HISTORY & LANDSCAPE CHANGE.
CA/U-5.   ISSN 0585-685X

STUDI DI LETTERATURA ISPANO-AMERICANA.
++STUDI LETT. ISPANO-AM.
UNIVERSITA COMMERCIALE LUIGI BOCCONI: ISTITUTO
DI LETTERATURA SPAGNOLA E ISPANO-AMERICANA.
MILAN & VARESE 1, 1967-
ISTITUTO SUBORD. TO FACOLA DI LINGUE E LETTER-
ATURA SPAGNOLA.
LO/U-1.   CA/U-1. 4, 1972-

STUDIA I MATERIALY DO DZIEJOW ZUP SOLNYCH
W POLSCE.
++STUD. & MATER. DZIEJOW SOLNYCH POL.
(POLAND) MINISTERSTWO KULTURY I SZTUKI:
ZARZAD MUZEOW I OCHRONY ZABYTKOW.
WIELICZKA 1, 1965-
ENGL. & RUSS. SUMM.
OX/U-1.

STUDIEN ZUR MODERNEN GESCHICHTE.
++STUD. MOD. GESCH.
[BERTELSMANN UNIVERSITATSVERLAG]
DUSSELDORF 1, [1971]-
MONOGR.
LO/N-1.

STUDIA MUSEOLOGICA.
++STUD. MUSEOL.
STATE CENTRAL MUSEUM (MONGOLIA).
ULAN-BATOR 1, 1968-
S/T: PAPERS ON MUSEOLOGY & MONGOLIAN STUDY.
LO/U14.

STUDI NOVECENTESCHI.
UNIVERSITA DI PADOVA: INSTITUTO DI FILOLOGIA E
LETTERATURA ITALIANA.
[MARSILIO]
PADUA 1(1), MR 1972-
S/T: QUADRIMESTRALE DI STORIA DELLA LETTERAT-
URA ITALIANA CONTEMPORANEA.
ED/N-1.   LD/U-1.   LO/U-1.   HL/U-1. 1(1-2;5), 1972-1973.

STUDIEN UND QUELLEN ZUR WELT KAISER FRIEDRICH
II.
++STUD. & QUELLEN WELT KAISER FRIEDRICH II.
COLOGNE 1, 1972-
OX/U-1.

STUDIES IN SCIENCE EDUCATION.
++STUD. SCI. EDUC.
UNIVERSITY OF LEEDS: CENTRE FOR STUDIES IN
SCIENCE EDUCATION.
LEEDS 1, 1974-
ANNU.
BH/U-3.   CA/U-1.   ED/N-1.   OX/U-1.   SW/U-1.

STUDIA SEMIOTICA. COLLECTA SEMIOTICA.
++STUD. SEMIOTICA.
[GEORG OLMS VERLAG]
 HILDESHEIM & NEW YORK 1, 1972-
 MONOGR. VARIOUS LANGUAGES.
 LO/N-1.

STUDIA THEOLOGICA RHENO-TRAIECTINA.   XXX
++STUD. THEOL. RHENO-TRAIECTINA.
 UTRECHT 1, 1955- 7, 1964.//
 OX/U-1.   ISSN 0585-5586

STUDIEN ZUR THEOLOGIE UND GEISTESGESCHICHTE
DES NEUNZEHNTEN JAHRHUNDERTS.
++STUD. THEOL. & GEISTESGESCH. NEUNZEHNTEN
 JAHRHUNDERTS.
 FRITZ THYSSEN-STIFTUNG: ARBEITSKREIS EVANGEL-
 ISCHE THEOLOGIE UND KATHOLISCHE THEOLOGIE.
[VANDENHOECK & RUPRECHT]
 GOTTINGEN 1, 1972-
 LO/N-1.

STUDIUM OVETENSE.
++STUD. OVETENSE.
 OVIEDO 1, 1973-
 OX/U-1.

SUID-AFRIKAANSE GEOGRAAF.   000
 SEE: SOUTH AFRICAN GEOGRAPHER.

SULU STUDIES.
++SULU STUD.
 JOLO NOTRE DAME OF JOLO COLLEGE: COORDINATED
 INVESTIGATION OF SULU CULTURE.
 JOLO, SULU 1, 1972-
 OX/U-1.   HL/U-3. 1, 1972- 2, 1973.

SUPERVISOR.   XXX
 SUBS (1971): SUPERVISORY MANAGEMENT.

SUPERVISORY MANAGEMENT.   XXX
++SUPERV. MANAGE.
 INSTITUTE OF SUPERVISORY MANAGEMENT.
 LICHFIELD 22(1), JA 1971- 23(1), 1972.//
 MON. PREV: SUPERVISOR FROM 1, 1950- 21, 1970.
 ED/N-1. 22(2), 1971-

SUPERVOL. A MONTHLY ITEM FOR VOLUNTEERS.
 COMMUNITY SERVICE VOLUNTEERS.
 LONDON NO.1, JL 1971-
 ED/N-1.

SUPPLEMENTUM EPIGRAPHICUM GRAECUM.   XXX
++SUPPL. EPIGRAPHICUM GRAECUM.
 LEYDEN 1, 1923- 25, 1971.//
 AB/U-1.   BL/U-1.   CA/U-1.   ED/N-1.   LO/U-1.   OX/U-1.

SURVEYS OF APPLIED ECONOMICS.
 SOCIAL SCIENCE RESEARCH COUNCIL (GB).
[MACMILLAN]
 LONDON 1, 1973-
 SPONS. BODY ALSO: ROYAL ECONOMIC SOCIETY.
 CA/U-1.

SURVIVAL KIT.
[STONEHART PUBL.]
 LONDON NO.1, 1973-
 ED/N-1. NO.20, 1974-   OX/U-1. NO.14, 1973-

SUSSEX FAMILY HISTORIAN.
++SUSSEX FAM. HIST.
 SUSSEX FAMILY HISTORY GROUP.
 BRIGHTON 1(1), 1973-
 ED/N-1.   OX/U-1.

SYMPOSIA MATHEMATICA.
++SYMP. MATH.
 ISTITUTO NAZIONALE DI ALTA MATEMATICA.
[ACADEMIC P.]
 LONDON &C. 1, 1969-
 ANNU. ENGL., FR., GER. & ITAL.
 GL/U-1.   HL/U-1.**   LO/N-4.   LO/N14.   NW/U-1.
 ISSN 0082-0725

SYNDROME IDENTIFICATION.
++SYNDROME IDENTIF.
 NATIONAL FOUNDATION - MARCH OF DIMES.
 WHITE PLAINS, N.Y. 1, 1973-
 LD/U-1.   LO/N13.   ISSN 0091-1747

SYNTHESIS & REACTIVITY IN INORGANIC & METAL-
ORGANIC CHEMISTRY.   XXX
++SYNTH. & REACT. INORG. & MET.-ORG. CHEM.
[DEKKER]
 NEW YORK 4, 1974-
 PREV: SYNTHESIS IN INORGANIC & METAL-ORGANIC
 CHEMISTRY FROM 1, 1971- 3, 1973.
 LO/N14.

SYSTEMES LOGIQUES.
++SYST. LOGIQUES.
 ECOLE POLYTECHNIQUE FEDERALE DE LAUSANNE:
 CHAIRE DE SYSTEMES LOGIQUES.
 LAUSANNE [NO.]1, N 1969-
 LO/N14.*

TAMKANG JOURNAL OF MATHEMATICS.
++TAMKANG J. MATH.
 TAMKANG COLLEGE OF ARTS & SCIENCES: INSTITUTE
 OF MATHEMATICS.
 TAIPEI 1, MR 1970-
 2/A.
 LO/N13.   ISSN 0049-2930

TARAXACUM.
 INTERNATIONAL YOUTH CENTRE FOR ENVIRONMENTAL
 STUDIES.
 AMSTERDAM 1, 1972-
 LO/R-5.

TARTUFFLES.   000
 SEE: CONNECTIONS.

TAYSIDE NEWS.
 DUNDEE NO.1, 1973-
 ED/N-1.   OX/U-1.

TEACHING ABOUT EUROPE.
++TEACH. EUR.
 UNIVERSITY OF SUSSEX: CENTRE FOR CONTEMPORARY
 EUROPEAN STUDIES.
 BRIGHTON 1(1), 1973-
 3/A.
 CA/U-1.   ED/N-1.   HL/U-2.   OX/U-1.

TEACHING LONDON KIDS.
++TEACH. LOND. KIDS.
 LONDON ASSOCIATION FOR THE TEACHING OF ENGLISH.
 LONDON [NO.1], S 1973-
 CA/U-1. NO.2, ‡1974A-   ED/N-1. NO.2, ‡1974A-

TEACHING SOCIOLOGY.
++TEACH. SOCIOL.
[SAGE PUBL.]
 BEVERLEY HILLS, CALIF. 1(1), OC 1973-
 2/A.
 BN/U-1.   GL/U-2.

TECHNICAL BULLETIN, OYSTER WATER BOTTOMS &
SEAFOODS DIVISION, WILD LIFE & FISHERIES COMM-
ISSION (LOUISIANA).
++TECH. BULL. OYSTER WATER BOTTOMS & SEAFOODS
 DIV. WILD LIFE & FISH. COMM. (LA).
 NEW ORLEANS NO.1, 1972-
 LO/N13.

TECHNICAL MEMORANDUM, ENVIRONMENTAL RESEARCH
LABORATORIES, NATIONAL OCEANIC & ATMOSPHERIC
ADMINISTRATION (US).
++TECH. MEMO. ENVIRON. RES. LAB. NATL. OCEANIC &
 ATMOS. ADM. (US).
 WASHINGTON, D.C. ERL WMPO-1, 1973-
 XS/N-1. 1, 1973.

TECHNICAL NEWS BULLETIN, NATIONAL BUREAU OF
STANDARDS (US).   XXX
 SUBS (1973): DIMENSIONS NBS.

TECHNICAL PAPER, DIVISION OF APPLIED GEOMECH-
ANICS, CSIRO (AUSTRALIA).   XXX
++TECH. PAP. DIV. APPL. GEOMECH. CSIRO (AUST.).
 MELBOURNE NO.8, 1970-
 PREV: TECHNICAL PAPER, DIVISION OF SOIL MECH-
 ANICS, CSIRO (AUSTRALIA) FROM NO.2, 1968- 7,
 1970.
 LO/N14.   ISSN 0069-7257

TECHNICAL PAPER, DIVISION OF SOIL MECHANICS,
CSIRO (AUSTRALIA).   XXX
++TECH. PAP. DIV. SOIL MECH. CSIRO (AUST.).
 MELBOURNE NO.2, 1968- 7, 1970 ...
 PREV: TECHNICAL PAPER, SOIL MECHANICS SECTION,
 CSIRO (AUSTRALIA) FROM NO.1, 1965. SUBS:
 TECHNICAL PAPER, DIVISION OF APPLIED GEOMECH-
 ANICS, CSIRO (AUSTRALIA).
 LO/N14.

TECHNICAL PAPER, INTERNATIONAL REFERENCE
CENTRE FOR COMMUNITY WATER SUPPLY (WHO).
++ TECH. PAP. INT. REF. CENT. COMMUNITY WATER
SUPPLY (WHO).
THE HAGUE NO.1, 1971-
LO/N14.

TECHNICAL PAPER, SCHOOL OF FORESTRY, DUKE
UNIVERSITY.
++ TECH. PAP. SCH. FOR. DUKE UNIV.
DURHAM, N.C. 1, 1973-
OX/U-3.

TECHNICAL PHOTOGRAPHY.
++ TECH. PHOTOGR.
[PTN PUBL. CORP.]
HEMPSTEAD, N.Y. 1, 1969-
MON.
LO/N14. CURRENT BOX ONLY.   ISSN 0040-0971

TECHNICAL REPORTS, SURVEILLANCE & INSPECTION
DIVISION, OFFICE OF RADIATION PROGRAMS (US).
++ TECH. REP. SURVEILL. & INSP. DIV. OFF. RADIAT.
PROGRAMS (US).
(UNITED STATES) ENVIRONMENTAL PROTECTION
AGENCY: OFFICE OF RADIATION PROGRAMS.
WASHINGTON, D.C. ORP/SID 71-1, 1971-
LO/N14.

TECHNICAL REVIEW, INDEPENDENT BROADCASTING
AUTHORITY.
++ TECH. REV. INDEP. BROADCAST. AUTH.
LONDON NO.1, S 1972-
OX/U-8.   SH/C-5.

TECHNOLOGY ASSESSMENT.
++ TECHNOL. ASSESS.
INTERNATIONAL SOCIETY FOR TECHNOLOGY ASSESSMENT
[GORDON & BREACH]
NEW YORK & LONDON 1, 1972-
Q.
LO/N14. CA/U-1. 2(2), 1974-   ED/N-1. 2(2), 1974-
XS/R10. 1(3), 1973-   ISSN 0092-2234

TECHNOLOGY MART.
++ TECHNOL. MART.
[THOMAS PUBL. CO.]
NEW YORK [1, 1971}
2M.
LO/N14. 2, 1972-   ISSN 0049-3198

TEIKETSU TO SETSUGO.
[NEJI NO SEKAI-SHA]
TOKYO NO.1, 1972-
ENGL. TITLE: FASTENING & JOINING.
LO/N13.

TELEVISION MONOGRAPHS, BRITISH FILM INSTITUTE.
++ TELEV. MONOGR. BR. FILM INST.
LONDON NO.1, 1973-
CA/U-1.   ISSN 0306-2929

TELONDE.
[THOMSON-CSF]
PARIS 1969-
Q. ENGL., FR. & SPAN.
LO/N-4. 1973(1}-   ISSN 0040-2834

TENSAI KENKYU HOKOKU: HOKAN.   XXX
NIHON TENSAI SHINKOKAI.
TOKYO NO.1, 1963- 14, 1973.//
JAP. WITH ENGL. SUMM. ENGL. TITLE: BULLETIN
OF SUGAR BEET RESEARCH: SUPPLEMENT.
LO/N13.

TERRE CUITE.   XXX
SUBS (1974): CAHIERS DE LA TERRE CUITE.

TEST VALLEY & BORDER ANTHOLOGY.
++ TEST VALLEY & BORDER ANTHOL.
ANDOVER LOCAL ARCHIVES COMMITTEE.
ANDOVER, HANTS. NO.1, 1973-
Q.
CA/U-1.   OX/U-1.   ISSN 0306-2023

TEXAS INTERNATIONAL LAW FORUM.   XXX
++ TEX. INT. LAW FORUM.
UNIVERSITY OF TEXAS: INTERNATIONAL LAW SOCIETY.
AUSTIN, TEX. 2, 1966- 6, 1971 ...
PREV: JOURNAL, INTERNATIONAL LAW SOCIETY,
UNIVERSITY OF TEXAS FROM 1, JA 1965. SUBS:
TEXAS INTERNATIONAL LAW JOURNAL. SOCIETY
SUBORD. TO: SCHOOL OF LAW.
OX/U15.   ISSN 0040-4381

TEXAS INTERNATIONAL LAW JOURNAL.   XXX
++ TEX. INT. LAW J.
UNIVERSITY OF TEXAS: INTERNATIONAL LAW SOCIETY.
AUSTIN, TEX. 7, 1971-
2/A. PREV: TEXAS INTERNATIONAL LAW FORUM FROM
2, 1966- 6, 1971. SOCIETY SUBORD. TO: SCHOOL
OF LAW.
OX/U15.

TEXTILE ASIA.
++ TEXT. ASIA.
[BUSINESS P. LTD.]
HONG KONG 1, OC 1970-
MON.
LO/N14. 5, 1974-   ISSN 0049-3554

TEXTS & STUDIES OF THE HISTORY OF CYPRUS.   000
SEE: KENTRON EPISTEMONIKON EREUMON.

THEATRO. DIMENE THEATRIKE EPITHEORESE.
ATHENS 1, D 1961-
CA/U-1.   ISSN 0495-4386

THEOLOGISCHE BERICHTE.
THEOLOGISCHE HOCHSCHULE CHUR.
[BENZIGER VERLAG]
ZURICH 1, 1972-
SPONS. BODY ALSO: THEOLOGISCHE FAKULTAT
(LUCERNE).
CA/U-1.

THEORY & SOCIETY.
++ THEORY & SOC.
[ELSEVIER]
AMSTERDAM 1, 1974-
Q.
AD/U-1.   BL/U-1.   CB/U-1.   ED/N-1.   ED/U-1.   EX/U-1.
LO/U-4.   MA/U-1.   NO/U-1.   SF/U-1.   SH/U-1.

THERMOPHYSICS NEWSLETTER.
++ THERMOPHYS. NEWSL.
PERDUE UNIVERSITY: THERMOPHYSICAL PROPERTIES
RESEARCH CENTER.
WEST LAFAYETTE, IND. [1, 1972}-
2M.
LO/N14. CURRENT BOX ONLY.

THIS.
IOWA CITY, NO.1, 1971-
LO/U-2.

THIS MONTH (GENEVA).
++ THIS MON. (GENEVA).
WORLD COUNCIL OF CHURCHES.
GENEVA 1, 1970-
S/T: MONTHLY EDITION OF THE ECUMENICAL PRESS
SERVICE.
OX/U-1. F 1971-

THIS MONTH (LONDON).
++ THIS MON. (LOND.).
LONDON 1(1), OC 1971-
ED/N-1.   OX/U-1.

TOCHNOST' 1 NADEZHNOST' KIBERNETICHESKIKH
SISTEM.
++ TOCH. & NADEZHNOST' KIBERN. SIST.
AKADEMIJA NAUK UKRAJINS'KOJI RSR: (INSTITUT
ELEKTRODINAMIKI).
KIEV 1, 1973-
LO/N13.

TOLSTOVSKIJ SBORNIK.
++ TOLSTOVSKIJ SB.
TUL'SKIJ GOSUDARSTVENNYJ PEDAGOGICHESKIJ
INSTITUT.
TULA 1, 1960-
LO/U15.

TORONTO SEMITIC TEXTS & STUDIES.
++ TORONTO SEMITIC TEXTS & STUD.
TORONTO 1, 1970-
OX/U-1.

TOURISM IN ENGLAND.
++ TOURISM ENGL.
ENGLISH TOURIST BOARD.
LONDON NO.1, 1970-
OX/U-1.   CA/U-1. NO.2, 1971-   ED/N-1. NO.2, 1971-

**TRANSACTIONS, AUSTRALIAN COLLEGE OF OPHTHAL-
MOLOGISTS.** XXX
++*TRANS. AUST. COLL. OPHTHALMOL.*
GLEBE, SYD. 1, 1969(1970)- 3, 1971(1972).
PREV: TRANSACTIONS, OPHTHALMOLOGICAL SOCIETY
OF AUSTRALIA FROM 1, 1939- 27, 1968. SUBS:
AUSTRALIAN JOURNAL OF OPHTHALMOLOGY. VOL.1
PUBLISHED JOINTLY WITH V.22 OF TRANSACTIONS OF
THE OPHTHALMOLOGICAL SOCIETY OF NEW ZEALAND.
LO/M17. OX/U-8.

**TRANSACTIONS, BRITISH CAVE RESEARCH ASSOC-
IATION.** XXX
++*TRANS. BR. CAVE RES. ASSOC.*
BRIDGEWATER, SOMERSET 1(1), 1974-
Q. PREV PART OF: TRANSACTIONS, CAVE RESEARCH
GROUP OF GREAT BRITAIN FROM 1, 1947- 15(4),
1973; & CAVE SCIENCE FROM NO.48, D 1971- 52,
N 1973.
ED/N-1. LO/N-2. LO/N13. OX/U-8. ISSN 0305-859X

**TRANSACTIONS OF THE BRITISH SOCIETY FOR THE
STUDY OF ORTHODONTICS.** XXX
SUBS (1973): PART OF BRITISH JOURNAL OF
ORTHODONTICS.

**TRANSACTIONS, CAVE RESEARCH GROUP OF GREAT
BRITAIN.** XXX
SUBS (1974) PART OF: TRANSACTIONS, BRITISH
CAVE RESEARCH ASSOCIATION.

**TRANSACTIONS, INDIAN INSTITUTE OF ADVANCED
STUDY.**
++*TRANS. INDIAN INST. ADV. STUDY.*
SIMLA 1, 1965-
OX/U13. ISSN 0073-6465

TRANSPORT FACTS & FIGURES.
GREATER LONDON COUNCIL: INTELLIGENCE UNIT.
LONDON NO.1, 1973-
LO/N-1.

**TRAVAUX ET RECHERCHES DE SCIENCES ECONOMIQUES:
RELATIONS INTERNATIONALES.**
++*TRAV. & RECH. SCI. ECON., RELAT. INT.*
FONDATION NATIONALE DES SCIENCES POLITIQUES
(FRANCE).
PARIS 1, 1972-
OX/U-1.

**TRAVAUX ET RECHERCHES DE SCIENCES POLITIQUES:
ECONOMIE FRANCAISE.**
++*TRAV. & RECH. SCI. POLIT., ECON. FR.*
FONDATION NATIONALE DES SCIENCES POLITIQUES
(FRANCE).
PARIS 1, 1973-
OX/U-1.

**TRAVAUX ET RECHERCHES DE SCIENCES POLITIQUES:
POLITIQUES ECONOMIQUES.**
++*TRAV. & RECH. SCI. POLIT., POLIT. ECON.*
FONDATION NATIONALE DES SCIENCES POLITIQUES:
(FRANCE).
PARIS NO.1, 1972-
OX/U-1.

TREATED WOOD PERSPECTIVES. XXX
++*TREATED WOOD PERSPECT.*
CANADIAN INSTITUTE OF TIMBER CONSTRUCTION.
OTTAWA P1, 1973-
PREV: MODERN WOOD FROM 1, JA 1959.
LO/N13.

TROPENMEDIZIN UND PARASITOLOGIE. XXX
++*TROPENMED. & PARASITOL.*
DEUTSCHE TROPENMEDIZINISCHE GESELLSCHAFT.
[GEORG THIEME VERLAG]
STUTTGART 25, 1974-
ENGL. & GER. WITH SUMM. IN BOTH LANG.
PREV: ZEITSCHRIFT FUR TROPENMEDIZIN
UND PARASITOLOGIE FROM 1, 1949/50- 24, 1973.
LO/N13.

TROPICAL FORESTRY RESEARCH NOTE.
++*TROP. FOR. RES. NOTE.*
(PAPUA & NEW GUINEA) DEPARTMENT OF FORESTS.
PORT MORESBY SR 1, 1973-
OX/U-3.

**TRUDY, INSTITUT FIZIOLOGII, AKADEMIJA NAUK
AZERBAJDZHANSKOJ SSR.** XXX
++*TR. INST. FIZ. AKAD. NAUK AZ. SSR.*
BAKU 10, 1968-
PREV: TRUDY, SEKTORA FIZIOLOGII, AKADEMII NAUK
AZERBAJDZHANSKOJ SSR FROM 1, 1956- 9, 1967.
LO/N13.

**TRUDY INSTITUTA STROITEL'NOJ FIZIKI, AKADEMIJA
STROITEL'STVA I ARKHITEKTURY SSSR.** XXX
SUBS (1969): NAUCHNYE TRUDY, NAUCHNO-ISSLEDO-
VATEL'SKIJ INSTITUT STROITEL'NOJ FIZIKI.

**TRUDY, KIRGIZSKIJ NAUCHNO-ISSLEDOVATEL'SKIJ
INSTITUT POCHVOVEDENIJA.**
++*TR. KIRG. NAUCHNO-ISSLED. INST. POCHVOVED.*
FRUNZE 1, 1969-
LO/N13.

**TRUDY, SEKTORA FIZIOLOGII, AKADEMII NAUK
AZERBAJDZHANSKOJ SSR.** XXX
SUBS (1968): TRUDY, INSTITUT FIZIOLOGII,
AKADEMIJA NAUK AZERBAJDZHANSKOJ SSR.

**TRUDY VSESOJUZNOGO JURIDICHESKOGO ZAOCHNOGO
INSTITUTA.**
++*TR. VSES. JURID. ZAOCHN. INST.*
VSESOJUZNYJ JURIDICHESKIJ ZAOCHNYJ INSTITUT.
MOSCOW 1, 1961-
GL/U-1. 6, 1966-

T.S. ELIOT NEWSLETTER.
++*T.S. ELIOT NEWSL.*
YORK UNIVERSITY (TORONTO): DEPARTMENT
OF ENGLISH.
TORONTO 1, 1974-
2/A.
LO/U-1.

TSU KUO. CHINA MONTHLY. XXX
UNION RESEARCH INSTITUTE (HONG KONG).
KOWLOON, HONG KONG NO.1, AP 1964-
MON. CHIN. WITH ENGL. CONTENTS LIST.
PREV: TSU KUO CHOU K'AN FROM 1 5/JA, 1953-
45(12), MR 1964.
LO/U14. NO.101-105, 1972. ISSN 0045-6756

TSU KUO CHON K'AN. XXX
SUBS (1964): TSU-KUO.

TUAIRISC. JOURNAL OF THE WOLFE TONE SOCIETY.
DUBLIN NO.1, MR 1973-
CA/U-1. ED/N-1. OX/U-1.

TUNGSTEN NEWS.
CLIMAX MOLYBDENUM CO.
NEW YORK 1962-
Q.
XS/R10. AP 1972- ISSN 0049-481X

TURBINE TECHNOLOGY & MARKETING NEWS. XXX
++*TURBINE TECHNOL. & MARK. NEWS.*
[GAS TURBINE PUBL.]
STAMFORD, CONN. 1, 1973-
PREV: TURBINE TECHNOLOGY FROM 1, 1969- 5, 1973
LO/N14.

TURKEY TODAY.
++*TURK. TODAY.*
UNION OF TURKISH PROGRESSIVES.
ILFORD, ESSEX NO.1, F 1973-
MON.
*CA/U-1.** ED/N-1. OX/U-1.*

TWENTIETH CENTURY (LONDON). XXX
LONDON 149, 1951- 179(1049), OC 1972.//
PREV: NINETEENTH CENTURY & AFTER FROM 49,
1901- 148, 1950.
AD/U-1. BH/P-1. BN/U-1. BR/P-1. CA/U-1. GL/U-1.
LV/P-1. MA/P-1.

TYDSKRIF VIR AARDYRYDSKUNDE. XXX
SUBS (1972): SOUTH AFRICAN GEOGRAPHER.

**TYDSKRIF, SUID-AFRIKAANSE VETERINERE VEREN-
IGING.** 000
SEE: JOURNAL, SOUTH AFRICAN VETERINARY ASSOC-
IATION.

TYNAGH MINER.
IRISH BASE METALS LTD.
DUBLIN 1(1), 1970-
CA/U-1. 4(2), 1972- ED/N-1. 4(2), 1972-

U ZRODEL WSPOLCZESNEJ STYLISTYKI.
UNIVERSYTET WARSZAWSKI: KATEDRA TEORII LITER-
ATURY.
WARSAW 1, 1966-
SPONS. BODY ALSO: POLSKA AKADEMIA NAUK: INST-
YTUT BADAN LITERACKICH.
ED/N-1.

UBIQUE.
 NEW YORK 1, 1968-
 5/A.
 DB/U-2.   ED/N-1. 7, 1973/74-   ISSN 0049-500X

UCHENYE ZAPISKI ASPIRANTOV (RIGA).   000
  SEE: ASPIRANTU ZINATNISKIE RAKSTI.

**UCHENYE ZAPISKI, VSESOJUZNYJ INSTITUT JURID-
ICHESKIKH NAUK.**   XXX
  SUBS (1964): UCHENYE ZAPISKI, VSESOJUZNYJ
  NAUCHNO-ISSLEDOVATEL'SKIJ INSTITUT SOVETSKOGO
  ZAKONODATEL'STVA.

**UCHENYE ZAPISKI, VSESOJUZNYJ NAUCHNO-ISSLED-
OVATEL'SKIJ INSTITUT SOVETSKOGO ZAKONODATEL'-
STVA.**   XXX
 *++UCH. ZAP. VSES. NAUCHNO-ISSLED. INST. SOV.
 ZAKON.
 MOSCOW 1, 1964-*
 PREV: UCHENYE ZAPISKI, VSESOJUZNYJ INSTITUT
 JURIDICHESKIKH NAUK FROM 1, 1940- 17, 1963.
 CC/U-1.   OX/U-1. 1965-

UGANDA LAW FOCUS.
 LAW DEVELOPMENT CENTRE (UGANDA).
 KAMPALA 1(1), OC 1972-
 S/T: A LAW QUARTERLY JOURNAL OF REVIEWS,
 OPINIONS & INFORMATION ON THE STATE & FUTURE
 DEVELOPMENT OF LAW IN UGANDA.
 LO/U14.

UKRAJINS'KYJ ISTORYK.
 ++UKR. ISTOR.
 NEW YORK NO.1, 1963-
 OX/U-1. NO.33/34, 1972-

UKRAJINS'KE MISTETSTVOZNAVSTVO.
 ++UKR. MISTETSTVOZNAV.
 AKADEMIJA NAUK UKRAJINS'KOJI RSR: INSTYTUT
 MISTETSTVOZNAVSTVA, FOL'KLORU I ETNOGRAFII.
 KIEV 1, 1967-
 LO/U15.

ULTRASOUND IN MEDICINE & BIOLOGY.
 ++ULTRASOUND MED. & BIOL.
 WORLD FEDERATION OF ULTRASOUND IN MEDICINE &
 BIOLOGY.
 [PERGAMON]
 OXFORD 1(1), S 1973-
 Q.
 CA/U-1.   ED/N-1.   OX/U-8.   ISSN 0301-5629

UNDERGROUNDING.
 [ASMAN CORP.]
 SHERMAN OAKS, CALIF. 1, 1972-
 2M.
 LO/N14. ‡W. 1(3), 1972; & 2(2), 1973A

**UNION OF BURMA JOURNAL OF LITERARY & SOCIAL
SCIENCES.**
 ++UNION BURMA J. LIT. & SOC. SCI.
 RANGOON 1, 1968-
 3/A.
 LO/N12.

**UNIVERSITY OF ALBERTA CLASSICAL & HISTORICAL
STUDIES.**
 ++UNIV. ALBERTA CLASS. & HIST. STUD.
 [UNIV. OF ALBERTA P.]
 EDMONTON NO.1, 1971-
 LO/N-1.

UNIVERSITY OF WASHINGTON BUSINESS REVIEW.   XXX
  SUBS (1972): JOURNAL OF CONTEMPORARY BUS-
  INESS.

UNIVERSITY OF WATERLOO BIOLOGY SERIES.
 ++UNIV. WATERLOO BIOL. SER.
 WATERLOO, ONT. NO.1, 1971-
 LO/N-2.

UNTERRICHTSPRAXIS.
 AMERICAN ASSOCIATION OF TEACHERS OF GERMAN.
 PHILADELPHIA, PA. 1(1), 1968-
 2/A. ENGL. & GER.
 GL/U-2. 6, 1973-   ISSN 0042-062X

UP AGAINST THE LAW.
 UP AGAINST THE LAW COLLECTIVE.
 LONDON NO.1, 1973-
 ED/N-1. NO.4, ‡1974A-   CA/U-1. NO.4, ‡1974A-

URBAN ABSTRACTS.   XXX
 ++URBAN ABSTR.
 GREATER LONDON COUNCIL: DEPARTMENT OF PLANNING
 & TRANSPORTATION.
 LONDON 1, 1974-
 PREV: PLANNING & TRANSPORTATION ABSTRACTS FROM
 NO.1, JL 1969- 50, F/MR 1974.
 BL/U-1.   CA/U-1.   ED/N-1.   GL/U-2.   HL/U-1.   LD/U-1.
 LO/U-3.   LO/U-3.   NO/U-1.   SF/U-1.   SO/U-1.

URBAN HISTORY YEARBOOK.
 ++URBAN HIST. YEARB.
 [LEICESTER UNIV. P.]
 LEICESTER 1974-
 AD/U-1.   CA/U-1.   CA/U-5.   GL/U-1.   HL/U-1.   LD/U-1.
 MA/P-1.   MA/U-1.   NO/U-1.   OX/U-1.   SA/U-1.   SH/U-1.
 ISSN 0306-0845

UROGALLO. REVISTA LITERARIA BIMESTRAL.
 MADRID NO.1, F 1970-
 NO.1 PRECEDED BY A PILOT ISSUE NO.0, D 1969.
 GL/U-2. NO.25, 1974-   MA/U-1. NO.7, 1971-

UROLOGICAL RESEARCH.
 ++UROL. RES.
 [SPRINGER]
 BERLIN &C. 1(1), 1973-
 Q.
 OX/U-8.

USPEKHI STROITEL'NOJ FIZIKI (MOSKVA).   000
  SEE: NAUCHNYE TRUDY, NAUCHNO-ISSLEDOVATEL'SKIJ
  INSTITUT STROITEL'NOJ FIZIKI.

**UURIMUSED, EKSPERIMENTAAL-BIOLOOGIA INSTITUUT,
EESTI NSV TEADUSTE AKADEMIA.**
 ++UURIM. EKSP.-BIOL. INST. EESTI NSV TEAD. AKAD.
 TALLIN 1, 1960-
 EST. OR RUSS. WITH ENGL. SUMM.
 LO/N13. ‡NO.A1, 1960; 2, 1962.

UV SPECTROMETRY GROUP BULLETIN.   XXX
 ++UV SPECTROM. GROUP BULL.
 [PYE UNICAM LTD.]
 CAMBRIDGE NO.1, 1973-
 PREV: PHOTOELECTRIC SPECTROMETRY GROUP BULL-
 ETIN FROM 1, 1949- 20, 1972.
 ED/N-1.   LO/N-4.   LO/S-3.

V POMOSHCH' PROEKTIROVSHCHIKU.
 ++V POMOSHCH' PROEKT.
 (UKRAINE) GOSUDARSTVENNYJ KOMITET PO DELAM
 STROITEL'STVA I ARKHITEKTURY.
 KIEV 1, 1966-
 CC/U-1. 1967-

VALUE ADDED TAX TRIBUNAL REPORTS.
 ++V.A.T. TRIB. REP.
 LONDON 1(1), JL 1973-
 Q.
 CA/U-1.   GL/U-1.   LO/U-3.   OX/U15.   RE/U-1. 1974-

VANDERBILT INTERNATIONAL.   XXX
 ++VANDERBILT INT.
 VANDERBILT UNIVERSITY: SCHOOL OF LAW.
 NASHVILLE 1, 1967- 4, 1971 ...
 SUBS: VANDERBILT JOURNAL OF TRANSNATIONAL LAW.
 OX/U15.   ISSN 0042-2525

VANDERBILT JOURNAL OF TRANSNATIONAL LAW.   XXX
 ++VANDERBILT J. TRANSNATL. LAW.
 VANDERBILT UNIVERSITY: SCHOOL OF LAW.
 NASHVILLE 5, 1971-
 2/A. PREV: VANDERBILT INTERNATIONAL FROM 1,
 1967- 4, 1971.
 OX/U15.

VANNET I NORDEN. WATER IN SCANDINAVIA.
 INTERNATIONAL HYDROLOGICAL DECADE: NORWEGIAN
 NATIONAL COMMITTEE.
 OSLO NO.1, 1972-
 JOINTLY SPONSORED BY THE NATIONAL COMMITTEES
 OF DENMARK, FINLAND, ICELAND & SWEDEN.
 XS/N-1.

**VEKOVE. BJULETIN NA BULGARSKOTO ISTORICHESKO
DRUZHESTVO.**
 SOFIA 1(1), 1972-
 LO/N-1.   OX/U-1.

VERTEX. THE MAGAZINE OF SCIENCE FICTION.
 [MANKIND PUBL. CO.]
 LOS ANGELES 1, AP 1973-
 2M.
 OX/U-1.   ISSN 0091-7257

VESNIK, ZAVOD ZA GEOLOSKA I GEOFIZICKA IST-
RAZIVANJA: SERIJA A: GEOLOGIJA.   xxx
++VESN. ZAVOD GEOL. & GEOFIZ. ISTRAZ., A.
 BELGRADE 18, 1960-
 PREV: PART OF ABOVE MAIN TITLE, OF WHICH
 NUMBERING IS CONTINUED.
 GL/U-1. 27, 1969-

VESNIK, ZAVOD ZA GEOLOSKA I GEOFIZICKA IST-
RAZIVANJA: SERIJA B: INZENJERSKA GEOLOGIJA I
HIDROGEOLOGIJA.
++VESN. ZAVOD GEOL. & GEOFIZ. ISTRAZ., B.
 [VZGH-A]
 BELGRADE 1, 1960-
 GL/U-1. 8, 1968-

VESNIK, ZAVOD ZA GEOLOSKA I GEOFIZICKA IST-
RAZIVANJA: SERIJA C: PRIMENJENA GEOFIZICKA.
++VESN. ZAVOD GEOL. & GEOFIZ. ISTRAZ., C.
 [VZGG-B]
 BELGRADE 1, 1960-
 GL/U-1. 10/11, 1969-.

VESTNIK MOSKOVSKOGO UNIVERSITETA: SERIJA 14:
VOSTOKOVEDENIE.
++VEST. MOSK. UNIV., 14.
 MOSKOVSKIJ GOSUDARSTVENNYJ UNIVERSITET.
 MOSCOW 1, 1970-
 LD/U-1.

VESTNIK VOENNOJ ISTORII. NAUCHNYE ZAPISKI.
++VEST. VOEN. ISTOR.
 (RUSSIA SSSR) MINISTERSTVO OBORONY: INSTITUT
 VOENNOJ ISTORII.
 MOSCOW 1, 1970-
 BH/U-1.   CA/U-1.   CC/U-1.   LO/U15.

VESTSI AKADEMII NAVUK BELARUSKAJ SSR: SERYJA
FIZIKA-MATEMATYCHNYKH NAVUK.
++VESTI AKAD. NAVUK B. SSR, FIZ.-MAT. NAVUK.
 AKADEMIJA NAUK BELARUSKAJ SSR.
 MINSK 1, 1965-
 TITLE ALSO IN RUSS.: IZVESTIJA AKADEMII NAUK
 BSSR: SERIJA FIZIKO-MATEMATICHESKIKH NAUK.
 LO/U-2. 1966-

VICTORIAN ENTOMOLOGIST.
++VICTORIAN ENTOMOL.
 MELBOURNE [NO.]1, 1972-
 LO/N-2.

VICTORIAN TEXTS.
 ST. LUCIA ·1, 1974-
 OX/U-1.

VIDEO & FILM COMMUNICATION.
++VIDEO & FILM COMMUN.
 [SCREEN DIGEST LTD.]
 LONDON NO.1, S 1974-
 MON.
 CA/U-1.   ED/N-1.   XS/R10.   ISSN 0305-2125

VIENTIANE NEWS.
 VIENTIANE [1], 1971-
 S/T: THE FIRST ENGLISH WEEKLY IN LAOS.
 HL/U-1.

VIETNAM MAGAZINE.
++VIETNAM MAG.
 VIETNAM COUNCIL ON FOREIGN RELATIONS.
 SAIGON [1, 1968]-
 CA/U-1. 2(4), 1969-   LO/U-1. 3(4), 1970-
 ISSN 0506-9777

VINE. A VERY INFORMAL NEWSLETTER ON LIBRARY
AUTOMATION.
 SOUTHAMPTON NO.1, OC 1971-
 AD/U-1. NO.7, 1973-   BL/U-1. NO.7, 1973-
 SA/U-1. NO.7, 1973-   SF/U-1. JE.1973-   ISSN 0305-5728

VITAL ECONOMIC TRENDS IN THE UNITED KINGDOM.
++VITAL ECON. TRENDS U.K.
 [INTERSTATS].
 CAMBERLEY, SURREY OC 1964-
 MON.
 GL/U-2. **   ISSN 0049-6553

VOL'NOE SLOVO. SAMIZDAT IZBRANNOE: DOC-
UMENTAL'NAJA SERIJA.
 [POSSEV-VERLAG]
 FRANKFURT AM MAIN 1, 1972-
 2M. NO.1-6, 1972 ISSUED AS SUBSERIES OF
 KHRONIKA TEKUSHCHIKH SOBYTIJ.
 EX/U-1.   GL/U-1.   HL/U-1.   LD/U-1.

VOLUNTARY ACTION RESEARCH.
++VOLUNTARY ACTION RES.
 [LEXINGTON BOOKS]
 LEXINGTON, MASS. 1972-
 ANNU. SUBSERIES OF VOLUNTARY ACTION RES-
 EARCH SERIES.
 CA/U-1. 1973-

VOPROSY ESTETIKI. SBORNIK STATEJ.
++VOPR. ESTETIKI.
 SARATOVSKIJ GOSUDARSTVENNYJ UNIVERSITET.
 SARATOV 1, 1963-
 GL/U-1.

VOPROSY FILOLOGII.
++VOPR. FILOL.
 INSTITUT MEZHDUNARODNYKH OTNOSHENIJ.
 MOSCOW 1, 1962-
 CC/U-1.   LD/U-1.   LO/U15.   SA/U-1.

VOPROSY FINNO-UGORSKOGO JAZYKOZNANIJA.
++VOPR. FINNO-UGORSKOGO JAZYKOZNANIJA.
 AKADEMIJA NAUK SSSR: INSTITUT JAZYKOZNANIJA.
 MOSCOW & LENINGRAD 1, 1962-
 TITLE VARIES: VOLS.1 & 2: VOPROSY SOVETSKOGO
 FINNO-UGROVEDENIJA.
 CA/U-1.   LO/U15.

VOPROSY ISTORII ESTONSKOJ SSR.   000
 SEE: EESTI NSV AJALOO KUSIMUSI.

VOPROSY ISTORIOGRAFII VSEOBSHCHEJ ISTORII.
SBORNIK STATEJ.
++VOPR. ISTOR. VSEOBSHCHEJ ISTOR.
 KAZANSKIJ GOSUDARSTVENNYJ UNIVERSITET.
 KAZAN 1, 1964-
 LO/U15.   OX/U-1.   CC/U-1. 1970-

VOPROSY KLASSICHESKOJ FILOLOGII.
++VOPR. KLASSICHESK. FILOL.
 MOSKOVSKIJ GOSUDARSTVENNYJ UNIVERSITET: KAFEDRA
 KLASSICHESKOJ FILOLOGII.
 MOSCOW 1, 1965-
 OX/U-1.   LO/U15. 3-4, 1971.

VOPROSY LITOLOGII I PETROGRAFII.
++VOPR. LITOL. & PETROGR.
 L'VOVSKOE GEOLOGICHESKOE OBSHCHESTVO.
 L'VOV 1, 1969-
 ENGL. SUMM.
 CA/U-2.   LO/N-2.   LO/N-4.

VOPROSY MORFOMETRII.
++VOPR. MORFOMETRII.
 SARATOVSKIJ GOSUDARSTVENNYJ UNIVERSITET.
 SARATOV 2, 1967-
 NO DATA AVAILABLE REGARDING VOL.1.
 LO/N13.

VOPROSY SOTSIOLOGII I OBSHCHESTVENNOJ PSIK-
HOLOGII.
++VOPR. SOTSIOL. & OBSHCHESTV. PSIKHOL.
 MOSKOVSKIJ GOSUDARSTVENNYJ UNIVERSITET.
 MOSCOW 1, 1970-
 GL/U-1.

VOPROSY SOVETSKOGO FINNO-UGROVEDENIJA.   000
 SEE: VOPROSY FINNO-UGORSKOGO JAZYKOZNANIJA.

VOPROSY TEORII I METODOV IDEOLOGICHESKOJ
RABOTY.   XXX
++VOPR. TEOR. & METODOV IDEOL. RAB.
 AKADEMIJA OBSHCHESTVENNYKH NAUK PRI TSK KPSS:
 KAFEDRA TEORII I METODOV IDEOLOGICHESKOJ RABOTY
 MOSCOW 1, 1972-
 PREV: VOPROSY TEORII I PRAKTIKI MASSOVYKH
 SREDSTV PROPAGANDY FROM 1, 1968- 4, 1971.
 BH/U-1.   CC/U-1.   GL/U-1.   OX/U-1.

VOPROSY TEORII PLAZMY.
++VOPR. TEOR. PLAZMY.
 GOSUDARSTVENNYJ KOMITET PO ISPOL'ZOVANIJU
 ATOMNOJ ENERGII SSSR.
 MOSCOW 1, 1963-
 LO/N13.   OX/U-8.

VYCHISLITEL'NAJA MATEMATIKA (KIEV).   000
 SEE: VYCHISLITEL'NAJA I PRIKLADNAJA MATEMATIKA

VYCHISLITEL'NAJA I PRIKLADNAJA MATEMATIKA.
++VYCHISL. & PRIKL. MAT.
KYJIVS'KYJ DERZHAVNYJ UNIVERSYTET [IM. T.G.
SHEVEHENKIA.
  KIEV 1, 1965-
  S/T: MEZHVEDOMSTVENNYJ NAUCHNYJ SBORNIK.
  TITLE VARIES: VOLS.1 & 2 PUBL. AS: VYCHISLIT-
  EL'NAJA MATEMATIKA.
  DB/S-1.   LO/N13. 3, 1967-

WALES YEARBOOK.
++WALES YEARBK.
[SAMUEL KNIGHT PUBL.]
  CARDIFF 1974/75(1974)-
  OX/U-1.   SA/U-1.   SW/U-1.   XW/C-4.

WAR MONTHLY.
++WAR MON.
[MARSHALL CAVENDISH LTD.]
  LONDON NO.1, AP 1974-
  CA/U-1.   ED/N-1.

WASHINGTON PAPERS.
++WASH. PAP.
GEORGETOWN UNIVERSITY: CENTER FOR STRATEGIC
& INTERNATIONAL STUDIES.
[LIBRARY P.]
  WASHINGTON, D.C. 1, 1972-
  CA/U-1.   OX/U-1.

WASTE DISPOSAL.   XXX
NATIONAL ASSOCIATION OF WASTE DISPOSAL CON-
TRACTORS.
[RHODES (PROMOTIONS)]
  MANCHESTER 1(1), 1967- 5(4), 1971 ...
  SUBS: POLLUTION TECHNOLOGY INTERNATIONAL.
  LO/N14. 4(4), 1970-   XS/R10. 5(2), 1971-

WATER IN SCANDINAVIA.   000
SEE: VANNET I NORDEN.

WATER SERVICES. THE JOURNAL OF RESOURCES,
SUPPLY, SEWAGE & EFFLUENT.   XXX
++WATER SERV.
[FUEL & METALLURGICAL JOURNALS]
  LONDON 78(935), 1974-
  MON. PREV: WATER & WATER ENGINEERING FROM 10,
  1908- 77(934), D 1973.
  ED/N-1.   LD/U-1.   LO/N14.   LO/U-2.   RE/U-1.   XS/R10.

WATER & WATER ENGINEERING.   XXX
SUBS (1974): WATER SERVICES.

WATERWORKS OFFICERS' ASSOCIATION JOURNAL.   XXX
++WATERWORKS OFF. ASSOC. J.
ASSOCIATION OF WATERWORKS OFFICERS.
  EXETER 9(7), 1971-
  PREV: WATERWORKS OFFICERS' JOURNAL FROM 1,
  1945- 9(6), 1971.
  LO/N14.

WATERWORKS OFFICERS' JOURNAL.   XXX
SUBS (1971): WATERWORKS OFFICERS' ASSOCIAT-
ION JOURNAL.

WEEKLY EPIDEMIOLOGICAL RECORD.
++WKLY. EPIDEMIOL. REC.
WORLD HEALTH ORGANIZATION.
  GENEVA 1973(1)-
  GL/U-2.

WEEKLY LIST OF PAPERS ON RADIATION CHEMISTRY.
++WKLY. LIST PAP. RADIAT. CHEM.
NATIONAL BUREAU OF STANDARDS (US): OFFICE OF
STANDARD REFERENCE DATA.
  WASHINGTON, D.C. 1, 1968-
  COMPILED BY THE RADIATION CHEMISTRY DATA
  CENTER, UNIVERSITY OF NOTRE DAME, INDIANA.
  LO/N14. 4, 1971-

WEIGHING & MEASUREMENT.   XXX
++WEIGH. & MEAS.
[SCALE JOURNAL PUBL. CO.]
  ROCKFORD, ILL. 58, 1974-
  PREV: SCALE JOURNAL FROM 1, 1914- 57, 1973.
  LO/N14.

WELDING RESEARCH NEWS.
++WELD. RES. NEWS.
WELDING RESEARCH COUNCIL.
  NEW YORK NO.1, 1974-
  GL/U-2.

WELSH ECONOMIC TRENDS.
++WELSH ECON. TRENDS.
(GREAT BRITAIN) WELSH OFFICE.
  CARDIFF NO.1, 1974-
  ANNU.
  CA/U-1.   CB/U-1.   HL/U-1.   LO/U-3.   OX/U-1.   SA/U-1.

WEN-T'I YU YEN-CHIU. ISSUES & STUDIES.
KUO CHI KUAN HSI YEN CHIU SO.
  TAIPEI 1, OC 1961-
  ENGLISH TITLE VARIES: ISSUES & RESEARCH;
  ISSUES & STUDIES.
  LD/U-1. 1(1), 1961; 6(11), 1967- 7(5), 1968;

WESSEX MAGAZINE.
++WESSEX MAG.
  WIMBORNE, DORSET [NO.1], JE/JL 1973-
  6/A.
  CA/U-1.   ED/N-1.   OX/U-1.   SO/U-1.

WEST AFRICAN ECONOMIST & BUSINESS REVIEW.
++WEST AFR. ECON. & BUS. REV.
[SPECIALIST & PROFESSIONAL P. LTD.]
  KINGSTON ON THAMES 1(1), 1971-
  S/T: THE INTERNATIONAL MAGAZINE FOR WEST
  AFRICA. EARLY ISSUES PUBL. IN LAGOS BY NIGER-
  IAN PUBLICATIONS.
  LO/U14. 1(2), 1971-

WESTERN NATURALIST.
++WEST. NAT.
RENFREWSHIRE NATURAL HISTORY SOCIETY.
  PAISLEY 1, 1972-
  S/T: A JOURNAL OF SCOTTISH NATURAL HISTORY.
  BL/U-1.   CA/U-1.   ED/N-1.   OX/U-1.

WHAT CAN THIS CHARLATAN BE TRYING TO SAY.   000
SEE: CHARLATAN.

WHAT CAR?
[HAYMARKET PUBL.]
  LONDON 1(1), N 1973-
  MON.
  CA/U-1. 1(2), 1973-

WHAT'S NEW. THE INDUSTRIAL PRODUCTS & EQUIPMENT
GUIDE.
[MORGAN-GRAMPIAN]
  LONDON S 1971-
  MON.
  ED/N-1.   OX/U-1.   LO/N14. CURRENT BOX ONLY.

WHO PESTICIDE RESIDUES SERIES.
++WHO PESTIC. RESIDUES SER.
WORLD HEALTH ORGANIZATION.
  GENEVA NO.1, 1972-
  CA/U-1.   GL/U-1.   LD/U-1.

WORK IN PROGRESS, DEPARTMENT OF ENGLISH,
AHMADU BELLO UNIVERSITY.
++WORK PROG. DEP. ENGL. AHMADU BELLO UNIV.
  ZARIA NO.1, 1972-
  LO/U14. NO.1, 1972.

WORK STUDY ø O & M ABSTRACTS.
++WORK STUDY ■ O & M ABSTR.
INSTITUTE OF WORK STUDY PRACTITIONERS.
[ANBAR PUBL.]
  WEMBLEY 1(1), 17/OC 1973-
  8/A.
  CA/U-1.   OX/U-1.   XS/R10.   ISSN 0305-0653

WORKERS' CONTROL BULLETIN.   XXX
++WORK. CONTROL BULL.
INSTITUTE FOR WORKERS' CONTROL.
  NOTTINGHAM OC 1973-
  PREV: BULLETIN, INSTITUTE FOR WORKERS' CONTROL
  FROM 1(1), [1968]- 10, 1972.
  CA/U-1.   LO/U-3.   ISSN 0306-7892

WORKING PAPERS IN SOCIOLOGY, DEPARTMENT OF
SOCIOLOGY & SOCIAL ADMINISTRATION, UNIVERSITY
OF DURHAM.
++WORK. PAP. SOCIOL. DEP. SOCIOL. & SOC. ADM.
UNIV. DURHAM.
  DURHAM NO.1, 1972-
  CA/U-1.

WORKS ENGINEERING.   XXX
++WORKS ENG.
[FUEL & METALLURGICAL JOURNALS LTD.]
  LONDON [NO.1], MY 1971- 22, 24/AP 1974 ...
  PREV: WORKS ENGINEERING & FACTORY SERVICES
  FROM 62(737), 1967- AP 1971. SUBS: POWER &
  WORKS ENGINEERING.
  LO/N14.   CA/U-1. NO.8, 1973-

**WORLD INDEX OF SOCIAL SCIENCE INSTITUTIONS.
REPERTOIRE MONDIAL DES INSTITUTIONS DE SCI-
ENCES SOCIALES.**
++*WORLD INDEX SOC. SCI. INST.*
UNESCO.
PARIS 1970-
ENGL. & FR. A SUPPL. TO: INTERNATIONAL SOCIAL
SCIENCE JOURNAL. UPDATED BY SUPPLEMENTS CALL-
ED AMENDMENTS.
LO/S10. OX/U-1.

WORLD MINING NEWSLETTER.
++*WORLD MIN. NEWSL.*
[MINING INTELLIGENCE]
LONDON [NO.1], OC 1973-
S/T: A MONTHLY SURVEY OF DEVELOPMENTS IN WORLD
MINING.
ED/N-1. ISSN 0306-1825

WORLD OUTLOOK.
ECONOMIST INTELLIGENCE UNIT.
LONDON 1974-
ANNU.
LO/U-3.

WORLD POLLEN & SPORE FLORA.
COLLEGIUM PALYNOLOGICUM SCANDINAVICUM.
STOCKHOLM 1, 1973-
2/A.
GL/U-1. LD/U-1. LO/N-4. RE/U-1. SH/U-1. SO/U-1.

WORLDWIDE LIST OF PUBLISHED STANDARDS. XXX
++*WORLDWIDE LIST PUBL. STAND.*
BRITISH STANDARDS INSTITUTION.
LONDON MR 1974-
MON. PREV: LIST OF OVERSEA STANDARDS FROM AP
1969- F 1974.
ED/N-1. GL/U-1. LO/N14. XS/R10.

WRIT. XXX
UNIVERSITY OF TORONTO: INNIS COLLEGE.
TORONTO 1, 1970-
2/A. PREV: ON THE BIAS. PRODUCED BY THE
COLLEGE'S WRITING LABORATORY.
OX/U-1.

WRITERS DIRECTORY.
++*WRIT. DIR.*
[ST. JAMES P.]
CHICAGO & LONDON 1971/73(1971)-
LO/U-1. GL/U-1. 1974/76(1973)- ISSN 0084-2699

WRITING ON THE WALL.
++*WRIT. WALL.*
LONDON NO.1, 1973-
6/A.
ED/N-1.

W.S.C.F. DOSSIER.
WORLD STUDENT CHRISTIAN FEDERATION.
GENEVA 1, 1973-
OX/U-1.

YA-CHOU WEN HUA. 000
SEE: ASIAN CULTURE QUARTERLY.

**YEARBOOK OF THE INTERNATIONAL FOLK MUSIC
COUNCIL.** XXX
++*YEARB. INT. FOLK MUSIC COUNC.*
[UNIV. OF ILLINOIS P.]
URBANA, ILL. &C. 1, 1969-
PREV: JOURNAL OF THE INTERNATIONAL FOLK MUSIC
COUNCIL FROM 1, 1949- 20, 1968.
LD/U-1. LO/S10. LO/U-1.

YOUTH SCENE.
YOUTH SERVICE INFORMATION CENTRE.
LEICESTER 1, D 1972-
ED/N-1. OX/U-1.

YOUTH SOCIAL WORK BULLETIN.
++*YOUTH SOC. WORK BULL.*
NATIONAL YOUTH BUREAU (GB).
LEICESTER 1(1), N/D 1973-
6/A.
CA/U-1. ED/N-1.

YOUTH IN SOCIETY.
++*YOUTH SOC.*
NATIONAL YOUTH BUREAU (GB).
LEICESTER NO.1, S/OC 1973-
ED/N-1. LO/S18. OX/U-1. SW/U-1.

Z KRALICKE TVRZE.
MUSEJNI SPOLEK PRO UCHOVANI BRATERSKYCH PAMATEK
A TISKU V KRALICICH NAD OSLAVOU.
BRNO 1, 1967-
OX/U-1.

ZABYTKI ARCHITEKTURY I BUDOWNICTWA W POLSCE.
++*ZABYTKI ARCHIT. & BUDOWNICTWA POL.*
(POLAND) MINISTERSTWO KULTURY I SZTUKI: OSRODEK
DOKUMENTACJI ZABYTKOW.
WARSAW 1, 1971-
OSRODEK DOKUMENTACJI SUBORD. TO: ZARZAD MUZEOW
I OCHRONY ZABYTKOW. ISSUED AS SUBSERIES OF
BIBLIOTEKA MUZEALNICTWA I OCHRONY ZABYTKOW.
OX/U-1. 2, 1972-

ZBORNIK: DEJINY ROBOTNICKEHO HNUTA. XXX
++*ZB., DEJINY ROBOTNICKEHO HNUTA.*
UNIVERZITA KOMENSKEHO: USTAV MARXIZMU-LENINIZMU
BRATISLAVA 3, 1972-
GER., RUSS. OR SLOVAK. PREV: ZBORNIK, USTAV
MARXIZMU-LENINIZMU UNIVERZITA KOMENSKEHO FROM
1, 1970- 2, 1971. CONT. PREV. NUMBERING.
OX/U-1.

**ZBORNIK PRAC, HYDROMETEOROLOGICKY USTAV V
BRATISLAVE.**
++*ZB. PRAC. HIDROMETEOROL. USTAV BRATISL.*
BRATISLAVA 1, 1972-
RUSS., GER., CZECH. OR SLOVAK SUMM.
XS/N-1.

**ZBORNIK, USTAV MARXIZMU-LENINIZMU UNIVERZITA
KOMENSKEHO.** XXX
++*ZB. USTAV MARXIZMU-LENINIZMU UNIV. KOMENSKEHO.*
BRATISLAVA 1, 1970- 2, 1971 ...
SUBS: ZBORNIK: DEJINY ROBOTNICKEHO HNUTA.
OX/U-1.

ZEITGESCHICHTE.
VIENNA &C. 1(1), 1973-
OX/U-1.

ZEITSCHRIFT FUR ARCHAOLOGIE DES MITTELALTERS.
++*Z. ARCHAOL. MITTELALTERS.*
[RHEINLAND VERLAG]
COLOGNE 1, 1973-
BL/U-1. CA/U-1. OX/U-1.

ZEITSCHRIFT FUR BIOLOGIE. XXX
++*Z. BIOL.*
[URBAN & SCHWARZENBERG]
MUNICH & BERLIN 1, 1865- 116, 1971.//
SUSPENDED BETWEEN 1944- 1949.
GL/U-1.* LO/U-2. LO/N13. 89, 1930-**
LO/N14. 36, 1910- 74(2), 1931.

ZEITSCHRIFT FUR GEOLOGISCHE WISSENSCHAFTEN.
++*ZEIT. GEOL. WISS.*
GESELLSCHAFT FUR GEOLOGISCHE WISSENSCHAFTEN DER
DDR.
BERLIN 1(1), 1973-
GL/U-1. LO/N-4. LO/N14. OX/U-8. LO/U-2. 2, 1974-

ZEITSCHRIFT FUR GERMANISTISCHE LINGUISTIK. XXX
++*Z. GER. LINGUIST.*
[GRUYTER]
BERLIN &C. 1(1), S 1973-
PREV: ZEITSCHRIFT FUR DEUTSCHE SPRACHE FROM
20(1/2), 1964- 27, 1971.
BN/U-1. CA/U-1. MA/U-1. SA/U-1.

**ZEITSCHRIFT FUR TROPENMED1Z1N UND
PARASITOLOGIE.** XXX
**SUBS(1974): TROPENMED1Z1N UND
PARASITOLOGIE.**

ZENTRALASIATISCHE STUDIEN.
++*ZENTRALASIAT. STUD.*
UNIVERSITAT BONN: SEMINAR FUR SPRACHE- UND
KULTURWISSENSCHAFT ZENTRALASIENS.
[VERLAG OTTO HARRASSOWITZ]
WIESBADEN 1, 1967-
ANNU.
LO/N12. OX/U-1. ISSN 0514-857X

**ZESZYTY NAUKOWE AKADEMII ROLNICZEJ: TECHNOL-
OGIA ROLNO-SPOZYWCZA.** XXX
++*ZESZ. NAUK. AKAD. ROLN., TECHNOL. ROLNO-
SPOZYW.*
WARSAW 8, 1973-
PREV: ZESZYTY NAUKOWE SZKOLY GLOWNEJ GOSPOD-
ARSTWA WIEJSKIEGO: TECHNOLOGIA ROLNO-SPOZYWCZA
FROM 1, 1960- 7, 1971.
CA/U11. ED/U-2. LO/N13. XS/R-6.** XY/N-1.**

**ZESZYTY NAUKOWE UNIWERSYTETU GDANSKIEGO:
CHEMIA.**
+ +ZESZ. NAUK. UNIW. GDANSK., CHEM.
UNIWERSYTET GDANSKI: WYDZIAL MATEMATYKI, FIZYKI
I CHEMII.
 GDANSK 1, 1971-
 ENGL. OR POL. WITH ENGL., FR., GER. OR POL.
 SUMM.
 LO/N14.

**ZESZYTY NAUKOWE UNIWERSYTETU GDANSKIEGO:
MATEMATYKA.**
+ +ZESZ. NAUK. UNIW. GDANSK., MAT.
UNIWERSYTET GDANSKI: WYDZIAL MATEMATYKI, FIZYKI
I CHEMII.
 GDANSK NO.1, 1971-
 ENGL. OR POL. WITH SUMM. IN THE OTHER LANGUAGE
 LO/N14.

ZHIVOTNYJ MIR BELORUSSKOGO POOZER'JA.
+ +ZHIVOTN. BELORUSS. POOZER'JA.
VITEBSKI PEDAHAHICHNY INSTYTUT: KAFEDRA
ZOOLOGII.
 MINSK 1, 1970-
 LO/N13. OX/U-8.

ZOOLOGISKA BIDRAG FRAN UPPSALA.   XXX
 SUBS (1973): ZOON.

ZOOLOGISKA BIDRAG FRAN UPPSALA: SUPPLEMENT.   XXX
 SUBS (1973): ZOON: SUPPLEMENT.

ZOON. A JOURNAL OF ZOOLOGY.   XXX
KUNGLIGA UNIVERSITET I UPPSALA: INSTITUTE OF
ZOOLOGY.
 UPPSALA 1, 1973-
 PREV: ZOOLOGISKA BIDRAG FRAN UPPSALA FROM 1,
 1911/12- 38, 1969.
 LO/N-2. LO/N13. MA/U-1. OX/U-8

ZOON: SUPPLEMENT.   XXX
KUNGLIGA UNIVERSITET I UPPSALA: INSTITUTE OF
ZOOLOGY.
 UPPSALA [NO.]1, 1973-
 PREV: ZOOLOGISKA BIDRAG FRAN UPPSALA: SUPPLE-
 MENT FROM [NO.]1, 1920- 2, 1972.
 LO/N-2. MA/U-1.

Index of Sponsoring Bodies

AKADEMIJA NAUK UKRAJINS'KOJI RSR: INSTYTUT
LITERATURY.
— PYTANNJA TEKSTOLOHIJI

AKADEMIJA NAUK UKRAJINS'KOJI RSR: INSTYTUT
MISTETSTVOZNAVSTVA, FOL'KLORU I ETNOGRAFII.
— UKRAJINS'KE MISTETSTVOZNAVSTVO.

AKADEMIJA NAUK UKRAJINS'KOJI RSR: INSTYTUT
MOVOZNAVSTVA.
— PYTANNJA MOVNOJI KUL'TURY.   XXX
— RIDNE SLOVO.   XXX

AKADEMIJA NAUK UKRAJINS'KOJI RSR: INSTITUT
POLUPROVODNIKOV.
— KVANTOVAJA ELEKTRONIKA (KIEV).

AKADEMIJA NAUK UZBEKSKOJ SSR.
— ISTORIJA RABOCHEGO KLASSA UZBEKISTANA.

AKADEMIJA NAVUK BELARUSKAJ SSR: INSTYTUT MOVAZ-
NAUSTVA.
— BELARUSKAJA LINHVISTYKA.

AKADEMIJA OBSHCHESTVENNYKH NAUK PRI TSK KPSS:
KAFEDRA ISTORII KPSS.
— LEKTSII PO ISTORII KPSS.

AKADEMIJA OBSHCHESTVENNYKH NAUK PRI TSK KPSS:
KAFEDRA TEORII I METODOV IDEOLOGICHESKOJ RABOTY
— VOPROSY TEORII I METODOV IDEOLOGICHESKOJ
RABOTY.   XXX

AKADEMIJA PEDAGOGICHESKIKH NAUK RSFSR.
— DEFEKTOLOGIJA.

AKADEMIA ROLNICZA (WARSAW).
— ZESZYTY NAUKOWE AKADEMII ROLNICZEJ: TECHNOL-
OGIA ROLNO-SPOZYWCZA.   XXX

ALL INDIA ASSOCIATION FOR CHRISTIAN HIGHER
EDUCATION.
— NEW FRONTIERS IN EDUCATION.

ALLIANZ VERSICHERUNGS.
— ALLIANZ BERICHTE FUR BETRIEBSTECHNIK UND
SCHADENVERHUTUNG.   XXX
— ERFAHRUNGSBERICHTE, ALLIANZ VERSICHERUNGS.   XXX

ALLIED IRISH BANKS LTD.
— ALLIED IRISH BANKS REVIEW.

AMERICAN ANTHROPOLOGICAL ASSOCIATION.
— AMERICAN ETHNOLOGIST.

AMERICAN ASSOCIATION OF THE PHILIPPINES.
— BULLETIN OF THE AMERICAN HISTORICAL COLLECT-
ION.

AMERICAN ASSOCIATION OF STATE HIGHWAY & TRANS-
PORTATION OFFICIALS.
— AMERICAN HIGHWAY & TRANSPORTATION MONTHLY.   XXX

AMERICAN ASSOCIATION OF TEACHERS OF GERMAN.
— UNTERRICHTSPRAXIS.

AMERICAN BIBLIOGRAPHICAL CENTER.
— ART BIBLIOGRAPHIES: CURRENT TITLES.

AMERICAN CONGRESS ON SURVEYING & MAPPING.
— AMERICAN CARTOGRAPHER.

AMERICAN FERN SOCIETY.
— NEWS & VIEWS, AMERICAN FERN SOCIETY.

AMERICAN GEOGRAPHICAL SOCIETY OF NEW YORK.
— UBIQUE.

AMERICAN HEART ASSOCIATION.
— CIRCULATION RESEARCH: SUPPLEMENT.

AMERICAN INSTITUTE OF ARCHITECTS.
— JOURNAL OF ARCHITECTURAL RESEARCH.   XXX

AMERICAN INSTITUTE OF ISLAMIC STUDIES.
— ISLAMIC STUDIES (DENVER).

AMERICAN INSTITUTE OF PHYSICS.
— INDEX TO THE LITERATURE OF MAGNETISM.

AMERICAN SOCIETY OF ANESTHESIOLOGISTS.
— ANESTHESIOLOGY BIBLIOGRAPHY.

AMERICAN SOCIETY FOR METALS.
— IRONMAKING & STEELMAKING.   XXX

AMERICAN SOCIETY OF MISSIOLOGY.
— MISSIOLOGY. AN INTERNATIONAL REVIEW.   XXX

AMIS DU MUSEE ROYAL DE L'AFRIQUE CENTRALE.
— AFRICA-TERVUREN.   XXX
— CONGO-TERVUREN.   XXX
SUBS (1961): AFRICA-TERVUREN.

AMNESTY INTERNATIONAL: BRITISH SECTION.
— BRITISH AMNESTY.   XXX

ANDOVER LOCAL ARCHIVES COMMITTEE.
— TEST VALLEY & BORDER ANTHOLOGY.

ANNAMALAI UNIVERSITY.
— SOUTHERN ECONOMIC REVIEW.

ANTHROPOLOGICAL RESEARCH CENTER OF NORTHERN
NEW ENGLAND.   000
SEE: FRANKLIN PIERCE COLLEGE: ANTHROPOLOGICAL
RESEARCH CENTER OF NORTHERN NEW ENGLAND.

ANTI DEAR FOOD CAMPAIGN.
— ANTI DEAR FOOD CAMPAIGNER.

APOSTOLIC FAITH CHURCH: GENERAL COUNCIL.
— HERALD OF GRACE.

ARCHIVO GENERAL DE LA NACION (GUATEMALA).
— BOLETIN, ARCHIVO GENERAL DE LA NACION
(GUATEMALA).

ARCHIVO NACIONAL (HONDURAS).
— ANALES, ARCHIVO NACIONAL (HONDURAS).

ARCTIC INSTITUTE OF NORTH AMERICA.
— INFORMATION NORTH.   XXX

(ARGENTINA) ARCHIVO GENERAL.
— REVISTA, ARCHIVO GENERAL (ARGENTINA).

(ARGENTINA) DIRECCION NACIONAL DEL ANTARTICO.
— ANTARTIDA.

ASIAN CULTURAL CENTRE (TAIPEI).
— ASIAN CULTURE QUARTERLY. YA-CHOU WEN HUA.

ASIAN CULTURAL CENTRE (TOKYO).
— ASIAN CULTURE. BULLETIN OF THE ASIAN CULT-
URAL CENTRE IN TOKYO.

ASLIB: AUDIOVISUAL GROUP.
— AUDIOVISUAL LIBRARIAN.   XXX

ASOCIACION COLUMBIANA DE GEOGRAFOS.
— CORREO GEOGRAFICO.

ASOCIACION COLOMBIANA DE INGENIEROS
AGRONOMOS.
— AGRICULTURA TROPICAL.   XXX

ASOCIACION MEXICANA DE SOCIOLOGICA.
— REVISTA INTERAMERICANA DE SOCIOLOGIA.

ASSOCIATION FOR THE ADVANCEMENT OF BALTIC
STUDIES.
— BULLETIN OF BALTIC STUDIES.   XXX
— JOURNAL OF BALTIC STUDIES.   XXX

ASSOCIATION FOR THE ADVANCEMENT OF MEDICAL
INSTRUMENTATION.
— JOURNAL, ASSOCIATION FOR THE ADVANCEMENT
OF MEDICAL INSTRUMENTATION.   XXX
— MEDICAL INSTRUMENTATION JOURNAL.   XXX

ASSOCIATION DES AMIS DES CAHIERS DU NOUVEAU
COMMERCE.
— NOUVEAU COMMERCE DE LA LECTURE.

ASSOCIATION DES AMIS DE LOUIS LECOIN.
— REFRACTAIRE.

ASSOCIATION POUR L'AVANCEMENT DES ETUDES IRAN-
IENNES.
— STUDIA IRANICA.

ASSOCIATION OF CARIBBEAN UNIVERSITY & RESEARCH
LIBRARIES.
— NEWSLETTER, ASSOCIATION OF CARIBBEAN UNIV-
ERSITY & RESEARCH LIBRARIES.
— PAPERS, ASSOCIATION OF CARIBBEAN UNIVERSITY &
RESEARCH LIBRARIES.

ASSOCIATION OF CLINICAL BIOCHEMISTS.
— CURRENT CLINICAL CHEMISTRY. A CURRENT AWARE-
NESS SERVICE FOR CLINICAL CHEMISTS & MEDICAL
BIOCHEMISTRY.

BOSTON UNIVERSITY: AFRICAN STUDIES CENTER.
— INTERNATIONAL JOURNAL OF AFRICAN HISTORICAL
STUDIES.   xxx

BOTANICAL SOCIETY OF PAKISTAN.
— PAKISTAN JOURNAL OF BOTANY.

(BRAZIL) DIRECCION NACIONAL DEL ANTARTICO.
— DIVULGACIONES, DIRECCION NACIONAL DEL ANTART-
ICO (BRAZIL).

(BRAZIL) MINISTERIO DA EDUCACAO E
CULTURA: CAMPANHA DE DEFESA DO
FOLCLORE BRASILEIRO.
— REVISTA BRASILEIRA DE FOLCLORE.

(BRAZIL) SECRETARIA DA RECEITA FEDERAL: CENTRO
DE INFORMACOES ECONOMICO.
— BOLETIM DO COMERCIO EXTERIOR.

BRISTOL CITY ART GALLERY.
— ABSTRACTS, BRISTOL CITY ART GALLERY.

BRITISH ASSOCIATION OF ORTHODONTISTS.
— BRITISH JOURNAL OF ORTHODONTICS.   xxx

BRITISH CALIBRATION SERVICE.
— MEASUREMENT FOCUS. BRITISH CALIBRATION SERVICE
NEWSLETTER.

BRITISH CAVE RESEARCH ASSOCIATION.   xxx
— BULLETIN, BRITISH CAVE RESEARCH ASSOCIATION. xxx
— TRANSACTIONS, BRITISH CAVE RESEARCH ASSOC-
IATION.   xxx

BRITISH ESPERANTO ASSOCIATION.
— ESPERANTO CONTACT.   xxx

BRITISH FILM INSTITUTE.
— TELEVISION MONOGRAPHS, BRITISH FILM INSTITUTE.

BRITISH HYDROMECHANICS RESEARCH ASSOCIATION.
— FLUID FLOW MEASUREMENT ABSTRACTS.

BRITISH HYDROMECHANICS RESEARCH ASSOCIATION:
FLUID ENGINEERING.
— CIVIL ENGINEERING HYDRAULICS ABSTRACTS.   xxx

BRITISH INSTITUTE OF INTERNATIONAL & COMPAR-
ATIVE LAW.
— GUIDES TO COMMON MARKET LAW.

BRITISH INSTITUTE OF MANAGEMENT.
— MANAGEMENT REVIEW & DIGEST.

BRITISH INSURANCE ASSOCIATION.
— INSURANCE FACTS & FIGURES.

BRITISH & IRISH COMMUNIST ORGANISATION.
— COMMUNIST REVIEW.

BRITISH LIBRARY: LENDING DIVISION.
— INTERNATIONAL POLYMER SCIENCE & TECHNOLOGY.

BRITISH LIBRARY OF POLITICAL & ECONOMIC
SCIENCE.   000
SEE: LONDON SCHOOL OF ECONOMICS & POLITICAL
SCIENCE: BRITISH LIBRARY OF POLITICAL &
ECONOMIC SCIENCE.

BRITISH MEDICAL ASSOCIATION.
— ABSTRACTS OF WORLD MEDICINE.   xxx

BRITISH MUSEUM (NATURAL HISTORY).
— BOTANY LEAFLET, BRITISH MUSEUM (NATURAL
HISTORY).
— ENTOMOLOGY LEAFLET, BRITISH MUSEUM (NATURAL
HISTORY).

BRITISH NATIONAL COMMITTEE ON LARGE DAMS.
— NEWS & VIEWS OF THE BRITISH NATIONAL COMMIT-
TEE ON LARGE DAMS.

BRITISH NUTRITION FOUNDATION LTD.
— BNF BULLETIN.   xxx

BRITISH PANTOMIME ASSOCIATION.
— PANTO! JOURNAL OF THE BRITISH PANTOMIME
ASSOCIATION.

BRITISH PTERIDOLOGICAL SOCIETY.
— BULLETIN, BRITISH PTERIDOLOGICAL SOCIETY.   xxx
— NEWSLETTER, BRITISH PTERIDOLOGICAL SOCIETY.   xxx

BRITISH SCHOOL OF ARCHAEOLOGY IN IRAQ.
— CUNEIFORM TEXTS FROM NIMRUD.

BRITISH SOCIETY OF PERIODONTOLOGY.
— JOURNAL OF CLINICAL PERIODONTOLOGY.

BRITISH SOCIETY FOR THE STUDY OF ORTHODONTICS.
— BRITISH JOURNAL OF ORTHODONTICS.   xxx
— TRANSACTIONS OF THE BRITISH SOCIETY FOR THE
STUDY OF ORTHODONTICS.   xxx
SUBS (1973): PART OF BRITISH JOURNAL OF
ORTHODONTICS.

(BRITISH SOLOMON ISLANDS) POSTS & TELECOMMUN-
ICATIONS DEPARTMENT.
— SOLOMON ISLANDS STAMP MAGAZINE.

BRITISH SPELEOLOGICAL ASSOCIATION.
— CAVE SCIENCE (1971).   ·xxx
— JOURNAL, BRITISH SPELEOLOGICAL ASSOCIATION.   xxx

BRITISH STANDARDS INSTITUTION.
— WORLDWIDE LIST OF PUBLISHED STANDARDS.   xxx

BROTHERHOOD OF SAINT HERMAN OF ALASKA.
— ORTHODOX WORD.

BROWNING INSTITUTE.
— BROWNING INSTITUTE STUDIES.

BRUNEL UNIVERSITY.
— BRUNEL BULLETIN.

(BUENOS AIRES, PROVINCE) COMISION DE INVEST-
IGACION CIENTIFICA.
— ANALES, COMISION DE INVESTIGACION CIENTIFICA
(BUENOS AIRES, PROVINCE).

BUILDING CENTRE GROUP.
— BULLETIN, BUILDING CENTRE GROUP.

(BULGARIA) MINISTERSTVO NA NARODNOTO ZDRAVE I
SOTSIALNITE GRIZHI.
— EKSPERIMENTALNA MEDITSINA I MORFOLOGIJA.

BULGARSKA AKADEMIJA NA NAUKITE: INSTITUT PO
SOTSIOLOGIJA.
— SOTSIOLOGICHESKI IZSLEDOVANIJA.   xxx
— SOTSIOLOGICHESKI PROBLEMI.   xxx

BULGARSKA AKADEMIJA NA NAUKITE: UNITED CENTRE
FOR RESEARCH & TRAINING IN HISTORY.
— BULGARIAN HISTORICAL REVIEW.

BULGARSKO ISTORICHESKO DRUZHESTVO.
— VEKOVE. BJULETIN NA BULGARSKOTO ISTORICHESKO
DRUZHESTVO.

BUND SCHWEIZERISCHER GARTEN- UND
LANDSCHAFTSARCHITEKTEN.
— ANTHOS. VIERTELJAHRES-ZEITSCHRIFT FUR
GARTEN- UND LANDSCHAFTSGESTALTUNG.

BUREAU DE RECHERCHES SOCIOLOGIQUES (TUNIS).
— ETUDES DE SOCIOLOGIE TUNISIENNE.

CAMBRIDGE SOCIETY FOR INDUSTRIAL ARCHAEOLOGY.
— CAMBRIDGE INDUSTRIAL ARCHAEOLOGY.

CAMBRIDGESHIRE COLLEGE OF ARTS & TECHNOLOGY.
— NUMBER 1.

CAMDEN HISTORY SOCIETY.
— NEWSLETTER, CAMDEN HISTORY SOCIETY.

(CANADA) DEPARTMENT OF AGRICULTURE: ENGINEERING
RESEARCH SERVICE.
— ERDA. ENGINEERING RESEARCH & DEVELOPMENT IN
AGRICULTURE.

(CANADA) DEPARTMENT OF AGRICULTURE: RESEARCH
BRANCH.
— REPORT, NEWFOUNDLAND SOIL SURVEY.

(CANADA) DEPARTMENT OF ENERGY, MINES &
RESOURCES.
— GEOS. A QUARTERLY CONCERNED WITH THE EARTH'S
RESOURCES.

(CANADA) FORESTRY SERVICE: LAURENTIAN FOREST
RESEARCH CENTRE.
— DOCUMENT, LAURENTIAN FOREST RESEARCH CENTRE,
FORESTRY SERVICE (CANADA).

(CANADA) NATIONAL HISTORIC SITES SERVICE.
— CANADIAN HISTORIC SITES. OCCASIONAL PAPERS
IN ARCHAEOLOGY & HISTORY.

(CANADA) NORTHERN SCIENCE RESEARCH GROUP.
— SOCIAL SCIENCE SERIES, NORTHERN SCIENCE RES-
EARCH GROUP (CANADA).

(CANADA) STATISTICS CANADA.   XXX
— COMMUNICATIONS SERVICE BULLETIN.

CANADIAN BAR ASSOCIATION.
— CANADIAN BAR NATIONAL.

CANADIAN INSTITUTE OF TIMBER CONSTRUCTION.
— TREATED WOOD PERSPECTIVES.   XXX

CANADIAN MUSIC CENTRE.
— MUSICANADA. NEWSLETTER OF THE CANADIAN MUSIC
CENTRE.   XXX
— NEWSLETTER, CANADIAN MUSIC CENTRE.   XXX

CANADIAN OTOLARYNGOLOGICAL SOCIETY.
— CANADIAN JOURNAL OF OTOLARYNGOLOGY. JOURNAL
CANADIEN D'OTOLARYNGOLOGIE.
— CANADIAN JOURNAL OF OTOLARYNGOLOGY: SUPPLE-
MENTS.

CANADIAN SOCIETY OF INHALATION THERAPY TECHNIC-
IANS.
— CANADIAN INHALATION THERAPY.   XXX
— RESPIRATORY TECHNOLOGY.   XXX

CANADIAN SOCIETY OF PETROLEUM GEOLOGISTS.
— MEMOIRS, CANADIAN SOCIETY OF PETROLEUM GEOL-
OGISTS.

CARLETON UNIVERSITY.
— CARLETON GERMANIC PAPERS.

CARNEGIE-MELLON UNIVERSITY: DEPARTMENT OF MOD-
ERN LANGUAGES.
— LATIN AMERICAN LITERARY REVIEW.

CAVE RESEARCH GROUP OF GREAT BRITAIN.   XXX
— CAVE SCIENCE.   XXX
SUBS (1967): JOURNAL, BRITISH SPELEOLOGICAL
ASSOCIATION.
— NEWSLETTER, CAVE RESEARCH GROUP OF GREAT
BRITAIN.   XXX
SUBS (1973): BULLETIN, BRITISH CAVE RESEARCH
ASSOCIATION.
— TRANSACTIONS, CAVE RESEARCH GROUP OF GREAT   XXX
BRITAIN.
SUBS (1974) PART OF: TRANSACTIONS, BRITISH
CAVE RESEARCH ASSOCIATION.

CENTRE FOR ADVANCED TELEVISION STUDIES.
— JOURNAL OF THE CENTRE FOR ADVANCED TELEVISION
STUDIES.

CENTRE AFRICAIN DE FORMATION ET DE RECHERCHE
ADMINISTRATIVES POUR LE DEVELOPPEMENT:
LIBRARY & DOCUMENTATION SERVICES.
— AFRICAN ADMINISTRATIVE ABSTRACTS.

CENTRAL ASIAN RESEARCH CENTRE.
— CENTRAL ASIAN MONOGRAPHS.

CENTRO AUXOLOGICO ITALIANO DI PIANCAVALLO.
— ACTA MEDICA AUXOLOGICA.

CENTRAL BANK OF THE PHILIPPINES: DEPARTMENT OF
ECONOMIC RESEARCH.
— PHILIPPINE FINANCIAL STATISTICS. QUARTERLY
BULLETIN.

CENTRE FOR BEHAVIOURAL ART.
— CONTROL MAGAZINE.

CENTRAL COFFEE RESEARCH INSTITUTE (INDIA).
— JOURNAL OF COFFEE RESEARCH.

CENTRE DE DOCUMENTATION ET D'ETUDES MONGOLES.
— ETUDES MONGOLES.

CENTRE FOR EDUCATIONAL DEVELOPMENT OVERSEAS.
— EDUCATIONAL DEVELOPMENT INTERNATIONAL.

CENTRAL ELECTRICITY GENERATING BOARD (GB).
— C.E.G.B. RESEARCH.

CENTRE ELECTRONIQUE HORLOGER.
— BULLETIN, CENTRE ELECTRONIQUE HORLOGER.   XXX

CENTRE FOR ENVIRONMENTAL STUDIES.
— RESEARCH PAPERS, CENTRE FOR ENVIRONMENTAL
STUDIES.

CENTRO DE ESTUDOS DE CABO VERDE.
— REVISTA DO CENTRO DE ESTUDOS DE CABO VERDE:
SERIE DE CIENCIAS BIOLOGICAS.

CENTRO DE ESTUDIOS HISTORICOS DE VIZCAYA.
— ESTUDIOS VIZCAINOS.

CENTRO DE ESTUDIOS LINGUISTICOS (BUENOS AIRES).
— ARCHIVO DE LENGUAS PRECOLOMBINAS.

CENTRO DE ESTUDIOS DEL PACIFICO (CHILE).
— REVISTA DE ESTUDIOS DEL PACIFICO.

CENTRE FOR INDIAN WRITERS.
— INDIAN WRITING TODAY.   XXX

CENTRO DE INVESTIGACION Y ACCION SOCIAL DE LA
COMPANIA DE JESUS (SANTO DOMINGO).
— ESTUDIOS SOCIALES. REVISTA DE INFORMACION Y
ORIENTACION SOCIAL.

CENTRE FOR LIBRARY SCIENCE & METHODOLOGY
(BUDAPEST).
— HUNGARIAN LIBRARY & INFORMATION SCIENCE
ABSTRACTS.

CENTRO NACIONAL DE INVESTIGACIONES DE CAFE
(COLOMBIA): SECCION DE DIVULGACION CIENTIFICA.
— BOLETIN TECNICO, SECCION DE DIVULGACION CIENT-
IFICA, CENTRO NACIONAL DE INVESTIGACIONES DE
CAFE (COLOMBIA).

CENTRE NATIONAL DE LA RECHERCHE SCIENTIFIQUE
(FRANCE).
— ARCHIVES DE SCIENCES SOCIALES DES RELIGIONS.   XXX
— ARCHIVES DE SOCIOLOGIE DES RELIGIONS.   XXX
SUBS (1973): ARCHIVES DE SCIENCES SOCIALES
DES RELIGIONS.

CENTRALNY OSRODEK TECHNIKI MEDYCZNEJ.
— PROBLEMY TECHNIKI W MEDYCYNIE.

CENTRE DE RECHERCHES EGYPTOLOGIQUES (PARIS).
— MEROITIC NEWSLETTER. BULLETIN D'INFORMATIONS
MEROITIQUES.

CENTRE DE RECHERCHE ET D'INFORMATION SOCIO-
POLITIQUES (BELGIUM).
— CONGO.   XXX

CENTRE FOR THE STUDY OF DEVELOPING SOCIETIES
(NEW DELHI).
— OCCASIONAL PAPERS, CENTRE FOR THE STUDY OF
DEVELOPING SOCIETIES (NEW DELHI).

CENTRO STUDI PER LE FONTI DELLA STORIA DELLA
CHIESA NEL VENTO.
— RICERCHE DI STORIA SOCIALE E RELIGIOSA.

CENTRE FOR STUDIES IN SOCIAL POLICY.
— DOUGHTY STREET PAPERS.

CENTRO STUDI DI STORIA SOCIALE E RELIGIOSA NEL
MEZZOGIORNO.
— RICERCHE DI STORIA SOCIALE E RELIGIOSA.

CENTRE TECHNIQUE DES TUILES ET BRIQUES.
— CAHIERS DE LA TERRE CUITE.   XXX
— TERRE CUITE.   XXX
SUBS (1974): CAHIERS DE LA TERRE CUITE.

CENTRE FOR WRITERS & JOURNALISTS FROM THE
EXPLOITED WORLD.
— LIBERATION STRUGGLE.

CESKOSLOVENSKA AKADEMIE VED: ARCHEOLOGICKY
USTAV.
— BULLETIN, ARCHEOLOGICKY USTAV, CESKOSLOVENSKA
AKADEMIE VED.

CESKOSLOVENSKA AKADEMIE VED: GEOGRAFICKY USTAV.
— STUDIA GEOGRAPHICA.

CESKOSLOVENSKA AKADEMIE VED: HISTORICKY USTAV.
— MEDIAEVALIA BOHEMICA.

CESKOSLOVENSKA AKADEMIE VED: USTREDNI ARCHIV.
— ARCHIVNI ZPRAVY, USTREDNI ARCHIV, CESKOSLOV-
ENSKA AKADEMIE VED.

CESKOSLOVENSKE USTREDI KNIZNI KULTURY.
— CESKOSLOVENSKE NEJKRASNEJSI KNIHY. THE MOST
BEAUTIFUL BOOKS OF CZECHOSLOVAKIA.

CEYLON: CONSERVATOR OF FORESTS.   XXX
— CEYLON FORESTER.   XXX
SUBS (1972): SRI LANKA FORESTER.

CHAMBRE SYNDICALE DES PRODUCTEURS D'ACIERS FINS
ET SPECIAUX.
— ACIERS SPECIAUX.

CHARLES LAMB SOCIETY.
— CHARLES LAMB BULLETIN: NS.   XXX
— C.L.S. BULLETIN.   XXX
  SUBS (1973): CHARLES LAMB BULLETIN:NS.

CHARTERED INSTITUTE OF PUBLIC FINANCE
& ACCOUNTANCY.
— LOCAL GOVERNMENT TRENDS.
— PUBLIC FINANCE & ACCOUNTANCY.   XXX

CHEMICAL & ALLIED PRODUCTS INDUSTRY TRAINING
BOARD (GB).
— INFORMATION PAPER, CHEMICAL & ALLIED PRODUCTS
  INDUSTRY TRAINING BOARD (GB).

CHEMICAL SOCIETY.
— INORGANIC CHEMISTRY OF THE MAIN-GROUP
  ELEMENTS.
— MOLECULAR STRUCTURE BY DIFFRACTION METHODS.

CHICAGO INSTITUTE FOR PSYCHOANALYSIS.
— ANNUAL OF PSYCHOANALYSIS.

CHICHESTER & DISTRICT ANGLING SOCIETY.
— BAIT.

CHILD POVERTY ACTION GROUP.
— POVERTY RESEARCH SERIES.

CHILDREN'S LITERATURE ASSOCIATION.
— CHILDREN'S LITERATURE.

CHILE SOLIDARITY CAMPAIGN.
— CHILE MONITOR.

CHRISTIAN PEACE CONFERENCE: INTERNATIONAL
SECRETARIAT.
— CHRISTIAN PEACE CONFERENCE.   XXX

CHUNG-KUO CHIEN-CHU HSUEH-HUI.
— CHIEN-CHU HSUEH-PAO. ARCHITECTURAL JOURNAL.

CHURCH MISSIONARY SOCIETY: YOUTH DEPARTMENT.
— ALIVE. CMS YOUTH MAGAZINE.

CHUZO GIJUTSO FUKYU KYOKU.
— JACT NYUSU.   XXX

CLIMAX MOLYBDENUM CO.
— TUNGSTEN NEWS.

COCOA CHOCOLATE & CONFECTIONERY ALLIANCE.
— ALLIANCE JOURNAL.   XXX

COLLEGE OF LIBRARIANSHIP, WALES.
— SPEL. SELECTED PUBLICATIONS IN EUROPEAN
  LANGUAGES.

COLLEGIUM PALYNOLOGICUM SCANDINAVICUM.
— WORLD POLLEN & SPORE FLORA.

COLORADO STATE UNIVERSITY: DEPARTMENT OF
AGRONOMY.
— BARLEY GENETICS NEWSLETTER.

COLUMBIA UNIVERSITY: INSTITUTE OF HUMAN RIGHTS.
— COLUMBIA HUMAN RIGHTS LAW REVIEW.   XXX

COLUMBIA UNIVERSITY: SCHOOL OF LAW.
— COLUMBIA HUMAN RIGHTS LAW REVIEW.   XXX

COMMERCIAL RABBIT ASSOCIATION.
— COMMERCIAL RABBIT.

COMMERCIAL UNION ASSURANCE COMPANY.
— HAND-IN-HAND. INTERNATIONAL JOURNAL OF THE
  COMMERCIAL UNION ASSURANCE COMPANY.

COMMISSION ON ORE-FORMING FLUIDS IN INCLUSIONS.
— PROCEEDINGS, COMMISSION ON ORE-FORMING FLUIDS
  IN INCLUSIONS.

COMMITTEE ON SPACE RESEARCH.
— SPACE RESEARCH.

COMMONWEALTH HUMAN ECOLOGY COUNCIL.
— C.H.E.C. NEWS.

COMMONWEALTH INSTITUTE OF BIOLOGICAL CONTROL.
— MISCELLANEOUS PUBLICATION, COMMONWEALTH INST-
  ITUTE OF BIOLOGICAL CONTROL.

COMMONWEALTH LIBRARY ASSOCIATION.
— COMLA NEWSLETTER.

COMMONWEALTH MAGISTRATES' ASSOCIATION.
— COMMONWEALTH JUDICIAL JOURNAL.

COMMONWEALTH SECRETARIAT.
— COMMONWEALTH ECONOMIC PAPERS.

COMMUNIST PARTY OF GREAT BRITAIN.
— LINK. COMMUNIST PARTY WOMEN'S JOURNAL.

COMMUNIST PARTY OF GREAT BRITAIN: HISTORY
GROUP.
— NEWSLETTER, HISTORY GROUP, COMMUNIST PARTY OF
  GREAT BRITAIN.

COMMUNITY RELATIONS COMMISSION (GB).
— EDUCATION & COMMUNITY RELATIONS.

COMMUNITY RELATIONS COMMISSION (GB): INFORMAT-
ION DEPARTMENT.
— CRC JOURNAL.

COMMUNITY SERVICE VOLUNTEERS.
— SUPERVOL. A MONTHLY ITEM FOR VOLUNTEERS.

CONFERENCE BOARD OF THE ASSOCIATED RESEARCH
COUNCILS: COMMITTEE ON INTERNATIONAL EXCHANGE
OF PERSONS.
— AMERICAN STUDIES. AN INTERNATIONAL NEWS-
  LETTER.   XXX

CONGRESSO PARA EL DESARROLLO CIENTIFICO, CULT-
URAL Y ECONOMICO DE IBEROAMERICA.
— DESARROLLO.

CONSEJO SUPERIOR UNIVERSITARIO CENTRO-
AMERICANO: PROGRAMA CENTROAMERICANO DE DESARR-
OLLO DE LAS CIENCIAS SOCIALES.
— ESTUDIOS SOCIALES CENTROAMERICANOS.

CONSEJO TECNICO DE INVERSIONES S.A. (BUENOS
AIRES).
— ECONOMIA ARGENTINA. + THE ARGENTINE ECONOMY.

CONSERVATIVE POLITICAL CENTRE.
— CPC OUTLINE SERIES.   XXX
— OVERSEAS REVIEW (LONDON, 1969).   XXX

CORNELL UNIVERSITY: LABORATORY OF ORNITHOLOGY.
— NEWSLETTER, PEREGRINE FUND.

CORSTORPHINE LIBERAL ASSOCIATION.
— CORSTORPHINE NEWSLETTER.

COUNCIL FOR BRITISH ARCHAEOLOGY: SCOTTISH
REGIONAL GROUP.
— CARNYX.

COUNCIL OF EUROPE: DIRECTORATE OF LEGAL
AFFAIRS.
— EXCHANGE OF INFORMATION ON RESEARCH IN EUROP-
  EAN LAW.

COUNCIL FOR EXCEPTIONAL CHILDREN.
— EXCEPTIONAL CHILD EDUCATION ABSTRACTS.

COUNCIL FOR POLITICAL STUDIES (INDIA).
— SOCIALIST PERSPECTIVE.

COUNTRYSIDE COMMISSION (GB).
— RECREATION NEWS.
— RECREATION NEWS: SUPPLEMENT.

CROWN ZELLERBACH.
— FORESTRY RESEARCH NOTE (CAMAS, WASH.).

CSIRO (AUSTRALIA).
— AUSTRALIAN JOURNAL OF PLANT PHYSIOLOGY.

CSIRO (AUSTRALIA): DIVISION OF APPLIED
GEOMECHANICS.   XXX
— TECHNICAL PAPER, DIVISION OF APPLIED GEOMECH-
  ANICS, CSIRO (AUSTRALIA).   XXX

CSIRO (AUSTRALIA): DIVISION OF FOOD RESEARCH.XX
— CSIRO FOOD RESEARCH QUARTERLY.   XXX

CSIRO (AUSTRALIA): DIVISION OF SOIL
MECHANICS.   XXX
— TECHNICAL PAPER, DIVISION OF SOIL MECHANICS,
  CSIRO (AUSTRALIA).   XXX

**CSIRO (AUSTRALIA): MINERALS RESEARCH LAB-
ORATORIES.**
— RESEARCH REVIEW, MINERALS RESEARCH LABORATOR-
IES, CSIRO (AUSTRALIA).

**(CUBA) EMBASSY, LONDON: PRESS & INFORMATION
DEPARTMENT.**
— CUBAN NEWS.

(CUBA) MINISTERIO DE LA INDUSTRIA ALIMENTICIA.
— INDUSTRIA ALIMENTICIA.

**(CZECHOSLOVAKIA) MINISTERSTVO CHEMICKEHO
PRUMYSLU.**
— PLASTY A KAUCUK.   XXX

DACORUM COLLEGE OF FURTHER EDUCATION.
— OCCASIONAL PAPERS, DACORUM COLLEGE OF FURTHER
EDUCATION.

DAG HAMMARSKJOLD LIBRARY.
— CURRENT BIBLIOGRAPHICAL INFORMATION.   XXX
— NEW PUBLICATIONS IN THE DAG HAMMARSKJOLD
LIBRARY.   XXX
SUBS (1971): PART OF CURRENT BIBLIOGRAPH-
ICAL INFORMATION.

DALARNAS MUSEUM.
— DALARNAS MUSEUMS SERIE AV SMASKRIFTER.

DALHOUSIE UNIVERSITY: FACULTY OF LAW.
— DALHOUSIE LAW JOURNAL.

DANIEL STEWART'S & MELVILLE COLLEGE (EDINBURGH)
— COLLEGIAN.

DANISH SOCIETY OF ACTUARIES.
— SCANDINAVIAN ACTUARIAL JOURNAL.   XXX

DAVIDSON POLYSAR LTD.
— POLYSAR PROGRESS.

**DELAWARR LABORATORIES LIMITED: INFORMATION
SERVICE.**
— NEWSLETTER, DELAWARR LABORATORIES LIMITED.

DELHI LIBRARY ASSOCIATION.
— INDIAN PRESS INDEX.

DERWENT ARCHAEOLOGICAL SOCIETY.
— RESEARCH REPORT, DERWENT ARCHAEOLOGICAL
SOCIETY.

**DEUTSCHE AKADEMIE DER KUNSTE: ABTEILUNG GES-
CHICHTE DER SOZIALISTISCHEN LITERATUR.**
— BEITRAGE ZUR GESCHICHTE DER DEUTSCHEN SOZIAL-
ISTISCHEN LITERATUR IM 20. JAHRHUNDERT.

**DEUTSCHE AKADEMIE DER WISSENSCHAFTEN ZU BERLIN:
INSTITUT FUR ORIENTFORSCHUNG.**
— MITTEILUNGEN, INSTITUT FUR ORIENTFORSCHUNG,
DEUTSCHE AKADEMIE DER WISSENSCHAFTEN ZU
BERLIN.   XXX

DEUTSCHE GESELLSCHAFT FUR AMERIKASTUDIEN.
— AMERIKASTUDIEN. AMERICAN STUDIES.   XXX
— AMERIKASTUDIEN: BEIHEFT.   XXX

DEUTSCHE GESELLSCHAFT FUR EISENBAHNGESCHICHTE.
— JAHRBUCH FUR EISENBAHNGESCHICHTE.

DEUTSCHES HISTORISCHES INSTITUT IN PARIS.
— FRANCIA. FORSCHUNGEN ZUR WESTEUROPAISCHEN
GESCHICHTE.

DEUTSCHER KALTETCHNISCHER VEREIN.
— KLIMA-KALTE-TECHNIK.   XXX

DEUTSCHER KONGRESS FUR AERZTLICHE FORTBILDUNG.
— DEUTSCHES MEDIZINISCHES JOURNAL.   XXX

DEUTSCHE TROPENMEDIZINISCHE GESELLSCHAFT.
— TROPENMEDIZIN UND PARASITOLOGIE.   XXX
— ZEITSCHRIFT FUR TROPENMED1Z1N UND   XXX
PARASITOLOGIE.
SUBS(1974): TROPENMED1Z1N UND
PARASITOLOGIE.

DIFFUSION INFORMATION CENTER.
— DIFFUSION & DEFECT DATA.   XXX

DIPUTACION FORAL DE ALAVA.
— ESTUDIOS DE ARQUELOGIA ALAVESA.

DIVINE LIGHT MISSION.
— DIVINE TIMES.

DONETS'KYJ BOTANICHNYJ SAD.
— INTRODUKTSIJA TA EKSPERYMENTAL'NA EKOLOHIJA
ROSLYN.

DONETSKIJ MEDITSINSKIJ INSTITUT.
— AKTUAL'NYE PROBLEMY PROFESSIONAL'NOJ PATOL
OGII.

DOUGLAS COLLEGE: DEPARTMENT OF ENGLISH.
— EVENT.

**DRUSTVO NA ARHIVSKITE RABOTNICI I ARHIVITE
VO SR MAKEDONIJA.**
— MAKEDONSKI ARHIVIST.

DUBLIN NATURALISTS' FIELD CLUB.
— FIELDFARE.

DUKE UNIVERSITY: SCHOOL OF FORESTRY.
— TECHNICAL PAPER, SCHOOL OF FORESTRY, DUKE
UNIVERSITY.

**DUNDEE & TAYSIDE CHAMBER OF COMMERCE &
INDUSTRY.**
— DUNDEE TAYSIDE. JOURNAL OF THE DUNDEE & TAY-
SIDE CHAMBER OF COMMERCE & INDUSTRY.

**DUSSELDORFER INSTITUT FUR AMERIKANISCHE VOELK-
ERKUNDE.**
— ETHNOLOGIA AMERICANA.

EAST AFRICA NATURAL HISTORY SOCIETY.
— EANHS BULLETIN.   XXX
— EANHS NEWSLETTER.   XXX

**EASTERN MICHIGAN UNIVERSITY: DEPARTMENT OF
ENGLISH.**
— ARNOLD NEWSLETTER.

**ECOLE CANTONALE D'HORTICULTURE: ASSOCIATION DES
ANCIENS ELEVES.**
— REVUE HORTICOLE SUISSE.   XXX

**ECOLE POLYTECHNIQUE FEDERALE DE LAUSANNE:
CHAIRE DE SYSTEMES LOGIQUES.**
— SYSTEMES LOGIQUES.

**ECOLE PRATIQUE DES HAUTES ETUDES (PARIS):
SECTION DES SCIENCES ECONOMIQUES ET SOCIALES.**
— MEMOIRES DE PHOTO-INTERPRETATION.

ECOLOGICAL SOCIETY OF AUSTRALIA.
— MEMOIRS, ECOLOGICAL SOCIETY OF AUSTRALIA.

ECONOMIST INTELLIGENCE UNIT.
— WORLD OUTLOOK.

EDINBURGH COMMUNITY RELATIONS COUNCIL.
— COMMUNITY NOW. MONTHLY NEWSLETTER OF THE
EDINBURGH COMMUNITY RELATIONS COUNCIL.

EDINBURGH NATURAL HISTORY SOCIETY.
— JOURNAL, EDINBURGH NATURAL HISTORY SOCIETY.   XXX

**EESTI NSV TEADUSTE AKADEMIA: EKSPERIMENTAAL-
BIOLOOGIA INSTITUUT.**
— UURIMUSED, EKSPERIMENTAAL-BIOLOOGIA INSTITUUT,
EESTI NSV TEADUSTE AKADEMIA.

(EIRE) METEOROLOGICAL SERVICE.
— AGROMETEOROLOGICAL MEMORANDUM, METEOROLOGICAL
SERVICE (EIRE).

EKONOMSKI INSTITUT.
— EKONOMSKE STUDIJE.

ELECTRICAL & ELECTRONIC RETAILERS' ASSOCIATION.
— ELECTRICAL RETAILER.

ENGLISH TOURIST BOARD.
— TOURISM IN ENGLAND.

ENOCH PRATT FREE LIBRARY.
— MENCKENIANA.

ENTOMOLOGICAL SOCIETY OF NIGERIA.
— NEWSLETTER, ENTOMOLOGICAL SOCIETY OF NIGERIA.

ENVIRONMENT INFORMATION CENTER.
— ENVIRONMENT ABSTRACTS.   XXX

ESSEX RIVER AUTHORITY.
— ANNUAL REPORT, ESSEX RIVER AUTHORITY.

ETHIOPIAN FORESTRY ASSOCIATION.
— ETHIOPIAN FORESTRY REVIEW.   XXX

ETHIOPIAN MANUSCRIPT MICROFILM LIBRARY.
— BULLETIN OF ETHIOPIAN MANUSCRIPTS.

EUROPEAN ASSOCIATION OF JAPANESE STUDIES.
— NEWSLETTER OF THE EUROPEAN ASSOCIATION FOR
JAPANESE STUDIES.   XXX

EUROPEAN COMMISSION OF HUMAN RIGHTS.
— ANNUAL REVIEW, EUROPEAN COMMISSION OF HUMAN
RIGHTS.

EUROPEAN MOVEMENT.
— FACTS (LONDON).

EUROPEAN PARLIAMENT: INFORMATION OFFICES.
— INFORMATION DIGEST, EUROPEAN PARLIAMENT.

EXCERPTA MEDICA FOUNDATION.
— EUROPEAN JOURNAL OF CARDIOLOGY.

FACULDADE DE CIENCIAS AGRARIAS DO PARA.
— DESARROLLO DEL TROPICO AMERICANO.

FACULDADE DE FILOSOFIA, CIENCIAS E LETRAS DE
PRESIDENTE PRUDENTE: DEPARTAMENTO DE MATEMATICA
— BOLETIM, DEPARTAMENTO DE MATEMATICA, FACUL-
DADE DE FILOSOFIA, CIENCIAS E LETRAS DE PRES-
IDENTE PRUDENTE.

FACULDADE DE ODONTOLOGIA DE SAO JOSE DOS
CAMPOS.
— REVISTA, FACULDADE DE ODONTOLOGIA DE SAO JOSE
DOS CAMPOS.

FAMILY HISTORY SOCIETY OF CHESHIRE.
— CHESHIRE FAMILY HISTORIAN.

FARLOW HERBARIUM OF CRYPTOGAMIC BOTANY.
— OCCASIONAL PAPERS OF THE FARLOW HERBARIUM OF
CRYPTOGAMIC BOTANY.

FEDERATION OF AFRO-ASIAN INSURERS & REINSURERS.
— F.A.I.R. REVIEW.

FEDERATION OF EUROPEAN BIOCHEMICAL SOCIETIES.
— INDEX OF BIOCHEMICAL REVIEWS.

FEDERATION INTERNATIONALE PHARMACEUTIQUE.
— JOURNAL MONDIAL DE PHARMACIE.   XXX

FONDATION NATIONALE DES SCIENCES POLITIQUES
(FRANCE).
— TRAVAUX ET RECHERCHES DE SCIENCES ECONOMIQUES:
RELATIONS INTERNATIONALES.
— TRAVAUX ET RECHERCHES DE SCIENCES POLITIQUES:
ECONOMIE FRANCAISE.
— TRAVAUX ET RECHERCHES DE SCIENCES POLITIQUES:
POLITIQUES ECONOMIQUES.

FONDATION NATIONALE DES SCIENCES POLITIQUES
(FRANCE): CENTRE D'ETUDES DES RELATIONS INTER-
NATIONALES.
— ANNEE AFRICAINE.

FONDATION NATIONALE DES SCIENCES POLITIQUES
(FRANCE): SERVICE D'ETUDES DE L'ACTIVITE ECON-
OMIQUE.
— ANNEE ECONOMIQUE.

FONDO PARA EL DESARROLLO DEL COCO, DE LA
COPRA Y DE LA PALMA AFRICANA.
— COCO Y PALMA.

FOOD & AGRICULTURAL ORGANIZATION (UN).
— CURRENT FOOD ADDITIVES LEGISLATION.   XXX

FORENINGEN DANMARKS FOLKEMINDER.
— FOLK OG KULTUR. ARBOG FOR DANSK ETNOLOGI OG
FOLKEMINDEVIDENSKAB.   XXX

FOREST FIRE RESEARCH INSTITUTE (CANADA).
— INFORMATION REPORT, FOREST FIRE RESEARCH INST-
ITUTE (CANADA).

FOREST MANAGEMENT INSTITUTE (CANADA).   XXX
— INFORMATION REPORT, FOREST MANAGEMENT INST-
ITUTE (CANADA).   XXX

FOREST PRODUCTS LABORATORY, VANCOUVER.
— INFORMATION REPORT, FOREST PRODUCTS LABORAT-
ORY (VANCOUVER).

FOREST PRODUCT RESEARCH & INDUSTRIES DEVELOP-
MENT COMMISSION (PHILIPPINES).
— FORPRIDE DIGEST.

FOUNDATION FOR ENVIRONMENTAL CONSERVATION.
— ENVIRONMENTAL CONSERVATION.

FOUNDATION FOR RESEARCH IN THE AFRO-AMERICAN
CREATIVE ARTS, INC.
— BLACK PERSPECTIVE IN MUSIC.

(FRANCE) EMBASSY, LONDON: PRESS & INFORMATION
SERVICE.
— BULLETIN MENSUEL D'INFORMATION, AMBASSADE DE
FRANCE A LONDRES.   XXX
SUBS (1974): NEWS FROM FRANCE.
— NEWS FROM FRANCE.   XXX

FRANKLIN INSTITUTE RESEARCH LABORATORIES.
— EXPLOSIVES & PYROTECHNICS.

FRANKLIN PIERCE COLLEGE: ANTHROPOLOGICAL RES-
EARCH CENTER OF NORTHERN NEW ENGLAND.
— MAN IN THE NORTHEAST.

FRIENDS OF THE LIBRARY, TRINITY COLLEGE,
DUBLIN.
— ANNUAL BULLETIN OF THE FRIENDS OF THE LIBRARY,
TRINITY COLLEGE, DUBLIN.   XXX
SUBS (1970): LONG ROOM.
— LONG ROOM. BULLETIN OF THE FRIENDS OF THE
LIBRARY, TRINITY COLLEGE, DUBLIN.   XXX

FRITZ THYSSEN-STIFTUNG: ARBEITSKREIS EVANGEL-
ISCHE THEOLOGIE UND KATHOLISCHE THEOLOGIE.
— STUDIEN ZUR THEOLOGIE UND GEISTESGESCHICHTE
DES NEUNZEHNTEN JAHRHUNDERTS.

FRITZ THYSSEN-STIFTUNG: ARBEITSKREIS KUNSTGES-
CHICHTE.
— STUDIEN ZUR KUNST DES NEUNZEHNTEN JAHRHUNDERTS.

GARDEN HISTORY SOCIETY.
— OCCASIONAL PAPERS, GARDEN HISTORY SOCIETY.

GENERAL TEACHING COUNCIL FOR SCOTLAND.
— GTC NEWS.

GEOGRAFICHESKOE OBSHCHESTVO SSSR: ALTAJSKIJ
OTDEL.
— IZVESTIJA, ALTAJSKIJ OTDEL, GEOGRAFICHESKOE
OBSHCHESTVO SSSR.

GEOGRAFICHESKOE OBSHCHESTVO SSSR: SEVERNYJ
FILIAL.
— PRIRODA I KHOZJAISTVO SEVERA.

GEOGRAFICHESKOE OBSHCHESTVO SSSR: ZABAJKAL'SKIJ
FILIAL.
— IZVESTIJA, ZABAJKAL'SKIJ FILIAL GEOGRAFICH-
ESKOGO OBSHCHESTVA SSSR.   XXX

GEOLOGICAL ASSOCIATION OF CANADA.
— GEOSCIENCE CANADA.   XXX
— PROCEEDINGS, GEOLOGICAL ASSOCIATION OF
CANADA.   XXX
SUBS (1974): GEOSCIENCE CANADA.

GEOLOGICAL SOCIETY OF AMERICA.
— GEOLOGY.

GEORGE WASHINGTON UNIVERSITY: DEPARTMENT OF
MEDICAL & PUBLIC AFFAIRS.
— POPULATION REPORT: SERIES B: INTERUTERINE
DEVICES.
— POPULATION REPORT: SERIES C-D: STERILIZATION.
— POPULATION REPORT: SERIES F: PREGNANCY TERM-
INATION.
— POPULATION REPORT: SERIES G: PROSTAGLANDINS.
— POPULATION REPORT: SERIES J: FAMILY PLANNING.

GEORGETOWN UNIVERSITY: CENTER FOR STRATEGIC
& INTERNATIONAL STUDIES.
— WASHINGTON PAPERS.

GESELLSCHAFT FUR GEOLOGISCHE WISSENSCHAFTEN DER
DDR.
— ZEITSCHRIFT FUR GEOLOGISCHE WISSENSCHAFTEN.

GLASGOW ARCHAEOLOGICAL SOCIETY.
— BULLETIN, GLASGOW ARCHAEOLOGICAL SOCIETY.

GLENS OF ANTRIM HISTORICAL SOCIETY.
— GLYNNS. JOURNAL OF THE GLENS OF ANTRIM HIST-
ORICAL SOCIETY.

GOSUDARSTVENNAJA BIBLIOTEKA SSSR IM. V.I.
LENINA: INFORMATSIONNYJ TSENTR PO PROBLEMAM
KUL'TURY I ISKUSSTVA.
— NOVAJA SOVETSKAJA LITERATURA PO ISKUSSTVU.
BIBLIOGRAFICHESKIJ UKAZATEL'.

GOSUDARSTVENNYJ KOMITET PO ISPOL'ZOVANIJU
ATOMNOJ ENERGII SSSR.
— VOPROSY TEORII PLAZMY.

GOSUDARSTVENNAJA PUBLICHNAJA NAUCHNO-TEKHNICH-
ESKAJA BIBLIOTEKA SSSR: NAUCHNO-BIBLIOGRAFICH-
ESKIJ OTDEL.
— EKONOMIKA I ORGANIZATSIJA PROMYSHLENNOGO PRO-
IZVODSTVA SIBIRI I DAL'NEGO VOSTOKA.

GRATZ COLLEGE (PHILADELPHIA).
— ANNUAL OF JEWISH STUDIES.

(GREAT BRITAIN) CIVIL SERVICE DEPARTMENT:
CENTRAL COMPUTER AGENCY.
— CENTRAL COMPUTER AGENCY GUIDE.

(GREAT BRITAIN) DEPARTMENT OF EDUCATION &
SCIENCE.
— EDUCATIONAL PRIORITY.

(GREAT BRITAIN) DEPARTMENT OF EDUCATION &
SCIENCE: LIBRARIES DIVISION.
— LIBRARY INFORMATION SERIES, DEPARTMENT OF
EDUCATION & SCIENCE (GB).

(GREAT BRITAIN) DEPARTMENT OF EMPLOYMENT &
PRODUCTIVITY.
— NEW EARNINGS SURVEY.

(GREAT BRITAIN) DEPARTMENT OF ENERGY.
— ENERGY TRENDS. A STATISTICAL BULLETIN.

(GREAT BRITAIN) DEPARTMENT OF HEALTH & SOCIAL
SECURITY.
— SOCIAL SECURITY STATISTICS.
— SOCIAL WORK SERVICE.

(GREAT BRITAIN) FOREIGN & COMMONWEALTH OFFICE:
INDIA OFFICE LIBRARY.   000
    SEE: (GREAT BRITAIN) INDIA OFFICE LIBRARY.

(GREAT BRITAIN) HOME OFFICE: SCOTTISH HOME &
HEALTH DEPARTMENT.
— FIRE PREVENTION GUIDE.

(GREAT BRITAIN) INDIA OFFICE LIBRARY.
— NEWSLETTER, INDIA OFFICE LIBRARY & RECORDS.

(GREAT BRITAIN) SCOTTISH EDUCATION DEPARTMENT:
CONSULTATIVE COMMITTEE ON THE CURRICULUM.
— BULLETIN, CONSULTATIVE COMMITTEE ON THE CURR-
ICULUM, SCOTTISH EDUCATION DEPARTMENT.

(GREAT BRITAIN) TREASURY.
— GOVERNMENT ECONOMIC SERVICE OCCASIONAL PAPERS.

(GREAT BRITAIN) WELSH OFFICE.
— WELSH ECONOMIC TRENDS.

GREATER LONDON COUNCIL: DEPARTMENT OF PLANNING
& TRANSPORTATION.
— PLANNING & TRANSPORTATION ABSTRACTS.   XXX
— URBAN ABSTRACTS.   XXX

GREATER LONDON COUNCIL: INTELLIGENCE UNIT.
— TRANSPORT FACTS & FIGURES.

GUILDHALL LIBRARY.
— GUILDHALL MISCELLANY.   XXX
    SUBS (1973): GUILDHALL STUDIES IN LONDON
    HISTORY.
— GUILDHALL STUDIES IN LONDON HISTORY.   XXX

(GUYANA) MINISTRY OF AGRICULTURE & NATURAL
RESOURCES: CENTRAL AGRICULTURAL STATION.
— AGRICULTURAL RESEARCH, GUYANA.

HAMPDEN-SYDNEY COLLEGE.
— POLITICAL SCIENCE REVIEWER.

HARVARD UNIVERSITY: LAW SCHOOL.
— HARVARD CIVIL RIGHTS - CIVIL LIBERTIES LAW
REVIEW.

HARVARD UNIVERSITY: MUSEUM OF COMPARATIVE
ZOOLOGY.
— SPECIAL OCCASIONAL PUBLICATIONS, MUSEUM OF
COMPARATIVE ZOOLOGY, HARVARD UNIVERSITY.

HATFIELD POLYTECHNIC.
— OCCASIONAL PAPERS, HATFIELD POLYTECHNIC.

(HAWAII) DEPARTMENT OF PLANNING & ECONOMICS
DEVELOPMENT.
— HAWAII ECONOMIC REVIEW.

HEALTH VISITORS' ASSOCIATION.
— HEALTH EDUCATION INDEX.

HEBREW UNION COLLEGE BIBLICAL & ARCHAEOLOGICAL
SCHOOL.
— ANNUAL, HEBREW UNION COLLEGE BIBLICAL & ARCH-
AEOLOGICAL SCHOOL.

HEBREW UNIVERSITY OF JERUSALEM.
— HEBREW UNIVERSITY STUDIES IN LITERATURE.

HELEN DWIGHT REID EDUCATIONAL FOUNDATION.
— SOCIOLOGY. REVIEWS OF NEW BOOKS.

HERTFORDSHIRE ARCHAEOLOGICAL COUNCIL.
— HERTFORDSHIRE ARCHAEOLOGICAL REVIEW.

HISTORICAL ASSOCIATION OF KENYA.
— HADITH.

HISTORICAL BREECHLOADING SMALLARMS ASSOCIATION.
— JOURNAL OF THE HISTORICAL BREECHLOADING SMALL-
ARMS ASSOCIATION.

(HONG KONG) DEPARTMENT OF AGRICULTURE &
FISHERIES.
— AGRICULTURE HONG KONG.   XXX

HUDDERSFIELD POLYTECHNIC: DEPARTMENT OF
GEOGRAPHY & GEOLOGY.
— LOCAL INFORMATION PAPER, DEPARTMENT OF
GEOGRAPHY & GEOLOGY, HUDDERSFIELD POLYTECHNIC.

HUMAN ERGOLOGY RESEARCH ASSOCIATION.
— JOURNAL OF HUMAN ERGOLOGY.

HUMAN SCIENCES RESEARCH COUNCIL (SOUTH
AFRICA).
— ANNOTATED BIBLIOGRAPHY OF RESEARCH IN
EDUCATION.

HUNTINGDON RESEARCH CENTRE.
— HRC GAZETTE.

HYDROMETEOROLOGICKY USTAV V BRATISLAVE.
— ZBORNIK PRAC, HYDROMETEOROLOGICKY USTAV V
BRATISLAVE.

(ILLINOIS) AGRICULTURAL EXPERIMENT STATION:
DEPARTMENT OF FORESTRY.
— FORESTRY RESEARCH REPORT, DEPARTMENT OF FOR-
ESTRY, AGRICULTURAL EXPERIMENT STATION
(ILLINOIS).

IMPERIAL CANCER RESEARCH FUND.
— RESEARCH USING TRANSPLANTED TUMOURS OF LABOR-
ATORY ANIMALS.

IMPERIAL COLLEGE OF SCIENCE & TECHNOLOGY.
— I C DIARY.

INDEPENDENT BROADCASTING AUTHORITY.
— TECHNICAL REVIEW, INDEPENDENT BROADCASTING
AUTHORITY.

(INDIA) ANTHROPOLOGICAL SURVEY.
— NEWSLETTER, ANTHROPOLOGICAL SURVEY (INDIA).

(INDIA) DEPARTMENT OF AGRICULTURE: DIRECTORATE
OF CASHEWNUT DEVELOPMENT.
— CASHEW NEWS TELLER.

INDIA OFFICE LIBRARY.   000
    SEE: (GREAT BRITAIN) INDIA OFFICE LIBRARY.

INDIAN ACADEMY OF GEOSCIENCE.   XXX
— JOURNAL OF THE INDIAN ACADEMY OF GEOSCIENCE.   XXX

INDIAN ACADEMY OF SCIENCES.
— PRAMANA. A JOURNAL OF PHYSICS.

INDIAN ARCHAEOLOGICAL SOCIETY.
— PURATATTVA.

INDIAN COUNCIL OF SOCIAL SCIENCE RESEARCH.
— ICSSR RESEARCH ABSTRACTS QUARTERLY.

INDIAN & EASTERN NEWSPAPER SOCIETY.
— INDIAN PRESS.

INDIAN GEOSCIENCE ASSOCIATION.
— JOURNAL OF THE INDIAN GEOSCIENCE ASSOCIATION.   XXX
    SUBS (1972): JOURNAL OF THE INDIAN ACADEMY
    OF GEOSCIENCE.

INDIAN INSTITUTE OF ADVANCED STUDY.
— TRANSACTIONS, INDIAN INSTITUTE OF ADVANCED
STUDY.

INDIAN INSTITUTE OF PACKAGING.
— PACKAGING INDIA.

INDIAN LAW INSTITUTE.
— ANNUAL SURVEY OF INDIAN LAW.

INDIAN MUSICOLOGICAL SOCIETY.
— JOURNAL OF THE INDIAN MUSICOLOGICAL SOCIETY.   XXX
— SANGEET KALA VIHAR: ENGLISH SUPPLEMENT.   XXX

INDIAN NATIONAL SCIENCE ACADEMY.
— PRAMANA. A JOURNAL OF PHYSICS.

INDIAN PHYSICS ASSOCIATION.
— PRAMANA. A JOURNAL OF PHYSICS.

INDIANA UNIVERSITY: FOLKLORE INSTITUTE.
— FOLKLORE FORUM.

INDIANA UNIVERSITY: RESEARCH CENTER FOR THE
LANGUAGE SCIENCES.
— SIGN LANGUAGE STUDIES.

INLAND FISHERIES SOCIETY OF INDIA.
— JOURNAL OF THE INLAND FISHERIES SOCIETY OF
INDIA.

INSTITUTE OF ANDEAN STUDIES.
— NAWPA PACHA.

INSTITUT FUR ASIENKUNDE (HAMBURG).
— CHINA AKTUELL.

INSTITUTE OF ASPHALT TECHNOLOGY.
— JOURNAL, INSTITUTE OF ASPHALT TECHNOLOGY.

INSTITUTE OF BRITISH CARRIAGE & AUTOMOBILE
MANUFACTURERS.
— IBCAM. JOURNAL OF THE INSTITUTE OF BRITISH
CARRIAGE & AUTOMOBILE MANUFACTURERS.   XXX
— INSTITUTE BULLETIN, INSTITUTE OF BRITISH
CARRIAGE & AUTOMOBILE MANUFACTURERS.   XXX
SUBS (1974): IBCAM.

INSTITUTE OF BRITISH GEOGRAPHERS.
— OCCASIONAL PUBLICATIONS, INSTITUTE OF BRITISH
GEOGRAPHERS.

INSTITUTO DE CIENCIA ANIMAL (CUBA).
— CUBAN JOURNAL OF AGRICULTURAL SCIENCE.   XXX

INSTITUTION OF CIVIL ENGINEERS.
— 1.C.E. ABSTRACTS.

INSTITUTO COLOMBIANO DE PEDAGOGICA.
— SERIE DIVULGACION, INSTITUTO COLOMBIANO DE
PEDAGOGICA.
— SERIE INVESTIGACIONES, INSTITUTO COLOMBIANO
DE PEDAGOGICA.

INSTITUTE OF COMMONWEALTH STUDIES.
— JOURNAL OF COMMONWEALTH & COMPARATIVE   XXX
POLITICS.

INSTITUTE OF DATA PROCESSING.
— DATA PROCESSING PRACTITIONER.

INSTITUTE OF ELECTRICAL & ELECTRONICS ENGINEERS
— IEEE TRANSACTIONS ON ACOUSTICS, SPEECH & SIG-
NAL PROCESSING.   XXX
— IEEE TRANSACTIONS ON AUDIO & ELECTROACOUSTICS.XX
— INDEX TO IEEE PERIODICALS.

INSTITUTION OF ELECTRICAL & ELECTRONICS ENG-
INEERS: CIRCUITS & SYSTEMS SOCIETY.
— IEEE TRANSACTIONS ON CIRCUITS & SYSTEMS.   XXX

INSTITUTION OF ELECTRONICS & TELECOMMUNICATION
ENGINEERS.   XXX
— JOURNAL OF THE INSTITUTION OF ELECTRONICS &
TELECOMMUNICATION ENGINEERS.   XXX

INSTITUTO DE ESTUDIOS POLITICOS (MADRID).
— REVISTA DE INSTITUTIONES EUROPEAS.

INSTITUTION OF FIRE ENGINEERS.
— FIRE ENGINEERS JOURNAL.   XXX
— QUARTERLY, INSTITUTION OF FIRE ENGINEERS: NEW
SERIES.   XXX
SUBS (1973): FIRE ENGINEERS JOURNAL.

INSTITUTE FOR FISCAL STUDIES.
— IFS NEWSLETTER.
— PUBLICATIONS, INSTITUTE FOR FISCAL STUDIES.

INSTITUTO FLORESTAL (BRAZIL).
— BOLETIM TECNICO, INSTITUTO FLORESTAL (BRAZIL).

INSTITUT FRANCAIS D'ARCHAEOLOGIE ORIENTALE.
— COLLECTION DES VOYAGEURS OCCIDENTAUX EN
EGYPTE.

INSTITUTION OF GAS ENGINEERS.
— GAS ENGINEERING & MANAGEMENT.   XXX

INSTITUTE OF GAS TECHNOLOGY.
— INTERNATIONAL GAS TECHNOLOGY HIGHLIGHTS.

INSTITUT FUR GESELLSCHAFTSWISSENSCHAFTEN: ZENT-
RALSTELLE FUR DIE PHILOSOPHISCHE INFORMATION
UND DOKUMENTATION.
— BIBLIOGRAPHIE PHILOSOPHIE.
— BIBLIOGRAPHIE PHILOSOPHIE: BEIHEFT.

INSTITUT HISTORIQUE ALLEMAND DE PARIS.   000
SEE: DEUTSCHES HISTORISCHES INSTITUT IN PARIS

INSTITUTE OF HYGIENE & EPIDEMIOLOGY (PRAGUE).
— CZECHOSLOVAK BIBLIOGRAPHY ON INDUSTRIAL HY-
GIENE & OCCUPATIONAL DISEASES.   XXX

INSTITUTE FOR INDUSTRIAL RESEARCH & STANDARDS
(EIRE).
— BUILDING PROGRESS.

INSTITUTO INTER-AMERICANO DE CIENCIAS
AGRICOLAS.   000
SEE: INTER-AMERICAN INSTITUTE OF
AGRICULTURAL SCIENCES.

INSTITUTO DE INVESTIGACION DE LOS RECURSOS
NATURALES RENOVABLES.
— SERIE FAUNA, INSTITUTO DE INVESTIGACION DE
LOS RECURSOS NATURALES RENOVABLES.

INSTITUT ISTORII SSSR.
— ISTORIJA I ISTORIKI. ISTORIOGRAFICHESKIJ
EZHEGODNIK.

INSTITUT ZA IZUCAVANJE RADNICKOG POKRETA.
— ISTORIJA RADNICKOG POKRETA, ZBORNIK RADOVA.

INSTITUTE OF JAMAICA.
— BULLETIN OF THE INSTITUTE OF JAMAICA: SCIENCE
SERIES.   XXX

INSTITUTE OF MANAGEMENT CONSULTANTS.
— MANAGEMENT CONSULTANT. JOURNAL OF THE INST-
ITUTE OF MANAGEMENT CONSULTANTS.

INSTITUTE OF MANPOWER STUDIES.
— IMS MONITOR. QUARTERLY REVIEW OF THE LABOUR
MARKET.

INSTITUTE OF MARINE RESEARCH (INDONESIA).   000
SEE: LEMBAGA PENELITIAN LAUT.

INSTITUTO DE MATEMATICAS PURAS Y APLICADAS
(LIMA).
— NOTAS DE MATEMATICAS.

INSTYTUT MECHANIKI PRECYZYJNEJ.
— POWLOKI OCHRONNE.   XXX
— PRACE INSTYTUTU MECHANIKI PRECYZYJNEJ.   XXX
SUBS (1973): POWLOKI OCHRONNE.
— JOURNAL OF THE INSTITUTE OF METALS.   XXX
SUBS (1974) PART OF: METALS TECHNOLOGY.

INSTITUT MEZHDUNARODNYKH OTNOSHENIJ.
— VOPROSY FILOLOGII.

INSTITUTE OF MUSICAL INSTRUMENT TECHNOLOGY.
— MUSICAL INSTRUMENT TECHNOLOGY.
— ‡PUBLICATIONS‡ INSTITUTE OF MUSICAL INST-
RUMENT TECHNOLOGY.   XXX

INSTITUTO NACIONAL DE PESQUISAS DA AMAZONIA
(BRAZIL).
— AMAZONIANA. LIMNOLOGIA ET OECOLOGIA REGION
ALIS SYSTEMAE FLUMINIS AMAZONAS.
— BIBLIOGRAFIA AMAZONICA. PUBLICACOES LIMNOL-
OGICAS ECOLOGICAS E DE CIENCIAS AFINS SOBRE A
REGIAO AMAZONICA.

INSTITUT NATIONAL DE LA RECHERCHE SCIENTIFIQUE
(TOGO).
— ETUDES TOGOLAISES: NOUVELLE SERIE.

INTERNATIONAL INSTITUTE FOR THE STUDY OF
RELIGIONS.
— JAPANESE JOURNAL OF RELIGIOUS STUDIES.   XXX

INTERNATIONAL LABOUR OFFICE.
— SOCIAL & LABOUR BULLETIN.

INTERNATIONAL MAIZE & WHEAT IMPROVEMENT CENTER.
— INFORMATION BULLETIN, INTERNATIONAL MAIZE &
WHEAT IMPROVEMENT CENTER.

INTERNATIONAL MULTIDISCIPLINARY RESEARCH
ASSOCIATION.
— MULTIDISCIPLINARY RESEARCH.

INTERNATIONAL OCCUPATIONAL SAFETY & HEALTH
INFORMATION CENTRE.
— CIS ABSTRACTS.

INTERNATIONAL PEACE RESEARCH INSTITUTE.
— PRIO STUDIES FROM THE INTERNATIONAL PEACE
RESEARCH INSTITUTE.

INTERNATIONAL PLANNED PARENTHOOD FEDERATION.
— PEOPLE.

INTERNATIONAL REFERENCE CENTRE FOR COMMUNITY
WATER SUPPLY.   000
SEE: WORLD HEALTH ORGANIZATION: INTERNAT-
IONAL REFERENCE CENTRE FOR COMMUNITY WATER
SUPPLY.

INTERNATIONAL SOCIETY FOR BURN INJURIES.
— BURNS. JOURNAL OF THE INTERNATIONAL SOCIETY
FOR BURN INJURIES.

INTERNATIONAL SOCIETY FOR EXPERIMENTAL
HEMATOLOGY.
— EXPERIMENTAL HEMATOLOGY (COPENHAGEN).

INTERNATIONAL SOCIETY FOR NEUROVEGETATIVE
RESEARCH.
— JOURNAL OF NEURAL TRANSMISSION.   XXX

INTERNATIONAL SOCIETY FOR TECHNOLOGY ASSESSMENT
— TECHNOLOGY ASSESSMENT.

INTERNATIONAL SOCIOLOGICAL ASSOCIATION.
— REVISTA INTERAMERICANA DE SOCIOLOGIA.

INTERNATIONAL WATERFOWL RESEARCH BUREAU.   XXX
— BULLETIN, INTERNATIONAL WATERFOWL RESEARCH
BUREAU.   XXX

INTERNATIONAL YOUTH CENTRE FOR ENVIRONMENTAL
STUDIES.
— TARAXACUM.

(IRAN) MINISTRY OF SCIENCE & HIGHER EDUCATION:
IRANIAN DOCUMENTATION CENTRE.
— CHAKIDAH. IRANDOC SCIENCE & SOCIAL SCIENCE
ABSTRACT BULLETIN.

IRISH ANGUS CATTLE SOCIETY.
— IRISH ANGUS HERD BOOK.

IRISH BASE METALS LTD.
— TYNAGH MINER.

IRISH CHAROLAIS CATTLE SOCIETY.
— IRISH CHAROLAIS HERD BOOK.

IRISH COMPUTER SOCIETY.
— NEWSLETTER, IRISH COMPUTER SOCIETY.

IRISH WILDBIRD CONSERVANCY.
— I.W.C. NEWS.   XXX

IRKUTSKIJ GOSUDARSTVENNYJ UNIVERSITET:
JURIDICHESKIJ FAKUL'TET.
— PROBLEMY BOR'BY S PRESTUPNOST'JU.

IRON & STEEL INSTITUTE.
— JOURNAL OF THE IRON & STEEL INSTITUTE.   XXX
SUBS (1974) PART OF: METALS TECHNOLOGY; &
IRONMAKING & STEELMAKING.

ISTITUTO NAZIONALE DI ALTA MATEMATICA.
— SYMPOSIA MATHEMATICA.

JAFFNA ARCHAEOLOGICAL SOCIETY.
— EPIGRAPHIA TAMILICA. A JOURNAL OF TAMIL EPI-
GRAPHY.

JAPAN SUGAR BEET IMPROVEMTNT FOUNDATION.   000
SEE: NIHON TENSAI SHINKOKAI.

JOCKEYS' ASSOCIATION OF GREAT BRITAIN.
— RACING WORLD.

JOLO NOTRE DAME OF JOLO COLLEGE: COORDINATED
INVESTIGATION OF SULU CULTURE.
— SULU STUDIES.

JUNTA DE INVESTIGACOES DO ULTRAMAR (PORTUGAL).
— GARCIA DE ORTA: SERIE DE BOTANICA.   XXX
— GARCIA DE ORTA: SERIE DE FARMACOGNOSIA.
— GARCIA DE ORTA: SERIE DE GEOGRAFIA.
— GARCIA DE ORTA: SERIE DE GEOLOGIA.
— GARCIA DE ORTA: SERIE DE ZOOLOGIA.

KAMER VAN KOOPHANDEL EN FABRIEKEN VOOR
AMSTERDAM.
— AMSTERDAM IN DE MARKT.

KANSAI DAIGAKU.
— KANSAI UNIVERSITY REVIEW OF ECONOMICS &
BUSINESS.

KANSAI UNIVERSITY.   000
SEE: KANSAI DAIGAKU.

KANSAS STATE UNIVERSITY: DEPARTMENT OF
MODERN LANGUAGES.
— JOURNAL OF SPANISH STUDIES: TWENTIETH CENTURY.

KANSAS STATE UNIVERSITY OF AGRICULTURE &
APPLIED SCIENCE: DEPARTMENT OF ECONOMICS.
— REGIONAL SCIENCE PERSPECTIVES.

KARL MARX-UNIVERSITAT (LEIPZIG).
— BEITRAGE ZUR TROPISCHEN LANDWIRTSCHAFT UND
VETERINARMEDIZIN.   XXX

KARLOVA UNIVERSITA V PRAZE.
— CESKOSLVENSKO-SOVETSKE VZTAHY.

(KAZAKH SSR) MINISTERSTVO VYSSHEGO I SREDNEGO
SPETSIAL'NOGO OBRAZOVANIJA.
— EKONOMIKA I PRAVO. SBORNIK STATEJ ASPIRANTOV
I SOISKATELEJ.

KAZANSKIJ GOSUDARSTVENNYJ UNIVERSITET.
— GRAVITATSIJA I TEORIJA OTNOSITEL'NOSTI.
— ISSLEDOVANIJA PO ELEKTROKHIMII, MAGNETOKHIMII
I ELEKTROKHIMICHESKIM METODAM ANALIZA.
— OCHERKI ISTORII POVOLZH'JA I PRIURAL'JA.
— VOPROSY ISTORIOGRAFII VSEOBSHCHEJ ISTORII.
SBORNIK STATEJ.

KEGWORTH VILLAGE ASSOCIATION.
— COGWORDS. BULLETIN OF THE KEGWORTH VILLAGE
ASSOCIATION.

KEMEROVSKIJ GOSUDARSTVENNYJ PEDAGOGICHESKIJ
INSTITUT.
— IZ ISTORII RUSSKOGO ROMANTIZMA.

KENYA LANGUAGE ASSOCIATION.
— LUGHA.

KENYA LIBRARY ASSOCIATION.
— MAKTABA.

KHAR'KOVSKIJ GOSUDARSTVENNYJ UNIVERSITET.
— ENERGETICHESKOE MASHINOSTROENIE.
— FIZIKA TVERDOGO TELA.

KIEVSKIJ NAUCHNO-ISSLEDOVATEL'SKIJ INSTITUT
OTOLARINGOLOGII.
— SOVREMENNYE PROBLEMY OTORINOLARINGOLOGII.

KINGSTON POLYTECHNIC: SCHOOL OF ARCHITECTURE.
— ARCHITECTURAL PSYCHOLOGY NEWSLETTER.

KIRGIZSKIJ NAUCHNO-ISSLEDOVATEL'SKIJ INSTITUTE
POCHVOVEDENIJA.
— TRUDY, KIRGIZSKIJ NAUCHNO-ISSLEDOVATEL'SKIJ
INSTITUT POCHVOVEDENIJA.

KODAK LTD.
— KODAK COLOUR LAB NOTES.

KOMMUNISTICHESKAJA PARTIJA SOVETSKOGO SOJUZA.
— EKONOMICHESKAJA GAZETA.   XXX

KOMMUNISTICHESKAJA PARTIJA SOVETSKOGO SOJUZA:
DAGESTANSKIJ OBLASTNOJ KOMITET.
— SOVETSKIJ DAGESTAN .

KOREAN NATIONAL COMMISSION FOR UNESCO.
— KOREA JOURNAL.

KOTSU ANZEN KOGAI KENKYUJO.
— KOTSU ANZEN KOGAI KENKYUJO HOKOKU.

KOZPONTI ELEMISZERIPARI KUTATO INTEZET.
— ELELMISZERTUDOMANY.   XXX

KRAJSKE STREDISKO LIDOVEHO UMENI VE STRAZNICI.
— NARODOPISNE AKTUALITY.

KRIO LITERARY SOCIETY.
— JOURNAL OF THE KRIO LITERARY SOCIETY.

KUNGLIGA UNIVERSITET I UPPSALA: INSTITUTE OF
ZOOLOGY.
— ZOON. A JOURNAL OF ZOOLOGY.   XXX
— ZOON: SUPPLEMENT.   XXX

KUO CHI KUAN HSI YEN CHIU SO.
— WEN-T'I YU YEN-CHIU. ISSUES & STUDIES.

KURUKSHETRA UNIVERSITY.
— SAMBHAVANA.

KUTZTOWN STATE COLLEGE.
— COMPASS (KUTZTOWN, PA.).

KYJIVS'KYJ DERZHAVNYJ UNIVERSYTET ‡IM. T.G.
SHEVEHENKIA.
— EKONOMICHNA HEOHRAFIJA.
— VYCHISLITEL'NAJA I PRIKLADNAJA MATEMATIKA.

KYJIVS'KYJ DERZHAVNYJ UNIVERSYTET: NAUKOVO-
DOSLIDNYJ SEKTOR.
— SBORNIK NAUCHNYKH RABOT, NAUCHNO-ISSLED-
OVATEL'SKIJ SEKTOR, KIEVSKIJ UNIVERSITET.

KYOTO SANGYO UNIVERSITY: SOCIETY OF ECONOMICS
& BUSINESS ADMINISTRATION.
— K.S.U. ECONOMIC & BUSINESS REVIEW.

LANCASTER ARCHAEOLOGICAL SOCIETY.
— CONTREBIS. BULLETIN OF THE LANCASTER ARCH-
AEOLOGICAL SOCIETY.

LATVIJAS PSR ZINATNU AKADEMIJA: ORGANISKAS
SINTEZES INSTITUTAS.
— EKSPERIMENTAL'NAJA I KLINICHESKAJA FARMAKO-
TERAPIJA.

LATVIJSKIJ GOSUDARSTVENNYJ UNIVERSITET.
— ASPIRANTU ZINATNISKIE RAKSTI.

LATVIJSKIJ NAUCHNO-ISSLEDOVATEL'SKIJ INSTITUT
LEGKOJ PROMYSHLENNOSTI.
— NAUCHNO-ISSLEDOVATEL'SKIE TRUDY, LATVIJSKIJ
NAUCHNO-ISSLEDOVATEL'SKIJ INSTITUT LEGKOJ
PROMYSHLENNOSTI.

LAW DEVELOPMENT CENTRE (UGANDA).
— UGANDA LAW FOCUS.

LEAGUE FOR SOCIALIST RECONSTRUCTION.   XXX
— SOCIALIST REPUBLIC.   XXX

LEMBAGA PENELITIAN LAUT.
— OCEANOGRAPHICAL CRUISE REPORT. OCEANOGRAPHIC
OBSERVATIONS IN INDONESIAN & ADJACENT SEAS.

LENINGRADSKIJ GOSUDARSTVENNYJ UNIVERSITET.
— ISTORIOGRAFIJA I ISTOCHNIKOVEDENIE ISTORII
STRAN AZII.
— LESOVODSTVO, LESNYE KUL'TURY I POCHVOVEDENIE.
— METODOLOGICZESKIE VOPROSY OBSHCHESTVENNYKH
NAUK.
— PROBLEMY BOR'BY PROTIV BURZHUAZNOJ IDEOLOGII.
— PROBLEMY ISTORICHESKOGO MATERIALIZMA.

LENINGRADSKIJ GOSUDARSTVENNYJ UNIVERSITET:
INSTITUT POVYSHENIJA KVALIFIKATSII
PREPODAVATELEJ OBSHCHESTVENNYKH NAUK.
— PROBLEMY ISTORIOGRAFII I ISTOCHNIKOVEDENIJA
ISTORII KPSS.

LEWIS CARROLL SOCIETY.
— JABBERWOCKY.

LIBRARY ASSOCIATION.
— RADIALS BULLETIN.

LIBRARY ASSOCIATION: AUDIOVISUAL GROUP.
— AUDIOVISUAL LIBRARIAN.   XXX

LIBRARY ASSOCIATION: HOSPITAL LIBRARIES &
HANDICAPPED READERS GROUP.
— HEALTH & WELFARE LIBRARIES QUARTERLY.   XXX

LIBRARY ASSOCIATION: LIBRARY EDUCATION GROUP.
— LEG NEWS. NEWSLETTER OF THE LIBRARY EDUCATION
GROUP OF THE LIBRARY ASSOCIATION.

LIBRARY ASSOCIATION: RARE BOOKS GROUP.
— NEWSLETTER, RARE BOOKS GROUP, LIBRARY ASSOC-
IATION.

LIBRARY OF CONGRESS (US): REFERENCE DEPARTMENT.
— FOREIGN NEWSPAPER REPORT.

LIETUVOS TSR MOKSLU AKADEMIJA: ISTORIJOS
INSTITUTAS.
— LIETUVOS ISTORIJOS METRASTIS.

LIFE UNDERWRITERS ASSOCIATION OF CANADA.
— FORUM (DON MILLS, ONT.).   XXX
— LIFE UNDERWRITERS NEWS.   XXX
SUBS (1971): FORUM (DON MILLS, ONT.).

LIGHT RAILWAY TRANSPORT LEAGUE.
— MODERN TRAMWAY & RAPID TRANSIT REVIEW.   XXX

LIGHTWEIGHT ENCLOSURES UNIT.
— AIR STRUCTURES BIBLIOGRAPHY/ LIGHTWEIGHT
ENCLOSURES UNIT.

LINCOLNSHIRE LOCAL HISTORY SOCIETY: INDUST-
RIAL ARCHAEOLOGY GROUP.
— LINCOLNSHIRE INDUSTRIAL ARCHAEOLOGY.   XXX
— NEWSLETTER, INDUSTRIAL ARCHAEOLOGY GROUP,   XXX
LINCOLNSHIRE LOCAL HISTORY SOCIETY.

LONDON ALTERNATIVE ANTHROPOLOGY GROUP.
— CRITIQUE OF ANTHROPOLOGY.

LONDON ASSOCIATION FOR THE TEACHING OF ENGLISH.
— TEACHING LONDON KIDS.

LONDON SCHOOL OF ECONOMICS & POLITICAL SCIENCE:
ASIAN CLUB.
— JOURNAL OF ASIAN INTEGRATION STUDIES.

LONDON SCHOOL OF ECONOMICS & POLITICAL SCIENCE:
BRITISH LIBRARY OF POLITICAL & ECONOMIC SCIENCE
— QUARTERLY LIST OF ADDITIONS IN RUSSIAN & EAST
EUROPEAN LANGUAGES, BRITISH LIBRARY OF POLIT-
ICAL & ECONOMIC SCIENCE.

LONDON SCHOOL OF ECONOMICS & POLITICAL SCIENCE:
RADICAL ECONOMICS DISCUSSION GROUP.
— JOURNAL OF THE RADICAL ECONOMICS GROUP,
LONDON SCHOOL OF ECONOMICS.

(LOUISIANA) WILD LIFE & FISHERIES COMMISSION:
OYSTER WATER BOTTOMS & SEAFOODS DIVISION.
— TECHNICAL BULLETIN, OYSTER WATER BOTTOMS &
SEAFOODS DIVISION, WILD LIFE & FISHERIES COMM-
ISSION (LOUISIANA).

LUNDS UNIVERSITET: INSTITUTE OF ART HISTORY.
— ARIS. ART RESEARCH IN SCANDINAVIA.

L'VIVS'KYJ NAUKOVO-DOSLIDNYJ INSTYTUT EPIDEM-
IOLOHIJI I MIKROBIOLOHIJI.
— FAKTORY VNESHNEJ SREDY I IKH ZNACHENIE DLJA
ZDOROV'JA NASELENIJA.

L'VOVSKIJ GOSUDARSTVENNYJ UNIVERSITET:
L'VOVSKOE GEOLOGICHESKOE OBSHCHESTVO.   000
SEE: L'VOVSKOE GEOLOGICHESKOE OBSHCHESTVO.

L'VOVSKOE GEOLOGICHESKOE OBSHCHESTVO.
— VOPROSY LITOLOGII I PETROGRAFII.

MAGYAR TUDOMANYOS AKADEMIA.
— ACTA ALIMENTARIA.   XXX

MAGYAR TUDOMANYOS AKADEMIA: FOLDRAJZTUDOMANYI
KUTATOCSOPORT.
— STUDIES IN GEOGRAPHY.   XXX
— STUDIES IN GEOGRAPHY IN HUNGARY.   XXX

MAINTENANCE ADVISORY SERVICE.
— MAINTENANCE MANAGEMENT.   XXX

MAKERERE INSTITUTE OF SOCIAL RESEARCH.
— POLICY ABSTRACTS & RESEARCH NEWSLETTER, MAK-
ERERE INSTITUTE OF SOCIAL RESEARCH.   XXX
— RESEARCH ABSTRACTS & NEWSLETTER, MAKERERE
INSTITUTE OF SOCIAL RESEARCH.   XXX

(MALAYSIA) MINISTRY OF LANDS & MINES: GEOL-
OGICAL SURVEY.
— MAP BULLETIN, GEOLOGICAL SURVEY (MALAYSIA).

MALAYSIAN AGRICULTURAL RESEARCH & DEVELOPMENT INSTITUTE.
— MARDI RESEARCH BULLETIN.

MALMO MUSEUM.
— ARSBOK, MALMO MUSEUM.

MARINE BIOLOGICAL ASSOCIATION OF THE UNITED KINGDOM.
— MARINE POLLUTION RESEARCH TITLES.

MARXIST-LENINIST ORGANISATION OF BRITAIN.   XXX
— CLASS AGAINST CLASS.   XXX
— RED FRONT. FOR WORKING-CLASS POWER, FOR A
SOCIALIST BRITAINI   XXX

MATICA SLOVENSKA V MARTINE.
— KNIZNICE A VEDECKE INFORMACIE.
— MATICNE CITANIE.

MATICA SLOVENSKA V MARTINE: BIOGRAFICKY USTAV.
— BIOGRAFICKE STUDIE.

MCMASTER UNIVERSITY: ASSOCIATION FOR 18TH-CENTURY STUDIES.
— PUBLICATIONS, ASSOCIATION FOR 18TH-CENTURY
STUDIES, MCMASTER UNIVERSITY.

MEAT RESEARCH INSTITUTE.
— SPECIAL REPORT, MEAT RESEARCH INSTITUTE.

MEDICAL UNION.
— MEDICAL UNION REVIEW.

METALS SOCIETY.
— IRONMAKING & STEELMAKING.
— METAL SCIENCE.   XXX
— METALS TECHNOLOGY.   XXX

(MEXICO) ARCHIVO GENERAL DE LA NACION.
— PUBLICACIONES, ARCHIVO GENERAL DE LA NACION
(MEXICO): SERIE II.

MID-CONTINENT REGIONAL SCIENCE ASSOCIATION.
— REGIONAL SCIENCE PERSPECTIVES.

MILK MARKETING BOARD.
— BETTER BREEDING.

MISSISSIPPI FOLKLORE SOCIETY.
— MISSISSIPPI FOLKLORE REGISTER.

MODERN LANGUAGE ASSOCIATION OF AMERICA: SEMINAR ON CHILDREN'S LITERATURE.
— CHILDREN'S LITERATURE.

MONASH UNIVERSITY.
— CIVIL ENGINEERING RESEARCH REPORTS, MONASH
UNIVERSITY.

MONASH UNIVERSITY: CHEMICAL ENGINEERING DEPARTMENT.
— REPORT, CHEMICAL ENGINEERING DEPARTMENT,
MONASH UNIVERSITY.

MONUMENTAL BRASS SOCIETY.
— BULLETIN OF THE MONUMENTAL BRASS SOCIETY.

MOSKOVSKIJ GOSUDARSTVENNYJ UNIVERSITET.
— ANALIZ ASSOTSIATIVNOJ DEJATEL'NOSTI GOLOVNOGO
MOZGA.
— EROZIJA POCHV I RUSLOVYE PROTSESSY.
— FIZIKA I FIZIKO-KHIMIJA ZHIDKOSTEJ.
— VESTNIK MOSKOVSKOGO UNIVERSITETA: SERIJA 14:
VOSTOKOVEDENIE.
— VOPROSY SOTSIOLOGII I OBSHCHESTVENNOJ PSIK-
HOLOGII.

MOSKOVSKIJ GOSUDARSTVENNYJ UNIVERSITET: INST-ITUT MEKHANIKI.
— NAUCHNYE TRUDY, INSTITUT MEKHANKIKI MOSKOV-
SKOGO GOSUDARSTVENNOGO UNIVERSITETA.

MOSKOVSKIJ GOSUDARSTVENNYJ UNIVERSITET: KAFEDRA GEOFIZICHESKIKH METODOV ISSLEDOVANIJA ZEMNOJKORY.
— GEOFIZICHESKIE ISSLEDOVANIJA.

MOSKOVSKIJ GOSUDARSTVENNYJ UNIVERSITET: KAFEDRA KLASSICHESKOJ FILOLOGII.
— VOPROSY KLASSICHESKOJ FILOLOGII.

MOSKOVSKOE GORODSKOE OBSHCHESTVO KOLLEKTSION-EROV.
— SOVETSKIJ KOLLEKTSIONER.

MUSEE ROYAL DE L'AFRIQUE CENTRALE.
— ARCHIVES D'ANTHROPOLOGIE. ARCHIEF VOOR ANT-
ROPOLOGIE.   XXX

MUSEJNI SPOLEK PRO UCHOVANI BRATERSKYCH PAMATEK A TISKU V KRALICICH NAD OSLAVOU.
— Z KRALICKE TVRZE.

MUSEO ETNOGRAFICO MUNICIPAL DAMASO ARCE.
— ACTUALIDAD ANTROPOLOGICA.

MUSEO NACIONAL (COSTA RICA).
— BRENESIA.

MUSEO NACIONAL DE ANTROPOLOGIA Y ARQUEOLOGIA (PERU).
— BOLETIN DEL MUSEO NACIONAL DE ANTROPOLOGIA Y
ARQUEOLOGIA (PERU).

MUSEUM OF ART (BALTIMORE).
— ANNUAL, MUSEUM OF ART (BALTIMORE).

MUZEUM TRUTNOV.
— KRKONOSE, PODKRKONOSI.

MYTHOPOETIC SOCIETY.
— MYTHLORE.

NAGASAKI AGRICULTURAL & FORESTRY EXPERIMENT STATION.   000
SEE: NAGASAKI-KEN SOGO NORIN SHIKENJO.

NAGASAKI-KEN SOGO NORIN SHIKENJO.
— NAGASAKI-KEN SOGO NORIN SHIKENJO KENKYU
HOKOKU: NOGYO BUMON.

NARODNA BIBLIOTEKA SR SRBIJE.
— BILTEN OBAVEZNOG PRIMERKA JUGOSLOVENSKE
KNJIGE.

NATIONAL ASSOCIATION OF BRASS BAND CONDUCTORS.
— SOUNDING BRASS ■ THE CONDUCTOR.   XXX

NATIONAL ASSOCIATION OF CORROSION ENGINEERS.
— MATERIALS PERFORMANCE.   XXX

NATIONAL ASSOCIATION OF HEALTH STUDENTS (GB).
— HEALTH TEAM.

NATIONAL ASSOCIATION OF WASTE DISPOSAL CON-TRACTORS.
— WASTE DISPOSAL.   XXX

NATIONAL BUREAU OF ECONOMIC RESEARCH (US).
— HUMAN BEHAVIOR & SOCIAL INSTITUTIONS.

NATIONAL BUREAU OF STANDARDS (US).
— DIMENSIONS NBS.   XXX
— TECHNICAL NEWS BULLETIN, NATIONAL BUREAU OF
STANDARDS (US).   XXX
SUBS (1973): DIMENSIONS NBS.

NATIONAL BUREAU OF STANDARDS (US): OFFICE OF STANDARD REFERENCE DATA.
— WEEKLY LIST OF PAPERS ON RADIATION CHEMISTRY.

NATIONAL CENTER FOR ATMOSPHERIC RESEARCH (US).
— ATMOSPHERIC TECHNOLOGY.   XXX

NATIONAL COAL BOARD (GB).
— COAL & ENERGY QUARTERLY.

NATIONAL COUNCIL ON CRIME & DELINQUENCY (US).
— CRIME & DELINQUENCY LITERATURE.   XXX
— INFORMATION REVIEW ON CRIME & DELINQUENCY.   XXX
— SELECTED HIGHLIGHTS ON CRIME & DELINQUENCY
LITERATURE.   XXX

NATIONAL COUNCIL FOR SPECIAL EDUCATION (GB).
— NEWSLETTER, NATIONAL COUNCIL FOR SPECIAL
EDUCATION (GB).

NATIONAL DEVELOPMENT CORPORATION (TANZANIA).
— JENGA.

NATIONAL EARTHQUAKE INFORMATION CENTER (US).
— EARTHQUAKE INFORMATION BULLETIN.

NATIONAL FERTILIZER DEVELOPMENT CENTER (US).
— FERTILIZER TRENDS.

NATIONAL FOUNDATION - MARCH OF DIMES.
— SYNDROME IDENTIFICATION.

NATIONAL FRONT STUDENTS ASSOCIATION.
— SPARK. DEVOTED TO A CORRECT INTERPRETATION
OF MARX.

NATIONAL GALLERY OF ART (US).
— ANNUAL REPORT, NATIONAL GALLERY OF ART (US).   XXX
— REPORT & STUDIES IN THE HISTORY OF ART, NAT-
IONAL GALLERY OF ART (US).   XXX
— STUDIES IN THE HISTORY OF ART, NATIONAL GALL-
ERY OF ART (US).   XXX

**NATIONAL GEOPHYSICAL & SOLAR-TERRESTRIAL DATA
CENTER (US).**
— KEY TO GEOPHYSICAL RECORDS DOCUMENTATION.

NATIONAL HAIRDRESSERS' FEDERATION.
— NATIONAL HAIRDRESSER.

NATIONAL HEART INSTITUTE (US).
— CEREBROVASCULAR BIBLIOGRAPHY.

**NATIONAL INFORMATION & DOCUMENTATION CENTRE
(EGYPT).**   XXX
— EGYPTIAN JOURNAL OF BOTANY (1972).   XXX
— EGYPTIAN JOURNAL OF PHARMACEUTICAL SCIENCES
(1972).   XXX

**NATIONAL INSTITUTE ON ALCOHOL ABUSE & ALCOHOL-
ISM (US).**
— ALCOHOL & HEALTH NOTES.
— ALCOHOL HEALTH & RESEARCH WORLD.

**NATIONAL INSTITUTE OF ENVIRONMENTAL HEALTH
SCIENCES (US).**
— ENVIRONMENTAL HEALTH PERSPECTIVES.

NATIONAL INSTITUTE OF MENTAL HEALTH (US).
— ALCOHOL & HEALTH NOTES.

**NATIONAL INSTITUTE OF NEUROLOGICAL DISEASES
& BLINDNESS (US).**
— CEREBROVASCULAR BIBLIOGRAPHY.

NATIONAL LIBRARY OF NIGERIA.
— INDEX TO NIGERIANA IN SELECTED PERIODICALS.   XXX

NATIONAL MUSEUM OF CANADA.
— ANNUAIRE DU MUSEE NATIONAL DU CANADA.

NATIONAL PAINT & COATINGS ASSOCIATION (US).   XXX
— ABSTRACT REVIEW, NATIONAL PAINT & COATINGS
ASSOCIATION.   XXX

**NATIONAL PAINT, VARNISH & LACQUER ASSOC-
IATION.**   XXX
— ABSTRACT REVIEW, NATIONAL PAINT, VARNISH &
LACQUER ASSOCIATION.   XXX
SUBS(1972): ABSTRACT REVIEW, NATIONAL PAINT
& COATINGS ASSOCIATION.

NATIONAL REPROGRAPHIC CENTRE FOR DOCUMENTATION.
— REPROGRAPHICS QUARTERLY.   XXX

NATIONAL SPELEOLOGICAL SOCIETY (US).
— BULLETIN, NATIONAL SPELEOLOGICAL SOCIETY.   XXX
• SUBS (1974): NSS BULLETIN.
— NSS BULLETIN. QUARTERLY JOURNAL OF THE NAT-
IONAL SPELEOLOGICAL SOCIETY.   XXX

NATIONAL STRATEGY INFORMATION CENTER (US).
— ANNUAL OF POWER & CONFLICT.

**NATIONAL TAIWAN UNIVERSITY: INSTITUTE OF OCEAN-
OGRAPHY.**
— ACTA OCEANOGRAPHICA TAIWANICA.

NATIONAL TRUST: WICKEN FEN LOCAL COMMITTEE.
— GUIDES TO WICKEN FEN.

NATIONAL WILDLIFE FEDERATION (US).
— INTERNATIONAL WILDLIFE.

NATIONAL YOUTH BUREAU (GB).
— YOUTH SOCIAL WORK BULLETIN.
— YOUTH IN SOCIETY.

**NAUCHNO DRUZHESTVO NA ANATOMITE, KHISTOLOZITE I
PATOLOZITE.**
— EKSPERIMENTALNA MEDITSINA I MORFOLOGIJA.

NAUCHNO DRUZHESTVO ZA FIZIOLOGICHESKI NAUKI.
— EKSPERIMENTALNA MEDITSINA I MORFOLOGIJA.

**NAUCHNO-ISSLEDOVATEL'SKIJ INSTITUT STROITEL'NOJ
FIZIKI.**
— NAUCHNYE TRUDY, NAUCHNO-ISSLEDOVATEL'SKIJ
INSTITUT STROITEL'NOJ FIZIKI.   XXX

**NAUCHNOIZSLEDOVATELSKI INSTITUT PO RADIOLOGIJA
I RADIATSIONNA KHIGIENA.**
— NAUCHNI TRUDOVE, NAUCHNOIZSLEDOVATELSKI INST-
ITUT PO RADIOLOGIJA I RADIATSIONNA KHIGIENA.

NENE VALLEY RESEARCH COMMITTEE.
— DUROBRIVAE. A REVIEW OF NENE VALLEY ARCH-
AEOLOGY.

**(NETHERLANDS) MINISTRY OF ECONOMIC AFFAIRS:
ECONOMIC INFORMATION SERVICE.**
— ECONOMIC TITLES.

(NEW SOUTH WALES) DEPARTMENT OF MOTOR TRANSPORT
— AUTOSAFE.

NEW YORK SHAKESPEARE FESTIVAL PUBLIC THEATER.
— PERFORMANCE.

NEW YORK UNIVERSITY: CENTER FOR SAFETY.
— SAFETY SCIENCE ABSTRACTS.

**(NEW ZEALAND) DEPARTMENT OF SCIENTIFIC &
INDUSTRIAL RESEARCH.**
— NEW ZEALAND JOURNAL OF EXPERIMENTAL AGRICULT-
URE.
— NEW ZEALAND JOURNAL OF ZOOLOGY.

**NEW ZEALAND LIBRARY ASSOCIATION: ARCHIVES
COMMITTEE.**
— ARCHIFACTS. BULLETIN OF THE ARCHIVES COMMITTEE
OF THE NEW ZEALAND LIBRARY ASSOCIATION.

NEWARK BETH ISRAEL HOSPITAL.   XXX
— JOURNAL, NEWARK BETH ISRAEL HOSPITAL.   XXX
SUBS (1969): JOURNAL, NEWARK BETH ISRAEL
MEDICAL CENTER.

NEWARK BETH ISRAEL MEDICAL CENTER.   XXX
— JOURNAL, NEWARK BETH ISRAEL MEDICAL CENTER.   XXX

**NIGERIAN INSTITUTE OF SOCIAL & ECONOMIC
RESEARCH.**
— RESEARCH NEWS, NIGERIAN INSTITUTE OF SOCIAL &
ECONOMIC RESEARCH.

NIHON SHERU MORUDO KYOKAI.
— SHERU MORUDO NYUSU. SHELL MOLD NEWS.   XXX

NIHON TENSAI SHINKOKAI.
— TENSAI KENKYU HOKOKU: HOKAN.   XXX

**NIIGATA DAIGAKU RIGAKUBU CHISHITSU KOBUTSUGAKU
KYOSHITSU.**
— NIIGATA DAIGAKU RIGAKUBU CHISHITSU KOBUTSU-
GAKU KYOSHITSU KENKYU HOKOKU. CONTRIBUTIONS,
DEPARTMENT OF GEOLOGY & MINERALOGY, NIIGATA
UNIVERSITY.

**NIIGATA UNIVERSITY: DEPARTMENT OF GEOLOGY &
MINERALOGY.**   000
SEE: NIIGATA DAIGAKU RIGAKUBU CHISHITSU
KOBUTSUGAKU KYOSHITSU.

NORDIC INSTITUTE OF FOLKLORE.   000
SEE: NORDISK INSTITUT FOR FOLKED'GTNING.

NORDISK AUDIOLOGISK SELSKAB.
— SCANDINAVIAN AUDIOLOGY.

NORDISK INSTITUT FOR FOLKED'GTNING.
— NIF NEWSLETTER.

NORDISKA MUSEET & SKANSEN.
— ACTA VERTEBRATICA.   XXX

**NORGES TEKNISK-NATURVITENSKAPELIGE FORSKNING-
SRAD.**
— NORWEGIAN MARITIME RESEARCH.   XXX

NORTH AMERICAN MYCOLOGICAL ASSOCIATION.
— MCILVAINEA.

NORTH CENTRAL FOREST EXPERIMENT STATION (US).
— GENERAL TECHNICAL REPORT, NORTH CENTRAL FOR-
EST EXPERIMENT STATION (US).

NORTH OF SCOTLAND HYDRO-ELECTRIC BOARD.
— HYDRO NEWS.

NORTH STAFFORDSHIRE LABOUR STUDIES GROUP.
— BULLETIN OF THE NORTH STAFFORDSHIRE LABOUR
STUDIES GROUP.

NORTHAMPTON DEVELOPMENT CORPORATION.
— PROGRESS IN EXPANDING NORTHAMPTON.

NORTHERN IRELAND CIVIL RIGHTS ASSOCIATION.
— CIVIL RIGHTS.

NORTHUMBERLAND WILDLIFE TRUST.
— ROEBUCK. JOURNAL OF THE NORTHUMBERLAND WILD-
LIFE TRUST.

NORTHWESTERN UNIVERSITY: SCHOOL OF LAW.
— JOURNAL OF CRIMINAL LAW & CRIMINOLOGY.　XXX
— JOURNAL OF POLICE SCIENCE & ADMINISTRATION.　XXX

NORWEGIAN SOCIETY OF ACTUARIES.
— SCANDINAVIAN ACTUARIAL JOURNAL.　XXX

NUFFIELD FOUNDATION GROUP ON RESEARCH & IN-
NOVATION IN HIGHER EDUCATION.
— NEWSLETTER, NUFFIELD FOUNDATION GROUP ON RES-
EARCH & INNOVATION IN HIGHER EDUCATION.

OBLASNI ZAVOD ZA ZASTITU SPOMENIKA KULTURE.
— STARINE KOSOVA I METOHIJE.

ODINANI MUSEUM.
— ODINANI. THE JOURNAL OF THE ODINANI MUSEUM.

OECD: DIRECTORATE OF AGRICULTURE & FOOD.
— OECD AGRICULTURAL REVIEW.　XXX

OECD: MANPOWER & SOCIAL AFFAIRS DIRECTORATE.
— OECD SOCIAL INDICATOR DEVELOPMENT PROGRAMME.

OECD: SECRETARIAT.
— MONETARY STUDIES SERIES.

(OHIO) DEPARTMENT OF AGRICULTURE.
— CERES (COLUMBUS, OHIO).

OMSKAJA VYSSHAJA SHKOLA MILITSII.
— PROBLEMY BOR'BY S PRESTUPNOST'JU.

ONTARIO COLLEGE OF PHARMACY.
— ON CONTINUING PRACTICE.

ONTARIO HISTORICAL SOCIETY.
— RESEARCH PUBLICATION, ONTARIO HISTORICAL
SOCIETY.

ORSZAGOS SZECHENY1 KONYVTAR.
— KULFOLDI MAGYAR NYELVU FOLYOIRATOK REPERT-
ORIUMA.

OTEMON GAKUIN DAIGAKU KEIZAIGAKUBU.
— OTEMON ECONOMIC STUDIES.

OTEMON GAKUIN UNIVERSITY: SCHOOL OF ECONOM-
ICS.　000
SEE: OTEMON GAKUIN DAIGAKU KEIZAIGAKUBU.

OVERSEAS DEVELOPMENT INSTITUTE.
— ODI REVIEW.

OXFORD UNIVERSITY FORESTRY SOCIETY.
— LAND (OXFORD).

OXFORD UNIVERSITY POETRY SOCIETY.
— OXFORD POETRY MAGAZINE.

PACIFIC SOUTHWEST FOREST & RANGE EXPERIMENT
STATION (US).
— GENERAL TECHNICAL REPORT, PACIFIC SOUTHWEST
FOREST & RANGE EXPERIMENT STATION (US).

PACIFIC TROPICAL BOTANICAL GARDENS.
— MEMOIRS, PACIFIC TROPICAL BOTANICAL GARDENS.

PAHLAVI UNIVERSITY.
— IRANIAN JOURNAL OF SCIENCE & TECHNOLOGY.

PAHLAVI UNIVERSITY: COLLEGE OF AGRICULTURE.
— IRANIAN JOURNAL OF AGRICULTURAL RESEARCH.

PAINT RESEARCH ASSOCIATION.
— PAINT TITLES.

PALACKEHO UNIVERSITA: PRIRODOVEDECKA FACULTA.
— ACTA UNIVERSITATIS PALACKIANAE OLOMUCENSIS:
GEOGRAPHICA-GEOLOGICA.　XXX

PAMATNIK NARODNIHO PISEMNICTVI.
— CESKOSLOVENSKE NEJKRASNEJSI KNIHY.

(PAPUA & NEW GUINEA) DEPARTMENT OF FORESTS.
— RESEARCH BULLETIN, DEPARTMENT OF FORESTS
(PAPUA & NEW GUINEA).
— TROPICAL FORESTRY RESEARCH NOTE.

(PAPUA & NEW GUINEA) DEPARTMENT OF INFORMATION
& EXTENSION SERVICES: BUREAU OF LITERATURE.
— NEW GUINEA WRITING.　XXX
— PAPUA NEW GUINEA WRITING.　XXX

PEACE PLEDGE UNION.
— NEWSLETTER, PEACE PLEDGE UNION.

PEP.　000
SEE: POLITICAL & ECONOMIC PLANNING.

PERCY FITZPATRICK INSTITUTE OF AFRICAN
ORNITHOLOGY.
— MONOGRAPHS, PERCY FITZPATRICK INSTITUTE OF
AFRICAN ORNITHOLOGY.

PERDUE UNIVERSITY: THERMOPHYSICAL PROPERTIES
RESEARCH CENTER.
— THERMOPHYSICS NEWSLETTER.

PETROLEUM INDUSTRY TRAINING BOARD.
— NEWS, PETROLEUM INDUSTRY TRAINING BOARD.

PETRONIAN SOCIETY.
— PETRONIAN SOCIETY NEWSLETTER.

PETROZAVODSKIJ INSTITUT GEOLOGII.
— PROBLEMY OSADOCHNOJ GEOLOGII DOKEMBRIJA.

(PHILIPPINES) NATIONAL ECONOMIC COUNCIL.
— PHILIPPINE ECONOMY BULLETIN.

PHYSICAL EDUCATION ASSOCIATION OF GREAT
BRITAIN & NORTHERN IRELAND.
— BRITISH JOURNAL OF PHYSICAL EDUCATION.　XXX
— LEAFLET, PHYSICAL EDUCATION ASSOCIATION OF
GREAT BRITAIN & NORTHERN IRELAND.　XXX
SUBS (1970) PART OF: BRITISH JOURNAL OF
PHYSICAL EDUCATION.

PICKLE PACKERS INTERNATIONAL, INC.
— PICKLE PAK SCIENCE.

(POLAND) MINISTERSTWO KULTURY I SZTUKI: OSRODEK
DOKUMENTACJI ZABYTKOW.
— ZABYTKI ARCHITEKTURY I BUDOWNICTWA W POLSCE.

(POLAND) MINISTERSTWO KULTURY I SZTUKI:
ZARZAD MUZEOW I OCHRONY ZABYTKOW.
— STUDIA I MATERIALY DO DZIEJOW ZUP SOLNYCH
W POLSCE.

POLICY STUDIES ORGANISATION.
— POLICY STUDIES JOURNAL.

POLISH MEDICAL ALLIANCE.
— POLISH MEDICAL SCIENCES & HISTORY BULLETIN.　XXX
SUBS (1973): POLISH MEDICAL SCIENCES &
HISTORY BULLETIN & ABSTRACTS.

POLITECHNIKA WROCLAWSKA: INSTYTUT TECHNOLOGII
BUDOWY MASZYN.
— PRACE NAUKOWE INSTYTUTU TECHNOLOGII BUDOWY
MASZYN POLITECHNIKI WROCLAWSKIEJ: STUDIA I
MATERIALY.

POLITICAL & ECONOMIC PLANNING.
— ANNUAL REPORT, POLITICAL & ECONONIC PLANNING.

POLJARNO-AL'PIJSKIJ BOTANICHESKIJ SAD.
— BOTANICHESKIE ISSLEDOVANIJA ZA POLJARNYM
KRUGOM.

POLSKA AKADEMIA NAUK: INSTYTUT BADAN LITERACK-
ICH.
— U ZRODEL WSPOLCZESNEJ STYLISTYKI.

POLSKA AKADEMIA NAUK: INSTYTUT BOTANIKI.
— ACTA PALAEOBOTANICA.

POLSKA AKADEMIA NAUK: KOMISJA TEORII I HISTORII
SZTUKI.
— FOLIA HISTORIAE ARTIUM.

POLSKA AKADEMIA NAUK: KOMITET BADAN MORZA.
— OCEANOLOGIA.

POLSKA AKADEMIA NAUK: ZAKLAD ZOOLOGII
SYSTEMATYCZNEJ.
— MONOGRAFIE FAUNY POLSKI.

POLYTECHNIC OF NORTH LONDON: SCHOOL OF
LIBRARIANSHIP.
— RESEARCH IN PROGRESS, SCHOOL OF LIBRARIANSHIP,
POLYTECHNIC OF NORTH LONDON.

PONTIFICIA UNIVERSIDAD CATOLICA DEL PERU:
DEPARTAMENTO DE HUMANIDADES.
— HUMANIDADES.

POWER OF WOMEN COLLECTIVE.
— POWER OF WOMEN.

PRINCETON UNIVERSITY.
— CONTRIBUTIONS FROM THE BIOLOGICAL LABORATOR-
IES, PRINCETON UNIVERSITY.						XXX

PROFESSIONAL REHABILITATION WORKERS WITH THE
ADULT DEAF.
— JOURNAL OF REHABILITATION OF THE DEAF.

PUBLIC HEALTH LABORATORY SERVICE BOARD (GB).
— MONOGRAPH SERIES, PUBLIC HEALTH LABORATORY
SERVICE BOARD (GB).

PUNJABI UNIVERSITY: DEPARTMENT OF LINGUISTICS.
— PAKHA SANJAM.

(QUEBEC) DEPARTMENT OF LANDS & FORESTS: RES-
EARCH SERVICE.
— NOTE, RESEARCH SERVICE, DEPARTMENT OF LANDS &
FORESTS (QUEBEC).

QUEENSLAND LAW SOCIETY.
— JOURNAL, QUEENSLAND LAW SOCIETY.

RAPTOR RESEARCH FOUNDATION, INC.
— RAPTOR RESEARCH.							XXX
— RAPTOR RESEARCH NEWS.						XXX

RED FRONT MOVEMENT.
— RED FRONT. BULLETIN OF THE RED FRONT
MOVEMENT.

REID EDUCATIONAL FOUNDATION.						000
SEE: HELEN DWIGHT REID EDUCATIONAL
FOUNDATION.

RENFREWSHIRE NATURAL HISTORY SOCIETY.
— WESTERN NATURALIST.

RESEARCH & DOCUMENTATION CENTRE.
— SCANNER. A FORTNIGHTLY DIGEST OF CURRENT
EVENTS IN THE SOUTH ASIAN SUBCONTINENT.

RESEARCH INSTITUTE OF INDUSTRIAL HYGIENE &
OCCUPATIONAL DISEASES (BRATISLAVA).
— CZECHOSLOVAK BIBLIOGRAPHY ON INDUSTRIAL HY-
GIENE & OCCUPATIONAL DISEASES.					XXX

RESEARCH INSTITUTE OF MEDICAL SCIENCE
OF KOREA.
— INDEX MEDICUS KOREA.

(RHODESIA) DEPARTMENT OF THE PRIME MINISTER:
SCIENTIFIC LIASION OFFICE.
— RHODESIA RESEARCH INDEX.

RHODESIA PIONEERS' & EARLY SETTLERS' SOCIETY.
— PIONEER. JOURNAL OF THE RHODESIA PIONEERS' &
EARLY SETTLERS' SOCIETY.

RIGAS POLITEHNISKAIS INSTITUTS: ARHITEKTURAS
KATEDRA.
— ARHITEKTURA UN PILSETBUVNIECIBA LATVIJAS PSR,
RAKSTU KRAJUMS.

RIZHSKIJ POLITEKHNICHESKIJ INSTITUT (RIGA).			000
SEE: RIGAS POLITEHNISKAIS INSTITUTS.

ROBERT GORDON'S INSTITUTE OF TECHNOLOGY: SCHOOL
OF BUSINESS MANAGEMENT STUDIES.
— BUSINESS EDUCATION REVIEW.

ROXBURGH, SELKIRK & PEEBLES CONSERVATIVE &
UNIONIST ASSOCIATION.
— BORDER TORY.

ROYAL ANTHROPOLOGICAL INSTITUTE.
— RAIN. ROYAL ANTHROPOLOGICAL INSTITUTE NEWS-
LETTER.

ROYAL AUSTRALIAN CHEMICAL INSTITUTE.
— REVIEWS OF PURE & APPLIED CHEMISTRY.				XXX

ROYAL COLLEGE OF PHYSICIANS & SURGEONS OF
CANADA.
— ANNALS OF THE ROYAL COLLEGE OF PHYSICIANS &
SURGEONS OF CANADA.

ROYAL ECONOMIC SOCIETY.
— SURVEYS OF APPLIED ECONOMICS.

ROYAL INSTITUTE OF BRITISH ARCHITECTS.
— ARCHITECTURAL COMPETITIONS NEWS.
— ARCHITECTURAL PERIODICALS INDEX.				XXX
— JOURNAL OF ARCHITECTURAL RESEARCH.				XXX
— RIBA LIBRARY BULLETIN.						XXX
SUBS (1973): PART OF ARCHITECTURAL PERIOD-
ICALS INDEX.

ROYAL INSTITUTION OF CHARTERED SURVEYORS.
— CHARTERED SURVEYOR: BUILDING & QUANTITY
SURVEYING QUARTERLY.
— CHARTERED SURVEYOR: LAND HYDROGRAPHIC & MIN-
ING QUARTERLY.
— CHARTERED SURVEYOR: URBAN QUARTERLY.

ROYAL MEDICO-PSYCHOLOGICAL ASSOCIATION.
— BRITISH JOURNAL OF PSYCHIATRY: SPECIAL
PUBLICATIONS.

ROYAL NORWEGIAN COUNCIL FOR SCIENTIFIC & IND-
USTRIAL RESEARCH.							000
SEE: NORGES TEKNISK-NATURVITENSKAPELIGE
FORSKNINGSRAD.

ROYAL ONTARIO MUSEUM.
— ARCHAEOLOGY MONOGRAPH, ROYAL ONTARIO MUSEUM.
— ETHNOGRAPHY MONOGRAPH, ROYAL ONTARIO MUSEUM.
— HISTORY, TECHNOLOGY & ART MONOGRAPH, ROYAL
ONTARIO MUSEUM.
— PAPERS, ROYAL ONTARIO MUSEUM: ARCHAEOLOGY.

ROYAL ONTARIO MUSEUM: DIVISION OF ART & ARCH-
AEOLOGY.
— OCCASIONAL PAPER, DIVISION OF ART & ARCHAEOL-
OGY, ROYAL ONTARIO MUSEUM.					XXX

ROYAL SCOTTISH MUSEUM.
— INFORMATION SERIES, ROYAL SCOTTISH MUSEUM:
NATURAL HISTORY.

ROYAL TOWN PLANNING INSTITUTE.
— PLANNER. JOURNAL OF THE ROYAL TOWN PLANNING
INSTITUTE.							XXX

RUBBER & PLASTICS RESEARCH ASSOCIATION OF GREAT
BRITAIN.
— INTERNATIONAL POLYMER SCIENCE & TECHNOLOGY.

RUBBER RESEARCH INSTITUTE OF SRI LANKA.			XXX
— ANNUAL REVIEW, RUBBER RESEARCH INSTITUTE
OF SRI LANKA.							XXX

(RUSSIA RSFSR) MINISTERSTVO PROSVESHCHENIJA.
— MATEMATIKA V SHKOLE.

(RUSSIA RSFSR) MINISTERSTVO VYSSHEGO
I SREDNEGO SPETSIAL'NOGO OBRAZOVANIJA.
— LESOVODSTVO, LESNYE KUL'TURY I POCHVOVEDENIE.

(RUSSIA SSSR) MINISTERSTVO GEOLOGII.
— PROBLEMY OSADOCHNOJ GEOLOGII DOKEMBRIJA.

(RUSSIA SSSR) MINISTERSTVO OBORONY: INSTITUT
VOENNOJ ISTORII.
— VESTNIK VOENNOJ ISTORII. NAUCHNYE ZAPISKI.

(RUSSIA SSSR) MINISTERSTVO VNESHNEJ
TORGOVLI.
— SBORNIK NORMATIVNYKH MATERIALOV PO
VOPROSAM VNESHNEJ TORGOVL1 SSSR.

(RUSSIA SSSR) MINISTERSTVO ZDRAVOOKHRANENIJA.
— KOSMICHESKAJA BIOLOGIJA I AVIAKOSMICHESKAJA
MEDITSINA.							XXX

(RUSSIA SSSR) MINISTERSTVO VYSSHEGO I SREDNEGO
SPETSIAL'NOGO OBRAZOVANIJA SSSR.
— NAUCHNYJ KOMMUNIZM.

SAFETY IN MINES RESEARCH ESTABLISHMENT.
— RESEARCH REPORT, SAFETY IN MINES RESEARCH
ESTABLISHMENT.							XXX
SUBS (1973): SMRE REPORT.
— SMRE REPORT.							XXX

SAINT MARY'S COLLEGE, BAYOMBONG.
— JOURNAL OF NORTHERN LUZON.

SALFORD LOCAL HISTORY SOCIETY.
— NEWSLETTER, SALFORD LOCAL HISTORY SOCIETY.

SALLSKAPET BOKVANNERNA.
— STOCKHOLMIANA.

SAN FERNANDO VALLEY STATE COLLEGE: DEPARTMENT
OF GEOGRAPHY.
— HISTORICAL GEOGRAPHY NEWSLETTER.

SANDOZ AG.
— SANDOZ BULLETIN.

**SARAGOSSA UNIVERSIDAD: SEMINARIO DE PREHISTORIA
Y PROTOHISTORIA.**
— MONOGRAFIAS ARQUEOLOGICAS.

SARATOVSKIJ GOSUDARSTVENNYJ UNIVERSITET.
— ISTORIOGRAFICHESKIJ SBORNIK.
— OSVOBODITEL'NOE DVIZHENIE V ROSSII.
— VOPROSY ESTETIKI. SBORNIK STATEJ.
— VOPROSY MORFOMETRII.

SAUDI ARABIAN NATURAL HISTORY SOCIETY.
— JOURNAL, SAUDI ARABIAN NATURAL HISTORY
SOCIETY.   XXX
— REPORT, SAUDI ARABIAN NATURAL HISTORY SOCIETY.XX

**SAVEZ MASINSKIH I ELEKTROTEHNICHIH INZENJERA I
TEHNICARA SRBIJE: DRUSTVO ZA GREJANJE, HLADENJE
I KLIMATIZACIJU.**
— KLIMATIZACIJA, GREJANJE, HLADENJE.

SCANDINAVIAN AUDIOLOGICAL SOCIETY.   000
SEE: NORDISK AUDIOLOGISK SELSKAB.

**SCHOOLS COUNCIL (GB): CAREERS EDUCATION & GUID-
ANCE PROJECT.**
— FRAMEWORK.

SCHOOLS COUNCIL (GB): PROJECT TECHNOLOGY.
— SCHOOL TECHNOLOGY.   XXX

**SCHWEIZERISCHE GESELLSCHAFT FUR UR- UND FRUH-
GESCHICHTE.**   XXX
— JAHRBUCH DER SCHWEIZERISCHEN GESELLSCHAFT FUR
UR- UND FRUHGESCHICHTE.   XXX

SCHWEIZERISCHE GESELLSCHAFT FUR URGESCHICHTE.XX
— JAHRBUCH DER SCHWEIZERISCHEN GESELLSCHAFT FUR
URGESCHICHTE.   XXX
SUBS (1966): JAHRBUCH DER SCHWEIZERISCHEN
GESELLSCHAFT FUR UR- UND FRUHGESCHICHTE.

SCIENCE POLICY FOUNDATION.
— SCIENCE & PUBLIC POLICY.   XXX

**SCIENCE RESEARCH COUNCIL (GB): ASTROPHYSICS
RESEARCH UNIT.**
— REPORT, ASTROPHYSICS RESEARCH UNIT, SCIENCE
RESEARCH COUNCIL (GB).

SCOTTISH CHILDREN'S BOOK ASSOCIATION.
— BOOK WINDOW.

SCOTTISH COUNCIL FOR CIVIL LIBERTIES.
— BOUNDARIES.

**SCOTTISH COUNCIL FOR POSTGRADUATE MEDICAL
EDUCATION.**
— POSTGRADUATE NEWS.

SCOTTISH COUNCIL OF TENANTS.
— SCOTTISH TENANT. NEWSPAPER OF THE SCOTTISH
COUNCIL OF TENANTS.

SCOTTISH INLAND WATERWAYS ASSOCIATION.
— SIWA NEWS.

SCOTTISH PROVIDENT INSTITUTION.
— SPI-GLASS. HOUSE MAGAZINE OF THE SCOTTISH
PROVIDENT INSTITUTION.

SHIRLEY INSTITUTE.
— MEMOIRS, SHIRLEY INSTITUTE.   XXX

SHUTEI KYOKAI SHUPPANBU.
— BOTO ENJINIARINGU. BOAT ENGINEERING.

SILK & ART SILK MILLS' RESEARCH ASSOCIATION.
— MAN-MADE TEXTILES IN INDIA.   XXX
— SILK & RAYON INDUSTRIES OF INDIA.   XXX
SUBS (1973): MAN-MADE TEXTILES IN INDIA.

(SINGAPORE) MINISTRY OF CULTURE.
— SINGAPORE BULLETIN.

SLASKI INSTYTUT NAUKOWY.
— STUDIA NAD EKONOMIKA REGIONU.

SLOVAK NATIONAL MUSEUM.   000
SEE: SLOVENSKE NARODNE MUZEUM V BRATISLAVA.

SLOVENSKA AKADEMIA VIED.
— ENTOMOLOGICKE PROBLEMY.

SLOVENSKA AKADEMIA VIED: USTAV STATU A PRAVA.
— EDICIA PROBLEMY A UVAHY: RAD PRAVNY.

SLOVENSKA ENTOMOLOGICKA SPOLECNOST.
— ENTOMOLOGICKE PROBLEMY.

SLOVENSKE NARODNE MUZEUM V BRATISLAVA.
— MUSIKETHNOLOGISCHE JAHRESBIBLIOGRAPHIE
EUROPAS. ANNUAL BIBLIOGRAPHY OF EUROPEAN
ETHNOMUSICOLOGY.

**SLOVENSKE NARODNE MUZEUM: NARODOPISNY
ODBOR.**
— NARODOPISNE ZBIERKY.

SLOVENSKE USTREDIE KNIZNEJ KULTURY.
— CESKOSLOVENSKE NEJKRASNEJSI KNIHY.

SMITHSONIAN INSTITUTION.
— RESEARCH REPORTS, SMITHSONIAN INSTITUTION.

SMITHSONIAN INSTITUTION: RIVER BASIN SURVEYS.
— PUBLICATIONS IN SALVAGE ARCHEOLOGY, RIVER
BASIN SURVEYS, SMITHSONIAN INSTITUTION.   XXX

SOCIAL SCIENCE RESEARCH COUNCIL (GB).
— EDUCATIONAL PRIORITY.
— SURVEYS OF APPLIED ECONOMICS.

SOCIALIST PARTY OF AUSTRALIA.
— AUSTRALIAN MARXIST REVIEW.

SOCIETE DES AMIS DE JEAN GIRAUDOUX.
— CAHIERS JEAN GIRAUDOUX.

SOCIETY FOR ANALYTICAL CHEMISTRY.
— ANALYTICAL SCIENCES MONOGRAPH.

SOCIETY OF ANALYTICAL PSYCHOLOGY.
— LIBRARY OF ANALYTICAL PSYCHOLOGY.

SOCIEDADE BRASILEIRA DE GEOLOGIA.
— BOLETIM DA SOCIEDADE BRASILEIRA DE GEOLOGIA.   XXX

SOCIETY OF COMPANY & COMMERCIAL ACCOUNTANTS.
— ACCOUNTANTS REVIEW.   XXX

SOCIETY FOR CO-OPERATIVE STUDIES.
— BULLETIN OF THE SOCIETY FOR CO-OPERATIVE
STUDIES.

SOCIEDADE ENTOMOLOGICA DO BRASIL.
— ANAIS, SOCIEDADE ENTOMOLOGICA DO BRASIL.

SOCIEDAD ESPANOLA DE OFTALMOLOGIA.   XXX
— ARCHIVOS DE LA SOCIEDAD ESPANOLA DE OFTALMOL-
OGIA.   XXX

SOCIETE D'ETUDES DES PAYS DU COMMONWEALTH.
— ECHOS DU COMMONWEALTH.

**SOCIETE FRANCAISE D'ANTHROPOLOGIE ET
D'ECOLOGIE HUMAINE.**
— CAHIERS D'ANTHROPOLOGIE ET D'ECOLOGIE HUMAINE.

SOCIETY FOR GENERAL MICROBIOLOGY.
— PROCEEDINGS OF THE SOCIETY FOR GENERAL MICRO-
BIOLOGY.   XXX

SOCIETY OF INDUSTRIAL TUTORS.
— INDUSTRIAL TUTOR.

SOCIETE INTERNATIONALE DE PEDODONTIE.   000
SEE: INTERNATIONAL ASSOCIATION OF DENTISTRY
FOR CHILDREN.

SOCIETY FOR LATIN AMERICAN STUDIES.
— BULLETIN OF THE SOCIETY FOR LATIN AMERICAN
STUDIES.   XXX
— INFORMATION BULLETIN, SOCIETY FOR LATIN AMER-
ICAN STUDIES.   XXX

SOCIETY FOR LIBYAN STUDIES.
— ANNUAL REPORT, SOCIETY FOR LIBYAN STUDIES.

**SOCIEDAD MEXICANA DE GEOGRAFIA Y
ESTADISTICA.**
— REVISTA INTERAMERICANA DE SOCIOLOGIA.

SOCIEDAD DE OFTALMOLOGICA HISPANO-AMERICANA.   XXX
— ARCHIVOS DE LA SOCIEDAD OFTALMOLOGICA HISPANO-
AMERICANA.   XXX
SUBS (1971): ARCHIVOS DE LA SOCIEDAD ESPAN-
OLA DE OFTALMOLOGIA.

SOCIETY FOR RENAISSANCE STUDIES.
— OCCASIONAL PAPERS, SOCIETY FOR RENAISSANCE STUDIES.

SOCIETY FOR RESEARCH INTO HIGHER EDUCATION.
— RESEARCH INTO HIGHER EDUCATION MONOGRAPHS.

SOCIETATEA STIINTELOR MEDICALE DIN R.P.R.
— MICROBIOLOGIA, PARAZITOLOGIA, EPIDEMIOLOGIA.   XXX
SUBS (1974): BACTERIOLOGIA, VIRUSOLOGIA, PARAZITOLOGIA, EPIDEMIOLOGIA.

SOCIETY FOR THE STUDY OF HUMAN BIOLOGY.
— ANNALS OF HUMAN BIOLOGY.

SOCIETY OF VERTEBRATE PALEONTOLOGY.
— BIBLIOGRAPHY OF VERTEBRATE PALEONTOLOGY.   XXX

SOIL & WATER MANAGEMENT ASSOCIATION.
— BASIC ASSET.

SOJUZ NA ISTORISKITE DRUSTVA NA SR MAKEDONIJA.
— ISTORIJA, SOJUZ NA ISTORISKITE DRUSTVA NA SR MAKEDONIJA.

(SOUTH AFRICA) ATOMIC ENERGY BOARD.
— NUCLEAR ACTIVE.

(SOUTH AFRICA) DEPARTMENT OF AGRICULTURE.
— FARMING IN SOUTH AFRICA.   XXX

SOUTH AFRICAN VETERINARY ASSOCIATION.   XXX
— JOURNAL, SOUTH AFRICAN VETERINARY ASSOCIATION.XX

SOUTH AFRICAN VETERINARY MEDICAL ASSOCIATION.XX
— JOURNAL, SOUTH AFRICAN VETERINARY MEDICAL ASSOCIATION.   XXX
SUBS (1972): JOURNAL, SOUTH AFRICAN VETERINARY ASSOCIATION.

(SOUTH AUSTRALIA) DEPARTMENT OF AGRICULTURE.
— AGRICULTURAL RECORD, DEPARTMENT OF AGRICULTURE (SOUTH AUSTRALIA).   XXX

(SOUTH AUSTRALIA) DEPARTMENT OF FISHERIES & FAUNA CONSERVATION.
— PUBLICATIONS, DEPARTMENT OF FISHERIES & FAUNA CONSERVATION (SOUTH AUSTRALIA).

SOUTH EAST ASIA IRON & STEEL INSTITUTE.
— SEAISI QUARTERLY.

SOUTH PACIFIC COMMISSION.
— STATISTICAL BULLETIN, SOUTH PACIFIC COMMISSION.

SOUTHEAST ASIA TREATY ORGANIZATION.   000
SEE: SEATO

SOUTHEASTERN FOREST EXPERIMENT STATION (US).
— GENERAL TECHNICAL REPORT, SOUTHEASTERN FOREST EXPERIMENT STATION (US).

SOUTHERN FOREST EXPERIMENT STATION (US).
— GENERAL TECHNICAL REPORT, SOUTHERN FOREST EXPERIMENT STATION (US).

SOUTHERN SUDAN ASSOCIATION.
— GRASS CURTAIN.

SPIRITUALIST ASSOCIATION OF GREAT BRITAIN.
— PSYCHIC RESEARCHER & SPIRITUALIST GAZETTE.   XXX
— SPIRITUALIST GAZETTE.   XXX
— SPIRITUALIST GAZETTE.   XXX

SPLITSKA NADBISKUPIJA.
— CRKVA U SVIJETU.

SPORTS COUNCIL (GB).
— SPORTS COUNCIL STUDIES.

SPRING MANUFACTURERS INSTITUTE.
— SPRINGS MAGAZINE.

SREDNEAZIATSKIJ NAUCHNO-ISSLEDOVATEL'SKIJ INSTITUT PRIRODNOGO GAZA.
— GEOLOGIJA GAZOVYKH MESTOROZHDENIJ.

SRPSKO SOCIOLOSKO DRUSTVO.
— SOCIOLOSKI PREGLED.

STANDING CONFERENCE ON LIBRARY MATERIALS ON AFRICA.
— AFRICAN RESEARCH & DOCUMENTATION.   XXX

STATE CENTRAL MUSEUM (MONGOLIA).
— STUDIA MUSEOLOGICA.

STATE UNIVERSITY COLLEGE OF NEW FREDONIA: DEPARTMENT OF FOREIGN LANGUAGES.
— NINETEENTH-CENTURY FRENCH STUDIES.

STATE UNIVERSITY COLLEGE (NEW PALITZ, N.Y.): DEPARTMENT OF AFRICAN STUDIES.
— CONCH REVIEW OF BOOKS.

STATE UNIVERSITY OF NEW YORK AT BINGHAMTON: DEPARTMENT OF ENGLISH.
— BOUNDARY 2. A JOURNAL OF POSTMODERN LITERATURE.

STUDENT ASSOCIATION FOR THE STUDY OF HALLUCINOGENS, INC.
— SPEED. THE CURRENT INDEX TO THE DRUG ABUSE LITERATURE.

STUDY GROUP ON EIGHTEENTH-CENTURY RUSSIA.   000
SEE: UNIVERSITY OF EAST ANGLIA: STUDY GROUP ON EIGHTEENTH-CENTURY RUSSIA.

SUSSEX FAMILY HISTORY GROUP.
— SUSSEX FAMILY HISTORIAN.

SWEDISH SOCIETY OF ACTUARIES.
— SCANDINAVIAN ACTUARIAL JOURNAL.   XXX

SWEDISH STATISTICAL ASSOCIATION.
— SCANDIANAVIAN JOURNAL OF STATISTICS THEORY & APPLICATIONS.

SWISS WILDLIFE INFORMATION SERVICE.
— KEY-WORD-INDEX OF WILDLIFE RESEARCH.

TAMKANG COLLEGE OF ARTS & SCIENCES: INSTITUTE OF MATHEMATICS.
— TAMKANG JOURNAL OF MATHEMATICS.

(TANZANIA) MINISTRY OF NATIONAL EDUCATION.
— LUGHA YETU.

TANZANIA INVESTMENT BANK.
— RASILIMALI. TANZANIA INVESTMENT OUTLOOK.

TARTU RIIKLIK ULIKOOL.
— EESTI NSV AJALOO KUSIMUSI.
— LINGUISTICA (TARTU).
— TAYSIDE NEWS.

TENNYSON SOCIETY.
— MONOGRAPH SERIES, TENNYSON SOCIETY.   XXX

TEXAS A & M UNIVERSITY.
— SEA GRANT 70'S.

THEOLOGISCHE FAKULTAT (LUCERNE).
— THEOLOGISCHE BERICHTE.

THEOLOGISCHE HOCHSCHULE CHUR.
— THEOLOGISCHE BERICHTE.

TOKYO DAIGAKU: INSTITUTE OF SPACE & AERONAUTICAL SCIENCE.
— SOUNDING ROCKET DATA IN JAPAN.

TOKYO DAIGAKU JISHIN KENKYUJO.
— STRONG-MOTION EARTHQUAKE RECORDS IN JAPAN.

TRAFFIC SAFETY & NUISANCE RESEARCH INSTITUTE (JAPAN).   000
SEE: KOTSU ANZEN KOGAI KENKYUJO.

TRANSPERSONAL ASSOCIATION.
— JOURNAL OF TRANSPERSONAL PSYCHOLOGY.

TRANSPORT & INDUSTRIAL WORKERS' UNION (TRINIDAD).
— SOCIALIST WORKER (TRINIDAD).

TREVITHICK SOCIETY.
— JOURNAL OF THE TREVITHICK SOCIETY.

TRIBHUVAN UNIVERSITY: CENTRE FOR ECONOMIC DEVELOPMENT & ADMINISTRATION.
— CEDA SAMACHAR. A NEWSLETTER.

TSENTRAL'NYJ GOSUDARSTVENNYJ ARKHIV LITERATURY I ISKUSSTVA SSSR.
— SBORNIK NEOPUBLIKOVANNYKH MATERIALOV.

TUL'SKIJ GOSUDARSTVENNYJ PEDAGOGICHESKIJ INSTITUT.
— TOLSTOVSKIJ SBORNIK.

TUSSOCK GRASSLANDS & MOUNTAIN LANDS INSTITUTE.
— REVIEW, TUSSOCK GRASSLANDS & MOUNTAIN LANDS INSTITUTE.

(UKRAINE) GOSUDARSTVENNYJ KOMITET PO DELAM
STROITEL'STVA I ARKHITEKTURY.
— V POMOSHCH' PROEKTIROVSHCHIKU.

(UKRAINE) MINISTERSTVO VYSSHOJI I SEREDN'OJI
SPETSIAL'NOJI OS'VITY.
— AVTOMATIZATSIJA PROEKTIROVANIJA V ELEKTRONIKE.
— EKONOMICHESKAJA GEOGRAFIJA.

(UKRAINE) MINISTERSTVO ZDRAVOOKHRANENIJA USSR.
— FAKTORY VNESHNEJ SREDY I IKH ZNACHENIE DLJA
ZDOROV'JA NASELENIJA.

UKRAINSKIJ ZAOCHNYJ POLITEKHNICHESKIJ INSTITUT.
— KONTROL I TEKHNOLOGIJA PROTSESSOV OBOGASH-
CHENIJA POLEZNYKH ISKOPAEMYKH.

UKRAINSKOE NAUCHNOE OBSHCHESTVO VRACHEJ-
OTOLARINGOLOGOV.
— SOVREMENNYE PROBLEMY OTORINOLARINGOLOGII.

UNESCO.
— CULTURES.   XXX
— WORLD INDEX OF SOCIAL SCIENCE INSTITUTIONS.
REPERTOIRE MONDIAL DES INSTITUTIONS DE SCI-
ENCES SOCIALES.

UNESCO: INTERNATIONAL INSTITUTE FOR EDUCATIONAL
PLANNING.   000
SEE: INTERNATIONAL INSTITUTE FOR EDUCATIONAL
PLANNING.

UNION CARBIDE CORPORATION.
— MOLECULAR SIEVE ABSTRACTS.

UNION OF CONSTRUCTION, ALLIED TRADES &
TECHNICIANS.
— JOB FINDER - BUILDING & CONSTRUCTION.

UNION FOR RADICAL POLITICAL ECONOMICS.
— REVIEW OF RADICAL POLITICAL ECONOMICS.

UNION RESEARCH INSTITUTE (HONG KONG).
— TSU KUO. CHINA MONTHLY.   XXX

UNION OF TURKISH PROGRESSIVES.
— TURKEY TODAY.

UNITED KINGDOM CHEMICAL INFORMATION SERVICE.
— INFOCAST.

UNITED KINGDOM NATIONAL DOCUMENTATION CENTRE
FOR SPORT, PHYSICAL EDUCATION & RECREATION.
— SPORTS DOCUMENTATION MONTHLY BULLETIN.   XXX

UNITED NATIONS CHILDREN'S FUND: EUROPEAN OFFICE
— CARNETS DE L'ENFANCE.   XXX
— CARNETS DE L'ENFANCE. ASSIGNMENT CHILDREN.   XXX

UNITED NATIONS INDUSTRIAL DEVELOPMENT ORGAN-
IZATION.
— FERTILIZER INDUSTRY SERIES, UNITED NATIONS
INDUSTRIAL DEVELOPMENT ORGANIZATION.

(UNITED STATES) BUSINESS & DEFENSE SERVICES
ADMINISTRATION.
— BDSA INDUSTRY TREND SERIES.

(UNITED STATES) DEPARTMENT OF COMMERCE: BUS-
INESS & DEFENSE SERVICES ADMINISTRATION.   000
SEE: (UNITED STATES) BUSINESS & DEFENSE
SERVICES ADMINISTRATION.

(UNITED STATES) ENVIRONMENTAL PROTECTION
AGENCY: OFFICE OF RADIATION PROGRAMS.
— TECHNICAL REPORTS, SURVEILLANCE & INSPECTION
DIVISION, OFFICE OF RADIATION PROGRAMS (US).

(UNITED STATES) GEOLOGICAL SURVEY.
— GEOPHYSICAL ABSTRACTS. ABSTRACTS OF CURRENT
LITERATURE PERTAINING TO THE PHYSICS OF THE
SOLID EARTH & TO GEOPHYSICAL EXPLORATION.   XXX

UNITED STATES INFORMATION AGENCY.
— HORIZONS U.S.A.   XXX

(UNITED STATES) INFORMATION SERVICE (GB).
— INSIGHT U.S.A.   XXX

(UNITED STATES) NATIONAL OCEANIC & ATMOSPHERIC
ADMINISTRATION.
— PROGRESS REPORT, INTERNATIONAL DECADE OF
OCEAN EXPLORATION.

(UNITED STATES) NATIONAL OCEANIC & ATMOSPHERIC
ADMINISTRATION: ENVIRONMENTAL DATA SERVICE.
— SEA GRANT 70'S.

(UNITED STATES) NATIONAL OCEANIC & ATMOSPHERIC
ADMINISTRATION: ENVIRONMENTAL RESEARCH
LABORATORIES.
— TECHNICAL MEMORANDUM, ENVIRONMENTAL RESEARCH
LABORATORIES, NATIONAL OCEANIC & ATMOSPHERIC
ADMINISTRATION (US).

UNITED STATES INTERNATIONAL UNIVERSITY:
CALIFORNIA WESTERN SCHOOL OF LAW.
— CALIFORNIA WESTERN INTERNATIONAL LAW JOURNAL.

UNIUNEA SOCIETATILER DE STIINTE MEDICALE.
— BACTERIOLOGIA, VIRUSOLOGIA, PARAZITOLOGIA,
EPIDEMIOLOGIA.   XXX

UNIVERSITY OF ABERDEEN: DEPARTMENT OF ECONOMIC
HISTORY.
— SCOTTISH ECONOMIC HISTORY NEWSLETTER.

UNIVERSITY OF ABERDEEN: DEPARTMENT OF POLITICAL
ECONOMY.
— ABERDEEN STUDIES IN DEFENCE ECONOMICS.

UNIVERSITE D'ABIDJAN.
— ANNALES DE L'UNIVERSITE D'ABIDJAN: SERIES I:
HISTOIRE.

UNIWERSYTET IM. ADAMA MICKIEWICZA W POZNANIU.
— STUDIA HISTORICA SLAVO-GERMANICA.

UNIVERSITY OF ADELAIDE: CENTRE FOR PRECAMBRIAN
RESEARCH.
— SPECIAL PAPERS, CENTRE FOR PRECAMBRIAN RES-
EARCH, UNIVERSITY OF ADELAIDE.

UNIVERSITY OF ASTON IN BIRMINGHAM: DEPARTMENT
OF METALLURGY.
— HEAT TREATMENT OF METALS.

UNIVERSIDAD DE BARCELONA: DEPARTMENTO DE
SOCIOLOGICOS.
— PAPERS. TRABAJOS DE SOCIOLOGIA.

UNIVERSITE DU BENIN: ECOLE DES LETTRES.
— ANNALES DE L'ECOLE DES LETTRES DE L'UNIV-
ERSITE DU BENIN.

UNIVERSITY OF BIRMINGHAM: DEPARTMENT OF GREEK.
— MANTATOPHOROS. BULLETIN OF MODERN GREEK
STUDIES.

UNIVERSITY OF BIRMINGHAM: INSTITUTE OF LOCAL
GOVERNMENT STUDIES.
— CORPORATE PLANNING.

UNIVERSITA DI BOLOGNA: ISTITUTO DI LINGUE E
LETTERATURE STRANIERE.
— SPICILEGIO MODERNO, ISTITUTO DI LINGUE E LETT-
ERATURE STRANIERE, UNIVERSITA DI BOLOGNA.

UNIVERSITAT BONN: SEMINAR FUR SPRACHE- UND
KULTURWISSENSCHAFT ZENTRALASIENS.
— ZENTRALASIATISCHE STUDIEN.

UNIVERSITY OF BRITISH COLUMBIA: FACULTY OF LAW.
— BULLETIN OF CANADIAN WELFARE LAW.

UNIVERSITY OF CALGARY.
— STUDIES IN LAND USE HISTORY & LANDSCAPE
CHANGE: NATIONAL PARK SERIES.

UNIVERSITY OF CALGARY: RESEARCH CENTRE FOR
CANADIAN ETHNIC STUDIES.
— CANADIAN ETHNIC STUDIES. BULLETIN/ETUDES
ETHNIQUES DU CANADA.

UNIVERSITY OF CALIFORNIA: AFRICAN STUDIES
CENTER.
— RESEARCH IN PROGRESS, AFRICAN STUDIES CENTER,
UNIVERSITY OF CALIFORNIA.

UNIVERSITY OF CALIFORNIA: EARTHQUAKE ENGINEER-
ING RESEARCH CENTER.
— ABSTRACT JOURNAL IN EARTHQUAKE ENGINEERING.

UNIVERSITY OF CALIFORNIA AT LOS ANGELES:
ENGLISH MEDIEVAL CLUB.
— COMITATUS. STUDIES IN OLD & MIDDLE ENGLISH
LITERATURE.

UNIVERSITY OF CALIFORNIA: PROJECT ON LINGUISTIC
ANALYSIS.
— JOURNAL OF CHINESE LINGUISTICS.

UNIVERSITY OF CAMBRIDGE: DEPARTMENT OF LAND ECONOMY.
— RESEARCH & PUBLICATIONS, DEPARTMENT OF LAND ECONOMY, UNIVERSITY OF CAMBRIDGE.

UNIVERSITY OF CAMBRIDGE: LIBRARY.
— HISTORICAL BIBLIOGRAPHY SERIES, CAMBRIDGE UNIVERSITY LIBRARY.
— NEWTON MANUSCRIPT SERIES, CAMBRIDGE UNIVERSITY LIBRARY.

UNIVERSITY OF CANTERBURY: BIOLOGICAL SOCIETY.
— MAURI ORA.

UNIVERSITA DI CATANIA: CENTRO DI STUDI E RICERCHE SUL MEZZOGIORNO E LA SICILIA.
— ANNALI DE MEZZOGIORNO.

UNIVERSITE CATHOLIQUE DE LOUVAIN: INSTITUT INTERFACULTE D'ETUDES MEDIEVALES.
— MEDIAEVALIA LOVANIENSIA: SERIES 1: STUDIA.

UNIVERSITE CATHOLIQUE DE LOUVAIN: INSTITUT DE LINGUISTIQUE.
— CAHIERS, INSTITUT DE LINGUISTIQUE, UNIVERSITE CATHOLIQUE DE LOUVAIN.

UNIVERSIDAD CATOLICA ANDRES BELLO: FACULTAD DE HUMANIDADES Y EDUCACION.
— MONTALBAN.

UNIVERSIDAD CENTRAL DE VENEZUELA: INSTITUTO DE CIENCIAS PENALES Y CRIMINOLOGICAS.
— ANUARIO, INSTITUTO DE CIENCIAS PENALES Y CRIMINOLOGICAS, UNIVERSIDAD CENTRAL DE VENEZUELA.

UNIVERSITY OF CHICAGO: DEPARTMENT OF BIOLOGY.
— EVOLUTIONARY THEORY.

UNIVERSITY COLLEGE, DAR ES SALAAM: INSTITUTE OF PUBLIC ADMINISTRATION.
— CASE STUDIES IN THE MANAGEMENT OF ECONOMIC DEVELOPMENT.

UNIVERSITA COMMERCIALE LUIGI BOCCONI: ISTITUTO DI LETTERATURA SPAGNOLA E ISPANO-AMERICANA.
— STUDI DI LETTERATURA ISPANO-AMERICANA.

UNIVERSITY COUNCIL FOR EDUCATIONAL ADMINISTRATION.
— EDUCATIONAL ADMINISTRATION QUARTERLY.

UNIVERSITY OF DELHI: DEPARTMENT OF SANSKRIT.
— INDOLOGICAL STUDIES. XXX
— JOURNAL, DEPARTMENT OF SANSKRIT, UNIVERSITY OF DELHI. XXX

UNIVERSITY OF DENVER: COLLEGE OF LAW. XXX
— DENVER LAW JOURNAL. XXX

UNIVERSITY OF DENVER: LAW CENTER. XXX
— JOURNAL, DENVER LAW CENTER. XXX

UNIVERSITY OF DURHAM: CENTRE FOR MIDDLE EASTERN & ISLAMIC STUDIES.
— OCCASIONAL PAPERS SERIES, CENTRE FOR MIDDLE EASTERN & ISLAMIC STUDIES, UNIVERSITY OF DURHAM.

UNIVERSITY OF DURHAM: DEPARTMENT OF SOCIOLOGY & SOCIAL ADMINISTRATION.
— WORKING PAPERS IN SOCIOLOGY, DEPARTMENT OF SOCIOLOGY & SOCIAL ADMINISTRATION, UNIVERSITY OF DURHAM.

UNIVERSITY OF EAST ANGLIA: CENTRE OF EAST ANGLIAN STUDIES.
— EAST ANGLIAN HISTORY & ARCHAEOLOGY: WORK IN PROGRESS.

UNIVERSITY OF EAST ANGLIA: CLIMATIC RESEARCH UNIT.
— CLIMATIC RESEARCH UNIT OCCASIONAL BULLETIN. XXX

UNIVERSITY OF EAST ANGLIA: STUDY GROUP ON EIGHTEENTH-CENTURY RUSSIA.
— NEWSLETTER, STUDY GROUP ON EIGHTEENTH-CENTURY RUSSIA.

UNIVERSITAS ECONOMICA WASAENSIS.
— ACTA WASAENSIA: GEOGRAPHY.

UNIVERSITY OF EXETER: INSTITUTE OF BIOMETRY & COMMUNITY MEDICINE.
— PUBLICATION, INSTITUTE OF BIOMETRY & COMMUNITY MEDICINE, UNIVERSITY OF EXETER.

UNIVERSITY FOLKLORE ASSOCIATION.
— FOLKLORE ANNUAL.

UNIWERSYTET GDANSKI: WYDZIAL MATEMATYKI, FIZYKI I CHEMII.
— ZESZYTY NAUKOWE UNIWERSYTETU GDANSKIEGO: CHEMIA.
— ZESZYTY NAUKOWE UNIWERSYTETU GDANSKIEGO: MATEMATYKA.

UNIVERSITA DI GENOVA: ISTITUTO DI ARCHITETTURA.
— QUADERNI DELL'ISTITUTO DI ARCHITETTURA DELL' UNIVERSITA DI GENOVA.

UNIVERSITY OF GLASGOW.
— DISCUSSION PAPERS IN ECONOMICS, UNIVERSITY OF GLASGOW.

UNIVERSIDAD DE GRANADA.
— CUADERNOS DE ESTUDIOZ MEDIEVALES.

UNIVERSITE DE GRENOBLE: CENTRE D'ETUDE ET DE RECHERCHE SUR L'ADMINISTRATION ECONOMIQUE ET L'AMENAGEMENT DU TERRITOIRE.
— AMENAGEMENT DU TERRITOIRE ET DEVELOPPEMENT REGIONAL.

UNIVERSITY OF HAWAII: HAROLD L. LYON ARBORETUM.
— LECTURES, HAROLD L. LYON ARBORETUM, UNIVERSITY OF HAWAII.

UNIVERSITY OF HULL.
— HUMBERSIDE STATISTICAL BULLETIN.

UNIVERSITY OF IDAHO: FOREST, WILDLIFE & RANGE EXPERIMENT STATION.
— STATION PAPERS, FOREST, WILDLIFE & RANGE EXPERIMENT STATION, UNIVERSITY OF IDAHO.

UNIVERSITY OF ILLINOIS AT URBANA-CHAMPAIGNE: CENTER FOR ADVANCED COMPUTATION.
— CAC DOCUMENT.

UNIVERSITY OF KHARTOUM: FACULTY OF ARTS.
— ADAB. JOURNAL OF THE FACULTY OF ARTS, UNIVERSITY OF KHARTOUM.

UNIVERZITA KOMENSKEHO (BRATISLAVA): FILOZOFICKA FACULTA.
— GRAECOLATINA ET ORIENTALIA.

UNIVERZITA KOMENSKEHO (BRATISLAVA): USTAV MARXIZMU-LENINIZMU.
— ZBORNIK: DEJINY ROBOTNICKEHO HNUTA. XXX
— ZBORNIK, USTAV MARXIZMU-LENINIZMU UNIVERZITA KOMENSKEHO. XXX

UNIVERSITA DI LECCE: BIBLIOTECA CENTRALE.
— QUADERNI DELLA BIBLIOTECA CENTRALE, UNIVERSITA DI LECCE.

UNIVERSITY OF LEEDS: CENTRE FOR STUDIES IN SCIENCE EDUCATION.
— STUDIES IN SCIENCE EDUCATION.

UNIVERSITY OF LEEDS: MUSEUM OF THE HISTORY OF EDUCATION.
— EDUCATIONAL ADMINISTRATION & HISTORY MONOGRAPHS.

UNIVERSITE LIBRE DE BRUXELLES: INSTITUT DE PHILOSOPHIE.
— ANNALES, INSTITUT DE PHILOSOPHIE, UNIVERSITE LIBRE DE BRUXELLES.

UNIVERSITE DE LIEGE: BIBLIOTHEQUE GENERALE.
— REPERTOIRE DES THESES DE DOCTORAT EUROPEENNES.

UNIVERSITE DE LIEGE: INSTITUT BOTANIQUE.
— ARCHIVES DE L'INSTITUT BOTANIQUE DE L'UNIVERSITE DE LIEGE. XXX

UNIVERSIDADE DE LISBOA: CENTRO DE ESTUDOS GEOGRAFICOS.
— FINISTERRA. REVISTA PORTUGUESA DE GEOGRAFIA.

UNIVERZA V LJUBLJANA: FILOZOFSKA FAKULTETA.
— ACTA NEOPHILOLOGICA.

UNIVERZA V LJUBLJANI: ODDELEK ZA MUZIKOLOGIJO FILOSOFSKE FAKULTE.
— MUZIKOLOSKI ZBORNIK.

ISB/ 22

UNIV   UNIV

**UNIVERSITY OF LONDON: SCHOOL OF ORIENTAL &
AFRICAN STUDIES.**
 — BULLETIN OF QUANTITATIVE & COMPUTER METHODS
   IN SOUTH ASIAN STUDIES.
 — INDONESIA CIRCLE.

UNIVERSIDAD DE LOS ANDES.
 — ACTUAL.

UNIVERSIDADE DO LOURENCO MARQUES.
 — REVISTA DE CIENCIAS MATEMATICAS: SERIE A.   XXX

UNIVERSITY OF MALAWI.
 — ODI. BILINGUAL QUARTERLY OF MALAWIAN WRITING.

UNIVERSITY OF MALAWI: HISTORY DEPARTMENT.
 — HISTORY IN MALAWI BULLETIN.

**UNIVERSITY OF MANCHESTER: INSTITUTE OF SCIENCE
& TECHNOLOGY.**   XXX
 — INTERNATIONAL JOURNAL OF MECHANICAL ENGINEER-
   ING EDUCATION.   XXX

UNIVERSITY OF MARYLAND: DEPARTMENT OF ENGLISH.
 — RESOURCES FOR AMERICAN LITERARY STUDY.

**UNIVERSITY OF MIAMI: ROSENSTIEL SCHOOL OF
MARINE & ATMOSPHERIC SCIENCE.**
 — SEDIMENTA.

UNIVERSITY OF MICHIGAN: LAW SCHOOL.
 — JOURNAL OF LAW REFORM.   XXX

UNIVERSITY OF MICHIGAN: MUSEUM OF ANTHROPOLOGY.
 — CONTRIBUTIONS IN HUMAN BIOLOGY, MUSEUM OF
   ANTHROPOLOGY, UNIVERSITY OF MICHIGAN.

**UNIVERSITY OF MOSUL: FACULTY OF AGRICULTURE &
VETERINARY SCIENCE.**
 — MESOPOTAMIA AGRICULTURE.   XXX
 — BOLETIN DEL INSTITUTO DE DERECHO COMPARADO,
   UNIVERSIDAD NACIONAL AUTONOMA DE MEXICO.   XXX
   SUBS (1968): BOLETIN MEXICANO DE DERECHO
   COMPARADO: NUEVA SERIE.

**UNIVERSIDADE NACIONAL AUTONOMA DE MEXICO:
INSTITUTO DE INVESTIGACIONES ESTETICAS.**
 — CUADERNOS DE HISTORIA DEL ARTE.

**UNIVERSIDAD NACIONAL AUTONOMA DE MEXICO: INST-
ITUTO DE INVESTIGACIONES JURIDICAS.**
 — BOLETIN MEXICANO DE DERECHO COMPARADO: NUEVA
   SERIE.   XXX

**UNIVERSIDAD NACIONAL DE LA PLATA: FACULTAD DE
CIENCIAS VETERINARIAS.**
 — ANALECTA VETERINARIA.   XXX
 — REVISTA, FACULTAD DE CIENCIAS VETERINARIAS,
   UNIVERSIDAD NACIONAL DE LA PLATA: TERCERA
   EPOCA.   XXX
   SUBS (1969): ANALECTA VETERINARIA.

**UNIVERSIDAD NACIONAL Y POPULAR DE BUENOS AIRES:
FACULTAD DE DERECHO Y CIENCIAS SOCIALES.**
 — CUADERNOS NACIONALES (BUENOS AIRES).
 — LIBERACION Y DERECHO.

UNIVERSITY OF NEW MEXICO.
 — JOURNAL OF ANTHROPOLOGICAL RESEARCH.   XXX
 — SOUTHWESTERN JOURNAL OF ANTHROPOLOGY.   XXX
   SUBS (1973): JOURNAL OF ANTHROPOLOGICAL
   RESEARCH.

UNIVERSITY OF NIGERIA: INSTITUTE OF EDUCATION.
 — REVIEW OF EDUCATION. A JOURNAL OF THE INST-
   ITUTE OF EDUCATION, UNIVERSITY OF NIGERIA.

UNIVERSITY OF OREGON: DEPARTMENT OF SOCIOLOGY.
 — INSURGENT SOCIOLOGIST.

UNIVERSITY OF OTTAWA.
 — CAHIERS D'HISTOIRE.

UNIVERSITY OF OTTAWA: FACULTY OF LAW.
 — JUSTINIEN. REVUE ANNUELLE DES INSTITUTIONS
   JURIDIQUES DU QUEBEC.   XXX
 — REVUE GENERALE DE DROIT.   XXX

**UNIVERSITY OF OXFORD: INSTITUTE OF AGRICULTURAL
ECONOMICS.**
 — FARMLAND MARKET.

**UNIVERSITY OF OXFORD: INSTITUTE OF ECONOMICS &
STATISTICS.**   XXX
 — OXFORD BULLETIN OF ECONOMICS & STATISTICS.   XXX

**UNIVERSITA DI PADOVA: FACOLTA DI ECONOMIA E
COMMERCIO IN VERONA.**
 — ANNALI DELLA FACOLTA DI ECONOMIA E COMMERCIO
   IN VERONA.

**UNIVERSITA DI PADOVA: INSTITUTO DI FILOLOGIA E
LETTERATURA ITALIANA.**
 — STUDI NOVECENTESCHI.

UNIVERSITA DEGLI STUDI DI PAVIA.
 — ANNALES CISALPINES D'HISTOIRE SOCIALE.

**UNIVERSITY OF THE PHILIPPINES: NATURAL SCIENCE
RESEARCH CENTER.**
 — KALIKASAN. PHILIPPINE JOURNAL OF BIOLOGY.

UNIVERSITY OF PITTSBURGH: DEPARTMENT OF HISTORY
 — PEASANT STUDIES NEWSLETTER.

**UNIVERSITY OF PITTSBURGH: UNIVERSITY CENTER FOR
INTERNATIONAL STUDIES.**
 — RUSSIAN HISTORY. HISTOIRE RUSSE.
 — SOUTHEASTERN EUROPE. L'EUROPE DU SUD EST.

UNIVERSIDADE DO PORTO: FACULDADE DE LETRAS.
 — REVISTA DA FACULDADE DE LETRAS, UNIVERSIDADE
   DO PORTO: SERIE DE HISTORIA.

**UNIVERSITY OF QUEENSLAND: DEPARTMENT OF
AGRICULTURE.**
 — AGRICULTURAL ECONOMICS & FARM MANAGEMENT
   OCCASIONAL PAPER.

**UNIVERSIDAD RAFAEL LANDIVAR: INSTITUTO DE
CIENCIAS POLITICO-SOCIALES.**
 — ESTUDIOS SOCIALES. REVISTA DE CIENCIAS
   SOCIALES.

**UNIVERSIDAD DE LA REPUBLICA (URUGUAY):
DEPARTAMENTO DE LITERATURA IBEROAMERICANA.**
 — REVISTA IBEROAMERICANA DE LITERATURA: 2S.

UNIVERSITY OF RHODESIA.   XXX
 — MONOGRAPHS IN POLITICAL SCIENCE.

UNIVERSITY OF RHODESIA: LIBRARY.
 — RHODESIA RESEARCH INDEX.

UNIVERSITA DI ROMA: ISTITUTO DI AUTOMATICA.
 — NOTIZIARIO, ISTITUTO DI AUTOMATICA, UNIV-
   ERSITA DI ROMA.

**UNIVERSITA DI ROMA: SCUOLA DI STUDI STORICO-
RELIGIOSI.**
 — RELIGIONI E CIVILTA.

UNIVERSIDAD DE SALAMANCA: FACULTAD DE MEDICINA.
 — ANALES DE LA FACULTAD DE MEDICINA, UNIV-
   ERSIDAD DE SALAMANCA.

UNIVERSIDAD DE SANTIAGO DE COMPOSTELA.
 — MONOGRAFIAS, UNIVERSIDAD DE SANTIAGO DE
   COMPOSTELA.

**UNIVERSIDADE DE SAO PAULO: FACULDADE DE MED-
ICINA VETERINARIA.**   XXX
 — REVISTA DA FACULDADE DE MEDICINA VETERINARIA,
   UNIVERSIDADE DE SAO PAULO.   XXX
   SUBS (1972): REVISTA DA FACULDADE DE MED-
   ICINA VETERINARIA E ZOOTECNIA, UNIVERSIDADE
   DE SAO PAULO.

**UNIVERSIDADE DE SAO PAULO: FACULDADE DE MED-
ICINA VETERINARIA E ZOOTECNIA.**   XXX
 — REVISTA DA FACULDADE DE MEDICINA VETERINARIA
   E ZOOTECNIA, UNIVERSIDADE DE SAO PAULO.   XXX

**UNIVERSITY OF SHEFFIELD: BIOMEDICAL INFORMATION
PROJECT.**
 — CYCLIC AMP.
 — ENZYME REGULATION.
 — RENAL PHYSIOLOGY.

UNIVERSITY OF SINGAPORE LAW SOCIETY.
 — ME JUDICE.   XXX
   SUBS (1969): PART OF SINGAPORE LAW REVIEW.
 — SINGAPORE LAW REVIEW.   XXX

UNIVERSITY OF SOUTH AFRICA.
 — MOUSAION 11.

UNIVERSITY OF THE SOUTH PACIFIC: LIBRARY.
 — LEGAL DEPOSIT ACCESSIONS, LIBRARY, UNIVERSITY
   OF THE SOUTH PACIFIC.

UNIVERSITY OF STIRLING.
 — BULLETIN, UNIVERSITY OF STIRLING.

VYSSHAJA PARTIJNAJA SHKOLA PRI TSK KPSS: KAFEDRA RUSSKOGO JAZYKA.
— IZ OPYTA PREPODAVANIJA RUSSKOGO JAZYKA NERUS-SKIM. SBORNIK NAUCHNOMETODICHESKIKH STATEJ.

WADIA INSTITUTE OF HIMALAYAN GEOLOGY.
— HIMALAYAN GEOLOGY.

WARWICKSHIRE NATURE CONSERVATION TRUST.
— OCCASIONAL PAPERS, WARWICKSHIRE NATURE CON-SERVATION TRUST.

WELDING RESEARCH COUNCIL.
— WELDING RESEARCH NEWS.

WEST BENGAL VETERINARY ASSOCIATION.
— INDIAN JOURNAL OF ANIMAL HEALTH.   XXX

WESTERN ASSOCIATION OF MAP LIBRARIES.
— INFORMATION BULLETIN, WESTERN ASSOCIATION OF MAP LIBRARIES.   XXX
— NEWSLETTER, WESTERN ASSOCIATION OF MAP LIBRARIES.   XXX

WESTERN ECONOMIC ASSOCIATION.
— ECONOMIC INQUIRY.   XXX

WISSENSCHAFTLICHE GESELLSCHAFT FUR EUROPARECHT.
— EUROPARECHT.

WOLFE TONE SOCIETY.
— TUAIRISC. JOURNAL OF THE WOLFE TONE SOCIETY.

WOLFSON HEAT TREATMENT CENTRE.
— HEAT TREATMENT OF METALS.

WORLD ALLIANCE OF REFORMED CHURCHES (PRESBYTER-IAN & CONGREGATIONAL).
— REFORMED WORLD.   XXX

WORLD COUNCIL OF CHURCHES.
— THIS MONTH (GENEVA).

WORLD FEDERATION OF ULTRASOUND IN MEDICINE & BIOLOGY.
— ULTRASOUND IN MEDICINE & BIOLOGY.

WORLD HEALTH ORGANIZATION.
— INTERNATIONAL HISTOLOGICAL CLASSIFICATION OF TUMOURS.
— PUBLIC HEALTH IN EUROPE.
— WEEKLY EPIDEMIOLOGICAL RECORD.
— WHO PESTICIDE RESIDUES SERIES.

WORLD HEALTH ORGANIZATION: IBADAN CARDIAC REGISTRY.
— CARDIOVASCULAR PROJECTS.

WORLD HEALTH ORGANIZATION: INTERNATIONAL REF-ERENCE CENTRE FOR COMMUNITY WATER SUPPLY.
— TECHNICAL PAPER, INTERNATIONAL REFERENCE CENTRE FOR COMMUNITY WATER SUPPLY (WHO).

WORLD MEETINGS INFORMATION CENTER.
— CURRENT PROGRAMS.

WORLD METEOROLOGICAL ORGANIZATION.
— GARP NEWSLETTER.
— GATE REPORT.
— OPERATIONAL HYDROLOGY REPORT.

WORLD STUDENT CHRISTIAN FEDERATION.
— W.S.C.F. DOSSIER.

WORLD ZIONIST ORGANIZATION: DEPARTMENT FOR EDUCATION & CULTURE IN THE DIASPORA.
— OROT. JOURNAL OF HEBREW LITERATURE.

WORSHIPFUL COMPANY OF STATIONERS & NEWSPAPER MAKERS.
— STATIONER & NEWSPAPER MAKER.

WRITERS & SCHOLARS INTERNATIONAL.
— INDEX ON CENSORSHIP.

WYE COLLEGE: CENTRE FOR EUROPEAN AGRICULTURAL STUDIES.
— REPORT, CENTRE FOR EUROPEAN AGRICULTURAL STUDIES, WYE COLLEGE.

WYZSZA SZKOLA NAUK SPOLECZNYCH: ZAKLAD BADAN SPOLECZNYCH PRZEMYSLU I KLASY ROBOTNICZEJ.
— SOCJOLOGICZNE PROBLEMY PRZEMYSLU I KLASY ROBOTNICZEJ.

YONSEI TAEHAKKYO (SEOUL): TONGSO MUNJE YON'-GUNON.
— JOURNAL OF EAST & WEST STUDIES.

YORK ARCHAEOLOGICAL TRUST.
— INTERIM. BULLETIN OF THE YORK ARCHAEOLOGICAL TRUST.

YORK UNIVERSITY (TORONTO): ATKINSON COLLEGE.
— EXILE. A LITERARY QUARTERLY.

YORK UNIVERSITY (TORONTO): DEPARTMENT OF ENGLISH.
— T.S. ELIOT NEWSLETTER.

YOUNG EXPLORERS' TRUST.
— ISLAND.

YOUNG FABIAN GROUP.
— PLEBS.

YOUNG LIBERAL MOVEMENT.
— LIBERATOR. A NEWSPAPER OF THE YOUNG LIBERAL MOVEMENT.

YOUNG UNITED FEDERALISTS.
— FEDERALIST (LONDON).

YOUTH SERVICE INFORMATION CENTRE.
— YOUTH SCENE.

ZAVOD ZA GEOLOSKA I GEOFIZICKA ISTRAZIVANJA.
— VESNIK, ZAVOD ZA GEOLOSKA I GEOFIZICKA IST-RAZIVANJA: SERIJA A: GEOLOGIJA.   XXX
— VESNIK, ZAVOD ZA GEOLOSKA I GEOFIZICKA IST-RAZIVANJA: SERIJA B: INZENJERSKA GEOLOGIJA I HIDROGEOLOGIJA.
— VESNIK, ZAVOD ZA GEOLOSKA I GEOFIZICKA IST-RAZIVANJA: SERIJA C: PRIMENJENA GEOFIZICKA.

ZAVOD ZA ZASTITU SPOMENIKA KULTURE SR CRNE GORE
— STARINE CRNE GORE.

ZENTRAAL RAT FUR ASIEN-, AFRIKA- UND LATEIN-AMERIKAWISSENSCHAFTEN IN DER DDR.
— ASIEN, AFRIKA, LATEINAMERIKA.

ZOOLOGISCHES FORSCHUNGSINSTITUT UND MUSEUM ALEXANDER KOENIG.
— BONNER ZOOLOGISCHE MONOGRAPHIEN.

Index of Library Symbols

AB——— ABERYSTWYTH.

AB/N–1 NATIONAL LIBRARY OF WALES. L/A/P
AB/U–1 UNIVERSITY COLLEGE OF WALES, GENERAL LIBRARY. L/˙A
AB/U–2 WELSH PLANT BREEDING STATION, PLAS GOGERDDAN, CARDS.

AD——— ABERDEEN.

AD/R–1 MACAULAY INSTITUTE FOR SOIL RESEARCH, CRAIGIEBUCKLER. L/˙A
AD/R–2 ROWETT RESEARCH INSTITUTE (REID LIBR.), BUCKSBURN, ABERDEENSHIRE. ⟨JT. LIBR. WITH: COMMONW. BUR. OF ANIM. NUTRITION⟩
AD/U–1 UNIVERSITY OF ABERDEEN (UNIV. LIBR.), KINGS COLLEGE. L/A/P
AD/U–2 MARISCHAL COLLEGE, ABERDEEN.

BD——— BRADFORD.

BD/U–1 UNIVERSITY OF BRADFORD (UNIV. LIBR.), RICHMOND RD., BRADFORD, YORKS. BD7 1DP.

BH——— BIRMINGHAM.

BH/C–1 NOW AS *BH/U–3*, Q.V.
BH/C–2 CITY OF BIRM. COLLEGE OF COMMERCE, ASTON ST., GOSTA GREEN, 4. L/A/XP
BH/C–3 SELLY OAK COLLEGES, 29. L/A/˙P
BH/F–1 AUSTIN MOTOR CO. LTD. (TECHNICAL INFORMATION BUREAU), BOX 41, GPO. L/˙A/˙P
BH/P–1 BIRM. CITY LIBRARIES (REFERENCE LIBR.), RATCLIFFE PLACE, 1. ˙L/A/P
BH/U–1 UNIVERSITY OF BIRM. (UNIV. LIBR.), EDGBASTON, 15. L/˙A/˙P
BH/U–2 INSTITUTE OF EDUCATION, UNIV. OF BIRM., 50, WELLINGTON RD., EDGBASTON, 15. L/A/˙P
BH/U–3 UNIVERSITY OF ASTON IN BIRMINGHAM, GOSTA GREEN, 4. ⟨PREV: (BIRM.) COLL. OF ADVANCED TECHNOLOGY⟩. XL/XF/A/P/M

BL——— BELFAST.

BL/C–1 STRANMILLIS COLLEGE, BELFAST, BT9 5DY. ˙L/XF/A/P/XM
BL/P–1 BELF. PUBLIC LIBRARY, ROYAL AVE., 1. L/A/P
BL/U–1 QUEENS UNIVERSITY OF BELF. L/˙A/P

BN——— BANGOR, NORTH WALES.

BN/U–1 UNIVERSITY COLLEGE OF NORTH WALES. L/˙A/P
BN/U–2 UNIV. COLL. OF NORTH WALES (SCIENCE LIBR.)

BR——— BRISTOL.

BR/C–1 BRIS. COLLEGE OF SCIENCE & TECHNOLOGY, ASHLEY DOWN, 7. L/A/P
BR/F–1 IMPERIAL TOBACCO GROUP (RES. DEP. LIBR.), RALEIGH RD., 3. L/˙A/˙P
BR/P–1 BRIS. CITY LIBRARIES (CENTRAL LIBR.), COLLEGE GREEN, 1. L/A/P
BR/U–1 UNIVERSITY OF BRIS., 8. L/˙A/P
BR/U–2 INSTITUTE OF EDUCATION, UNIV. OF BRIS., 19 BERKELEY SQUARE, 8.
BR/U–3 ENGINEERING LABORATORIES, UNIV. OF BRIS., UNIVERSITY WALK, 8.
BR/U–4 (LONG ASHTON) RESEARCH STATION, DEP. OF AGRIC. & HORTIC., UNIV. OF BRIS., LONG ASHTON. L/˙A/P

BT——— BRIGHTON.

BT/C–1 BRIGHTON COLLEGE: FACULTY OF ARTS & DESIGN, GRAND PARADE, 7. L/A/˙P
BT/U–1 UNIVERSITY OF SUSSEX, FALMER. L/˙A/˙P

CA——— CAMBRIDGE.

CA/M–1 DEP. OF PATHOLOGY, UNIV. OF CAMBRIDGE, (KANTHACK LIBR.), TENNIS COURT RD. L/˙A/˙P
CA/M–2 PHYSIOLOGICAL LABORATORY, UNIV. OF CAMB., DOWNING ST. ˙L/˙A/P
CA/M–3 PSYCHOLOGICAL LABORATORY, DEP. OF EXPERIMENTAL PSYCHOL., UNIV. OF CAMB., DOWNING ST. ˙L/˙A/˙P
CA/M–4 SCHOOL OF VETERINARY MEDICINE, UNIV. OF CAMB., MADINGLEY RD. ˙L/˙A/˙P
CA/M–5 INSTITUTE OF ANIMAL PHYSIOLOGY (AGRICULTURAL RESEARCH COUNCIL), BABRAHAM. L/˙A/˙P
CA/P–1 CAMB. CITY LIBRARIES (CENTRAL LIBR.), GUILDHALL. L/A/˙P
CA/R–1 LOW TEMPERATURE RESEARCH STATION, DOWNING ST. ˙L/˙A/XP ⟨NOW FOOD RESEARCH INSTITUTE, COLNEY LANE, NORWICH, & MEAT RESEARCH INSTITUTE, LANGFORD, BRISTOL⟩
CA/R–2 PLANT BREEDING INSTITUTE, TRUMPINGTON. ˙L/˙A
CA/S–1 TYNDALE LIBRARY FOR BIBLICAL RESEARCH (TYNDALE FELLOWSHIP FOR BIBLICAL RES.), TYNDALE HOUSE, 36 SELWYN GARDENS, CAMB. XL/˙A/XP/XM
CA/U–1 UNIVERSITY LIBRARY, CAMBRIDGE. ˙L/˙A/P
CA/U–2 SCIENTIFIC PERIODICALS LIBRARY ⟨PREV: CAMBRIDGE PHILOSOPHICAL LIBRARY⟩, BENE'T STREET.
CA/U–3 FACULTY OF ARCHAEOLOGY & ANTHROPOLOGY (HADDON LIBRARY), UNIV. OF CAMBRIDGE, DOWNING ST. L/˙A/˙P
CA/U–4 DEP. OF ENGINEERING, UNIV. OF CAMBRIDGE, TRUMPINGTON ST. ˙L/˙A/˙P
CA/U–5 DEP. OF GEOGRAPHY, UNIV. OF CAMBRIDGE, DOWNING PLACE. XL/˙A/XP
CA/U–6 DEP. OF ZOOLOGY (BALFOUR LIBRARY), UNIV. OF CAMBRIDGE, DOWNING ST. ˙L/˙A/XP
CA/U–7 BOTANY SCHOOL, UNIV. OF CAMBRIDGE, DOWNING ST. L/˙A/˙P
CA/U–8 CHRISTS COLLEGE. XL/˙A/P
CA/U–9 INSTITUTE OF EDUCATION, UNIV. OF CAMB., SHAFTESBURY RD. ˙L/A
CA/U10 MOLTENO INSTITUTE OF BIOLOGY & PARASITOLOGY, DOWNING ST. ˙L/˙A/XP
CA/U11 DEPARTMENT OF AGRICULTURAL SCIENCE & APPLIED BIOLOGY, UNIV. OF CAMBRIDGE. ˙L/˙A/˙P
CA/U12 SCOTT POLAR RESEARCH INSTITUTE, LENSFIELD RD. ˙L/˙A/P
CA/U13 SQUIRE LAW LIBR., OLD SCHOOLS. XL/˙A/˙P
CA/U14 SEDGWICK MUSEUM, DOWNING ST. XL
CA/U15 DEP. OF GENETICS, UNIV. OF CAMBRIDGE
CA/U37 INSTITUTE OF CRIMINOLOGY, UNIV. OF CAMB., WEST RD., CB3 9DT.

CB——— CANTERBURY.

CB/U–1 UNIVERSITY OF KENT AT C'BURY. L/A/˙P

CC——— COLCHESTER.

CC/U–1 UNIVERSITY OF ESSEX, P.O. BOX NO. 24, WIVENHOE PARK, COLCHESTER, CO4 3UA.

CO——— CORK.

CO/U–1 UNIVERSITY COLLEGE, CORK. ˙L/˙A/˙P

CR——— CARDIFF.

CR/M–1 WELSH NATIONAL SCHOOL OF MEDICINE, HEATH PARK, CARDIFF, CF4 4XN.
CR/N–1 NATIONAL MUSEUM OF WALES. L/A
CR/S–1 CARDIFF NATURALISTS SOCIETY, C/O NAT. MUS. OF WALES. *L/*A/XP
CR/U–1 UNIVERSITY COLLEGE OF SOUTH WALES & MONMOUTHSHIRE, CATHAYS PARK. L/*A/*P

CV——— COVENTRY.

CV/C–1 LANCHESTER POLYTECHNIC. L/P/XM
CV/F–1 COURTAULDS LTD. (TECHNICAL INFORMATION BUREAU), FOLESHILL RD. L/*A/*P
CV/U–1 UNIVERSITY OF WARWICK. L/*A/XP

DB——— DUBLIN.

DB/S–1 ROYAL IRISH ACADEMY, 19 DAWSON ST., 2. L(THRU ICLS)/F(THRU ICLS)/*A/P/XM
DB/U–1 TRINITY COLLEGE LIBRARY, DUBLIN 2. XL/*A/P
DB/U–2 UNIVERSITY COLLEGE, DUBLIN, EARLSFORT TERRACE, 2. L/A/P

DN——— DUNDEE.

DN/R–1 SCOTTISH HORTICULTURAL RESEARCH INSTITUTE, MYLNEFIELD, INVERGOWRIE. L/*A/P
DN/U–1 UNIVERSITY OF DUNDEE, DD1 4HN. L/*A/XP

DR——— DURHAM

DR/U–1 UNIVERSITY OF DURHAM (UNIV. LIBR.) L/*A/XP
DR/U–2 INSTITUTE OF EDUCATION, UNIV. OF DUR., OLD SHIRE HALL.

ED——— EDINBURGH.

ED/M–1 ROYAL COLLEGE OF PHYSICIANS OF EDINB., 9 QUEEN ST., 2. *L/A/P
ED/M–2 ROYAL (DICK) SCHOOL OF VETERINARY STUDIES, SUMMERHALL.
ED/N–1 NATIONAL LIBRARY OF SCOTLAND, 1. XL/*A/P
ED/P–1 EDINB. PUBLIC LIBRARIES (CENTRAL LIBR.), GEORGE IV BRIDGE, 1. *L/A/P
ED/R–1 POULTRY RESEARCH CENTRE (AGRIC. RES. COUN.), KINGS BUILDINGS, WEST MAINS RD., EDINB. 8. L/*A/P
ED/R–2 ANIMAL BREEDING LIBRARY, WEST MAINS RD., EDINB. 9. (JT. LIBR. OF: ANIMAL BREEDING RES. ORG. (ARC); (&) COMMONW. BUR. OF ANIM. BREEDING & GENETICS) L/*F/A/P
ED/R–3 ROYAL OBSERVATORY, BLACKFORD HILL, 9. L/*A/*P
ED/S–1 ROYAL SCOTTISH GEOGRAPHICAL SOCIETY, 10 RANDOLPH CRESCENT, 3. L/XA/P
ED/S–2 ROYAL SOCIETY OF EDINB., 22 GEORGE ST., EDINB. 2. L/A/P
ED/U–1 UNIVERSITY OF EDINB. (UNIV. LIBR.), OLD COLLEGE, SOUTH BRIDGE, 8. L/*A/P
ED/U–2 EDINB. SCHOOL OF AGRICULTURE, WEST MAINS RD, 9. L/*A/P
ED/U–3 HERIOT-WATT UNIVERSITY, CHAMBERS ST., 1. L/*A/*P

EX——— EXETER.

EX/U–1 UNIVERSITY OF EXETER (ROBOROUGH LIBR.) L/*A/*P
EX/U–2 INSTITUTE OF EDUCATION, UNIV. OF EX., GANDY ST.

GA——— GALWAY.

GA/U–1 UNIVERSITY COLLEGE, GALWAY. L/A/XP

GL——— GLASGOW.

GL/C–1 NOW AS *GL/U–2*, Q.V.
GL/C–2 NOW AS *GL/U–3*, Q.V.
GL/M–1 ROYAL COLLEGE OF PHYSICIANS & SURGEONS, 242 VINCENT ST., C2.
GL/P–1 MITCHELL LIBRARY, NORTH ST., C3. *L/A/P
GL/R–1 NATIONAL ENGINEERING LABORATORY, EAST KILBRIDE. NLLST (XY/N–1) MUST BE TRIED FIRST FOR ANY ITEM. *L/F/*A/*P/*M
GL/U–1 UNIVERSITY OF GLASGOW, W2. L/*A/P
GL/U–2 UNIVERSITY OF STRATHCLYDE (ANDERSONIAN LIBR.), MCCANCE BUILDING, RICHMOND ST., GLASGOW, G1 1XQ. *L/*A/P
GL/U–3 SCOTTISH COLLEGE, UNIV. OF STRATHCLYDE (PREV: SCOTT. COLL. OF COMMERCE) (COLL. LIBR.), PITT ST., C2. L/*A/P

HL——— HULL.

HL/P–1 KINGSTON UPON HULL PUBLIC LIBRARIES (CENTRAL LIBR.), ALBION ST. L/A/P
HL/U–1 UNIVERSITY OF HULL (BRYNMOR JONES LIBR.) COTTINGHAM RD. L/*A/P
HL/U–2 INSTITUTE OF EDUCATION, UNIV. OF HULL, 173 COTTINNGHAM RD. L/A/P

LA——— LANCASTER.

LA/U–1 UNIVERSITY OF LANCASTER (UNIV. LIBR.), BAILRIGG, LANCS. L/*A/*P

LB——— LOUGHBOROUGH, LEICS.

LB/C–1 LOUGHB. COLLEGE OF FURTHER EDUCATION. *L/A/*P (PREV AS *XE/C–1*)
LB/U–1 LOUGHB. UNIVERSITY OF TECHNOLOGY. L/*A/*P (PREV AS *XE/C–2*)

LC——— LEICESTER.

LC/C–1 CITY OF LEICESTER POLYTECHNIC L/A/P
LC/P–1 LEIC. CITY LIBRARIES, BISHOP ST. L/A/P
LC/U–1 UNIVERSITY OF LEIC., UNIVERSITY RD. *L/*A/*P
LC/U–2 SCHOOL OF EDUCATION, UNIV. OF LEIC., 21 UNIVERSITY RD. L/*F/A/*P/XM

LD——— LEEDS.

LD/P–1 LEEDS CITY LIBRARIES (CENTRAL LIBR.), 1. XL/A/P

LD/T–1   COAL TAR RESEARCH ASSOCIATION, OXFORD ROAD, GOMERSAL. *L/*A/*P

LD/T–2   WOOL INDUSTRIES RESEARCH ASSOCIATION, TORRIDON, HEADINGLEY LANE, 6. L/*F/*A/P/XM

LD/U–1   UNIV. OF LEEDS (BROTHERTON LIBRARY), 2. L/*A/P

LD/U–2   INSTITUTE OF EDUCATION, UNIV. OF LEEDS, LEEDS 2. L/*A/XP

LN——   LONDONDERRY.

LN/U–1   MAGEE UNIVERSITY COLLEGE. L/A/*P

LO——   LONDON.

LO/C–1   ACTON TECHNICAL COLLEGE, HIGH ST., W3. L/*A

LO/C–2   NOW AS LO/U21, Q.V.

LO/C–3   POLYTECHNIC OF THE SOUTH BANK, BOROUGH RD., LONDON, SE1. *L/*A/*P

LO/C–4   CHELSEA COLLEGE OF SCIENCE & TECHNOLOGY. MANRESA RD, SW3. L/*A/P

LO/C–5   EALING TECHNICAL COLLEGE, ST. MARYS RD. W5. L/*A/XP

LO/C–6   ENFIELD COLLEGE OF TECHNOLOGY, QUEENSWAY, ENFIELD, MIDDX. L/A/XP

LO/C–7   HORNSEY COLLEGE OF ART, CROUCH END HILL, N8. L/*A/XP

LO/C–8   ISLEWORTH POLYTECHNIC, LONDON RD., ISLEWORTH, MIDDX. L/A/P

LO/C–9   JEWS COLLEGE, 11 MONTAGU PLACE, MONTAGU SQUARE, W1. *L/*A/XP

LO/C10   KINGSTON COLLEGE OF TECHNOLOGY, PENRHYN RD, KINGSTON/THAMES, SURREY. L/A/*P

LO/C11   NATIONAL COLLEGE OF FOOD TECHNOLOGY, ST GEORGES AVE, WEYBRIDGE, SURREY. *L/*A/P

LO/C12   NATIONAL COLLEGE FOR HEATING, VENTILATING, REFRIGERATION & FAN ENGINEERING, BORO POLYTECH, BOROUGH RD, SE1. L/*A

LO/C13   NOW AS LO/U18, Q.V.

LO/C14   NORTHERN POLYTECHNIC, HOLLOWAY, N7. (JT. LIBR. WITH: NAT. COLL. RUBBER TECHNOL.)

LO/C15   POLYTECHNIC OF CENTRAL LONDON, 309 REGENT ST., W1R 8AL.

LO/C16   ST MARYS COLLEGE, STRAWBERRY HILL, TWICKENHAM. L/*A/XP

LO/C17   NORTH EAST LONDON POLYTECHNIC, FOREST RD., LONDON, E17 4JB. L/A/P

LO/C18   THAMES POLYTECHNIC, WELLINGTON ST., WOOLWICH, LONDON, SE18. L/XA/P

LO/C19   NOW AS LO/U20, Q.V.

LO/C20   MARIA ASSUMPTA TRAINING COLLEGE, 23 KENSINGTON SQ, W8. *L/*A

LO/F–1   BRITISH INSULATED CALLENDERS CABLES LTD (RESEARCH DEP.), 38 WOOD LANE, W12. L/XA/*P

LO/F–2   DECCA RADAR LTD. (RESEARCH LABS.), LYON RD., HERSHAM, WALTON/THAMES, SURREY. *L/*A/*P

LO/F–3   EMI ELECTRONICS LTD. (EMI CENTRAL TECH. LIBR.), BLYTH RD., HAYES, MIDDX. L/*A/*P

LO/F–4   ENGLISH ELECTRIC HOUSE, STRAND, WC2. *L/*A/*P

LO/F–5   GEORGE WIMPEY & CO. LTD. (CENTRAL LAB.), LANCASTER RD, SOUTHALL, MIDDX. L/XA/*P

LO/F–6   HAWKER SIDDELEY DYNAMICS LTD. (TECH. LIBR.), WELKIN HOUSE, CHARTERHOUSE SQ., EC1. L/XA/XP

LO/F–7   IBM UNITED KINGDOM LTD., 101 WIGMORE STREET, W.I. *L/*A/*P

LO/F–8   KODAK LTD. (RESEARCH LAB.), WEALDSTONE, HARROW, MIDDX. *L/XA

LO/F–9   METAL BOX CO. LTD. (RESEARCH DIV.), KENDAL AVE., WESTFIELDS RD., W3. *L/XA/P

LO/F10   BROOKE BOND OXO LIBRARY, 20 SOUTHWARK BRIDGE RD., SE1. L/*A/*P

LO/F12   ILFORD LTD. (RESEARCH LIBR.), 7-9 RODEN ST., ILF., ESSEX. L/XA/*P

LO/F13   LLOYDS & BOLSA INTERNATIONAL BANK LTD., 100 PALL MALL, SW1Y 5HP. XL/*A/*P/XM

LO/F14   SHELL INTERNATIONAL PETROLEUM CO. LTD. (CENTRAL INF. SERVICES), SHELL CENTRE, SE1.

LO/M–1   CHARING CROSS HOSPITAL MEDICAL SCHOOL (LIBRARY), FULHAM PALACE ROAD, W6 8RF. L/*A/P

LO/M–2   GUYS HOSPITAL MEDICAL SCHOOL (WILLS LIBR.), SE1. L/*A/P (*L HOSP. DEPS.)

LO/M–3   INSTITUTE OF CANCER RESEARCH, (CHESTER BEATTY RES. INST.), ROYAL CANCER HOSPITAL, FULHAM RD., SW3. L/*A/P

LO/M–4   INSTITUTE OF CHILD HEALTH, HOSP. FOR SICK CHILDREN, GT. ORMOND ST., WC1. L/*A/*P

LO/M–5   INSTITUTE OF DERMATOLOGY, ST. JOHNS HOSP. FOR DISEASES OF THE SKIN, LISLE ST., WC2. *L/*A/*P

LO/M–6   INSTITUTE OF LARYNGOLOGY & OTOLOGY 330/2 GRAYS INN RD., WC1. XL/*A/P

LO/M–7   INSTITUTE OF PSYCHOANALYSIS, 63 NEW CAVENDISH ST., W1. *L/*A/XP

LO/M–8   LISTER INSTITUTE OF PREVENTIVE MEDICINE, CHELSEA BRIDGE RD., SW1. L/*A/P

LO/M–9   LONDON HOSPITAL MEDICAL COLLEGE, TURNER ST., E1. *L/*A/*P

LO/M10   LONDON SCHOOL OF HYGIENE & TROPICAL MEDICINE, KEPPEL ST., WC1. *L/*A

LO/M11   MIDDLESEX HOSPITAL MEDICAL SCHOOL, MORTIMER ST., W1. L/XA/P

LO/M12   NATIONAL INSTITUTE FOR MEDICAL RESEARCH (MEDICAL RESEARCH COUNCIL), THE RIDGEWAY, MILL HILL, NW7. L/XA/P

LO/M13   ROYAL COLLEGE OF PHYSICIANS OF LONDON, 11 ST. ANDREWS PLACE, NW1. *L/*A/P

LO/M14   ROYAL COLLEGE OF SURGEONS OF ENGLAND, LINCOLNS INN FIELDS, WC2. L/*A/P

LO/M15   ROYAL COLLEGE OF VETERINARY SURGEONS (MEMORIAL LIBR.), 32 BELGRAVE SQ., SW1. L/*A/P

LO/M16   ROYAL FREE HOSPITAL SCHOOL OF MEDICINE, 8 HUNTER ST., WC1. L/XA/P

LO/M17   ROYAL SOCIETY OF MEDICINE, 1 WIMPOLE ST., W1. XL/*A

LO/M18   ROYAL VETERINARY COLLEGE, ROYAL COLLEGE ST., NW1. L/*A/*P

LO/M19   ST. BARTHOLOMEWS HOSPITAL MEDICAL COLLEGE, WEST SMITHFIELD, EC1. L/*A/P

LO/M20   ST. THOMAS'S HOSPITAL MED. SCHOOL, SE1. L

LO/M21   SCHOOL OF DENTAL SURGERY (STOBIE MEMORIAL LIBR.), R. DENTAL HOSP. OF LONDON, LEICESTER SQ., WC2. *L/*A/*P

LO/M22   SCHOOL OF PHARMACY, 29/39 BRUNSWICK SQ., WC1. L/*A/*P

LO/M23   UNIVERSITY COLLEGE HOSPITAL MEDICAL SCHOOL, UNIVERSITY ST., WC1. *L/XA/*P

LO/M24   WELLCOME HISTORICAL MEDICAL LIBRARY, EUSTON RD., NW1. *L/A/P

LO/M25   WELLCOME RESEARCH LABORATORIES, LANGLEY COURT, BECKENHAM, KENT. *L/*A/*P

LO/M26   CENTRAL VETERINARY LABORATORY, MIN. OF AGRIC., FISH & FOOD, NEW HAW, WEYBRIDGE, SURREY. L/*A/XP

LO/M27   DEPARTMENT OF HEALTH & SOCIAL SECURITY, ALEXANDER FLEMING HOUSE, ELEPHANT & CASTLE, SE1.

LO/M28   OFFICE OF HEALTH ECONOMICS, MERCURY HOUSE, 195 KNIGHTSBRIDGE, SW7. *L/*A/P

LO/M29   MEDICAL RESEARCH COUNCIL LABORA-TORIES, WOODMANSTERNE RD., CARSHALTON, SY. *L/P

LO/M30   ROYAL POSTGRADUATE MEDICAL SCHOOL OF LONDON, HAMMERSMITH HOSP., DUCANE RD., W12. L/*A

LO/M31 KINGS COLLEGE HOSPITAL MEDICAL SCHOOL, DENMARK HILL, SE5. L/*F/*A/*P

LO/M32 BRITISH MEDICAL ASSOCIATION, TAVISTOCK SQUARE, WC1. XL/XF/*A/P

LO/M33 INSTITUTE OF PSYCHIATRY, DE CRESPIGNY PARK, DENMARK HILL, SE5. L/XA/XP

LO/M34 BRITISH DENTAL ASSOCIATION, 64 WIMPOLE ST., W1. L/*F/*A/P/XM

LO/N–1 BRITISH LIBRARY: REFERENCE DIVISION, GREAT RUSSELL ST., WC1 3DG.⟨PREV: BRITISH MUSEUM⟩ XL/*A/P

LO/N–2 BRITISH MUSEUM (NATURAL HISTORY), CROMWELL RD., SW7. XL/*A/P

LO/N–3 NOW AS XY/N–1, Q.V.

LO/N–4 SCIENCE MUSEUM LIBRARY, SW7. XL/*A/P (*L THROUGH NLL ST).

LO/N–5 DEPARTMENT OF TRADE & INDUSTRY, KINGSGATE HOUSE, VICTORIA ST., SW1. ⟨PREV: MIN. OF TECHNOLOGY⟩

LO/N–6 MINISTRY OF AGRICULTURE, FISHERIES & FOOD (MAIN LIBR.), 3 WHITEHALL PLACE, SW1. ` L/A/XP

LO/N–7 DEPARTMENT OF TRADE & INDUSTRY (CENT. LIBR.), ⟨PREV. MIN. OF TECH.⟩ ST. GILES HIGH ST., LONDON, WC2. L/*A/P

LO/N–8 INSTITUTE OF GEOLOGICAL SCIENCES ⟨PREV: GEOLOGICAL SURVEY & MUSEUM⟩ , EXHIBITION ROAD, SW7. *L/A/P/M

LO/N–9 NOW AS *LO/N14*, Q.V.

LO/N10 DEPARTMENT OF TRADE & INDUSTRY, 1 VICTORIA ST., SW1. ⟨PREV: BOARD OF TRADE⟩

LO/N11 DEPARTMENT OF EDUCATION & SCIENCE, 38 BELGRAVE SQUARE, SW1.

LO/N12 INDIA OFFICE LIBRARY, KING CHARLES ST., SW1. *L/A/P

LO/N13 BRITISH LIBRARY: SCIENCE REFERENCE LIBRARY: BAYSWATER BRANCH, 10, PORCHESTER GARDENS, QUEENSWAY, W2 4DE. ⟨PREV: NATIONAL REFERENCE LIBRARY FOR SCIENCE AND INVENTION⟩XL/A/P

LO/N14 BRITISH LIBRARY: SCIENCE REFERENCE LIBRARY: HOLBORN BRANCH ⟨PATENT OFFICE LIBRARY⟩, 25, SOUTHAMPTON BUILDINGS, CHANCERY LANE, WC2A 1AW. ⟨PREV: NATIONAL REFERENCE LIBRARY FOR SCIENCE AND INVENTION⟩XL/A/P

LO/N15 VICTORIA & ALBERT MUSEUM, SW7

LO/N16 IMPERIAL WAR MUSEUM, LAMBETH RD., SE1.

LO/N17 FOREIGN & COMMONWEALTH OFFICE, SANCTUARY BUILDINGS, GREAT SMITH ST., SW1.

LO/N35 PROCUREMENT EXECUTIVE (MIN. DEFENCE), 1-13 ST. GILES HIGH ST., LONDON WC2H 8LD.

LO/P–1 BERMONDSEY DISTRICT LIBRARY (SOUTH-WARK PUB. LIBR.), SPA RD., SE16. L/A/*P

LO/P–2 CHELSEA PUBLIC LIBRARY (KENSINGTON & CHELSEA PUB. LIBR.), MANRESA RD., SW3. L/A/P

LO/P–3 EALING CENTRAL LIBRARY, WALPOLE PARK, W5. *L/A/*P

LO/P–4 EAST HAM LIBRARY (NEWHAM PUB. LIBR.), HIGH ST. SOUTH, E6. L/A/XP

LO/P–5 FINSBURY LIBRARY (ISLINGTON PUBLIC LIBRARIES), 245 ST. JOHN ST., EC1. L/A/*P

LO/P–6 GUILDHALL LIBRARY, EC2. *L/A/P

LO/P–7 HACKNEY CENTRAL LIBRARY, MARE ST., E8. L/A/*P

LO/P–8 HAMMERSMITH PUBLIC LIBRARIES (CENTRAL LIBR.), SHEPHERD'S BUSH RD., W6. L/A/*P

LO/P–9 BARNET PUBLIC LIBRARIES (CENT. LIBR.), THE BURROUGHS, NW4. L/A/P

LO/P10 HOLBORN CENTRAL LIBRARY (CAMDEN PUB. LIBR.), 32/38 THEOBALDS RD., WC1. L/A/P

LO/P11 HORNIMAN MUSEUM & LIBRARY, LONDON RD., FOREST HILL, SE23. Ł/A/XP

LO/P12 LAMBETH PUBLIC LIBRARIES (TATE CENTRAL LIBR.), BRIXTON OVAL, SW2. *L/*A/*P

LO/P13 LEWISHAM PUBLIC LIBRARIES, 170 BROMLEY ROAD, SE6. L/A/P

LO/P14 PADDINGTON DISTRICT LIBRARY (WEST-MINSTER PUB. LIBR.), PORCHESTER RD., W2. L/A/P

LO/P15 WESTMINSTER PUBLIC LIBRARIES, CENTRAL LIBRARY, MARYLEBONE RD., NW1. L/A/P

LO/P16 SHOREDITCH DISTRICT LIBRARY (HACKNEY PUB. LIBR.), PITFIELD ST., N1. L/A/XP

LO/P17 NEWINGTON DISTRICT LIBRARY & CUMING MUSEUM (SOUTHWARK PUB. LIBR.), WALWORTH RD., SE17. L/A/P

LO/P18 TOTTENHAM PUBLIC LIBRARY (HARINGEY PUB. LIBR.), 391 HIGH RD., N17. L/A/P

LO/P19 WEST HAM LIBRARY (NEWHAM PUB. LIBR.), WATER LANE, STRATFORD, E15. L/A/P

LO/P20 WESTMINSTER PUBLIC LIBRARIES (CENTRAL REFERENCE LIBR.), ST. MARTINS ST., WC2. *L/A/P

LO/P21 WILLESDEN CENTRAL LIBRARY (BRENT PUB. LIBR.), HIGH RD., NW10. L/A/*P

LO/P22 WIMBLEDON PUBLIC LIBRARY (MERTON PUB. LIBR.), HILL RD., SW19. L/A/*P

LO/P23 WOOLWICH PUBLIC LIBRARY (GREENWICH PUB. LIBR.), CALDERWOOD ST., SE18. L/A/P

LO/P24 BATTERSEA PUBLIC LIBRARY (WANDSWORTH PUB. LIBR.), 265 LAVENDER HILL, SW11. L/A/P

LO/R–1 ANTI-LOCUST RESEARCH CENTRE, COLLEGE HOUSE, WRIGHTS LANE, W8. *L/*A/XP

LO/R–2 COMMONWEALTH INSTITUTE OF ENTO-MOLOGY, 56 QUEENS GATE, SW7. *L/*A/*P

LO/R–3 COMMONWEALTH MYCOLOGICAL INSTITUTE, FERRY LANE, KEW, SURREY. L/XA/P

LO/R–4 ⟨NATIONAL CHEMICAL LABORATORY, NOW INCORP. INTO NAT. PHYSICAL LABORATORY⟩

LO/R–5 NATURE CONSERVANCY, 19 BELGRAVE SQ., SW1.

LO/R–6 TROPICAL PRODUCTS INSTITUTE, 56-62 GRAYS INN RD., WC1.

LO/R–7 SCIENCE RESEARCH COUNCIL, STATE HOUSE, HIGH HOLBORN, WC1. L/F/*A/*P

LO/S–1 BRITISH INSTITUTE OF MANAGEMENT, 80 FETTER LANE, EC4. *L/*A/P

LO/S–2 CENTRE FOR EDUCATIONAL TELEVISION OVERSEAS, NUFFIELD LODGE, REGENTS PARK, NW8. L/XA/*P

LO/S–3 CHEMICAL SOCIETY, BURLINGTON HOUSE, W1. *L/*A/P

LO/S–4 INSTITUTE OF ACTUARIES, STAPLE INN HALL, HIGH HOLBORN, WC1. L/*A/XP

LO/S–5 INSTITUTE OF PRODUCTION ENGINEERS, 10 CHESTERFIELD ST., W1. *L/*A/*P

LO/S–6 LINNEAN SOCIETY OF LONDON, BURLINGTON HOUSE, W1. L/*A/P

LO/S–7 LONDON LIBRARY, 14 ST. JAMES'S SQ., SW1. *L/XA/*P

LO/S–8 METROPOLITAN POLICE LABORATORY, NEW SCOTLAND YARD, SW1. *L/*A

LO/S–9 POLISH LIBRARY, 9 PRINCES GARDENS, SW7. *L/*A/P

LO/S10 ROYAL ANTHROPOLOGICAL INSTITUTE, 6 BURLINGTON GARDENS, LONDON W1X 2EX. L/*A/XP

LO/S12 ROYAL ENTOMOLOGICAL SOCIETY OF LONDON, 41 QUEENS GATE, SW7. *L/*A/P

LO/S13 ROYAL GEOGRAPHICAL SOCIETY, KENSING-TON GORE, SW7. L/*A/P

LO/S14 ROYAL INSTITUTE OF INTERNATIONAL AFFAIRS, CHATHAM HOUSE, 10 ST. JAMES'S SQ., SW1. XL/*A/P

LO/S15 ROYAL INSTITUTE OF PUBLIC ADMINISTRA-TION, 24 PARK CRESCENT, W1. L/XA/XP

LO/S16 ROYAL INSTITUTION OF CHARTERED SURVEYORS, 12 GREAT GEORGE ST., SW1. L/*A/*P

LO/S17 GEOLOGICAL SOCIETY OF LONDON, BURLINGTON HOUSE, W1. *L/*A/*P

LO/S18 TAVISTOCK LIBRARY (TAVISTOCK CLINIC & TAVISTOCK INST. OF HUMAN RELATIONS JT. LIBR.), 3 DEVONSHIRE ST., W1. L/*A/XP

LO/S19 ZOOLOGICAL SOCIETY OF LONDON, REGENTS PARK, NW1. *L/*A/XP

LO/S20 ROYAL INSTITUTION OF GREAT BRITAIN, 21 ALBEMARLE ST., W1. *L/*A/*P

LO/S21 INSTITUTE OF WELDING, 54 PRINCES GATE, SW7. L/A/P ⟨NOW THE WELDING INSTITUTE, ABINGTON HALL, ABINGTON, CAMB.⟩

LO/S22 ASLIB, 3 BELGRAVE SQ., SW1.

LO/S23   INTERNATIONAL WOOL SECRETARIAT, WOOL HOUSE, CARLTON GARDENS, SW1. L/*A/P

LO/S24   CHARTERED INSURANCE INSTITUTE, THE HALL, 20 ALDERMANBURY, EC2. L/XF/*A/XP/XM

LO/S25   ROYAL BOTANIC GARDENS, KEW, RICHMOND, SURREY. *L/*A/*P

LO/S26   COMMONWEALTH INSTITUTE LIBRARY, KENSINGTON HIGH ST., W8. L/*F/A/*P/XM

LO/S27   HISPANIC & LUSO-BRAZILIAN COUNCILS, CANNING HOUSE, 2 BELGRAVE SQ., SW1

LO/S28   INSTITUTE OF BANKERS, 10 LOMBARD ST., EC3.

LO/S29   GERMAN INSTITUTE, 51 PRINCES GATE, SW7. L/A/XP

LO/S30   FOLKLORE SOCIETY, C/O UNIVERSITY COLLEGE LONDON, GOWER ST., WC1.

LO/S74   INTERNATIONAL PLANNED PARENTHOOD FEDERATION, 18-20 LOWER REGENT ST., LONDON, SW1. XL/XF/*A/XP/XM

LO/T-1   NOW AS XS/N-2, Q.V.

LO/T-2   BRITISH LAUNDERERS RESEARCH ASSOCIATION LABS., HILL VIEW GARDENS, NW4. *L/*A/P

LO/T-3   GAS COUNCIL, WATSON HOUSE, PETERBOROUGH ROAD, SW6. L/XA/*P

LO/T-4   MINING RESEARCH ESTABLISHMENT (NATIONAL COAL BOARD), WORTON RD., ISLEWORTH, MIDDX. *L/XA/*P <NOW CLOSED>

LO/T-5   RESEARCH ASSOCIATION OF BRITISH PAINT, COLOUR & VARNISH MANUFACTURERS, PAINT RESEARCH STATION, WALDEGRAVE RD., TEDDINGTON, MIDDX. L/*A/*P

LO/U-1   UNIVERSITY OF LONDON (GOLDSMITHS LIBR.), SENATE HOUSE, WC1. *L/*A/P

LO/U-2   UNIVERSITY COLLEGE LONDON, GOWER ST., WC1. L/*A/P

LO/U-3   LONDON SCHOOL OF ECONOMICS & POLITICAL SCIENCE (BR. LIBR. OF POLIT. & ECON. SCI.), HOUGHTON ST., WC2. L/*A/P

LO/U-4   BEDFORD COLLEGE, REGENTS PARK, NW1. L/*A/XP

LO/U-5   BIRKBECK COLLEGE, MALET ST., WC1. L/*A/XP

LO/U-6   IMPERIAL COLLEGE OF SCIENCE & TECHNOLOGY (LYON PLAYFAIR LIBR.), 180 QUEENS GATE, SW7. L/*A/*P

LO/U-7   INSTITUTE OF CLASSICAL STUDIES, UNIV. OF LOND., 31/34 GORDON SQ., WC1. L/*A/XP

LO/U-8   INSTITUTE OF COMMONWEALTH STUDIES, UNIV. OF LOND., 27 RUSSELL SQ., WC1. XL/*A/XP

LO/U-9   INSTITUTE OF EDUCATION, UNIV. OF LOND., 11-13 RIDGMOUNT ST., WC1.

LO/U10   INSTITUTE OF GERMANIC STUDIES, UNIV. OF LOND., 29 RUSSELL SQ., WC1. XL/*A/*P

LO/U11   KINGS COLLEGE LONDON, STRAND, WC2. L/*A/*P

LO/U12   QUEEN MARY COLLEGE, MILE END RD., E1. L/*A/P

LO/U13   ROYAL HOLLOWAY COLLEGE, ENGLEFIELD GREEN, SURREY. L/*A/*P

LO/U14   SCHOOL OF ORIENTAL & AFRICAN STUDIES, UNIV. OF LOND., WC1. L/A/*P

LO/U15   SCHOOL OF SLAVONIC & EAST EUROPEAN STUDIES, UNIV. OF LOND., WC1. XL/*A/*P

LO/U16   WESTFIELD COLLEGE, NW3. *L/*A/*P

LO/U17   WARBURG INSTITUTE, WOBURN SQ., WC1.

LO/U18   THE CITY UNIVERSITY, < PREV: NORTHAMPTON COLL. OF ADV. TECHNOL.> (SKINNERS LIBR.), ST. JOHN ST., EC1. *L/*F/*A/P/XM

LO/U19   INSTITUTE OF HISTORICAL RESEARCH, UNIV. OF LOND., SENATE HOUSE, WC1. XL/XF/*A/P/M

LO/U20   BRUNEL UNIVERSITY OF TECHNOLOGY <PREV: BRUNEL COLL.> ,WOODLANDS AVE., ACTON, W3. L/*A/*P

LO/U21   UNIVERSITY OF SURREY, GUILDFORD, SURREY. *L/*A/P

LO/U22   INSTITUTE OF UNITED STATES STUDIES, UNIV. OF LOND., 31 TAVISTOCK SQ., WC1.

LO/U23   INSTITUTE OF LATIN AMERICAN STUDIES, UNIV. OF LOND., 31 TAVISTOCK SQ., WC1.

LO/U24   INSTITUTE OF ADVANCED LEGAL STUDIES, UNIV. OF LOND., 25 RUSSELL SQ., WC1.

LO/U25   INSTITUTE OF ARCHAEOLOGY, UNIV. OF LOND., 31-34 GORDON SQ., WC1.

LO/U26   COURTAULD INSTITUTE OF ART, 20 PORTMAN SQ., W1.

LV——   LIVERPOOL.

LV/P-1   LIV. PUBLIC LIBRARIES (CENTRAL LIBR.), WILLIAM BROWN ST., 3. *L/A/*P

LV/U-1   UNIV. OF LIVERPOOL (UNIV. LIBRARY), 3. L/*A/*P

LV/U-2   INSTITUTE OF EDUCATION, UNIV. OF LIV., 1 ABERCROMBY SQUARE, 7.

MA——   MANCHESTER.

MA/C-1   NOW AS MA/U-3, Q.V.

MA/F-1   CARBORUNDUM CO. LTD., (TECHNICAL LIBR.), TRAFFORD PARK, 17. L/XA/P

MA/P-1   MANC. PUBLIC LIBRARIES (CENTRAL LIBR.), ST. PETERS SQUARE, 2. *L/A/P

MA/S-1   JOHN RYLANDS LIBRARY, DEANSGATE, 3. XL/*A/P

MA/T-1   TEXTILE INSTITUTE, 10 BLACKFRIARS ST., 3. *L/*A/*P

MA/T-2   COTTON, SILK & MAN-MADE FIBRES RESEARCH ASSOCIATION, (SHIRLEY INST.), DIDSBURY, MANC. 20. L(THRU NCL)/*A/XP

MA/U-1   UNIVERSITY OF MANCHESTER (UNIV. LIBR.), OXFORD RD., 13. L/*A/P

MA/U-2   UNIV. (OF MANC.) SCHOOL OF EDUCATION.

MA/U-3   UNIVERSITY OF MANCHESTER INSTITUTE OF SCIENCE & TECHNOLOGY<PREV: MANCHESTER COLL. OF SCI. & TECHNOL.>, SACKVILLE ST., MANC. 1.

MA/U-4   MANCHESTER BUSINESS SCHOOL, BOOTH ST. WEST, MANCHESTER, M15 6PB.

NO——   NOTTINGHAM.

NO/P-1   NOTTINGHAM CITY LIBRARY, SOUTH SHERWOOD ST. L/A/P

NO/T-1   HOSIERY & ALLIED TRADES RESEARCH ASS., 7 GREGORY BLVD. L/*A/P

NO/U-1   UNIVERSITY OF NOTTINGHAM, UNIVERSITY PARK. L/*A/P

NO/U-2   INSTITUTE OF EDUCATION, UNIV. OF NOTT., UNIVERSITY PARK.

NR——   NORWICH.

NR/P-1   NORWICH PUBLIC LIBRARIES (CENT. LIBR.), BETHEL ST. L/A/P

NR/U-1   UNIVERSITY OF EAST ANGLIA.

NW——   NEWCASTLE/TYNE.

NW/P-1   NEWC./TYNE CITY LIBRARIES (CENT. LIBR.), NEW BRIDGE ST., 1. *L/*A/*P

NW/U-1   UNIVERSITY OF NEWCASTLE UPON TYNE <PREV: KINGS COLL. (UNIV. OF DURHAM)>, (UNIV. LIBR.). L/*F/*A/P/M

NW/U-2   INSTITUTE OF EDUCATION, UNIV. OF NEWC./TYNE, ST. THOMAS ST. L/A/*P

OX—— OXFORD.

OX/U–1 BODLEIAN LIBRARY. *L/*A/P

OX/U–2 ASHMOLEAN MUSEUM. XL/*A/P

OX/U–3 COMMONWEALTH FORESTRY INSTITUTE (&) DEP. OF FORESTRY, UNIV. OF OXFORD (JT. LIBR.), SOUTH PARKS RD. *L/*A/*P

OX/U–4 DEP. OF AGRICULTURE, UNIV. OF OXFORD, PARKS RD. L/*A/XP

OX/U–5 FACULTY OF HISTORY, UNIV. OF OXFORD, MERTON ST. L/*A/XP

OX/U–6 INSTITUTE OF EDUCATION, UNIV. OF OXFORD, 15 NORHAM GARDENS.

OX/U–7 MUSEUM OF THE HISTORY OF SCIENCE, OLD ASHMOLEAN BUILDING, BROAD ST. *L/A/*P

OX/U–8 RADCLIFFE SCIENCE LIBRARY. *L/*A/P

OX/U–9 RHODES HOUSE. *L/*A/P

OX/U10 SCHOOL OF GEOGRAPHY, UNIV. OF OXFORD, MANSFIELD RD. L/*A/*P

OX/U11 UNIVERSITY COLLEGE, OXFORD. *L/*A/XP

OX/U12 DEP. OF ZOOLOGY & COMPARATIVE ANATOMY, UNIV. OF OXFORD.

OX/U13 INDIAN INSTITUTE, UNIV. OF OXFORD.

OX/U14 INSTITUTE OF COMMONWEALTH STUDIES, UNIV. OF OXFORD, QUEEN ELIZABETH HOUSE, 20/21 ST. GILES.

OX/15 LAW LIBRARY. (PART OF BODLEIAN LIBR.)

OX/U16 INSTITUTE OF ECONOMICS & STATISTICS, UNIV. OF OXFORD <PREV: INST. OF STATISTICS>, ST. CROSS BLDG., MANOR RD. XL/*A/*P

OX/U17 NUFFIELD COLLEGE. *L/*A/*P

OX/U18 ST. ANTONY'S COLLEGE.

OX/U19 TAYLOR INSTITUTION, UNIV. OF OXFORD, ST. GILES ST., OXFORD.

OX/U24 INSTITUTE OF AGRICULTURAL ECONOMICS, UNIV. OF OXFORD, DARTINGTON HOUSE, LITTLE CLARENDON ST., OX1 2HP.

RE—— READING.

RE/F–1 GILLETTE INDUSTRIES LTD. (RESEARCH LABS.), 454 BASINGSTOKE RD. L/*A/*P

RE/P–1 READING PUBLIC LIBRARIES, BLAGRAVE ST. L/A/*P

RE/R–1 NATIONAL INSTITUTE FOR RESEARCH IN DAIRYING, SHINFIELD.

RE/U–1 UNIVERSITY OF READING. *L/*A/XP

RE/U–2 INSTITUTE OF EDUCATION, UNIV. OF READ.

SA—— ST. ANDREWS.

SA/U–1 UNIVERSITY OF ST. ANDREW'S. (UNIV. LIBR.) L/A/P

SF—— SALFORD, LANCS.

SF/U–1 UNIVERSITY OF SALFORD <PREV: ROYAL COLL. OF ADV. TECHNOL>, SALF. 5. XL/XF/A/P

SH—— SHEFFIELD.

SH/C–5 SHEFFIELD POLYTECHNIC, CENT. LIBR., HOWARD ST., SHEFFIELD.

SH/P–1 SHEFFIELD CITY LIBRARIES (CENT. LIBR., GEN. REF. LIBR.), SURREY ST., 1.

SH/T–1 BROWN-FIRTH RESEARCH LABORATORIES (HATFIELD LIBR.), PRINCESS ST., 4. L/*A/*P

SH/T–2 JOINT LIBRARY OF GLASS TECHNOLOGY (BR. GLASS IND. RES. ASS.; SOC. OF GLASS TECHNOL.; DEP. OF GLASS TECHNOL., UNIV. OF SHEFF.), ELMFIELD, NORTHUMBERLAND RD., 10. *L/*A/P

SH/T–3 SAFETY IN MINES RESEARCH ESTABLISHMENT, OFF BROAD LANE, 3. L/*A/*P

SH/U–1 UNIVERSITY OF SHEFFIELD (UNIV. LIBR.), WESTERN BANK, 10. *L/*A

SH/U–2 INSTITUTE OF EDUCATION, UNIV. OF SHEFF., SHEFF. 10.

SH/U–3 UNIV. OF SHEFFIELD (APPLIED SCIENCE LIBRARY), ST. GEORGE'S SQ., 1. L/*A/P

SL/U–1 FOR THIS SYMBOL READ *SF/U–1* (SEE ABOVE).

SO—— SOUTHAMPTON.

SO/F–1 BRITISH-AMERICAN TOBACCO CO. LTD. (RES. & DEV. ESTAB.), REGENTS PARK RD.

SO/P–1 SOUTHAMPTON PUBLIC LIBRARIES (CENTRAL LIBR.), CIVIC CENTRE. L/A/P

SO/U–1 UNIVERSITY OF SOUTHAMPTON. L/*A/P

SO/U–2 INSTITUTE OF EDUCATION, UNIV. OF SOUTH., L/*A/P

SW—— SWANSEA.

SW/P–1 SWANSEA PUBLIC LIBRARIES (CENT. LIBR.), ALEXANDRA RD. L/A

SW/U–1 UNIVERSITY COLLEGE OF SWANSEA, SINGLETON PARK. L/*A/*P

XE—— EAST MIDLANDS (LIBRARY) REGION.

XE/C–1 NOW AS *LB/C–1*, Q.V.

XE/C–2 NOW AS *LB/U–1*, Q.V.

XE/C–3 ROYAL AIR FORCE COLLEGE, TRENCHARD HALL LIBR. <PREV: R.A.F. TECH. COLL., HENLOW, BEDS>, CRANWELL, SLEAFORD, LINCS.

XE/F–1 FISONS LTD. (HEAD OFFICE), HARVEST HOUSE, FELIXSTOWE, SUFFOLK. L/*A

XE/F–2 FISONS FERTILIZERS LTD., LEVINGTON RES. STATION, IPSWICH, SUFFOLK. L/XA/P

XE/F–3 ENGLISH ELECTRIC DIESELS LTD., RUSTON SUB-GROUP, P.O. BOX 46, LINCOLN. L/*A/P

XE/F–4 STAVELEY IRON & CHEMICALS CO. LTD. (RES. DEP., TECH. LIBR.), NR. CHESTERFIELD. L/*A/*P

XE/P–1 ARNOLD (NOTTS.) PUBLIC LIBRARY. L/A/*P

XE/P–2 CHESTERFIELD PUBLIC LIBRARY, STEPHENSON MEMORIAL HALL, CORPORATION ST., CHESTERFIELD, DERBS. *L/A/XP

XE/P–3 GREAT YARMOUTH CENTRAL LIBRARY. L/A/*P

XE/P–4 NORTHAMPTON CENTRAL PUBLIC LIBRARY, ABINGTON ST. L/A/XP

XE/P–5 WORKSOP (NOTTS.) PUBLIC LIBRARY & MUSEUM. L/A/*P

XE/P–6 MANSFIELD (NOTTS.) PUBLIC LIBRARY, CENTRAL LIBR., LEEMING ST. L/A/XP

XE/R–1 HOUGHTON POULTRY RESEARCH STATION, HOUGHTON, HUNTS. *L/*A/XP

XL—— LANCASHIRE & CHESHIRE (NW LIBR. REGION).

XL/C–1 NOW AS *SF/U–1*, Q.V.

XL/F–1 FISONS PHARMACEUTICALS LTD. <PREV: BENGER LABS >, HOLMES CHAPEL, CHES. L

XL/M–1 DEVA HOSPITAL, MEDICAL LIBRARY, LIVERPOOL RD., CHESTER. *L/*A/XP

XL/P–1 BARROW-IN-FURNESS PUBLIC LIBRARY. L/A/P

XL/P–2 BOOTLE PUBLIC LIBRARIES, CENT. LIBR., ORIEL RD., BOOTLE 20, LANCS. L/*A/*P

XL/P–3 BURNLEY PUBLIC LIBRARIES, CENTRAL LIBR., GRIMSHAW ST. L/A/*P

XL/P-4 ECCLES PUBLIC LIBRARIES, CHURCH ST., ECCLES, LANCS. *L/*A/P

XL/P-5 MAYER PUBLIC LIBRARY, BEBINGTON, WIRRAL, CHES. L/A/XP

XL/P-6 ST. HELENS PUBLIC LIBRARIES, CENT. LIBR., ST. HELENS, LANCS. L/A/P

XL/P-7 SOUTHPORT PUBLIC LIBRARY, ATKINSON CENTRAL LIBR., LORD ST. *L/A/*P

XL/P-8 STOCKPORT PUBLIC LIBRARIES, CENT. LIBR., WELLNGTON RD. SOUTH. L/A/P

XL/P-9 WARRINGTON PUBLIC LIBRARY, MUSEUM ST. L/A/P

XL/P10 WIGAN CENTRAL LIBRARY, RODNEY ST. L/A/P

XL/P11 FLEETWOOD (LANCS.) CENTRAL LIBRARY, DOCK ST. L/A/XP

XL/T-1 UNITED KINGDOM ATOMIC ENERGY AUTHORITY, REACTOR GROUP HQ, LIBR. & INF. DEP., RISLEY, WARRINGTON, LANCS. L/XA/*P

XM—— MIDLANDS, WEST, (LIBRARY) REGION.

XM/F-1 ASSOCIATED ENGINEERING LTD., GROUP RES. & DEV., CAUSTON, RUGBY, WARWICKS. *L/*A/P

XM/F-2 GKN GROUP RESEARCH LAB., BIRMINGHAM NEW RD., LANESFIELD, WOLVERHAMPTON. L/*P

XM/P-1 OSWESTRY PUBLIC LIBRARY, ARTHUR ST., OSWESTRY, SALOP. L/A

XM/P-2 SHROPSHIRE COUNTY LIBRARY, WYLE COP, SHREWSBURY. L/A/*P

XM/P-3 SMETHWICK PUBLIC LIBRARIES, CENT. LIBR., SMETHWICK 41, STAFFS. L/A

XM/P-4 STOKE-ON-TRENT PUBLIC LIBRARIES, CENTRAL LIBRARY, BETHESDA ST., HANLEY. L/A/XP

XM/P-5 WALSALL CENTRAL LIBRARY, LICHFIELD ST. L/A/*P

XM/P-6 WARWICKSHIRE COUNTY LIBRARY, THE BUTTS, WARWICK. L/A/P

XM/P-7 WEST BROMWICH PUBLIC LIBRARY, HIGH ST., W. BROM., STAFFS. L/A/*P

XM/P-8 WOLVERHAMPTON PUBLIC LIBRARIES, CENTRAL LIBR., SNOW HILL, WOLV., STAFFS. L/A/XP

XM/P-9 DUDLEY PUBLIC LIBRARIES, CENT. LIBR., L/A/*P

XM/R-1 NATIONAL VEGETABLE RESEARCH STATION, WELLESBOURNE, WARWICKS. L/*A/*P

XM/T-1 BRITISH CERAMIC RESEARCH ASSOCIATION, MELLOR MEMORIAL LIBR., QUEENS RD., PENKHULL, STOKE/TRENT, STAFFS. L/*A/P

XN—— NORTHERN (LIBRARY) REGION.

XN/P-1 SUNDERLAND PUBLIC LIBRARIES, CENTRAL LIBR., BOROUGH RD. L/A/P

XN/R-1 FRESHWATER BIOLOGICAL ASSOCIATION, FERRY HOUSE, FAR SAWREY, AMBLESIDE, WESTMORL. *L/*A/*P

XN/R-2 DOVE MARINE LABORATORY, CULLERCOATS, NORTH SHIELDS, NORTHUMB. *L/*F/*A/XP BUT P & M BY SENDING MATERIAL TO *NW/U-1*

XN/S-1 LIBRARY OF JAPANESE SCIENCE & TECHNOLOGY, 24 DUKE ST., WHITLEY BAY, NORTHUMB. L/A/XP

XN/T-1 UNITED KINGDOM ATOMIC ENERGY AUTHORITY, REACTOR GROUP, WINDSCALE WORKS, SELLAFIELD, SEASCALE, CUMB. L/XA/*P

XS—— SOUTH EASTERN (LIBRARY) REGION.

XS/C-1 FIRE SERVICE COLLEGE, WOTTON HOUSE, ABINGER COMMON, DORKING, SURREY. L/*A

XS/C-2 HATFIELD POLYTECHNIC (& HERTFORDSHIRE COUNTY COUNCIL TECH. LIBR. INF. SERV.), HATFIELD, HERTS. *L/*A/P

XS/C-3 COLLEGE OF AERONAUTICS, CRANFIELD, BEDFORD. L/*A/P

XS/C-4 EWELL COUNTY TECHNICAL COLLEGE, REIGATE RD., EWELL, SURREY. L/A/P

XS/C-5 NOW AS *XE/C-3*, Q.V.

XS/F-1 COSSOR ELECTRONICS LTD., CENTR. LIBR., THE PINNACLES, HARLOW, ESSEX. L/XA

XS/F-2 ELLIOTT BROTHERS (LONDON) LTD., AIRPORT WORKS, TECH. LIBR., ROCHESTER, KENT. L/XA/*P

XS/F-3 GLAXO RESEARCH LTD., SEFTON PARK, STOKE POGES, BUCKS. L/XA/*P

XS/F-4 PLANT PROTECTION LTD., JEALOTT'S HILL RES. STN., BRACKNELL, BERKS. L/XA/XP

XS/F-5 JOHN LAING RESEARCH & DEVELOPMENT LTD., MANOR WAY, BOREHAM WOOD, HERTS. L/*A/*P

XS/F-6 MARCONI INSTRUMENTS LTD., LONGACRES, ST. ALBANS, HERTS. *L/XA/*P

XS/F-7 MILES LABORATORIES LTD., STOKES COURT, STOKE POGES, BUCKS. *L/XA/P

XS/F-8 PAN BRITANNICA INDUSTRIES LTD., BRITANNICA HOUSE, WALTHAM CROSS, HERTS. *L/*F/XA/*P/XM

XS/F-9 STANDARD TELECOMMUNICATION LABORATORIES LTD., TECH. LIBR., LONDON RD., HARLOW, ESSEX. L/*A

XS/F10 TATE & LYLE REFINERIES LTD., RESEARCH LAB., RAVENSBOURNE, WESTERHAM RD., KESTON, KENT. L/*A/P

XS/F11 BEECHAM RES. LAB., VITAMINS RES. STN., WALTON OAKS, TADWORTH, SURREY. L/XA/P

XS/F12 WH ALLEN & SONS & CO. LTD., QUEENS ENGINEERING WORKS, TECH. LIBR., BEDFORD. L/*A/P

XS/F13 HAWKER SIDDELEY DYNAMICS LTD., TECH. LIBR., MANOR RD., HATFIELD, HERTS. *L/XA/P

XS/F14 JOHN WYETH & BROTHER LTD., HUNTERCOMBE LANE SOUTH, TAPLOW, MAIDENHEAD, BERKS. L/XA/*P

XS/F15 VICKERS RESEARCH LTD., SUNNINGHILL, ASCOT, BERKS. L

XS/F16 SMITH KLINE & FRENCH LABORATORIES LTD., WELWYN GARDEN CITY, HERTS. L/XA/*P

XS/N-1 METEOROLOGICAL OFFICE, LONDON RD., BRACKNELL, BERKS. L/A/*P

XS/N-2 NAVAL SCIENTIFIC & TECHNICAL INFORMATION CENTRE (MIN. OF DEFENCE), BLOCK B, STATION SQ. HOUSE, ST. MARY CRAY, ORPINGTON, KENT. <PREV: *LO/T-1*>

XS/P-1 BUCKINGHAMSHIRE COUNTY LIBRARY, HIGHBRIDGE RD., AYLESBURY, BUCKS. L/A/P

XS/P-2 DARTFORD PUBLIC LIBRARIES, CENTRAL PARK, DARTFORD, KENT. L/A/P

XS/P-3 ESSEX COUNTY LIBRARY, TECH. LIBR. SERV., GOLDLAY GARDENS, CHELMSFORD, ESSEX. L/A/P

XS/P-4 GILLINGHAM PUBLIC LIBRARY, CENT. LIBR., HIGH ST., GILL., KENT. L/A/*P

XS/P-5 THURROCK CENTRAL LIBRARY, OR SETT RD., GRAYS, ESSEX. L/A/P

XS/R-1 DITTON LABORATORY (AGRICULTURAL RESEARCH COUNCIL), LARKFIELD, MAIDSTONE, KENT. L/XA/*P

XS/R-2 EAST MALLING RESEARCH STATION (JT. LIBR. WITH: COMMONW. BUR. OF HORTICULTURE & PLANTATION CROPS), EAST MALLING, MAIDSTONE, KENT. L/*A/*P

XS/R-3 FULMER RESEARCH INSTITUTE LTD., STOKE POGES, BUCKS. L/*A/*P

XS/R-4 GRASSLAND RESEARCH INSTITUTE, HURLEY, BERKS. XL/*A/XP

XS/R-5 JOHN INNES INSTITUTE, BAYFORDBURY, HERTFORD, HERTS. L/*A/P

XS/R-6 NATIONAL INSTITUTE OF AGRICULTURAL ENGINEERING, WREST PARK, SILSOE, BEDS. L/A/*P

XS/R-7 PEST INFESTATION LABORATORY, LONDON RD., SLOUGH, BUCKS. *L/*A/P

XS/R-8 ANIMAL VIRUS RESEARCH INSTITUTE <PREV: RESEARCH INSTITUTE (ANIMAL VIRUS DISEASES)>, PIRBRIGHT, WOKING, SURREY. L/XF/*A/*P/XM

XS/R–9 WARREN SPRING LABORATORY, GUNNELS WOOD RD., STEVENAGE, HERTS. *L/*A/XP
XS/R10 ATOMIC ENERGY RESEARCH ESTABLISHMENT (UKAEA RESEARCH GROUP), HARWELL, DIDCOT, BERKS. *L/*A/*P
XS/R11 NATIONAL INSTITUTE OF OCEANOGRAPHY, WORMLEY, GODALMING, SURREY.
XS/R12 ROTHAMPSTED EXPERIMENTAL STATION, HARPENDEN, HERTS. L/*F/A/P/M (SUPPLIES XEROX ONLY OF PER. ARTS. UP TO 10 PP.)
XS/R14 COMMONWEALTH BUREAU OF HELMINTHOLOGY, THE WHITE HOUSE, 103 ST. PETERS ST., ST. ALBANS.
XS/T–1 BREWING INDUSTRY RESEARCH FOUNDATION, NUTFIELD, REDHILL, SURREY. *L/*A/P
XS/T–2 BRITISH COAL UTILISATION RESEARCH ASSOCIATION, RANDALLS RD., LEATHERHEAD, SURREY. *L/*A/*P
XS/T–3 SIRA INSTITUTE, SOUTH HILL, CHISLEHURST, KENT, BR7 5EH. L/*A/*P
XS/T–4 ELECTRICAL RESEARCH ASSOCIATION (BR. ELEC. & ALLIED IND. RES. ASS.), CLEEVE RD., LEATHERHEAD, SURREY. *L/XA/*P
XS/T–5 MILITARY ENGINEERING EXPERIMENTAL ESTABLISHMENT, MEXE TECH. LIBR., BARRACK RD., CHRISTCHURCH, HANTS. L/XA/P
XS/T–6 PIRA (PRINTING & PACKAGING DIV.), RANDALLS RD., LEATHERHEAD, SURREY. *L/*A/P
XS/T–7 ROYAL AIRCRAFT ESTABLISHMENT, BEDFORD. L/XA
XS/T–8 SERVICES ELECTRONICS RESEARCH LABORATORY, BALDOCK, HERTS. L/*A/*P
XS/T–9 RADIOCHEMICAL CENTRE (UNITED KINGDOM ATOMIC ENERGY AUTHORITY), WHITE LION RD., AMERSHAM, BUCKS. L/XA/XP
XS/T10 HEATING & VENTILATING RESEARCH ASS., INFORMATION OFFICE, OLD BRACKNELL LANE, BRACKNELL, BERKS
XS/T11 BRITISH FOOD MANUFACTURING INDUSTRIES RESEARCH ASS., LEATHERHEAD, SURREY.
XS/U–1 WYE COLLEGE, NR. ASHFORD, KENT. *L/*A

XW—— WESTERN, SOUTH, (LIBRARY) REGION.

XW/C–1 HEYTHROP COLLEGE, CHIPPING NORTON, OXON. *L/*A/XP
XW/C–2 ROYAL AGRICULTURAL COLLEGE, CIRENCESTER, GLOUCS. L/*A/*P
XW/C–3 PORTSMOUTH POLYTECHNIC, HAMPSHIRE TCE., PORTSMOUTH, HANTS.
XW/C–4 ROYAL MILITARY COLLEGE OF SCIENCE, SHRIVENHAM, SWINDON, WILTS. L/*A/P
XW/P–1 BOURNEMOUTH PUBLIC LIBRARIES, CENTRAL LIBR., LANSDOWNE, BOURN., HANTS. L/A/P
XW/P–2 BRIDGWATER PUBLIC LIBRARY, BINFORD PLACE, BRIDGW., SOMERSET. L/A/P
XW/P–3 GLOUCESTER CITY LIBRARIES, BRUNSWICK RD. L/A/P
XW/P–4 HAMPSHIRE COUNTY LIBRARY HQ., NORTH WALLS, WINCHESTER. L/A/P
XW/P–5 SOMERSET COUNTY LIBRARY HQ., MOUNT ST., BRIDGWATER, SOMERSET. L/A/P
XW/P–6 SWINDON PUBLIC LIBRARIES, CENT. LIBR., REGENT CIRCUS, SWIN., WILTS. L/A/P
XW/P–7 TAUNTON PUBLIC LIBRARY, CORPORATION ST., TAUNTON, SOMERSET. L/A/P

XW/S–1 COMMONWEAL COLLECTION, 112 WINCHCOMBE ST., CHELTENHAM, GLOUCS. L/F/A/XM
XW/T–1 ROYAL AIRCRAFT ESTABLISHMENT, FARNBOROUGH, HANTS. L/*A/P

XY—— YORKSHIRE (LIBRARY REGION).

XY/C–1 HUDDERSFIELD COLLEGE OF EDUCATION (TECHNICAL) <PREV: TRAINING COLL. FOR TECHNICAL TEACHERS>, HOLLY BANK RD., LINDLEY. L/*A/*P
XY/F–1 BRITISH BELTING & ASBESTOS LTD., LIBR. & INF. SERV., CLECKHEATON, YORKS. L/*A/P
XY/N–1 BRITISH LIBRARY: LENDING DIVISION, BOSTON SPA, WETHERBY, YORKS. LS23 7BQ. <FORMED BY AMALGAMATION OF NATIONAL LENDING LIBRARY AND NATIONAL CENTRAL LIBRARY> L/A/P
XY/P–2 TEESIDE PUBLIC LIBRARIES, CENT. LIBR., VICTORIA SQUARE, MIDDLESBOROUGH. L/A/P
XY/P–3 WEST RIDING COUNTY LIBRARY HQ, BALNE LANE, WAKEFIELD, YORKS. L/A/P
XY/P–4 ROTHERHAM PUBLIC LIBRARY, HOWARD ST., ROTH., YORKS. L/A/*P

YK—— YORK.

YK/U–1 UNIVERSITY OF YORK (J.B. MORRELL LIBR.), HESLINGTON, YORK. L/A/P

ZN—— NORTHERN IRELAND.

ZN/P–1 ARMAGH PUBLIC LIBRARY, ABBEY ST. *L/*A/XP

ZS—— SCOTLAND.

ZS/F–1 BP CHEMICALS LTD., BO'NESS RD., GRANGEMOUTH, STIRLINGSHIRE. L/*A/P
ZS/P–1 CARNEGIE PUBLIC LIBRARY, AYR. L/A/XP
ZS/P–2 FRASERBURGH PUBLIC LIBRARY, KING EDWARD STREET, FRAS., ABERDEENSHIRE. L/A/*P
ZS/T–1 DOUNREAY EXPERIMENTAL REACTOR ESTABLISHMENT, THURSO, CAITHNESS. L/XA/P
ZS/T–2 SCIENTIFIC DOCUMENTATION CENTRE LTD., HALBEATH HOUSE, DUNFERMLINE, FIFE. L/*A/P
ZS/U–1 WEST OF SCOTLAND AGRICULTURAL COLLEGE, OSWALD HALL, AUCHINCRUIVE, AYR. L/*A/*P

ZW—— WALES.

ZW/F–1 MIDLAND SILICONES LTD., BARRY, GLAMORGAN. L/XA/P
ZW/M–1 PNEUMOCONIOSIS RESEARCH UNIT (MEDICAL RESEARCH COUNCIL), LLANDOUGH HOSPITAL, PENARTH, GLAMORGAN. L/*A/P
ZW/P–1 NEWPORT (MON.) PUBLIC LIBRARY, CENTRAL LIBR., DOXK ST. L/A/P
ZW/P–2 WREXHAM PUBLIC LIBRARY, QUEEN SQUARE, WREXHAM, DENBS. L/A/XP